The Problem of *De Facto States* in International Relations in Africa

INTERNATIONAL RELATIONS IN ASIA, AFRICA AND THE AMERICAS

The series International Relations in Asia, Africa and the Americas is edited by the Centre for International Studies and Development of the Jagiellonian University in Kraków.

Edited by Andrzej Mania & Marcin Grabowski

Vol. 20

Robert Kłosowicz / Joanna Mormul

The Problem of *De Facto* *States* in International Relations in Africa

PETER LANG

Berlin - Bruxelles - Chennai - Lausanne - New York - Oxford

Bibliographic Information published by the Deutsche Nationalbibliothek
The Deutsche Nationalbibliothek lists this publication in
the Deutsche Nationalbibliografie; detailed bibliographic
data is available in the internet at http://dnb.d-nb.de.

Library of Congress Cataloging-in-Publication Data
A CIP catalog record for this book has been applied for at the
Library of Congress.

This book is the result of a research project financed
by the National Science Centre (Narodowe Centrum
Nauki), Poland, grant ID: 2017/25/B/HS5/00958.

Cover illustration: Copyright Kłosowicz Robert.

ISSN 2511-588X
ISBN 978-3-631-90235-6 (Print)
E-ISBN 978-3-631-92115-9 (E-Book)
E-ISBN 978-3-631-92116-6 (E-PUB)
DOI 10.3726/2b1963

© 2024 Peter Lang Group AG, Lausanne
Published by Peter Lang GmbH, Berlin, Deutschland

info@peterlang.com - www.peterlang.com

This publication has been peer reviewed.
www.peterlang.com

Contents

6   Contents

Robert Kłosowicz, Joanna Mormul

Introduction

"We live in a world of states, but some territories and the people who live in them fall between the cracks. From Palestine to Somaliland to Taiwan, there are a number of disputed lands that formed as a result of conflict and do not fit neatly into the established global order. Millions of people live in places not generally recognized as states within the international system." – Thomas de Waal (2018, p. 5).

The issue of unrecognised states / *de facto states* in international relations has been the subject of intense scholarly debate for many years. In Africa, the formation of the first unrecognised states has to do with colonial legacy and subsequent decolonisation, which kept the newly formed African states within the artificial boundaries established on the continent by European colonisers. Another period in which unrecognised states appear in greater numbers is linked to the end of the Cold War and the collapse of the communist federations of the USSR and Yugoslavia. A number of internal conflicts occurred in Africa during this period. A consequence of this political situation was the state disintegration of Somalia and the declaration of secession by Somaliland within the borders of the former British colony. Paradoxically, both presently existing unrecognised states on the African continent, Western Sahara and Somaliland, aspire to operate as independent entities within colonial borders (Kłosowicz 2017, pp. 175-176). Western Sahara seeks to assert its claim as the successor to *Sáhara Español*, while Somaliland aims to establish sovereignty within the confines of the former British Somaliland Protectorate.

Lack of external sovereignty does not necessarily mean that there is no chance for unrecognised states to function in international space, and actors such as Somaliland and Western Sahara, for example, seek to carve out a niche for themselves in an international system based on external sovereignty. Indeed, the international system is still largely based on a clear division between sovereign states and non-sovereign actors. In international relations theory, sovereignty has traditionally been seen as the ability to exercise political authority over a defined territory and population independently of other actors. State sovereignty is seen to include independence in both internal and external affairs. With the exception of the Arctic and Antarctic regions, the world order as we know it today consists of states that are internationally recognised and control territories clearly delimited by internationally agreed boundaries. Thus, the problem of unrecognised states is treated as an anomaly, which does not fit the prevailing model for the academic study of this issue for the perspective of political science and international relations. However, the media report on the problems of unrecognised states almost every day, whether in the context of Somaliland, Western Sahara, Nagorno-Karabakh, Taiwan, or Northern Cyprus. It is also important to note that the problems of unrecognised states translate into concrete issues for neighbouring states, entire regions and even the world order in international relations. This confronts the international community with the problem of how to address the issue of unrecognised states, which pose a challenge not only in terms of security, but also international law, with their emergence undermining the territorial integrity of another state and challenging the established international order. The process of the formation of unrecognised states can be spontaneous – due to a region's desire to become independent through secession, or externally inspired.

For the most part, these are territories that have often achieved *de facto* independence (not always through armed conflict) but have failed to gain international recognition as independent states. Despite their challenge to the principle of territorial integrity, unrecognised states do not seek to undermine the system of sovereign states or create alternative forms of statehood. Rather, *de facto states* seek a place in a system that does not, in principle, accept them as members of the international community. Consequently, there is no formally recognised mechanism by which an unrecognised entity can legally make the transition to a 'recognised' state, as such a mechanism would logically require states to establish consent to rules that could have the effect of undermining their own territorial integrity (Walker 1998; Rutland 2007).

Unrecognised states are in many ways "places that do not exist", absent from maps, although in reality they function, for example, in media reports – not only on the occasion of spectacular events. Somaliland may serve as such an example of a state that is not a marked entity on maps, yet in the popular media and in political circles, it functions as a functioning entity in the Horn of Africa.

Unrecognised states, especially those on the "periphery", sometimes fall into oblivion until the situation in their area escalates, which catches the attention of the international community and the media. Such an example is the outbreak of hostilities in Nagorno-Karabakh, which lasted from late September to early November 2020 (Second Nagorno-Karabakh War), followed by the blockade of the Lachin corridor, which has continued uninterrupted since 12 December 2022 and is causing a humanitarian crisis in the Nagorno-Karabakh area. Other examples include the riots and armed clashes between the Moroccan army and the POLISARIO Front on the border between Mauritania and Western Sahara, which is under Moroccan occupation, taking place from mid-November 2020 to the present day (mid-2023), or the internal unrest and armed fighting in Somaliland over Laascaanood and the Sool region in the first half of 2023. These are just three recent high-profile examples of how situations involving unrecognised states can escalate rapidly. In addition, most reports on unrecognised states tend to view them precisely through the prism of threats to international security and link them to the problem of dysfunctional or even failing states. Here, the example of Somaliland is typical, as this entity emerged after the breakdown of Somalia's state structures. Other unrecognised entities, on the other hand, are sometimes seen as puppets of the larger powers that use them to increase and consolidate their regional influence (Transnistria, Abkhazia, and Ossetia) (Lynch 2002).

What then is an unrecognised state and how does it differ from other anomalies in the international system? Unrecognised states have often been classified as dysfunctional entities, formed as a result of the dysfunctionality or disintegration of larger states from which they have emerged as a result of secessions caused by aspirations for independence or deep internal crisis. However, as Nina Caspersen (2012) notes, they cannot be qualified as "shadow states" (Reno 1999), "black spots" (Stanislawski 2008) or "insurgent states" (McColl 1969). Some unrecognised states such as Somaliland control all the territory they claim and within which they have managed to build state institutions. In other words, they have reached a level of statehood based on a degree of *de facto* internal sovereignty (Caspersen 2012, p. 15). Moreover, unrecognised states demonstrate a clear desire for full independence and want to become part of the world of sovereign states (Stanislawski 2008). This latter factor also distinguishes them from autonomous regions. The unrecognised states are not satisfied with their current status, which, moreover, is threatened by the fact that their internal sovereignty is not accepted *de jure*, either by what can be referred to as the "mother state" from which they have separated or by the international community.

A large part of this publication is devoted to the issue of Western Sahara, which is a special case of an unrecognised state on the African continent. The case of Western Sahara shows that defining unrecognised states in terms of their *de facto* independence, their attempts at institution-building, their aspirations for *de jure* independence and their lack of international recognition leaves researchers with a number of borderline cases. Some authors, such as Nina Caspersen and Gareth Stansfield (2012) or Deon Geldenhuys (2009) do not include Western Sahara (the Sahrawi Arab Democratic Republic, SADR) and Palestine as *de facto states*, stating that while these entities are more widely recognised than most unrecognised states, they do not meet one of the basic criteria of control of territory.

According to Caspersen, an unrecognised state should control at least two-thirds of the territory to which it claims rights, including key regions and major urban centres. Meanwhile, the SADR controls only 20 per cent of the territory it claims, while the rest is under Moroccan control, including the capital and all major urban centres. Although Western Sahara is recognised by 47 states (as of end-2022), in the past the Sahrawi Arab Democratic Republic was recognised by 84 UN member states, but, of these, 36 have since "frozen" or "withdrawn" recognition and one of the states has ceased to exist (Yugoslavia) (USC: "SADR Recognition", Web). Thus, according to Caspersen (2012), it does not meet the criteria of an unrecognised state. Nonetheless, it remains an open question whether the case of Western Sahara can be considered a typical example of an unrecognised state according to the criteria cited earlier. The majority of instances of unrecognised states in Africa arose through secession when they broke away from the mother state, as was the case with Eritrea, South Sudan,[1] Somaliland or – historically – Katanga and Biafra. However, these seem to be very different situations from the case of Western Sahara, which was not part of Morocco but instead a Spanish colony at the time of decolonisation and, in accordance with the right to self-determination of peoples and the principle of *uti possidetis* that has guided decolonisation processes on the African continent since 1964, declared independence within its colonial borders. The territory of Western Sahara was occupied by Morocco against the will of the Sahrawi people, and certainly without consulting them, so none of the examples cited fit its case. The trouble of how to qualify the case of Western Sahara disrupts concepts and theories trying to sort out the issue of unrecognised states. Western Sahara's problem lies mainly in the fact that, although it had the right to exist as an independent international entity, it was never provided the possibility to do so. The current authorities of the Sahrawi Arab Democratic Republic and the administration managing the Sahrawi refugee camps are in exile, in an area belonging to Algeria in the province of Tindouf. Significantly, the SADR is a member of the African Union and maintains several official diplomatic missions worldwide. The Sahrawis themselves do not wish to be defined as an unrecognised state under occupation, similar to the approach taken by the Palestinians. Thus, it is by no means a coincidence that the case of Western Sahara is often referred to in the literature as unfinished decolonisation (Kosidło 2012; Shelley 2004).

---

[1] Both Eritrea and South Sudan were eventually recognised internationally and are functioning as fully internationally recognised states.

The case of the Sahrawi Arab Democratic Republic is often juxtaposed with the contested statehood of Palestine. Both entities have unilaterally declared independence, and their claims to statehood have garnered widespread international recognition, with their liberation movements enjoying international legitimacy. However, in neither case has this titular recognition translated into full-fledged membership in the global community. Furthermore, both Palestine and Western Sahara exhibit limited internal sovereignty due to foreign occupation of their territories. The Sahrawi government operates in exile, similar to the Palestinian leadership before 1994, while a significant portion of the population in both cases remains displaced as refugees in neighbouring countries. Nevertheless, the international community appears to have acquiesced to the status quo in Western Sahara. Despite Morocco's violation of a fundamental principle of international law by denying Western Sahara the right to self-determination, it has emerged relatively unscathed (Geldenhuys 2009, pp. 190-207). However, it is worth noting that Western Sahara is further distinguished from other unrecognised states by being delineated as a separate entity on the majority of political maps, unlike Somaliland, for instance, which is often depicted as part of Somalia.

Within its eleven chapters, the publication delves into the intricacies of the situation of African *de facto states* in the past and present. The first one, authored by Robert Kłosowicz and entitled "Fragmentation, Autonomy, and Secession in Africa on the example of *de facto*, *puppet* and autonomous states", presents the issue of unrecognised states in Africa from the decolonisation period to the present day, taking into account African specificities related to colonial and post-colonial legacies. The second chapter by Robert Kłosowicz and Agnieszka Czubik, "Controversy over the international subjectivity of *de facto states*", discusses the problem of unrecognised states in contemporary public international law scholarship. In the third chapter, "International relations of *de facto states*", Joanna Mormul and Kateřina Ženková Rudincová conduct theoretical reflections on the international relations of states that lack or enjoy only a certain degree of international recognition, leading to their international activity being problematic and often limited. In the fourth chapter, entitled "Foreign policy of a *de facto state* - the Sahrawi Arab Democratic Republic and its diplomatic struggle", Joanna Mormul presents the SADR's foreign policy, its declared and actual objectives, the current international environment, and the consequences of the activities undertaken by Sahrawi diplomacy. The fifth chapter, by Joanna Mormul, "The population of a *de facto state* – the case of the Sahrawi people in the protracted refugee situation", is devoted to the protracted refugeedom of Sahrawis in Algeria, which is often presented as a unique refugee situation. Chapter six, "The issue of Western Sahara in the international relations of states bordering on its territory – Morocco, Algeria and Mauritania", written by Robert Kłosowicz and Joanna Mormul, analyses the problem of Western Sahara in political relations between the states directly bordering its territory, drawing attention to the fact that the main axis of the Western Sahara conflict in regional terms runs between the state occupying the Western Saharan territories (Morocco) and the state supporting the cause of Western Sahara's independence, Algeria. In this situation, Mauritania, which is politically and economically weakest, is under pressure from both Rabat and Algiers, but also from the Sahrawis living in Mauritania. In chapter seven, "North African states not bordering Western Sahara in the face of the problem of its independence – Tunisia, Libya and Egypt", Robert Kłosowicz and Ewa Szczepankiewicz-Rudzka describe the problem of the Western Sahara in the policies of other North African states, of which Libya – at least until the outbreak of the Arab Spring – pursued a policy of support for the Sahrawi cause, while Tunisia – a policy of positive neutrality. In chapter eight, "The problem of *de facto* states in Africa from the historical perspective. The case of Katanga", Robert Kłosowicz describes the first case of the emergence by secession of an unrecognised state in Africa during the decolonisation period and analyses this case study from the perspective of the 60 years that have passed since these events. Chapter nine written by Robert Kłosowicz, Joanna Mormul and Kateřina Ženková Rudincová, entitled "The international relations of Somaliland", is an analysis of Somaliland's foreign policy, the main objective of which is to obtain international recognition, while developing bilateral relations, especially economic ones, with states willing to recognise Somaliland *de facto*, though not *de iure*. Chapter ten by Robert Kłosowicz, "Cooperation of unrecognised states in international relations on the example of the Republic of Somaliland and the Republic of China (Taiwan). A model for an unofficial approach to diplomacy", presents a special case of international cooperation between two unrecognised states, which are not only struggling to achieve international recognition, but are also identified as rebellious provinces of the states from which they have seceded. The eleventh chapter by Robert Kłosowicz and Edyta Chwiej, entitled "*Proto-state* as a consequence of unfinished decolonisation. The case of Azawad and West Papua" is a comparative study of two geopolitical units referred to in the literature as proto-states: West Papua in Southeast Asia and Azawad in Africa.

References

Caspersen, Nina: *Unrecognized states. The struggle for sovereignty in the modern international system*. Polity Press: Cambridge, 2012.

Caspersen, Nina / Stansfield, Gareth (eds.): *Unrecognized States in the International System*. (Exeter Studies in Ethno Politics Series). G. Stansfield (ed.). Routledge: London & New York, 2011.

De Waal, Thomas: *Uncertain ground. Engaging With Europe's De Facto States and Breakaway Territories*. Carnegie Endowment for International Peace: Washington, D.C., 2018.

Geldenhuys, Deon: *Contested States in World Politics*. Palgrave Macmillan: London, 2009.

Kłosowicz, Robert: *Konteksty dysfunkcyjności państw Afryki Subsaharyjskiej*. Wydawnictwo Uniwersytetu Jagiellońskiego: Kraków, 2017.

Kosidło, Adam: *Sahara Zachodnia. Fiasko dekolonizacji czy sukces podboju? 1975–2011*. Wydawnictwo Uniwersytetu Gdańskiego: Gdańsk, 2012

Lynch, Dov: "Separatist states and post-Soviet conflicts", *International Affairs* 4, 2002, pp. 831-848.

McColl, Robert W.: "The insurgent state: Territorial bases of revolution, *Annals of the Association of American Geographers* 59 (4) 1969, pp. 613-631.

Reno, William: *Warlord Politics and African States*. Lynne Reinner: Boulder, 1999.

Rutland, Peter. "Frozen conflicts, frozen analysis". (Paper presented at the International Studies Association, Chicago, 1 March 2007), retrieved 14.08.2023, from https://www.scribd.com/document/253058977/Peter-Rutland-Frozen-Conflicts.

Shelley, Toby: *Endgame in Western Sahara. What future for Africa's last colony?* Zed Books/War on Want: London & New York, 2004

Stanislawski, Bartosz H.: "Para-States, Quasi States, and Black Spots: Perhaps Not States, But Not 'Ungoverned Territories', Either", *International Studies Review* 10 (2) 2008, pp. 366-396.

USC: "SADR Recognitions". Centro de Estudos do Sahara Occidental da USC, retrieved 16.8.2023, from https://www.usc.es/en/institutos/ceso/RASD_Reconocimientos.html.

Walker, Edward: "No peace, no war in the Caucasus: Secessionist conflicts in Chechnya, Abkhazia and Nagorno-Karabakh". (Occasional Paper, Belfer Center for Science and International Affairs, Harvard Kennedy School, February 1998), retrieved 14.08.2023, from https://www.belfercenter.org/sites/default/files/files/publication/no_peace_no_war_csia_occasional_paper_1998.pdf.

Robert Kłosowicz

Chapter 1. Fragmentation, Autonomy, and Secession in Africa on the Example of *De Facto*, *Puppet* and Autonomous States[1]

The chapter aims to present the issue of unrecognised states in Africa from decolonisation to the present day within the context of African specificities related to colonial and post-colonial legacies, with special emphasis on the cases of Western Sahara and Somaliland. The focus of the chapter lies on the historical conditions surrounding the formation of *de facto states* in Africa. The author analyses existing literature on the issue, as well as draws conclusions from field research conducted on the continent. While a significant number of currently recognised states have emerged through unilateral secession in the past, the situation of *de facto states* emerging in the post-decolonisation period differs, as the international community does not recognise their statehood and regards them as illegitimate entities that contravene international law and the territorial integrity of recognised states. *De facto states* are viewed as a threat to the international order, as their existence could potentially lead to further fragmentation of the international system.

Keywords: *de facto states*, *puppet states*, autonomous states, secession, recognition, sovereignty, African states

In Africa, almost all examples of secessions and the formation of unrecognised states are linked to colonial legacy, followed by the decolonisation process, which froze the previous order established on the continent by European states. Somaliland and Western Sahara are such cases in point of unrecognised states in Africa. Somaliland has been operating without international recognition since 1991, i.e., 32 years, while the Sahrawi Arab Democratic Republic (SADR) since 1976, i.e., 47 years. However, the situation in Somaliland and Western Sahara is significantly different. According to some researchers, the territorial criterion is important and determines whether we can talk about a *de facto state*. Caspersen claims that *"First, the requirement for de facto independence and territorial control excludes cases such as Western Sahara (Sahrawi Arab Democratic Republic) which otherwise has a number of similarities with the unrecognized states"* (Caspersen

---

1   This chapter is the result of a research project financed by the National Science Centre (Narodowe Centrum Nauki), Poland, grant ID: 2017/25/B/HS5/00958.

2012, p. 9). Somaliland has permanent control over the territory and the people who inhabit it, while also maintaining full internal legitimacy as the people of Somaliland identify with and support the authorities. In addition, elections of authorities are held regularly in Somaliland and the state provides basic services. Meanwhile, the Sahrawi Arab Democratic Republic authorities are based in the refugee camps in an area belonging to the neighbouring state of Algeria (province of Tindouf). Only 20% of the Western Saharan territory is under the control of the POLISARIO Front, which is the representative organisation but also the liberation movement of the Sahrawi people. Since its proclamation of statehood in February 1976, Western Sahara has been recognised by 84 UN member states but 36 of them have withdrawn or suspended their recognition over the past 47 years. Several states that do not recognise the Sahrawi Arab Democratic Republic nonetheless recognise the POLISARIO Front as the legitimate representative of the population of the Western Sahara. Indeed, its functioning depends on the support of Algiers. In turn, the camps are maintained by the international community, which provides humanitarian aid mainly through UN agencies, but also via NGOs from around the world. At the UN General Assembly in November 1979, Resolution 34/37 was adopted, reaffirming the inalienable right of the people of Western Sahara to self-determination and recognising the POLISARIO Front as representative of the indigenous population (UN General Assembly 1979). Currently, the UN classifies Western Sahara as "a Non-Self-Governing Territory" under Chapter XI of the UN Charter, and it has been well established and acknowledged by the UN itself that it is not the appropriate authority to recognise states under international law (UN Committee on Information from Non-Self-Governing Territories: "Report…"; UN: "Charter of the United Nations", Arts. 73-74; UN Secretary General 1950).

Both *de facto states*, Somaliland and Western Sahara, manage to sustain themselves through external support from a powerful neighbour. In the case of Somaliland, this support comes from Ethiopia, while for the Sahrawi Arab Democratic Republic, it is provided by Algeria. As previously noted, Algerian assistance is pivotal, as without it, the SADR would be unable to function altogether (Kłosowicz 2015b, p. 90). In addition, in the case of Somaliland, its existence is influenced by the institutional weakness of the state from which Hargeisa declared its secession, i.e., Somalia, which has been in circumstances of statehood and territorial disintegration since the 1990s and recently returned to the first (worst) place in the ranking of fragile states conducted by the think tank Fund for Peace (Fragile States Index: 2023, Web). In contrast, Western Sahara faces the Kingdom of Morocco as its adversary. Morocco, a prominent state in the Maghreb region, also holds considerable influence in African international relations. Additionally,

Morocco served as a steadfast ally of the West, particularly France and the US, throughout the Cold War, cementing its significance on the global stage.

The description of the cases of Somaliland and Western Sahara can be analysed through the lens of considerations undertaken by P. Kolstø (2006), who looks at *de facto states* through the prevailing prism of the nation-state model, i.e., internal and external sovereignty, comparing the extent to which *de facto states* fulfil these conditions. This should take into account the assumption that modern nation states enjoy a dual sovereignty: internal to their own citizens and external to other states. Their internal sovereignty conditions the extent to which the authorities are recognised by the population of the territory which is under the control of the government and has a monopoly on the collection of taxes from the population in exchange for the provision of basic services, such as welfare and security. External sovereignty determines the extent to which the authorities are recognised as the sole representative of the people in the international arena. Some would-be states lack internal sovereignty, as in the case of the Sahrawi Arab Democratic Republic: although the vast majority of the Sahrawi population supports the POLISARIO Front, it does not fulfil the basic tasks required in terms of providing services and protecting its citizens, with only 20% of the territory under its control (so-called Liberated Territories) and its seat of power located outside its borders, managing also the refugee camps situated in the Tindouf province of Algeria.[2]

The situation differs quite significantly for Somaliland, which has internal sovereignty, controls its own territory, has a government recognised by the population that fulfils the basic tasks of a state. In the case of Somaliland, the refusal of recognition is not based on any assessment of their internal sovereignty. Instead, the reason is that this *de facto state* has separated itself from a recognised state, which does not accept this loss of territory. In the case of such countries as Somalia, the state does not in fact meet the conditions of internal sovereignty, as its state structures are in disintegration and the central government does not control its territory. Therefore, the secessionist states can be said to lack external sovereignty, and the flagship example in Africa of such a *de facto state* is precisely Somaliland (Kolstø 2006). As rightly noted by P. Kolstø (2006), these two deviations from the norm of the nation-state model are very different, even diametrically opposed to each other.

---

2   Field work conducted by the author in the Rabouni, Smara and Boujdour camps, May 2016; According to the UNHCR data, the number of Sahrawi in camps located in Algeria amounts to 173,600 in 2018 (UNHCR 2018, Web).

Robert H. Jackson, in his book *Quasi-states: Sovereignty, International Relations and the Third World* (1993), addressed the issues of states with only external sovereignty by drawing attention to the fact that most of the European colonies in Africa that gained independence in the 1950s and 1960s were poorly, or even not at all, prepared for independence, lacked even the most basic infrastructure, and did not have elites with sufficient professional training and social responsibility, capable of running state governance. In the past, states were created through war and diplomacy, and those that could not cope disintegrated and disappeared from the map. However, post-colonial states continue to exist even in the absence of the basic characteristics that were considered necessary for statehood in the past, because they are sustained:

> *Quasi-states* are kept from collapsing by leaning on an external scaffolding of international recognition, not by any internal structure of institutions and laws. Being protected by international law against external intrusions, quasi-states possess only external or negative sovereignty. (Kolstø 2006, p. 748; Jackson 1993, p. 41)

Taking Jackson's concepts into account, the vast majority of post-colonial states in Africa were quasi-states and even today several of them can be safely described as such. The example of contemporary Somaliland and Somalia illustrates this paradox very clearly. Somaliland has no international recognition and has internal sovereignty, while the state from which it has declared secession, Somalia, whose statehood is in a state of disintegration, is sustained only by external sovereignty (Fragile States Index: 2023, Web). Although Jackson touched on a very important topic, the term "quasi state" has not caught on in the literature and today the states he describes appear under the name of "failed state", "fragile state", "collapsed state", "dysfunctional state", while the term "quasi-state" is seen as an equivalent to "*de facto state*" or "unrecognised state" (Kolstø 2006; Kłosowicz / Mormul 2013, p. 18).

In Africa, the formation of unrecognised states has to do with the colonial legacy, followed by decolonisation, which preserved the artificial borders established on the continent by European states. Both currently existing unrecognised states want to function as independent states within colonial borders (Kłosowicz 2017, pp. 175-176): the SADR as heir to *Sáhara Español*, while Somaliland within the borders of the former *British Somaliland Protectorate*. Currently, it seems Somaliland's chances of international recognition are greater, while the frozen Western Sahara issue appears to be unresolvable, and each passing year moves the SADR further away from both independence and international recognition.

Another issue are periods when *de facto states* appear in greater numbers, sometimes in whole series. One such example in the history of international relations when such a phenomenon intensified, occurred in the 1990s, following the end of the Cold War and the collapse of the communist federations of the USSR and Yugoslavia. In the former Soviet Union republic of Moldova, we have the Pridnestrovian Moldavian Republic (Transnistria); and in Azerbaijan – the Nagorno-Karabakh Republic (Republic of Artsakh). Georgia has the dubious distinction of being the home of two quasi-states: Abkhazia and South Ossetia. In former Yugoslavia, there is Kosovo, Republika Srpska in Bosnia, and in the past, there was Republika Srpska Krajina in Eastern Croatia. Significantly, this was also when Africa saw the collapse of the communist regime of Mohamed Siad Barre in Somalia and the disintegration of that state, resulting in the formation of Somaliland within the borders of the former British colony. Prior to this, another such period were the decolonisation years in Africa, which stretches back in time as the process began in the 1950s in North Africa and lasted until the mid-1970s, when the former Portuguese colonies finally gained their independence.[3]

There have been several secessions in Africa over the decades following the start of decolonisation, with two successful ones – Eritrea (1993) and South Sudan (2011) and two near-successful ones that lasted for several years and resulted in unrecognised states – Katanga in Congo (1960-1963) and Biafra in Nigeria (1967-1970).[4] The last two *de facto states* lost their struggle for independence, and the example of Katanga will be further analysed in a separate chapter of the book[5]. However, in the period after the decolonisation of the African continent, other geopolitical entities also emerged, which their governments defined as states although they were not internationally recognised and did not even meet the criterion of a *de facto state*, but rather qualified under other categories of quasi-states. Such examples include puppet states, which in Africa include the Bantustans established by South Africa between 1976 and 1981. If we assume that a *de facto state* should have territory, authority, a population, and self-reliance, with its only deficiency being the lack of international recognition, then the puppet state possessed all these attributes except self-reliance and, of course, international recognition. What, then, is a puppet state in essence? It is an internationally unrecognised state that *de jure* possesses the attributes of independence, but *de facto* is entirely dependent on an external force. A puppet state thus

---

3   Angola, Mozambique, Guinea Bissau, Cape Verde, São Tomé and Príncipe.

4   Eritrea, despite not formally declaring independence after its territory was liberated from the Ethiopians in May 1991, was considered to be a *de facto state* in 1991–1993 (Caspersen / Stansfield (eds.) 2011, p. 4).

5   Chapter 8.

has nominal sovereignty, with another state effectively controlling it through economic or military dependence, in this case the Republic of South Africa.

In the literature, the most frequently cited positions shaping the view on unrecognised states include the texts of Robert H. Jackson (1993), Scott Pegg (1998), Nina Caspersen (2012), and Pål Kolstø (2006), who, in addressing the problem of the existence of unrecognised states, refer to internal as well as external conditions that can be matched to specific cases of *de facto states* in Africa, both current and historical ones, occurring in the period after the decolonisation of Africa in the 1960s. P. Kolstø (2006, pp. 753-758) defines the existence and stability of a *de facto state* on the basis of such factors as: a) the support of the population; b) the reliance on one's own military power as a basis for independence; c) the weakness of the parent state (from which the secession took place); d) the support of a patron state (or states), which may be overt or covert; e) the involvement of the international community in the process of conflict resolution around the *de facto state*.

In the African context, as regards the territory of an unrecognised state and the people living in that territory, the issue is complicated because it is closely linked both to the pre-colonial history of African states and to the colonial legacy of being dominated by European powers. The modern idea of borders was unknown in pre-colonial Africa, as they did not exist in the form of lines or planes, but often ran through areas of uninhabited buffer zones, which nobody claimed and ethnic groups moved freely through. Due to the low population density, large areas of available land and extensive agriculture, sub-Saharan Africans did not invest their efforts in cultivating the land, as they could move to other areas at any time. The lack of demographic pressure meant that battles over territory were quite rare and were not the most important determinants of existing African states in the pre-colonial era. In sub-Saharan Africa, state power manifested itself primarily in the control of as much of the population as possible, rather than in territorial sovereignty.

As mentioned, the boundaries of the colonies in sub-Saharan Africa were drawn on maps at the discretion of European negotiators, often as a result of a compromise between Old Continent states. More than half of these were simply straight lines or circular arcs, cutting across territories that had belonged for centuries to particular ethnic groups and tribes involved in cattle herding or agriculture. There were often tribes that had been in conflict with each other for generations within the boundaries of a single colony. There is no doubt that European states thus left their mark on the entire continent, and this historical legacy can still be observed today, even in international law accepting the principle of *uti possidetis*, which stipulated the immutability of the borders of former colonies as one of the conditions for recognising the independence of African states (Dudkiewicz 2012, p. 80).

Consequently, today's African states are primarily a legacy of the geopolitics of the late 19th century, when European powers competed for colonial control of Africa, i.e., territory, population, and resources, setting the boundaries of their properties without regard to ethnic, linguistic, religious and cultural issues. This is well reflected in the words of politicians speaking about Nigeria, such as the statement made by Obafemi Awolowo, who was Prime Minister of Western Nigeria under British rule:

> Nigeria is not a nation, it is a mere geographical expression. There are no "Nigerians" in the same sense as there are "English" or "Welsh" or "French". The word Nigeria is merely a distinctive appellation to distinguish those who live within the boundaries of Nigeria from those who do not. (Meredith 2011, p. 23)

Abubakar Tafawa Balewa, who became the first Prime Minister of Nigeria, similarly stated in 1947:

> …since the amalgamation of Southern and Northern provinces in 1914 Nigeria has existed as one country only on paper …. It is still far from being united. Nigeria's unity is only a British intention for the country. (Ekpu 2017, Web)

Sir Arthur Richards, who served as Governor of Nigeria from 1943 to 1948, commented on the same issue in the following words:

> It is only the accident of British suzerainty which had made Nigeria one country. It is still far from being one country or one nation socially or even economically… socially and politically there are deep differences between the major tribal groups. They do not speak the same language and they have highly divergent customs and ways of life and they represent different stages of culture. (Ekpu 2017, Web)

The artificial borders of post-colonial states in Africa have given rise to ethnic separatism, as exemplified by the secessions of Biafra, Katanga, South Sudan and Cabinda, as well as to separatism stemming from the colonial legacy but relating to different traditions of political elite formation and state and legal culture, as exemplified by Somaliland, whose population is ethnically, culturally, linguistically and religiously identical to that of Somalia. Factors that increase the pull towards self-determination can include historical traditions of independence, as in the case of Katanga (The Yeke Kingdom, Luba Empire), Cabinda (The Kingdom of Loango), or the impacts of previous colonial territorial constructs (Somaliland, Eritrea, Western Sahara). Groups that have strong traditions of independence even dating back to pre-colonial times or that have lost their autonomy in the recent past are more likely to be separatist than those that did not have such traditions. It should also be noted that the boundary between the movement for autonomy (South Kasai) and the movement for secession (Katanga) is fluid. Both use similar language referring to historical traditions, the ethnic factor, or territorial issues (Krawczuk 2019, pp. 332-333). According to some theories, ethnic awakening, of which ethnic separatism is an extreme form, can be both an expression of the aspirations of political elites seeking a greater share of power (Eritrea, Somaliland) and an expression of frustration in response to the political and economic marginalisation of an ethnic group (Eritrea) or of a population living in a particular territory (Somaliland). Finally, it might be the result of an awareness of possessing rich deposits and a reluctance to share income with other regions (Cabinda, Katanga, Biafra).

As mentioned, at the time of the decolonisation of Africa, the principle of *uti possidetis iuris* was adopted at the Organisation of African Unity (OAU) in 1964, which was intended to guarantee the inviolability of the borders of the newly created states and prevent conflict between African countries. From the outset, however, separatist tendencies became apparent, whether driven by a desire to unite ethnic groups separated by colonial (and now state) borders or to gain independence by seizing regions rich in natural resources. Even in the early days of the formation of independent states in sub-Saharan Africa, there was internal fighting, as exemplified by the civil war in the Belgian Congo and the failed secession of Katanga. The principle of *uti possidetis* took on particular significance during the decolonisation of Africa and was an endorsed practice for many years, with the OAU categorically opposing the secession of territories that were part of the Congo, Sudan, Nigeria, Ethiopia, or Angola. The legitimacy of the application of the *uti possidetis* principle was not questioned throughout the Cold War period. The exception was the recognition by four African states of the secession of Biafra from Nigeria, announced in May 1967.[6]

As the last 50 years of history have shown, this principle has not protected the states of the region from internal conflicts and separatist movements. The problem of secessionism in contemporary Africa in the context of post-colonial borders maintained by the *uti possidetis* principle is still relevant, as illustrated by the examples of resurgent separatist tendencies in Biafra (Nigeria), Cabinda (Angola), Azawad (Mali) or Somaliland (Somalia), which continue to seek international recognition, political independence, or greater autonomy. The Western Sahara issue differs in that this territory was under Spanish rule during the colonial period and was subsequently annexed by Morocco in the mid-1970s,

---

6 The Ivory Coast, Gabon, Tanzania, and Zambia.

thereby disrupting the decolonisation process of the region. A departure from the principle adopted during the decolonisation period of the immutability of post-colonial borders in Africa was made only in the cases of Eritrea and South Sudan, which gained political independence after decades of fighting. The Republic of Somaliland has continued to await international recognition for the last 32 years, after declaring independence in May 1991. In recent years, there have also been calls for secession in other African countries, such as in Uganda, where some politicians and the population of the area where the traditional kingdom of Buganda was located have expressed aspirations for independence, or in the north-western regions of Cameroon, where Ambazonian separatists in the Anglophone regions have become active (Kashambuzi 2011, Web; Cohen 2014, p. 419; Różański 2023, pp. 171-196).

It is worth noting that most separatist movements in sub-Saharan Africa have their roots in the colonial era, with the people of regions such as Cabinda (a former Portuguese colony), Western Sahara (a former Spanish colony) and Somaliland (a former British colony) wanting independence within colonial-era borders. During the decolonisation period, Cabinda, located at the mouth of the Congo River flowing into the Atlantic Ocean, was a Portuguese exclave only nominally part of the Portuguese colony of Angola. After its declaration of independence, it was occupied by Angolan troops.[7] The same fate befell Western Sahara, which had been a Spanish colony (Spanish Sahara) and was then occupied by Moroccan and Mauritanian troops after the Spanish withdrew.[8] Somaliland belonged to the United Kingdom during the colonial period, after which it voluntarily entered into a state union with Somalia (a former Italian colony) during the decolonisation period, and has been unsuccessfully seeking international recognition since breaking away from Somalia in 1991 (Wanyonyi 2016, pp. 46-47). In turn, in Cameroon there are growing tensions between areas that were trust territories of Britain and France, respectively, during the colonial period (Crisis24 2020, Web).

---

7 Administratively, Cabinda was a part of the Portuguese colony of Angola as of the 1950s.

8 Ultimately, Mauretania – under pressure from the Organisation of African Unity and because of the high cost of the conflict – withdrew from Western Sahara, but the territory was then occupied by Moroccan troops, who continue to occupy it today.

Table 1. Largest ethnic groups divided among countries in sub-Saharan Africa.

Name of the ethnic group	Countries they inhabit	Population
Fulani/Fulbe	Mauritania, Burkina Faso, Mali, Chad, Sudan, Niger, Cameroon, Central African Republic, Guinea, Guinea Bissau, Togo, Ivory Coast, Benin, Sierra Leone, Senegal	41.4 million
Yoruba	Nigeria, Benin, Ghana, Togo, Ivory Coast	50.1 million
Hausa	Benin, Ghana, Chad, Cameroon, Niger, Nigeria	56 million
Oromo	Ethiopia, Sudan, Kenya	44.5 million
Igbo	Nigeria, Equatorial Guinea, Cameroon, Ghana	37.1 million
Akan	Ghana, Ivory Coast, Togo, Liberia	20 million
Somali	Somalia, Ethiopia, Kenya, Djibouti	30 million
Bantu, Chewa-Sena	Malawi, Zambia, Mozambique, Zimbabwe, Republic of South Africa	23 million
Bantu, Central-Luba	Democratic Republic of Congo, Angola, Zambia	22,4 million

Source: Own compilation based on the *Joshua Project* ("People Groups", Web)

As mentioned, the creation of Eritrea and South Sudan is, thus far, the only major change on the map of sub-Saharan Africa after the decolonisation period which is in clear contradiction to the principle of *uti possidetis*. It is also worth noting that Morocco's annexation of Western Sahara was also a violation of the *uti possidetis* principle, and to this day it remains an unresolved political issue both regionally and globally (Byrne / Engelbert 2014, p. 3). Another departure from the principle of immutability of post-colonial borders involved the merger of Tanganyika and Zanzibar in 1964, although this was done peacefully (Calvo-coressi 2002, p. 706).

South Sudan's independence has prompted a return in the international community to reflection on the real legal meaning of the principle and the future of its application in Africa (Fagbayibo 2012, Web). Increasingly, voices are being raised about the need to move away from the principle of *uti possidetis*, as it does not lead to the fulfilment of its assumptions and does not make it possible for African states to adapt their borders to topographical and ethnic realities, which would allow the natural processes of state-building on the continent to develop unhindered. This topic was addressed by G. Pascal Zachary in an article titled "Africa Needs a New Map", which appeared in the magazine *Foreign Policy* in April 2010:

> Silence about borders has become Africa's pathology, born in the era of strongman leaders that followed decolonialization. Loath to lose any of their newly independent land, the continent's leaders upheld a gentleman's agreement to favor "stability" over change. Today, the unfortunate result is visible in nearly every corner of Africa: from a divided Nigeria, to an ungovernable Democratic Republic of the Congo (DRC), to the very real but unrecognized state in Somaliland. Borders created through some combination of ignorance and malice are today one of the continent's major barriers to building strong, competent states. No initiative would do more for happiness, stability, and economic growth in Africa today than an energetic and enlightened redrawing of these harmful lines. (…) Rethinking the borders could go far to quelling some of these conflicts. Countries could finally be framed around the de facto geography of ethnic groups. The new states could use their local languages rather than favoring another ethnicity's or colonial power's tongue. Rebel secessionist movements would all but disappear, and democracy could flourish more easily when based upon policies, rather than simple identity politics. On top of that, new states based on ethnic lines would by default be smaller, more compact, and more manageable for governments on a continent with a history of state weakness. (Zachary 2010, Web)

However, opponents of abandoning the *uti possidetis* principle note that while the principle is imperfect, ceasing its application could result in the outbreak of numerous intra- and inter-state conflicts with tragic consequences for the population, entailing the death and suffering of millions of people and the Balkanization of the sub-Saharan African subcontinent (Smith 2011, Web). Some, like Arthur S. Gakwandi (1996), have gone in the opposite direction, seeking even greater integration and proposing a new political map of Africa that would include only seven major states. According to such thinkers, this would solve current problems, such as border disputes, refugees, or weak and poor landlocked states. Yet others, like Ifeanyi A. Menkiti, believe that the existence of state territories in Africa within post-colonial borders is a secondary issue. The philosopher sees the future of the common, successful coexistence of different peoples primarily from the perspective of the existence of a state of justice within it. Thus, for Menkiti, it is not the integrity of modern African states that is the primary value, but how the life of societies within those states will be organised, because if the lives of citizens are arranged within a just state, it will become possible for different peoples to coexist in a single country within post-colonial borders or to bring about peaceful settlements of their division (see Trzciński 2013, pp. 75-76).

Although borders may eventually need to be redrawn, we do not have to do so right now. Social justice is still a powerful silent partner in the preservation of state boundaries. If the African state earns the respect of its citizens through the achievement of justice in the public domain, then it may not matter whether Africa remains as is, with its present boundaries, or is adjusted back to its earlier arrangements. What is important is that citizens feel secure in their persons and that they know their life prospects are not being dismantled by the very state that is supposed to be advancing them (Menkiti 2001, p. 146, qtd after Trzciński 2010, p. 2).

Biafra, the renaissance of separatism

Nigeria's oil-rich Biafra is an example of secessionism which has revived with renewed vigour in the past two years. Secession took place as early as May 30, 1967, when the military governor of the Eastern Region with the Igbo people as its dominant ethnic group, Lieutenant Colonel Chukwuemeka Odumegwu Ojukwu, announced its separation from Nigeria and the formation of the independent Republic of Biafra. The immensely devastating civil war lasted two and a half years and cost the lives of around two million people. The secessionist resistance was sustained by foreign aid. Contrary to the OAU's position, Biafran independence was also recognised by some African countries – Gabon, Tanzania, Ivory Coast and Zambia (Leśniewski 1996, p. 410). Support was also provided by European countries, such as Portugal, who granted access to airports in Lisbon, Guinea-Bissau or São Tomé and Príncipe, and France, whose government allowed clandestine arms deliveries to the rebellious province. The Biafran affair has become the subject of great interest to world public opinion and a symbol of the heroic and unequal struggle for independence (Piłaszewicz 2006, pp. 344-345; Meredith 2011, pp. 193-205). The conflict demonstrated the weakness of both the OAU and the UN. Throughout the war, both organisations attempted to bring the parties to an agreement, but the lack of unity in both institutions, as well as the interests of outside states, mainly the USSR, the USA, France, the

UK, and Portugal, did not help in resolving the conflict. The issue was also not clear-cut from the point of view of international law, since, on the one hand, the secession of Biafra contradicted the principle of *uti possidetis* (Article III, paragraph 3 of the OAU Charter – 1963) and the resolution of the Assembly of Heads of State and Government of the OAU (1964) (Srogosz 2011, p. 64); however, on the other hand, it did not interfere with the right to the self-determination of peoples. Moreover, the decision to secede was made by the region's legitimate government. The Biafra issue appears to have been sacrificed to ensure the permanence of the post-colonial arrangement in Africa and to prevent a domino effect that would have led to further attempts at secession across the continent, which could have resulted in the Balkanisation of Africa and numerous internal wars (Leśniewski 2000, p. 410).

Currently, the Igbo population in Nigeria constitutes 18% of 182 million inhabitants (UN, Department of Economic and Social Affairs, Population Division 2015, p. 16). 2017 marks the fiftieth anniversary of the secession, which left a lasting mark on the ethnic group, and the memory of the struggle has survived in subsequent generations. This is reflected in the numerous organisations that have emerged in recent years in Nigeria that operate in the Niger Delta region, some of which are peaceful in nature, while others resort to various forms of armed struggle: Ethnic Minorities Organization of Nigeria, the November 1985 Movement, the Urhobo Youth Movement, the Movement for Emancipation of Niger Delta – MEND, the Niger Delta Volunteer Force – NDVF, the Niger Delta Vigilante – NDV and the Niger Delta Strike Force – NDSF (Tycholiz 2010, pp. 190-191). The current leader of the secessionists is Nnamdi Kanu, who heads the Indigenous People of Biafra (IPOB) movement, established in 2012. The voice of the movement is the online Radio of Biafra (Radio Biafra), based in London. IPOB's goal is to peacefully agitate for the independence of Biafra, which as a state would be established within pre-colonial borders. IPOB leaders believe that the lack of shared values between Biafra and other regions of Nigeria makes it impossible to remain within a single state union. In October 2015, Kanu was arrested by the Nigerian Security Service and was imprisoned until the end of April 2017. He is a typical representative of the younger generation of Biafran independence supporters, already born after the Nigerian civil war. This generation is frustrated by corruption and bad governance and is looking to sever ties with the Nigerian state. According to observers, the fact that the Biafran issue is being raised once again should rather be seen as a consequence of, and even in a sense a metaphor for, a Nigerian state sinking into dysfunctionality, unable to cope with Boko Haram terrorists declaring the establishment of an independent caliphate in the northern part of the country, carrying out bloody bombings in public places and kidnapping students from public schools with impunity. The young Igbo generation believes that eventual independence will give them prospects for a better life in their own country, rich in oil. Meanwhile, Nigerian President Muhammadu Buhari, who served as an officer in the government troops during the civil war against Biafran secession, officially announced that he is not considering the possibility of Biafra seceding from Nigeria. The situation in the south of the country is becoming more tense and there is a real threat that the nightmare of civil war could become a reality (Wambu 2016, p. 82; Siollun 2016, pp. 20-21). In 2016, a new organization emerged that opted to adopt a form of armed struggle - the Niger Delta Avengers (NDA) (Niger Delta Avengers 2016, Web). This organization is a consolidation of previously inactive paramilitary groups that were formerly operating under the MEND umbrella. According to its official website, the NDA strongly advocates secession and has announced it will increase armed operations (Niger Delta Avengers 2017, Web).

In September 2017, President Muhammadu Buhari launched Operation Python Dance II in the southeast. It was ostensibly implemented to combat crime, but later turned into a tool of repression against unarmed members of the Indigenous People of Biafra. In the same month, the Nigerian government declared the Indigenous People of Biafra outlawed, but the organisation's activities did not cease. In December 2020, the organization established its paramilitary wing, known as the Eastern Security Network. According to the media and publicity secretary of the Indigenous People of Biafra, Comrade Emma Powerful, "the network was mandated to defend what he described as Biafraland by counteracting the activities of suspected armed Fulani herdsmen against peasant farmers and local communities" (The Conversation 2021, Web). During the government of President Muhammadu Buhari (2015-2023), separatist tendencies in the Biafra region grew exponentially, due to his political nominations, which were largely criticised in the south as they favoured individuals from the northern part of the country (Sahara Reporters 2015, Web). A second contributing factor was the location of important infrastructure investments in the country. One example was the railroad construction works, in which the Port Harcourt-Maiduguri rail project was completely neglected, while another was the National Assembly's approval of a huge infrastructure development plan without allocating a single project for the southeast zone (The Conversation 2021, Web).

Currently, mainly the Igbo and the Yoruba support separatism, but that could change soon. Several groups in northern Nigeria, as well as former national political leaders, unofficially admit that keeping Biafra in the federation is not worth another civil war. Meanwhile, separatist tendencies are also widespread among the Igbo diaspora, which translates into financial and material support for separatist movements in the country (Campbell / Quinn 2021, Web).

In addition, the rising separatism among the Yoruba might soon complicate Nigeria's relations with Benin, which is inhabited in 12.3 % by this ethnic group (World Directory of Minorities and Indigenous Peoples: "Benin", Web; Embassy of Benin, Washington DC: "Culture beninoise", Web). In addition, Biafran separatists have established cooperation with separatist movements in Northern Cameroon, which translates into mobilising supporters through social media, and clashing with government security forces in both countries, threatening both states with destabilisation (Craig 2021).

The separatist exclave of Cabinda

An exclave of Angola, Cabinda is separated from that country's territory by a narrow strip belonging to the Democratic Republic of Congo. The conflict began in August 1975, when Cabinda declared independence from Portugal, and three months later the troops of independent Angola and supporting Cuban troops occupied its territory. Angola then declared that Cabinda was an integral part of its territory. Angolan troops occupied the main cities, while the Front for the Liberation of the Enclave of Cabinda (*Frente para a Libertação do Enclave de Cabinda* – FLEC) exercised control in the provinces. Since then, the armed conflict has continued, with interruptions and varying degrees of intensity. The main obstacle to Cabinda's independence appears to be its large oil deposits. Indeed, the province produces 60% of Angola's oil, which accounts for half of the country's GDP. Cabinda also has other natural wealth in the form of gold, diamond, and uranium deposits (Kłosowicz 2015a). The population of the province amounts to 600,000 inhabitants, which constitutes 2.4 % of Angola's total population consisting of 25 million citizens (UN, Department of Economic and Social Affairs, Population Division 2015, p. 13). With such rich oil resources, if it were independent, the citizens of Cabinda would be among the richest in the world in terms of per capita GDP income. The prospect of the potential wealth of the province's population appears to be a stronger motivation in separatist aspirations than ethnic identification, but the separatist movement in Cabinda is relatively weak, both in terms of internal armed potential and international support.[9] Currently, the entire territory of the province is controlled by the Angolan military. In 2002,

---

9   During the Apartheid period, FLEC supported the Republic of South Africa to destabilise the political situation in Angola.

Angola's 30,000-strong armed forces carried out a major operation against FLEC guerrillas and destroyed their main bases, including those on the territory of the Democratic Republic of Congo (then emersed in the chaos of civil war). The last of the more high-profile incidents to draw the world's attention to the Cabinda problem was the shelling in January 2010 by FLEC guerrillas of a coach carrying the Togo football team, which was travelling to the Africa Cup of Nations being held in Angola. As a result of the shelling, three people were killed and several injured (BBC News 2010, Web). In July 2020, clashes occurred between separatists from FLEC and the Angolan Armed Forces, resulting in multiple fatalities in the Cabinda enclave (Crisis24 2020, Web).

The Autonomous Mining State of South Kasai (1960-1961)

An interesting case of seeking independence but without declaring an act of independence was that of South Kasai, a province that is part of the Congo (now the Democratic Republic of Congo). Even before the Republic of Congo declared independence (June 1960), steps towards broad autonomy were taken by the province of South Kasai, rich in mineral deposits, mainly diamonds.[10] Initially, South Kasai officially only sought broad autonomy, hoping that the turmoil in the Congo over its newly won independence and then the secession of Katanga would help it achieve its goal of eventual full independence. It was waiting for developments in Congo and Katanga. However, unlike Katanga, South Kasai did not explicitly declare full independence from the Republic of Congo. Rather, it introduced something resembling self-governance in the province; the title 'autonomous state' was also chosen not coincidentally, as it was intended to give the impression that secession was not a rejection of Congolese sovereignty. In practice, South Kasai had much more independence than a normal province and the steps taken were in fact a separation from Congo. Deputies from the province initially refused to sit in the Congolese parliament in Léopoldville and no taxes were transferred to the Congolese central budget (Ndikumana, Emizet 2005, pp. 67-68). The leader and main proponent of South Kasai, Albert Kalonji, who before decolonisation represented a faction of the National Movement of the Congo-Kalonji (*Mouvement National Congolais-Kalonji* – MNC-K), a nationalist organization, exploited ethnic tensions between his own Baluba ethnic group to create a state in the south-eastern Kasai region inhabited overwhelmingly by the

---

10 The South Kasai Province had a one third share of global diamond mining until the mid-1970s.

Baluba ethnic group. He was able to gain wide support for this purpose from local chiefs. Internationally, he portrayed secession as the result of persecution and the failure of the Congolese government to sufficiently protect the Baluba people in the rest of Congo.

Antagonism between the Baluba and Lulua ethnic groups began to grow significantly in December 1957, when the Baluba won the Luluaoburg (now Kananga) municipal elections. The Lulua, on the other hand, won the provincial parliamentary elections in 1959. This turned into a crisis in the relations between the Baluba and Lulua when the local administration proposed to resettle Baluba farmers from Lulua lands to their indigenous territories in South Kasai. This sparked fierce clashes in mid-October 1959. The central government dispatched a team to calm the situation and resolve the conflict during an improvised conference with representatives of the two feuding ethnic groups. At the conference, the suggestion was made that some 100,000 Baluba farmers should return to their native lands in South Kasai as this would help to resolve the conflict. Although indeed some Baluba farmers did return to South Kasai, this was not the end of problems. Kalonji was disappointed by the support shown for the Lulua by the central government represented by Patrice Lumumba, which was in a sense the result of a political alliance for the purposes of the electoral struggle between Lumumba representing the MNC and the Lulua supporting him (Ndikumana / Emizet 2005, pp. 67-68).

When riots broke out across the Belgian Congo, leading to chaos, the Autonomous State of South Kasai was proclaimed on 9 August 1960, with Bakwanga (now Mbuji-Mayi) as its capital. Kalonji became president, declaring secession from the Congo and calling for the return of the Baluba living in the rest of the Congo to their 'homeland'. Like Katanga, South Kasai, after declaring secession in August 1960, was supported by foreign powers, notably Belgium, and financed by the *Société Minière du Bécéka*, which, like the *Union Minière du Haut-Katanga* (UMHK), was part of the *Société Générale de Belgique* (Vanthemsche 2012, p. 244). In addition to its links with the UMHK, its subsidiary *De Beers* also had a strong interest in the diamond mining business in Kasai province. In September 1960, there was even a conversation between Harry Oppenheimer, a South African businessman and founder of the Anglo-American Company, extensively involved in diamond mining, and representatives of the South Kasai government, who asked him to support the secession (Pfister 2005, p. 35).

The attempted secession of South Kasai was not only economically motivated, but also ideologically and ethnically, as the leader, Albert Kalonji, who had previously been a prominent activist in the Congolese National Movement, came into conflict with Patrice Lumumba over the future state system. Lumumba advocated a strong central government, while Kalonji wanted a federation in which provinces within ethnic boundaries would have wide autonomy. Furthermore, in South Kasai, the Baluba ethnic group constituted the majority of the population. There was also the issue of the impact of the Belgians, who wanted to secure the diamond-rich areas of Kasai (*Société internationale forestière et minière du Congo*). The former colonisers, in the new political situation of the decolonisation of Congo, decided to pursue their interests within the federal structure of the Congolese state, with a weak central government. Moïse Tshombe, president of the secessionist African state of Katanga, supported the initiative for the secession of South Kasai and even considered, together with Kalonji, the creation of a confederation of Katanga and South Kasai. These two areas together constitute a quarter of Congo's territory and are by far the richest in mineral resources (Van Reybrouck 2016, pp. 39-391)[11].

On 12 April 1961, South Kasai was proclaimed a kingdom and Albert Kalonji was named King Albert I. This was a reference to the Baluba Kingdom established in the early 16th century, which was subsequently conquered by the Basonge tribes and revived around 1585. At the end of the 19th century, the country was conquered by the Belgians and incorporated into their colony of the Belgian Congo. Soon after the declaration of secession, the first battles between the South Kasai army and the Congolese army took place. The armed clashes were accompanied by massacres committed by the Congolese army against the civilian population. The Congolese army's expedition to South Kasai is believed to have ended with the massacre of 3,000 Baluba people and the flight of some 250,000. UN Secretary-General Dag Hammarskjöld called the Congolese army's actions one of the most blatant cases of violation of fundamental human rights, bearing the hallmarks of genocide (Van Reybrouck 2016, p. 391). At the end of 1962, South Kasai was reincorporated into the Democratic Republic of Congo (Encyclopedia Britannica: "Democratic Republic of the Congo...", Web).

South Kasai sought full independence, only choosing not to officially break ties with the Congo for tactical reasons. However, all political actions as well as those linked to the symbolic sphere, such as the reference to the historic Baluba Kingdom, show that these were aspirations directed towards the creation of an independent state of the people from the ethnic Baluba group. However, the actions of the UN supported by African states, the non-aligned countries movement and the USA, as well as the defeat of the separatists in Katanga, ultimately sealed the fate of South Kasai.

---

11 More on the State of Katanga in Chapter 8.

Although South Kasai has not made a formal declaration of independence, it can be considered in terms of a *de facto state*, as by not insisting on a formal declaration of independence, today entities such as Taiwan, the Kurdistan Region of Iraq are treated as *de facto states*. In this situation, the absence of a formal declaration of independence may be a strategic attempt to increase the room for manoeuvre and the prospect of international support. Such considerations were evident in Abkhazia, which only formally declared independence in 1999, despite having been a *de facto state* since 1993. Eritrea also only declared independence in 1993 after an independence referendum, despite having actually been independent since 1991 (Caspersen and Stansfield 2011, p. 4).

"Independent" Bantustans as an example of *puppet states* in South Africa (1976 – 1994)

A *puppet state, puppet regime, puppet government* or *dummy government* is a state that is *de jure* independent but *de facto* completely dependent upon an outside power and subject to its orders. *Puppet states* have nominal sovereignty, but a foreign power effectively exercises control through economic or military support. This is the name given in the literature to the unrecognised states that were the Bantustans created between 1976 and 1981 by the racist South African regime (Phillips, Chipkin 2014, Web).

The name Bantustan comes from the name of a group of African tribes classified as a Negroid race, living on the steppes in central and southern Africa. Another name used was 'homelands', and they made up 13.8% of South Africa's total area. These territories were carved out of the Republic of South Africa between 1971 and 1981 to be home to particular groups of black people (Egerö 1991). However, these regions, which were formally intended to be independent states or at least regions with a high degree of autonomy within South Africa, were in fact a tool of apartheid's racist policy – a permanent division of the country into separate political-territorial organisms governed by their own laws and customs, since in fact the idea of Bantustanisation embodied the far-reaching goal of territorial apartheid (Malinowski 1988, p. 148).

The principal purpose of these states was to remove South African citizenship from the Xhosa, Tswana, and Venda peoples. When in 1976, Transkei was declared an independent country, the 1.6 million Xhosa people living in this Bantustan and the 1.3 million inhabiting "white territories" lost South African citizenship (Meredith 2011, p. 423). Following the proclamation of independence in four successive Bantustans between 1976 and 1981, it is thought that as many as 8 million Africans, or about one third of the black population of

South Africa at the time, lost their South African citizenship.[12] The Bantustans had no chance of becoming independent states, as they were largely located in infertile areas and devoid of natural resources (with the exception of Bophuthatswana), lacked developed infrastructure and industry, which prevented them from achieving economic independence. The South African rand was the official currency of these quasi-states. The geography of the Bantustans made little sense as most comprised scattered and fragmented pieces of land broken up into many separate territories, e.g., the Bophuthatswana Bantustan consisted of 19 areas scattered across three provinces. This division of the Bantustans prevented their integration and development. Furthermore, they were also overpopulated (Meredith 2011, p. 422). They were governed by people who were dependent on and fully controlled by South African authorities. They also did not have the support of their compatriots. This led to these governments and quasi-states to be completely dependent on Pretoria. The South African authorities granted 'formal independence' to four Bantustans – Transkei, Bophuthatswana, Venda, and Ciskei. None of these quasi states joined either the UN or any other international organisation. In a wave of democratic change in 1994, these four Bantustans were reincorporated into South Africa on 27 April 1994, while the autonomy of the others was revoked. A brief description of the 'independent' Bantustans follows.

The concept of Bantustans was not new as in colonial times the British created a quasi-state within South Africa officially known as New Griqualand, which was located between the Umzimkulu and Kinira rivers, south of the Sotho Kingdom. New Griqualand existed from the early 1860s until the late 1870s, when the territory was occupied by the British Empire and became a colony in 1874 and was then administratively incorporated into the neighbouring Cape Colony (Egerö 1991, pp. 6-8, 12-16; Khapoya 1980, pp. 28-30).

Transkei – a Bantustan created in 1963 for the Xhosa people covering an area of 42,900 km². It was located within the borders of the modern Eastern Cape Province. It formally became independent on 26 October 1976, with Umtata as the capital of the Bantustan. Its population in 1985 was 3 million. Even before the declaration of independence in May 1976, the South African Parliament passed the Republic of Transkei Constitution Act of 1976 as the basis for the declaration of independence, which was subsequently approved by the Transkei Legislative Assembly. In September, South African Prime Minister John Vorster and Kaiser Daliwonga Mathanzima signed more than 70 bilateral agreements in Pretoria

---

12 Blacks – 24.9 million, 74.1% (O'Malley: "Demographic Characteristics of South Africa...", Web)

on all areas of relations between South Africa and the Transkei. The declaration of independence was attended by South African President Nicolaas Johannes Diederichs and parliamentarians from Taiwan and Chile (Malinowski 1986, p. 219). In the constitution of Transkei, equal electoral rights were guaranteed to all citizens regardless of their skin colour. The official language was Xhosa, with English and Sotho also allowed as official languages (Gąsowski 2006, p. 196).

In order to gain support in the eyes of the population, Prime Minister Kaiser Daliwonga Mathanzima even made territorial claims to the South African government resulting in the incorporation of the town of Port Saint Johns into Transkei. In February 1978, this leader threatened – "as part of a deepening of sovereignty" – that the Transkei would sever all diplomatic relations with South Africa, including the non-aggression pact between them, if all members of the South African Defence Force seconded to the Transkei army did not leave the Bantustan within a month. This political theatre was soon over, with Mathanzima backing down from his demands in the face of Transkei's dependence on South African economic aid. Despite efforts for international recognition, no country in the world, except South Africa, recognised its independence. Moreover, the proclamation of Transkei independence was met with widespread international condemnation. African states were particularly vocal in strongly condemning the South African government. The UN General Assembly on 27 October 1976 did not recognise the declaration of independence of the so-called independent Transkei and described it as "invalid" (Gąsowski 2006; Malinowski 1986).

1. *Strongly condemns* the establishment of bantustans as designed to consolidate the inhuman policies of *apartheid*, to destroy the territorial integrity of the country, to perpetuate white minority domination and to dispossess the African people of South Africa of their inalienable rights;

2. *Rejects* the declaration of "independence" of the Transkei and declares it invalid;

3. *Calls upon* all Governments to deny any form of recognition to the so-called independent Transkei and to refrain from having any dealings with the so-called independent Transkei or other bantustans;

4. *Requests* all States to take effective measures to prohibit all individuals, corporations and other institutions under their jurisdiction from having any dealings with the so-called independent Transkei or other bantustans. (UN General Assembly 1976)

Bophuthatswana, officially the Republic of Bophuthatswana – a Bantustan created in 1972 for the Tswana peoples, from the transformation of the Tswanaland Bantustan that existed since 1968. It gained independence on 6

December 1977 following a similar procedure to Transkei the year before. It had an area of 41.7 km² and a population of 1.7 million in 1985, with an average population density of 41.3 inhabitants per km². Its territory was a scattered mosaic of enclaves spread over the Cape Province, the Free State of Orania, and the Transvaal. The seat of government was Mmabatho. Unlike the other Bantustans, the new state had considerable economic potential, with mines where two-thirds of the total platinum production in the Western world was extracted. It was also rich in asbestos, granite, vanadium, chromium, and manganese. The Bantustan was financially dependent on Pretoria, which also had an 'advisory' voice in diplomatic and defence matters (Time 1977, Web).

The Republic of Bophuthatswana was not recognised by any country in the world except South Africa and the Transkei Bantustan. However, despite its official isolation, the Mmabatho government managed to establish a trade mission in Tel Aviv, Israel and to do business with neighbouring Botswana. Bophuthatswana maintained an unofficial embassy in Israel in the 1980s, with the Bantustan's president, Lucas Mangope, meeting important Israeli political figures of the time, such as Moshe Dayan, during visits to Israel. United Nations Secretary-General Kurt Waldheim said that he "strongly deplored" the establishment of "another so-called independent tribal homeland in pursuance of the discredited policies of apartheid" (Time 1977, Web) and in resolution A/RES/32/105N, passed on 14 December 1977, the United Nations General Assembly linked Bophuthatswana's "so-called 'independence'" to South Africa's "stubborn pursuit" of its policies, and called upon all governments to "deny any form of recognition to the so-called 'independent' bantustans" (UN General Assembly 1977).

Venda – a Bantustan created in 1973 for the Shona, from the transformation of the territory of VhaVenda, which had existed since 1969. It gained independence on 13 September 1979. The capital was originally located in Sibasa and was moved to Thohoyandou in 1979. The Bantustan covered an area of 6,900 square kilometres and had a population of 460,000 in 1985, with 66.7 inhabitants per square kilometre.

Ciskei – a Bantustan for the Xhosa peoples, created in 1972 from the territory of Ciskei, which had existed since 1968. It gained independence on 4 December 1981, with an area of 7,500 km² and a population of 1,088,476. The country's capital was Bisho (Egerö 1991, p. 8).

The international community did not fall for Pretoria's political manoeuvre, and the issue of their status under international law was researched and described in the legal and political literature of the time, as aptly summarized by Henry J. Richardson (1978) in the article *Self-Determination, International Law and the South African Bantustan Policy*:

„The general question of the legal consequences of the continuing unlawful re-tention of control by the Pretoria regime over an adjacent territory has been thor-oughly explored by the International Court of Justice in its Advisory Opinion on Namibia. Although the facts there concern the relationship between South Af-rica and an international territory, the policies underpinning the Court's holding as to the resulting legal consequences are applicable to the Transkei situation. Since domestic apartheid now clearly violates the same major international pol-icies that the analogous "exported apartheid" policy has been held to violate, the consequent treatment of Africans in and around the Transkei, whether it is now an unrecognized territory of ambiguous status or a province of the South African state, must be assessed under policies substantially identical to those adduced by the Court in Namibia. This is especially so in that both cases feature sustained coercion by South Africa which is simultaneously the sine qua non of that government's continuing control over the people involved and imper-missible as a matter of law in its objectives, strategies and outcomes. Analogous legal consequences, mutatis mutandis, for member states of the United Nations would seem to follow. These consequences would clearly encompass a duty of nonrecognition of the Transkei's change in status, including the refusal to send special missions or diplomatic envoys to the Transkei. They would encompass a duty to refuse to enter into treaty relations, or maintain those already in force…." (Richardson 1978, p. 218).

Table 2. List of unrecognised states in Africa since decolonisation.

Unrecognised state	The state from which secession was declared	Date of dec-laration of independence	Period of existence of unrecogni-sed state	Current statehood attribution
Katanga	Congo	11 July 1960	1960–1963	Democratic Republic of Congo
Rhodesia	Great Britain	11 November 1965	1965–1980	Zimbabwe
Biafra	Nigeria	30 May 1967	1967–1970	Nigeria
Cabinda	Portugal	1 August 1975	1975	Angola

Unrecognised state	The state from which secession was declared	Date of declaration of independence	Period of existence of unrecognised state	Current statehood attribution
Western Sahara (Sahrawi Arab Democratic Republic)	Spain	27 February 1976	1976 – to this day (controlling only 20% of the territory)	Morocco
Transkei	Republic of South Africa	26 October 1976	1976–1994	Republic of South Africa
Bophuthatswana	Republic of South Africa	6 December 1977	1977–1994	Republic of South Africa
Venda	Republic of South Africa	13 September 1979	1979–1994	Republic of South Africa
Ciskei	Republic of South Africa	4 December 1981	1981–1994	Republic of South Africa
Somaliland	Somalia	18 May 1991	1991 – to this day (controlling 100% of the territory)	Formally, it belongs to Somalia, but it is *de facto* independent
Eritrea	Ethiopia	24 May 1991 is considered to be the date of gaining independence	1991–1993 (1993 – achieved international recognition)	Eritrea
Anjouan	The Comoros	26 October 1997	1997–2002	The Comoros (autonomy)
Jubaland	Somalia	3 September 1998	1998–2013	Somalia (autonomy)
Azawad	Mali	12 July 2012	2012	Mali

Prepared by the author based on *Unrecognized States since World War II* (Caspersen / Stansfield 2011, p. 4).

Conclusions

As demonstrated in this chapter, unresolved territorial or ethnic conflicts around established and evolving *de facto states* pose serious challenges to regional and international stability, through the involvement of various external actors. The international community is struggling to find adequate responses to the subsequent challenges of *de facto states* and secession-related conflicts (Berg / Toomla 2009). Although the main actors in the international system generally oppose unilateral secession, in some cases they encourage *de facto states* to engage at various levels of international cooperation, an example of which is the cooperation of the United Nations Office on Drugs and Crime with Somaliland to combat piracy off the coast of Somalia (Kosienkowski 218, pp. 171-217). International organisations (IOs), such as the United Nations (UN), the Organisation for Security and Cooperation in Europe (OSCE), the European Union (EU) and the member states of these organisations, despite their apparent activities, actually do little to effectively address the problem of unrecognised states, which in fact remains in the hands of the strongest players in the region or the global powers.

In sub-Saharan Africa since 1960, three scenarios can be distinguished regarding the paths of emergence of unrecognised or autonomous states. They have emerged as the result of an initial decolonisation process (Rhodesia, Cabinda, Western Sahara), due to the breakdown of collapsed states (Somaliland) or through secession and armed conflict (Eritrea, South Sudan, Katanga, Biafra, Azawad). Several were reintegrated as a result of armed action (Katanga, South Kasai, Biafra, Cabinda). Two of the *de facto states* existed only episodically for a few months – South Kasai and Cabinda. Most of these entities existed for several or more years, Rhodesia – 15 years (1965-1980), Katanga – 3 years (1960-1963), Biafra – 3 years (1967-1970). As mentioned, only two cases – Eritrea and South Sudan – gained international recognition and joined the United Nations. As can clearly be observed, the first wave of *de facto states* resulting from secession is directly linked to decolonisation. It is also interesting to note that some of the *de facto states* in sub-Saharan Africa want to secede and return to colonial boundaries – Eritrea has already done so, while Somaliland is currently in such a situation. Cabinda has also put forward such a postulate. Despite their lack of international recognition, everything indicates that *de facto states* are not just temporary anomalies, but rather form a permanent part of the international system (Relitz 2019, pp. 313-314).

In the cotemporary international system, sanctions for interference with the territorial integrity of recognised states are so severe that even the weakest states are guaranteed independence (Kolstø 2006, p. 727). *De facto states* are in a situation in which they are still at risk of losing their territories and being reincorporated into the states from which they seceded. Geldenhuys (2009, p. 44) points out that among *de facto states*, although their origins vary considerably, unilateral secession is a common feature. Secession is a global phenomenon in the international system. According to Griffiths (2016, p.1) "We are truly living in an age of secession". As successful secessions can have a knock-on effect, *de facto states* are seen as a threat to the international order as such a situation could lead to further fragmentation of the international system. For example, natural resource sovereignty may be an essential component of a people's claim to a territory of its own (Dietrich 2018, p. 30). Secessionist movements can threaten the existence of any state, especially those whose origins are already based on shaky colonial foundations (Mylonas, 2015). Thus, *de facto states* appear to be a particular expression of the progressive fragmentation and destabilisation of the international system. They undermine the territorial integrity of recognised states, which is a cornerstone of the international system.

One might then ask what factors determine the relative positions of *de facto states*? Does the legality of secession, democratic governance, and external patronage matter? Secession, in fact, although legally taboo, can provide a basis for advocacy towards recognition when it is a last resort in the face of grave injustices (Berg / Toomla 2009, p. 43). The desire to preserve stable states and a stable international system favours the preservation of the current order at the expense of national self-determination. States, as the main elements of the international system, still have the decision-making power to recognise a secessionist *de facto state* and undoubtedly prioritise territorial integrity over self-determination. This is very well illustrated by the example of Eritrea, which eventually gained international recognition, but this only happened after Ethiopia agreed to allow Eritreans to choose independence in a referendum in 1993, even though it had actually gained independence two years earlier in 1991 after a 30-year war of independence and due to controlling all of its own territory. Thus, the consent of the Ethiopian authorities only made it possible to achieve what a three-decade-long war could not and finally gained factual independence. The same scenario was repeated in 2011 in South Sudan, which obtained the right to an independence referendum in agreements signed with the central government in Khartoum. Thus, the primacy of territorial integrity favours the status quo and the stability of the international system and is prioritised over the right to self-determination (Fabry 2012).

References

Bartmann, Barry: "Political Realities and Legal Anomalies. Revisiting the Politics of International Recognition". In: Bahcheli, Tozun / Bartmann, Barry / Srebrnik, Henry F. (eds.): *De Facto States. The Quest for Sovereignty.* Routledge: London-New York 2004, pp. 13–32.

BBC News: "Three dead after gun attack on Togo football team", *BBC News* 9.1.2010, retrieved 17.9.2016, from http://news.bbc.co.uk/2/hi/africa/8449 978.stm.

Berg, Eiki / Toomla, Raul: "Forms of Normalisation in the Quest for De Facto Statehood", *The International Spectator* 44 (4) 2009, pp. 27-45, DOI: 10.1080/03932720903351104.

Byrne, Heather / Englebert, Pierre: "Shifting Grounds for African Secessionism?" (Paper prepared as conclusion chapter for: Tomas, Jordi / Zeller, Wolfgang (eds.): *Secessionism in Africa.* Palgrave: London, 2014), retrieved 11.2.2016, from https://pierreenglebert.files.wordpress.com/2014/01/byrne-englebert-african-secessions-jan-2014.pdf.

Calvocoressi, Peter: *Polityka międzynarodowa 1945-2000.* Książka i Wiedza: Warszawa, 2002.

Campbell, John / Quinn, Nolan: "What's Behind Growing Separatism in Nigeria?", *Council on Foreign Affairs* 3.8.2021, retrieved 17.7.2023, from https://www.cfr.org/article/whats-behind-growing-separatism-nigeria.

Caspersen, Nina: *Unrecognized states. The struggle for sovereignty in the modern international system.* Polity Press: Cambridge, 2012.

Caspersen, Nina / Stansfield, Gareth (eds.): *Unrecognized States in the International System.* (Exeter Studies in Ethno Politics Series). Routledge: London and New York, 2011.

Cohen, Saul Bernard: *Geopolitics. The Geography of International Relations.* Rowman & Littlefield Publishers: Lanham, Boulder, New York, London, 2015.

Craig, Jess: "Separatist Movements in Nigeria and Cameroon Are Joining Forces", *Foreign Policy* 20.5.2021, retrieved 18.7.2023, from https://foreignpolicy.com/2021/05/20/separatists-nigeria-cameroon-biafra-ipob-ambazonia-anglophone-joining-forces/.

Crawford, J.: *The Creation of States in International Law.* Oxford University Press: 2006.

Crisis24: "Angola: Fatal clashes between separatists and security forces in Cabinda province July 28", *Crisis24* 29.7.2020, retrieved 19.7.2023, from https://crisis24.garda.com/alerts/2020/07/angola-fatal-clashes-between-separatists-and-security-forces-in-cabinda-province-july-28.

Crisis24: "Cameroon: Separatist activism likely to continue in the Southwest and Northwest regions through at least mid-2023", *Crisis24* 4.1.2023, retrieved 16.7.2023, from https://crisis24.garda.com/alerts/2023/01/cameroon-separat ist-activism-likely-to-continue-in-the-southwest-and-northwest-regions-through-at-least-mid-2023.

Dietrich, Frank. "Natural Resources, Collective Self-Determination, and Secession". *Law, Ethics and Philosophy*, 2018, Vol. 6, pp. 28-56, DOI: 10.31009/ LEAP.2018.V6.02

Dudkiewicz, Hubert: „Prawo międzynarodowe w kwestii państwa upadłego". In: Kłosowicz, Robert (ed.): *Problem upadku państw w stosunkach międzynaro-dowych*. Wydawnictwo Uniwersytetu Jagielońskiego: Kraków 2012, pp. 67-86.

Egerö, Bertil: *South Africa's Bantustans. From dumping grounds to battlefronts.* The Nordic Africa Institute: Uppsala, 1991, retrieved 10.7.2023, from https:// www.files.ethz.ch/isn/102661/4.pdf.

Ekpu, R.: "Geographical expression: So what?", *The Guardian* 15.8.2017, retrieved 30.7.2023, from https://guardian.ng/opinion/geographical-express ion-so-what/

Embassy of Benin, Washington DC: "Culture beninoise", retrieved 18.7.2023, from https://beninembassy.us/culture-beninoise/.

Encyclopedia Britannica: "Democratic Republic of the Congo – Government and society", *Encyclopedia Britannica*, retrieved 20.5.2022, from ttps://www. britannica.com/place/Democratic-Republic-of-the-Congo.

Fabry, Mikulas: "The contemporary practice of state recognition: Kosovo, South Ossetia, Abkhazia, and their aftermath", *Nationalities Papers*, 40 (5) 2012, pp. 661-676, DOI: 10.1080/00905992.2012.705266.

Fagbayibo, Babatunde: "South Sudan, *uti possidetis* rule and the future of state-hood in Africa", *AfricLaw* 26.4.2012, retrieved 20.7.2015, from https://afric law.com/2012/04/26/south-sudan-uti-possidetis-rule-and-the-future-of-statehood-in-africa/.

Fund for Peace: Fragile States Index 2023, retrieved 10.08.2023, from https://fra gilestatesindex.org/global-data/.

Gakwandi, Arthur, S.: "Towards a New Political Map of Africa". In: Asiwaju, A.I. (ed.): *Pan Africanism: Politics, Economy and Social Change in the Twenty-First Century.* Hurst: London, 1996, pp. 252–259.

Gąsowski, Andrzej: *RPA*. Trio: Warszawa, 2006.

Geldenhuys, Deon: *Contested States in World Politics*. Palgrave Macmillan: Basing-stoke, 2009.

Griffiths, Ryan D.: *Age of Secession: The International and Domestic Determinants of State Birth*. Cambridge University Press: Cambridge 2016.

Joshua Project: "People Groups", retrieved 16.7.2023, from https://joshuaproject.net/people_groups.

Jackson, Robert H.: *Quasi-states: Sovereignty, International Relations and the Third World*. University of British Columbia: Vancouver, 1993.

Kashambuzi, E.: *"The likely impact of Buganda secession"*, United Democratic Ugandans 2011, retrieved 18.9.2016, from http://udugandans.org/cms/media-section/538-the-likely-impact-of-buganda-secession.

Khapoya, V. B.: "Bantustans in South Africa: The Role of the Multinational Corporations", *Journal of Eastern African Research & Development* 10 (1-2) 1980, pp. 28-49.

Kłosowicz, Robert: "Can Cabinda follow the example of South Sudan? The problem of secessionism in contemporary Africa in the context of the 'uti possidetis' principle". In: Oppenheimer, J. / Pereira Leite, J. / Mah, L. (eds.): *Espaço Lusófono (1974 /2014): Trajectórias Económicas e Políticas – Textos*. CEsA – Centro de Estudos sobre África, Ásia e América Latina CSG – Investigação em Ciências Sociais e Gestão Instituto Superior de Economia e Gestão / Universidade de Lisboa: Lisboa, 2015a, pp. 169-185.

Kłosowicz, Robert: "The Role of Ethiopia in the Regional Security Complex of the Horn of Africa", *Ethiopian Journal of Social Sciences and Language Studies*, 2 (2) 2015b, pp. 83-97.

Kłosowicz, Robert / Mormul, Joanna: *Erytrea i jej wpływ na sytuację polityczną w Rogu Afryki*. Wydawnictwo Unniwersytetu Jagiellońskiego: Kraków, 2018.

Kłosowicz, Robert / Mormul, Joanna: "Pojęcie dysfunkcyjności państw, geneza i definicje". In: Kłosowicz, Robert (ed.): *Państwa dysfunkcyjne i ich destabilizujący wpływ na stosunki międzynarodowe*. Wydawnictwo Uniwersytetu Jagiellońskiego: Kraków, 2013, pp. 11-36.

Kolstø, Pål: "The Sustainability and Future of Unrecognized Quasi-States", *Journal of Peace Research* 43 (6) 2006, pp. 723-740.

Kosienkowski, Marcin: *Współpraca społeczności międzynarodowej z państwami de facto. Studium przypadków*. Wydawnictwo KUL: Lublin, 2018.

Krawczuk, Marcin: "Oblicza separatyzmu etnicznego w Etiopii". In: Marczewska-Rytko, Maria / Pomarański, Marcin (eds.): *Ruchy separatystyczne*. Wydawnictwo Uniwersytetu Marii Curie-Skłodowskiej: Lublin, 2019, p. 331-346

Leśniewski, Michał: "Biafra 1966–1970". In: Bartnicki, Andrzej (ed.): *Zarys dziejów Afryki i Azji 1869-1996. Historia Konfliktów*. Książka i Wiedza: Warszawa 2000, pp. 402-411.

Malinowski, Marek Jan: *Białe mocarstwo Czarnego Lądu*. Wydawnictwo Ministerstwa Obrony Narodowej: Warszawa, 1986.

Malinowski, Marek Jan: *Republika Południowej Afryki. Przemiany wewnętrzne i ich międzynarodowe uwarunkowania.* PWN: Warszawa, 1988.

Menkiti, Ifeanyi A.: "Normative Instability as Source of Africa's Political Disorder". In: Kiros, Teodros (ed.): *Explorations in African Political Thought: Identity, Community, Ethics.* Routledge: London, 2001, pp.133-149.

Meredith, Martin: *The State of Africa. A History of the Continent Since Independence.* Simon & Schuster: London-New York, 2011.

Mylonas, Harris: *De Facto States Unbound,* PONARS Euroasia, 10.8.2015, retrieved 29.7.2023, from https://www.ponarseurasia.org/de-facto-states-unbound/.

Ndikumana, Léonce / Emizet, Kisangani F.: "The Economics of Civil War: The Case of Democratic Republic of Congo". In: Collier, Paul / Sambanis, Nicholas (eds.): *Understanding Civil War: Africa. Evidence and Analysis.* Washington 2005, pp. 63-88.

Niger Delta Avengers: "Open Letter to President Muhammadu Buhari" 20.10.2016, retrieved 10.1.2017, from http://www.nigerdeltaavengers.org/.

Niger Delta Avengers: "Operations Walls of Jericho and Hurricane Joshua" 6.01.2017, retrieved 10.1.2017, from http://www.nigerdeltaavengers.org/.

O'Malley: "Demographic Characteristics of South Africa in the Late 1980s", retrieved 11.07.2023, from https://omalley.nelsonmandela.org/index.php/site/q/03lv02424/04lv03370/05lv03389.htm.

Pfister, Roger: *Apartheid South Africa and African States: From Pariah to Middle Power, 1961-1994.* Tauris Academic Studies: London, 2005.

Phillips, Laura, Chipkin, Ivor: „Bantustans are dead – long live the Bantustans", *Mail&Guardian* 10.7.2014, retrieved 16.7.2023, from https://mg.co.za/article/2014-07-10-bantustans-are-dead-long-live-the-bantustans/.

Piłaszewicz, Stanisław: "Nigeria". In: Łazowski, Zygmunt: *Państwa Afryki Zachodniej: fakty, problemy stabilizacji i rozwoju, polskie kontakty.* Vol. I. Wydawnictwo Towarzystwa Polsko-Nigeryjskiego: Warszawa, 2006, pp. 298 367.

Relitz, Sebastian: "The stabilisation dilemma: conceptualising international responses to secession and de facto states", *East European Politics* 35 (3) 2019, pp. 311-331.

Richardson J. Henry: "Self-Determination, International Law and the South African

Bantustan Policy", *Columbia Journal of Transnational Law* 17, 1978, pp. 185-220, retrieved 22.9.2023, from https://www.repository.law.indiana.edu/cgi/viewcontent.cgi?article=3214&context=facpub.

Różański, Jarosław: *Republika Federalna Ambazonii. Poszukiwanie tożsamości kulturowej i politycznej anglojęzycznych mieszkańców Kamerunu*, Wydawnictwo Naukowe UKSW: Warszawa 2023.

Sahara Reporters: "Buhari's Lopsided Appointments Split the North, His Supporters", *Sahara Reporters* 29.8. 2015, retrieved 16.7.2023, from https://saharareporters.com/2015/08/29/buhari%E2%80%99s-lopsided-appointments-split-north-his-supporters.

Siollun, Max: "Half a loaf, and half of yellow sun", *New African* 558 (Feb.) 2016, pp. 20–21.

Smith, David: "Will Sudan vote herald balkanisation of Africa?", *The Guardian* 7.1.2011, retrieved 12.9.2016, from https://www.theguardian.com/world/2011/jan/07/sudan-vote-balkanisation-africa.

Srogosz, Tomasz: "Charakter prawny *uti possidetis* w prawie międzynarodowym", *Państwo i Prawo* 66(6), 2011, pp. 64-76.

The Conversation: "A breakdown of Biafra separatism, and where Kanu fits into the picture", *The Conversation* 18.8.2021, retrieved 16.7.2023, from https://theconversation.com/a-breakdown-of-biafra-separatism-and-where-kanu-fits-into-the-picture-166235.

Time: "The Birth of Bophutha Tswana", *Time* 19.12.1977, retrieved 10.7.2023, from https://web.archive.org/web/20081215121824/http://www.time.com/time/magazine/article/0,9171,945848,00.html.

Trzciński, Krzysztof: *Demokratyzacja w Afryce Subsaharyjskiej. Perspektywa zachodnioafrykańskiej myśli politycznej*. Oficyna Wydawnicza Aspra-JR: Warszawa, 2013.

Trzciński, Krzysztof: "The Future of the Multi-Ethnic African State: On the Perspective of Ifeanyi A. Menkiti", *Hemispheres. Studies on Cultures and Societies* 25, 2010, retrieved 2.7.2023, from https://depot.ceon.pl/bitstream/handle/123456789/18426/Menkiti_Rawls_Africa_borders_justice_peoples.pdf?sequence=1&isAllowed=y

Tycholiz, Wojciech: "Kryzys w Delcie Nigru". In: Kopiński, Dominik / Polus, Andrzej (eds.): *Zgubne transakcje. Fatal Transactions. Surowce mineralne a rozwój państw afrykańskich*. Difin: Warszawa, 2010, pp. 190-203.

UN: "Charter of the United Nations", retrieved 19.11.2022, from https://www.un.org/en/about-us/un-charter/full-text.

UN Committee on Information from Non-Self-Governing Territories: "Report of the Committee on Information from Non-Self-Governing Territories, U.N. General Assembly on its Eighteenth Session, U.N. G.A.O.R. Supplement No. 14 (A/5514)", retrieved 20.11.2022, from https://digitallibrary.un.org/record/719840.

UN, Department of Economic and Social Affairs, Population Division: "Total population by sex in 2015 and sex ratio by country in 2015", *World Population Prospects* 2015, retrieved 5.2.2017, from https://esa.un.org/unpd/wpp/publi cations/files/key_findings_wpp_2015.pdf.

UN General Assembly: "Bantustans", *General Assembly* Thirty-second session, 102nd plenary meeting: A/RES/32/102 – 14.12.1977, retrieved 5.2.2017, from https://documents-dds-ny.un.org/doc/RESOLUTION/GEN/NR0/313/40/ PDF/NR031340.pdf?OpenElement

UN General Assembly: "Policies of apartheid of the Government of South Africa. The So-Called Independent Transkei and Other Bantustans", *General Assembly* Thirty- first Session, 42nd plenary meeting: A/RES/31/42 – 26.10.1976, retrieved 19.11.2022, from https://digitallibrary.un.org/record/637263.

UN General Assembly: "Question of Western Sahara", Resolutions adopted by the General Assembly at its 34th session: A/RES/34/37 – 21.11.1979, retrieved 20.11.2013, from http://www.un.org/documents/ga/res/34/a34res37.pdf.

UNHCR: "Saharawi Refugees in Tindouf, Algeria: Total In-Camp Population. Official Report", March 2018, Centro de Estudos do Sahara Occidental da USC, retrieved 5.10.2021, from https://www.usc.gal/export9/sites/webin stitucional/gl/institutos/ceso/descargas/UNHCR_Tindouf-Total-In-Camp-Population_March-2018.pdf.

UN Secretary-General: "Letter dated 8th Mar. 1950 from the Secretary-General to the President of the Security Council transmitting a memorandum on the legal aspects of the problem of representation in the U.N.", U.N. Doc. S/1466 (19.3.1950).

Van Reybrouck, David: *Kongo. Opowieść o zrujnowanym kraju.* W.A.B: Warszawa, 2016.

Vanthemsche, Guy: *Belgium and the Congo, 1885–1980.* Cambridge: Cambridge University Press, 2012.

Wambu, Onnyekachi: "The ghost of Biafra", *New African* 557 (Jan.) 2016, p. 82.

Wanyonyi, Edward. "Somaliland: Quest for international recognition", *New African* 558 (Feb.) 2016, pp. 46–47.

World Directory of Minorities and Indigenous Peoples: "Benin", retrieved 18.7.2023, from https://minorityrights.org/country/benin/.

Zachary, G. Pascal: "Africa Needs a New Map. It's time to start seeing the redrawing of the continent's colonial borders as an opportunity, not a threat", *Foreign Policy* 26.4.2010, retrieved 15.9.2022, from https://foreignpolicy.com/2010/ 04/26/africa-needs-a-new-map/.

Robert Kłosowicz, Agnieszka Czubik

Chapter 2. Controversy Over the International Subjectivity of *De Facto States*[1]

The potential international recognition or refusal to acknowledge the newly formed state may attract interest from various ostensibly neutral actors in the field of international relations. This renders the issue of legal recognition of an existing entity – namely, a *de facto state* – highly contentious, forming the focal point of this chapter. Additionally, the chapter aims to explore how an unrecognised state differs from other anomalies within the international system. The international community grapples with how to address the challenge posed by unrecognised states, which not only present security concerns but also raise legal dilemmas, as their emergence undermines the principles of international law by encroaching upon the territorial integrity of established states and the prevailing international order. The analysis presented in this chapter integrates perspectives from both public international law and political science.

Keywords: *de facto states*, unrecognised states, international subjectivity, public international law, Western Sahara, Sahrawi Arab Democratic Republic

Introduction

The problem of the recognition of a state as a subject of international law has been raised for decades in the science of contemporary public international law. The recognition of an existing entity that exercises undoubtedly independent state authority over a population and a given territory is crucial not only from a theoretical perspective, but also in practice. When a new participant appears on the international scene, with certain rights and the ability to assume obligations defined by international law, the balance of power in the region shifts. Therefore, the recognition of the new state's subjectivity will gradually influence the global situation, including, for example, international economic relations. Hence, the possible recognition of the newly formed state or au rebours refusal to recognise it may be of interest to various, seemingly neutral actors in the area of international relations. This makes the problem of legal recognition of an actually

---

1   This chapter is the result of a research project financed by the National Science Centre (Narodowe Centrum Nauki), Poland, grant ID: 2017/25/B/HS5/00958.

existing entity – a *de facto state* – quite controversial, and it is to this issue that this chapter is devoted.

1. The concept of international subjectivity

1.1. Definitional problems

The notion of subjectivity is extremely interesting in the context of the controversy surrounding the very concept in public international law. The literature on the subject indicates that there are no guidelines in this area of law that would unambiguously define what a subject of international law ought to be and what rules ought to apply to determine international legal subjectivity (Bierzanek / Symonides 1998, p. 121). In other words, the procedure for the creation of such a new subject does not exist at all. It is assumed that international law only plays the role of a witness to, or observer of, the "creation of the subject," which is considered a historical fact (Bierzanek / Symonides 1998, p. 126). Nevertheless, this historical fact takes place in a specific international environment and geopolitical situation. This raises the question of how other actors in international relations will react to the emergence of the new entity and what bearing their reaction will have for its subjectivity in the international arena. This question is clearly part of the long-lasting dispute in public international law about the declaratory or constitutive character of the recognition of a new international entity. In the context of the qualification of this entity as a state, the question arises as to whether it came into existence upon recognition by other states or whether it already existed before (Jessup 1949, p. 43). Another problem concerns the extent of the entity's powers prior to recognition and whether it can be called a state. The two aforementioned theories of recognition differ fundamentally on this issue. The constitutive theory assumes that the existence of a state depends on its recognition by the international community, whereas, according to the declarative one, recognition by other actors in the international arena merely implies the acknowledgement of its existence (Czapliński / Wyrozumska 1999, p. 230). What the supporters of both theories agree on is that the creation of a state is a historical fact (Saganek 2015, p. 116). It seems that in the current geopolitical situation the importance of the constitutive theory is on the decline due to the fact that membership in the international community is losing its "club" character. The club theory, i.e. the doctrine that membership in the association of states on the international stage is granted on the principle of co-optation, formally expressed as international recognition, seems to be losing its relevance (Schwarzenberger 1960, p. 65). Equally questionable is the qualification of all recognised states in today's world as civilised, which, according to Lassa Oppenheim's theory, gave them the right to sit "in the club." The question must be asked whether there is "but one important system" of public international law, as T. J. Lawrence described the still-dominant Eurocentric view (Lawrence 1910, p. 3). The cited author argued that there are more systems of international law, but that there is "a great gulf" between those other than the Eurocentric one (based on "the views of civilised Europeans and Americans") (Lawrence 1910, p. 4). Such an approach is contradicted by the views found in more recent international law scholarship, which recognises the existence of so-called "pseudo-regimes" in pre-colonial relations that preceded the emergence of the "Grotian" (Westphalian) system of public international law. The European "progenitorship" of the law of nations can, therefore, be questioned to some extent, as can the notion of the superiority of European norms of "civilised" states (Muszyński 2019, pp. 18-20). Worth noting are also the publications created in the current of the so-called "global history of international law," which present the history of international law taking into account the autonomous development of norms in different regions of the world (Srogosz 2020). Within this current, scholars of the movement known as Third World Approaches to International Law (TWAIL), who mostly come from post-colonial states, point to the existence of international law institutions developed by African peoples. In the context of the subject matter analysed in this chapter, the question arises as to the impact of this doctrine on the perception of subjectivity in public international law. What is more, some scholars have questioned the entire realist paradigm and its basic canons as limitations on our thinking about global politics at a time of new challenges. Consequently, there have been voices in the last two decades heralding the twilight of the role of the state in international relations in favour of non-state actors. It has been pointed out that the state, locked into the Westphalian model, is a rather ineffective actor, often incapable of meeting the new challenges. The post-Cold War crisis of many sub-Saharan African states, among others, which manifested itself in internal weakness, chaos and even disintegration of state structures, has been cited as one evidence of the weakness of the Westphalian system (Łoś-Nowak 2013, p. 102). An interesting case seems to be the question of the subjectivity of Western Sahara and Somaliland – "entities" situated on the African continent, whose statehood should be assessed taking into account the principles and specificities developed on this continent. This would entail the need to re-evaluate (read from a new perspective, considering the specificities of the region) the classic criteria of international legal subjectivity, which refer to population, territory and the existence of an effective sovereign authority. Meanwhile, the delimitation of the borders of both Western Sahara and British

Somaliland was the result of agreements between colonial states, which paid little attention to local ethnic or tribal conditions or ways of life. In the former case, the territory of today's Western Sahara was subject to bargaining between France and Spain, which affected the nomadic lifestyle of peoples who had been travelling freely in the area for centuries ("The Treaty of November 27, 1912, Between France and Spain Concerning Morocco"). In the latter case, the delimitation of the territory of present-day Somaliland was the result of negotiations between Great Britain, France, Italy, and Ethiopia, which resulted in the division of the large Somali ethnic group and dispersing its population across four European colonies. Moreover, under the Anglo-Ethiopian treaty of 1897, Great Britain ceded the north-eastern part of the Hawd Plateau, a traditional Somali grazing area, to Ethiopia in order to "strengthen and render more effective and profitable the friendship between the two kingdoms," according to its preamble (Ullendorf 1966; Lewis 2009, pp. 28-29). This is important because the modern idea of borders was alien to pre-colonial Africa, where they did not exist in the form of lines or planes, but often ran through areas of uninhabited buffer zones, which no one claimed and where ethnic groups moved freely, especially groups that led nomadic lifestyles (and it is this type of nomadic populations that we find in the aforementioned Spanish Sahara and British Somaliland). The lack of demographic pressure meant that battles over territory were rare and they were not the most important determinants of the existence of African states in the pre-colonial era. In Sub-Saharan Africa, state power manifested itself primarily in the ability to control large populations rather than territories. Meanwhile, Europeans colonising Africa saw the continent mainly as a coastline, whereas the territories extending further inland were perceived as terra incognita. Only the territories of today's north African states, South Africa and the eastern and western African coastal strips were reasonably well mapped. Hence, it is hardly surprising that both the long coastal strip of the Spanish Sahara in the north-west and British Somaliland in the east of the continent fitted into this pattern. As mentioned earlier, the borders of the colonies in Sub-Saharan Africa were drawn on maps at the discretion of European negotiators, often as a result of compromises between Old Continent states. More than half of them are perfectly straight lines or compass-drawn arcs that cut across territories that had belonged to concrete ethnic groups and tribes for centuries. In the case of both the Spanish Sahara and British Somaliland, colonisers divided between them territories that were ethnically, religiously, and linguistically coherent. In the case of Somali-inhabited areas, these were divided between British Somaliland, Italian Somali and French Somali (Djibouti). In addition, some of the Somali-inhabited areas came under the rule of Ethiopia (Ogaden) and some under the rule of the

British colony of Kenya. There is no doubt that European states have thus left their mark on the entire continent, and this historical legacy is reflected today in the international law principle of *uti possidetis*, which stipulates that in order to recognise their independence, African states had to accept the territorial boundaries of the administrative divisions or territories they possessed prior to their independence (Dudkiewicz 2012, p. 80). Consequently, today's African states are mostly rooted in the geopolitics of the late 19th century, when European powers competed for colonial control of Africa, i.e. territory, population, and resources, drawing the boundaries of their colonies without regard to ethnic, linguistic, religious, and cultural issues.

In the context of reflections on international subjectivity, it should further be indicated that the classical definition referred to an unquestioned and intuitive subject on the international scene, namely the state. Until the Second World War, in the age of "lone states," it was qualified as an exclusive subject of international law (Perkowski 2008, p. 22). This exclusivity meant having primary and full international law subjectivity. The role of public international law was limited to regulating relations between states. A change in this regard occurred in 1949, when the International Court of Justice issued an advisory opinion in the so-called "reparation case" (UN General Assembly 1949, A/RES/365). This opinion admitted the possibility of existence of non-state actors in the international arena, in this case – international organisations. Their subjectivity can vary in scope and is dependent on the will of states. The emergence of new actors in the international space in mid-20th century (e.g. the United Nations, the World Bank, the International Monetary Fund) led to the establishment of new rules of world politics. Joseph Stiglitz puts it very aptly in his book *Making Globalization Work*:

> The nation-state, which has been the center of political and (to a large extent) economic power for the past century and a half is being squeezed today—on one side, by the forces of global economics, and on the other side, by political demands for devolution of power. […] In effect, economic globalization has outpaced political globalization. We have a chaotic, uncoordinated system of global governance without global government, an array of institutions and agreements dealing with a series of problems, from global warming to international trade and capital flows (Stiglitz 2006, p. 21).

The classical criteria of international legal subjectivity are no longer applicable to all categories of international actors. It seems that it was the broadening of the concept of international subjectivity to include international organisations that gave rise to the revolutionisation of the very notion of international subjectivity, leading to the formulation of scholarly views according to which international subjectivity can now be obtained after having fulfilled the criterion of existence or being a subject of international law norms. According to contemporary theories, effectiveness is of ever-increasing importance for international legal subjectivity (Perkowski 2008, p. 233). It matters for the possible de facto subjectivity of states because, as it became apparent following the aforementioned advisory opinion of the International Court of Justice, the previously unchallenged and established concept of international subjectivity was gradable and could be reformulated. It heralded a revolution that would take place in the following decades, reaching its apogee now, when entities such as an individual, a large multinational corporation or a non-governmental organisation are beginning to appear within the category of "international subjects" in some scientific theories. Applying the classical criteria of international subjectivity to entities such as, for example, Western Sahara or Somaliland, even taking into account the TWAIL perspective, does not lead to a generally acceptable answer concerning their subjectivity, whereas with the application of the so-called new criteria of subjectivity, the chances of granting legal international subjectivity to these entities seem to be greater. This is due to the fact that one of the new criteria of international legal subjectivity is effectiveness, which is also one of the determinants for qualifying an entity as a *de facto state*.

1.2 Historical attempts to categorise state subjects

It is possible to note attempts throughout the historical development of public international law to categorise states according to certain criteria, more often than not justified by the specifics of the era in which such categorisation was made. In ancient Roman times, orbis terrarum was divided in terms of the influence that the Roman emperor had over a given territory. In the Middle Ages, there was a very clear division into Christian nations (and then states) and those with a "pagan" status. This division into "civilised nations" and "uncivilised" ones was connected with the possibility of colonising "uncivilised" peoples, permissible under classical international law (Symonides 2019, pp. 47-48). Echoes of this thinking could be traced all the way to Article 22 of the Covenant of the League of Nations, which emphasises the "sacred trust of civilisation," i.e. the idea that the "tutelage" of "peoples not yet able to stand by themselves under the strenuous conditions of the modern world [...] should be entrusted to advanced nations who by reason of their resources, their experience or their geographical position can best undertake this responsibility, and who are willing to accept it." The Covenant further envisaged that the character of this mandate "must differ according to the stage of the development of the people, the geographical situation of the territory, its economic conditions and other similar circumstances." It recognised that communities formerly belonging to the Turkish Empire could be recognised as provisionally independent due to the "stage of development" they had reached. With regard to the Central African peoples, the arrangements adopted in the Covenant implied that their lower "stage of development" meant that

> the Mandatory must be responsible for the administration of the territory under conditions which will guarantee freedom of conscience and religion, subject only to the maintenance of public order and morals, the prohibition of abuses such as the slave trade, the arms traffic and the liquor traffic, and the prevention of the establishment of fortifications or military and naval bases and of military training of the natives for other than police purposes and the defence of territory, and will also secure equal opportunities for the trade and commerce of other Members of the League ("Article 22, League of Nations: The Covenant of the League of Nations").

As for other territories, including those located in South-West Africa, it was considered that because of the "sparseness of their population, or their small size, or their remoteness from the centres of civilisation, or their geographical contiguity to the territory of the Mandatory," it was permissible to apply the laws of the Mandatory and de facto treat these lands as "integral portions" of the Mandatory's territory. However, the quoted Article 22 of the Covenant also indicates the necessity for the Mandatory to act in the interests of the indigenous peoples ("Article 22, League of Nations: The Covenant of the League of Nations"). It therefore seems that Eurocentrism was still very evident in 1919. Another manifestation of this way of thinking was the British argumentation when discussing the admission of Abyssinia to the League of Nations. Britain eventually agreed to it, but with great reluctance, stressing that it was too "barbaric" to enter the international community as an equal state. A similar position was held by Italy, which regarded Abyssinia as too "immature" to become a member of the League of Nations, and therefore unable to share "equal rights and obligations with other civilised states (Zajączkowski 2020, pp. 130-131)."

It has been accepted in contemporary public international law scholarship that the term "civilised nations" is an anachronism and a relic of Eurocentrism, incongruent with the current composition of the international community, which includes the now independent states of Africa and Asia (Symonides 2019, p. 48). It is a reflection of the 19th-century assumption that the global international community includes only so-called civilised states.

1.3 The "new state"

The regulations of the Covenant of the League of Nations, an emanation of the post-Versailles order, would give rise to the concept of the "new state." In view of its emergence, a division into "new states" and "old states" must be assumed. The latter included states counted among the 19th-century "powers," whereas the former included entities that emerged in Eastern Europe as a result of the breakout of previously existing states. In this context, the literature raises the question of whether the "new state" became a new institution of international law and whether it had a different legal status from other states (Kocot 1961, p. 86). Kazimierz Kocot writes that the doctrine that the "new state" ought to be considered an institution of "the public law of Europe" was formulated by Georges Clemenceau in a letter to Poland's Prime Minister Ignacy Paderewski. Clemenceau pointed out that in "the public law of Europe" there was a long-established procedure that a newly created state, or a state whose territory has increased considerably, should be "jointly and formally" recognised by the Great Powers. This recognition was in turn connected with the requirement that the "new state" had to accept binding international obligations with regard to the application of "certain principles of government." According to Thomas Woodrow Wilson, these were supposed to relate to the protection of the rights of national minorities in the newly formed states, but David Lloyd George saw them as guarantees that the "new states" would comply with the standards of "civilised states" (Mantoux 1992, p. 441). This position resulted from the assumption made by the representatives of the Great Powers at the Paris Peace Conference that there existed a principle of international custom in the "public law of Europe," according to which "in Eastern Europe the establishment of new States was a matter of general interest, which required the formal recognition of the Great Powers." Such recognition was granted subject to certain conditions, which in turn was intended to ensure that the "new states" respected the principles shared by all civilised nations (Temperley 1921, p. 116). In 1919, the Committee on New States was established in order to address the issues related to the creation of "new states" and the protection of minority rights in them (Fink 1995, pp. 197-205). These initiatives were intended to create a new category of entity in public international law – the "new state." In the context of the subject addressed in this chapter, this attempt is highly relevant as it relates to the genesis of state creation in the international arena. Nevertheless, even if its proponents wanted it to become a legal institution, its historical existence ended with the adoption of the UN Charter, which introduced the equality of states in the international arena ("Charter of the United Nations" 1945, 1 UNTS XVI, art. 1, para. 2). The principle of equality of states precludes the possibility of different subcategories implying a different scope of international subjectivity.

The term "new state" was reformulated after the Second World War, when it was applied to states created as a result of decolonisation on the assumption that they are full and equal members of the international community (Kocot 1961, p. 88). Conceived in this way, the notion of the "new state" precludes the existence of a new institution of public international law, even if its existence is justified in political science or the science of international relations.

2. The status of a de facto state in public international law

2.1 Categories of states distinguished in political science

It is worth noting that after the Second World War, different "variations" on the category of the state emerged in the political sciences. The creation of subcategories within the category of the state in these sciences is associated with the fact that the object of their study is also the factual state, not only the normative state. On the grounds of classical international law, such a distinction is not possible due to the existence of a homogeneous category of the state, while in reality the members of the international community are not perfectly and fully equal.

Such a situation gives rise to the distinction of subcategories within the category of the state in political science and international relations studies. An example of this practice is the category of "unrecognised states." This concept refers to a geopolitical entity that exercises authority performing state functions over a territory inhabited by a specific population, not necessarily homogeneous in terms of nationality, but one that tends to support this authority. Nevertheless, this entity is not recognised by other actors in international relations. For proponents of the theory of the constitutive role of recognition with regard to the creation of a state and, consequently, its subjectivity, the absence of such recognition will preclude the qualification of a given entity as a "state" in the international arena. Meanwhile, the reality of the international community is much more complex, and the global state system is not as neatly organized as it might appear. The lack of external sovereignty does not necessarily eliminate the possibility for a state to function in the international space, and entities such as Somaliland are trying to carve out a niche for themselves in the international system based on external sovereignty. Indeed, the international system is still largely based on a division into sovereign states and non-sovereign actors, and in the theory of international relations sovereignty has traditionally been viewed as the ability to exercise political authority over a given territory and population independently of other actors. State sovereignty includes independence in internal and external affairs. With the exception of the Arctic and Antarctic regions, the Earth's surface is carefully divided between entities that are internationally recognised and control territories that are unambiguously delineated by internationally agreed borders – or at least this is how the global state system tends to be portrayed. Therefore, the problem of unrecognised states is treated as an anomaly that contradicts the model for the academic study of this issue in the political science and international relations. What is also important to note is that the problems of unrecognised states translate into problems for neighbouring states and entire regions – Western Sahara (Maghreb area), Somaliland (Horn of Africa, Gulf of Aden), Northern Cyprus (Eastern Mediterranean, Greece, Turkey), Taiwan (Indo-Pacific area), and sometimes even into global international relations, as is the case with Taiwan (Washington-Beijing tension) or Northern Cyprus (conflict between NATO states – Greece and Turkey). The populations of unrecognised states become, against their own will, the real victims of regional and global rivalries (Shelby 2004, p. 199).

The international community faces the problem of how to approach the issue of unrecognised states, which pose a challenge not only in terms of security but also in terms of international law, as their emergence goes against its principles by undermining the territorial integrity of another state and the established international order. Such a new entity may emerge spontaneously, due to the desire of people in a given area to become independent through secession (Somaliland, Katanga, Biafra), or be externally inspired (Ossetia or Abkhazia). However, in the case of Katanga, Somaliland or Western Sahara, the states opposing secession take the view that this situation does not result from the population's desire for independence, but from an externally inspired rebellion. Regarding the State of Katanga, Congo-Léopoldville accused Belgium, Northern Rhodesia, and South Africa of instigating its secessionist aspirations; Somalia sees Ethiopia's inspiration for Somaliland's independence; and in the Western Sahara case, Morocco blames Algeria (Haskin 2005, p. 28; Boehme 2005, pp. 4-19). The problem is further complicated by the fact that unrecognised states have not infrequently been used in the game of the global and regional powers. Therefore, Western Sahara was part of both the Cold War rivalry between the US and the West with the USSR and the so-called Eastern Bloc, and at the regional level – of Morocco and Algeria (Kłosowicz 2022, pp. 57-70). The question of Somaliland is part of the rivalry between the US and the Western world and China, and regionally – between Ethiopia, Eritrea, Sudan, and Egypt (Kine 2021; Meservey 2021).

Despite the challenge posed by them to the principle of territorial integrity of established states, unrecognised states do not seek to undermine the sovereign states system or create alternative forms of statehood. Rather, *de facto states* try to secure their place in a system that does not, in principle, accept them as members of the international community. Consequently, there is no formally recognised mechanism by which an unrecognised entity can legally make the transition to a "recognised" state, as such a mechanism would logically require states to consent to procedures that could result in their own territorial weakening. Many of such entities therefore exist in a limbo state, "without war and without peace," and the problem of their international non-recognition has been characterized as either unresolved (Somaliland) or unresolvable (Western Sahara). They largely exist in a situation of forgotten conflicts on the geographical periphery – which is the case of both Somaliland and Western Sahara (Walker 1998; Rutland 2007).

Unrecognised states are in many respects "places that do not exist," absent from maps, although they actually function, for example in media reports, and not only on the occasion of spectacular events. Somaliland may be an example of an entity that, although unmarked on maps, functions in popular media and political debate as a *de facto state* in the Horn of Africa. Western Sahara, on the other hand, is distinguished from other unrecognised states by the fact that some political maps mark it as a separate entity (usually in a different colour, with the notation "territory occupied by Morocco" or "territory of undetermined status").

Unrecognised states, particularly those situated on what is commonly referred to as the periphery, occasionally fade into obscurity along with their myriad issues until circumstances in their regions escalate, drawing the attention of the international community and the media. Instances such as the outbreak of hostilities in Nagorno-Karabakh in 2020 and the unrest along the border between Mauritania and Western Sahara, which is under Moroccan control, serve as examples of situations involving non-recognised states that have the potential to erupt into violence. In fact, most reports on so-called non-recognised states are characterised by a tendency to view them through the prism of threats to international security or to associate them with the problem of dysfunctional or even failed states. The example of Somaliland is typical here, as it emerged following the disintegration of Somalia's state structures. Other unrecognised entities may be seen as puppets of the larger powers that use them to gain their regional influence (Nagorno-Karabakh, Transnistria, Abkhazia, and Ossetia) (Lynch 2002, pp. 831-848).

What then is an unrecognised state and how does it differ from other anomalies in the international system? As already mentioned, unrecognised states have often been classified as dysfunctional entities or entities formed as a result of dysfunctionality or break-up of the larger states from which they broke away as a result of secessions resulting from aspirations for independence or deep internal crises (Jackson 1996, pp. 21-26; Kolstø 2006, pp. 723-725). Some unrecognised states, such as Somaliland, exercise control over the entire territory they claim and on which they have managed to build state institutions. In other words, they have achieved a level of statehood based on a degree of actual internal sovereignty (Caspersen 2012, p. 15). Moreover, they demonstrate a clear desire for full independence and aspire to become part of the world of sovereign states (Stanislawski 2008). This last factor distinguishes them from autonomous regions. Unrecognised states are not satisfied with their current status; moreover, this status is threatened by the fact that their internal sovereignty is not de jure accepted, either by the so-called parent state from which they have seceded or by the international community. Therefore, most scholars define unrecognised states on the basis of three criteria. First, they have achieved de facto independence, which they have maintained for at least two years; they control most of the territory to which they claim rights, including key regions. With that said, this territorial control is not necessarily absolute; the size of the territory they control can vary over time. Secondly, they have not gained international recognition, and even if they are recognised by some states, they are still not full members of the international system of sovereign states (Kosovo – recognised by 117 states; Western Sahara – by 47 states; Taiwan – by 12 states and the Vatican). A separate category of "partially recognised states," such as Abkhazia, South Ossetia or Northern Cyprus, is usually not taken into account here, as they have been created and are recognised by the patron state, in this case, respectively, Russia and Turkey, and a number of states that are practically excluded from the international community due to their policies (support for terrorism, drastic human rights violations). The last criterion is their demonstrated aspiration for full de jure independence, either through a formal declaration of independence, through an organised referendum, or other actions or declarations that show a clear desire for independent existence. Defining unrecognised states in terms of their de facto independence, their attempts at institution-building, their aspirations for de jure independence and their lack of international recognition faces researchers with a number of borderline cases (Caspersen 2012, p. 8). Some authors, such as Caspersen and Gareth Stansfield or Deon Geldenhuys, do not take into account, for example, Western Sahara (Sahrawi Arab Democratic Republic, SADR) and Palestine, concluding that while these entities are more widely recognised than most non-recognised states, they do not meet one of the basic criteria – of controlling their territory (Caspersen / Stansfield 2011; Geldenhuys 2009). According to Caspersen, a non-recognised state should control at least two-thirds of the territory to which it claims rights, including key regions and major urban centres. Meanwhile, the SADR controls only 20% of the territory it claims, while the rest is under Moroccan control, including the capital and all major urban centres. Although Western Sahara is recognised by 47 states (as of December 2022), the SADR was recognized by 84 UN member states in the past, but since then 36 of them have "frozen" or "withdrawn" this recognition and one ceased to exist (Rosner-Merker 2021; Dasgupta 2000, pp. 2914-2917). Thus, in light of the abovementioned criteria, the SADR does not fit the definition of a non-recognised state (Caspersen 2012, p. 8). However, the question remains open as to whether the case of Western Sahara can be considered as a typical example of a non-recognised state according to the criteria cited earlier. The vast majority of states considered unrecognised were created through secession when they broke away from the parent state, as was the case with Eritrea, South Sudan, Somaliland, or historically Katanga and Biafra. However, these seem to be very different situations from the case of Western Sahara. Western Sahara was not part of Morocco (unless, that is, we go back to the ancient times of the Almoravid dynasty in the 11th/12th century). At the time of decolonisation, it was a Spanish colony and, in accordance with the principles of decolonisation and self-determination, it declared independence. Its territory was occupied by Morocco against the will of the Sahrawi people. Therefore, none of the examples cited above fits its case. The problem with how to qualify the case of Western Sahara undermines the order of concepts and theories aiming to address the question of unrecognised states. Western Sahara's misfortune is mainly that, although it had the right to exist as an independent entity, it never did so as a de jure state. The current authorities of the Sahrawi Arab Democratic Republic and the administration managing the Sahrawi refugee camps are in exile, in an area belonging to Algeria in the Tindouf province. The Sahrawis themselves do not wish to be defined as an unrecognised state, but as an occupied one, just as the Palestinians have done for a long time. The case of Western Sahara is often described in the literature as an example of unfinished decolonisation (Kosidło 2012; Shelby 2004).

For the sake of argument, it should be pointed out that another category of states distinguished in political science comprises dysfunctional states. As far as their subjectivity is concerned, this is not in question, whereas the attributes of their statehood, particularly the existence of an effective authority, have disappeared or are in a state of collapse. Their subjectivity results from their previous position as a full-fledged, legitimate, and recognised participant in international relations. Robert H. Jackson utilizes the term "quasi-states" to denote dysfunctional states characterized by weak and ineffective public institutions, low levels of economic development, and a lack of national unity and social legitimacy for actions taken by public authority. However, the international community does not dispute the international legal subjectivity of these states, even if it is merely formal. They are recognized internationally as equal actors, notwithstanding their deficiency in "basic empirical capacities". According to Scott Pegg, such a state "has a flag, an ambassador, a capital city, and a seat at the United Nations General Assembly, but it does not function positively as a viable governing entity" (Pegg 2021, p. 1). The territorial scope of a dysfunctional state's exercise of power is often limited to the capital city, as exemplified by the case of Somalia in recent years.

2.2. The concept of the *de facto state*

De facto states, which are typically secessionist entities, exercise effective jurisdiction over a population within a defined territory for an extended period of time and are capable of establishing relations with other states; moreover, they seek full constitutional independence and universal international recognition as sovereign states. The term was coined by Scott Pegg (1998), whose coherent concept of these entities in political science became the basis for further research in this area by other authors (Pegg 2017). Pegg points out that the same normative logic that justifies the existence of dysfunctional states is used to deny the legitimacy of *de facto states* in the international arena. Undeniably, despite the question of legality in the international arena, *de facto states* do interact with the international community. This raises the question of the approach to such entities under public international law. Already in 1976 James Crawford argued that

> if international law withholds legal status from effective illegal entities, the result is a legal vacuum undesirable both in practice and in principle. But this assumes that international law does not apply to *de facto* illegal entities; and this is simply not so. Relevant international legal rules can apply to *de facto* situations here as elsewhere (Crawford 1976, p. 145).

In other words, according to Crawford, even entities that do not qualify as states cannot take actions contrary to public international law. They are obliged to comply with peremptory norms public international law, just as states are. A different assumption would mean that peremptory norms, absolutely binding on all participants in the international arena, are not applicable on the territory of de facto states.

2.3. The impact of international recognition on the legal nature of the *de facto state*

Public international law does not regulate the creation of a state, as this is a matter of fact (Bierzanek / Symonides 1998, p. 126). Nevertheless, when it comes to the functioning of the international community, the existence of those organisational entities that have not received international recognition is problematic. Under this assumption, the international community appears as a relational and relative reality. In the context of the subject under consideration, international recognition stems from the prior recognition of a given participant in international relations as an entity with the character of state. This assumption means that a given organisational unit may be categorised as a state by some actors, while others may not recognise it as such. What follows is that the very concept of the international community is not precise – for it is not possible to define its composition in a way that would be acceptable to all its participants. The lack of international recognition for an organisational entity has a different meaning on the grounds of constitutive theory, whose assumptions seem to be passing into historical oblivion. According to this theory, the existence of a state is contingent upon the recognition of the international community. The difficulty in applying this concept stems, for example, from the relationality and relativity of the international community and, moreover, from the unclear rules that apply to the question of international recognition. After all, this unilateral act of the state has a predominantly political dimension. If recognition depends on the individual interests of a state or a group of states at a particular time, it is difficult to argue that the lack of international subjectivity results from the lack of recognition. It seems that the declaratory concept is more legitimate in this context, as it assumes that recognition merely confirms the state's subjectivity, which has actually occurred as a result of a historical fact. However, even under the declaratory concept, the lack of recognition complicates the situation of a *de facto state* in the international arena. This does not mean, however, that certain actions taken by these states cannot receive international recognition. This view became established first with regard to unrecognised governments, and then – to organisational entities whose status was debatable.

2.4. Attributes of implied subjectivity of *de facto states*

2.4.1. *Jus tractatuum*

It seems that the earliest historically accepted acts of organisational units without the status of a state were those which consisted in the exercise of the jus tractatuum, i.e. the right to conclude international treaties. As early as the mid-19th century, European states were already concluding bilateral agreements with social structures that had a territorial base and a defined and unified social structure (Brownlie 1984, p. 362). Studies focusing on unrecognised states emphasise that legal doctrine generally agrees that non-recognition does not preclude certain treaty relations with the non-recognised entity (Zaręba 2020, p. 320). Hence, bilateral agreements between a *de facto state* and one of the recognising states are not excluded, despite the lack of international recognition from other states. Being devoid of full subjectivity in the sphere of treaty-making power, the term "quasi-treaty" intercourse is sometimes applied to denote its not entirely clear nature under public international law (Zaręba 2020, p. 320). Following this line of reasoning, one should therefore rather speak of jus quasi-tractatuum. Sometimes states wishing to enter into a treaty with a *de facto state* act through legal entities such as associations or foundations, whose functioning is based on the principles of domestic law. The implementation of agreements concluded in this way takes place by introducing the changes resulting from these agreements into the national legal order. In the same manner, when the subject of an agreement is commercial relations, a commercial law company may act as the entity entering into such an agreement. Agreements on international scientific cooperation are concluded by scientific and research entities, which also operate on the basis of domestic law. A special solution is the conclusion of agreements by lower-level state administration units. As far as the subject of international agreements concluded by *de facto states* is concerned, it seems that they may cover almost the entirety of international relations, as in the case of Taiwan (Zaręba 2020, p. 328 et seq.). However, classical public international law excludes the possibility of bilateral agreements between a non-recognised entity and a non-recognising entity that would concern strictly political issues and could indicate the existence of a lasting political alliance or amity (Lauterpacht 1947, pp. 405-406). With regard to *de facto states*, the problem is more complicated, as they are operating on the international stage with partial recognition. In view of this, the question arises as to whether they are able to conclude bilateral agreements concerning the totality of international relations and alliances with states that recognise them. It seems that, on the basis of the relativistic concept, it may be assumed that such states conclude international agreements by exercising their jus tractatuum and not just their jus quasi-tractatuum. Thus, an agreement concluded by them will be qualified as a treaty and not as a political deal.

As far as multilateral agreements are concerned, *de facto states* exercise their jus tractatuum to a more limited extent than in the case of bilateral agreements. Historically, the former emerged later, as multilateral cooperation usually takes place in the forum of, or under the inspiration of, international organisations – which appeared on the international scene relatively late. With the exception of experiments undertaken within the framework of the League of Nations, they developed after the Second World War. In fact, international bodies with a universal character, such as the League of Nations or the United Nations, were originally conceived as a kind of "brake" preventing *de facto states* from joining multilateral agreements. They advised their member states not to enter into treaty relations with entities whose statehood was not internationally confirmed. This policy was set out in the legal acts of these bodies or in international agreements adopted under their auspices, which admitted as its members only those states that already belonged to, for example, the UN or its specialised bodies. Such a regulation constituted a barrier to entities whose international subjectivity was contested, notwithstanding the impossibility of their joining these organisations, which was clear at their establishment and does not seem to be about to change any time soon. It seems that *de facto states* are more likely to enter into multi-lateral agreements in the forum of regional international organisations, for they may find it easier to obtain at least partial recognition at this level. Regional recognition of a *de facto state* may also imply the possibility of its accession to re-gional organisations. This is the case of Palestine and Western Sahara, which, due to their widespread support in the region, have respectively joined the League of Arab States and the African Union (formerly the Organisation of African Unity). This means that they are parties to multilateral agreements, namely the founding treaties or agreements establishing international organisations. Incidentally, the case of the Sahrawi Arab Democratic Republic reveals striking similarities with the disputed statehood of Palestine. Neither of them declared secession from an existing state, but each declared unilateral independence. Both entities' claims to statehood have received widespread international recognition, and their libera-tion movements have enjoyed international legitimacy. However, in neither case has titular recognition translated into full-fledged membership in the world com-munity. Moreover, both Palestine and Western Sahara were characterised by lim-ited internal sovereignty due to foreign occupation of their territories, with the SADR being in an even worse position than Palestine. Morocco, which occupied and formally annexed Western Sahara, categorically rejected the right of state-hood for this entity, whereas Israel, at the very least, acknowledged the concept of the Palestinian National Authority, which administers areas "A" and "B" in the West Bank as per the Oslo Accords. Another parallel is that the SADR govern-ment is based in exile, as was the Palestinian leadership before 1994. These two entities have also had to contend with the fact that a large part of their popula-tions live as refugees in neighbouring countries. Compared to Palestine, the fate of Western Sahara has always been a peripheral international issue. In practice, the international community seems to have accepted the status quo in Western Sahara, as indicated by its passivity towards Morocco. By denying Western Sahara the right to self-determination, Morocco has violated a fundamental principle of international law, yet it has suffered virtually no consequences for doing so (Geldenhuys 2009, pp. 190-207; Shelly 2004, pp. 198-202).

There seems to be greater acceptability of the accession of internationally contested states to those instruments which are constitutive for the international community, such as the Geneva Conventions of 1949. Some unrecognised states of the Eastern Bloc acceded to these conventions in the 1950s, which, in the case of one of them, the German Democratic Republic, was welcomed by the USA, even though it did not recognize the GDR. In the context of *de facto states*, an interesting case on the possibility of acceding to the 1949 Geneva Conventions is that of Algeria, which, had the concept of *de facto states* existed in the 1960s, could have fulfilled its principles in the reality of the time. Algeria expressed its wish to accede to the Geneva Conventions in 1960. Its application was communicated to the contracting parties, including France, which protested against it, leading to a kind of "suspension" of the procedure until France accepted Algerian independence (Distefano / Henry 2015, p. 168). As far as Palestine is concerned, its 1989 application for accession to the 1949 Geneva Conventions was first rejected on the grounds of uncertainty as to the "existence or non-existence of a Palestinian state," but the one submitted in 2014 was accepted, which is associated in the literature with a significant increase in Palestine's international recognition (Mielus 2014, pp. 51-69).

If the adoption of certain international agreements by the widest possible range of entities is considered to be of paramount importance to the international community, certain creativity may be shown in terms of proposed solutions with regard to the identification of potential parties to these agreements. In June 2015, POLISARIO Front made a unilateral declaration on behalf of the people of Western Sahara that it undertook to apply the 1949 Geneva Conventions and Additional Protocol I to the conflict between it and the Kingdom of Morocco. The declaration was addressed to the Swiss Federal Council, the depositary of the Geneva Conventions and its Additional Protocols, which accepted it and notified to the governments of state parties. Such a declaration can only be made by a body representing a nation involved in an armed conflict referred to in Article 1(4) of Additional Protocol I. Its acceptance implies recognition that POLISARIO Front and Morocco are in a situation covered by Article 1(4) of Additional Protocol I, i.e. an armed conflict in which peoples are fighting against colonial domination, alien occupation, or racist regimes ("Military Occupation of the Western Sahara" 2017, Web).

Another interesting solution was the 1960 proposal formulated by the United States and the United Kingdom concerning parties to the Partial Nuclear Test Ban Treaty. They advocated defining the future parties to this agreement as "any state or authority." However, this solution was not adopted due to being contrary to public international law. Had such a standard been introduced, the concept of "any authority" could have been interpreted as authority exercised by a *de facto state*.

As the examples cited above demonstrate, the implementation of jus tractatuum by *de facto states* in terms of multilateral agreements is clearly present in the international arena. However, the accession of a *de facto state* to a multilateral agreement cannot be viewed as tantamount to their recognition by the other states-parties to the same agreement, which may refuse to recognise them.

2.4.2. *Jus legationis*

Under public international law, the establishment of diplomatic relations is regulated by Article 2 of the 1961 Vienna Convention on Diplomatic Relations. This article explicitly refers to relations between states, stipulating that the establishment of permanent diplomatic missions shall be by mutual consent of those states. It is generally accepted in doctrine that states whose subjectivity is not unquestionable in the international arena cannot maintain diplomatic relations. If, despite the lack of recognition, diplomatic relations have been established, and a diplomatic mission is established on the territory of a *de facto state*, such actions will amount to an implicit recognition of that state (Dynia 2017, pp. 102-103). However, cases of the establishment of diplomatic relations with entities with contested subjectivity are sporadic.

The issue of consular relations of states is regulated in Article 2 of the 1963 Vienna Convention on Consular Relations ("Vienna Convention on Consular Relations" 1963). It is generally accepted that "diplomatic relations are official, peaceful intercourses between sovereign states or other entities that mutually recognise each other" (Sutor 2019, p. 100). They are carried out by government officials forming part of the foreign service of a state (Sutor 2019, p. 100). Consular relations occur in the intercourse between two states in order to carry out consular functions. They are possible if the head of the consular office is granted consular status in the host state. It is symbolically performed by issuing an exequatur in a formalised procedure defined by the laws of the states concerned. However, with regard to de facto regimes views have been formulated that the tacit acceptance of the consular officer of the sending state implies the possibility for him or her to exercise consular functions in a non-recognised state (Quigly 2008, p. 96). In the 19th century, the United Kingdom and the United States made attempts to send consular officials to emerging states in Latin America, which had not yet been recognised by them, with a request for an exequatur. This request, however, was not accepted by the authorities of the *de facto states*, due to the lack of recognition of their independence by the requesting state. There was also the case of British consuls who, during the American Civil War, exercised their functions in Confederate territory without obtaining an exequatur from its authorities, which were not recognised by Britain. This example is provided by Lauterpacht, who also points out that in order for the consuls to be able to act, they had to limit their activity to purely consular functions and not question the actions of the Confederate government (Lauterpacht 1947, p. 387). There have also been cases where the request for an exequatur was not formulated at all, yet the performance of consular functions continued without the recognition of the newly formed state (Graham 1939, p. 297). After the Second World War, due to the creation of many new states and the tensions between the Eastern and Western blocs translating into politically conditioned conflicts in many regions of the world, the practice with regard to the exercise of the "consular right" in *de facto states* varied. In some cases, consular offices were established without the recognition of the state in which they functioned. In others, consular offices continued to function after changes of sovereign power in a particular territory, although an unambiguously clear statement as to the non-recognition of the host state could result in non-recognition of the sending state's officials as consular officials (Sutor 2019, pp. 471 et seq.). An appeal to members of the international community to sever consular relations may be prompted by the recognition that the state in question is de facto illegitimate due to the incompatibility of the assumptions under which it operates with public international law. Szymon Zaręba points out that while in the 1980s and 1990s there did exist the practice of establishing consular offices in the unrecognised newly created states of the former Yugoslavia, this practice has not been observed on the international arena in the last twenty years (Zaręba 2020, p. 299).

Conversely, already in the 19th century *de facto states* also made attempts to send their consular officials to other states; this practice was continued in the 20th century and until today. Clearly, the obvious aim of this activity was to strengthen their position in the international arena. As in the case of sending consular officials to *de facto states*, there is no uniform practice in this regard, not even with regard to the reception of consular officials from *de facto states* by the same states. In 1819, the United States refused to issue an exequatur to the consul for the United Provinces of the Rio de la Plata because of their non-recognition. A century later, after the First World War, the same country granted permission for consular officials from Lithuania, Latvia, and Estonia to reside on their territory without an exequatur, clearly indicating that granting an exequatur was impossible because it would be tantamount to recognizing the entities in question (Chen 1951, pp. 199-200, fn. 51; Graham 1939). It seems that political factors played, and continue to play, a crucial role when it comes to the solutions adopted each time.

Limiting official diplomatic and consular relations with *de facto states* is not tantamount to the absence of any intercourse. Zaręba uses the term "quasi-diplomatic" and "quasi-consular" relations but does not distinguish between quasi-diplomatic and quasi-consular establishments, pointing out that strict categorisation is unjustified due to the lack of terminological uniformity and different status of entities that bear identical or very similar names. The Somaliland government maintains informal representations in some countries. These missions, however, do not have diplomatic status under the provisions of the Vienna Convention on Diplomatic Relations. Although the Somali authorities do not fully control their territory, they strongly oppose the opening of diplomatic missions in Somaliland (Economist Intelligence Unit 2022, Web).

The Sahrawi Arab Democratic Republic has, since its proclamation, established diplomatic relations with a number of states, mainly in Africa and Latin America, which have recognised its independence. The Sahrawi Arab Democratic Republic was recognized by 84 UN member states, but 36 of them have withdrawn or suspended their recognition. Several states that do not recognise the SADR nonetheless recognise POLISARIO Front as the legitimate representative of the population of the Western Sahara. The exact number of states that recognise the Sahrawi Arab Democratic Republic is difficult to ascertain due to the fact that some of them have resumed recognition, as Bolivia did in 2021 and Colombia in 2022. Conversely, some states (mainly African) no longer recognise the SADR and in fact do not maintain relations with it, but have not officially confirmed this, not wanting to risk worsening relations with Morocco on the one hand and Algeria on the other. It is understood that some seventeen states take an "unknown position." The SADR officially maintains embassies in 22 states, the majority of them in Africa and Latin America. In addition, the SADR (POLISARIO Front) maintains an extensive network of representatives, also in countries that do not recognise the SADR as a sovereign state (Sahrawi Embassy in Addis Abeba, Web). The status of these missions and their tasks depend on the agreements between the states concerned. The practice also shows that the absence of agreements in this respect results in the closure of the post on the territory of the state "allegedly" hosting the foreign mission. Algeria also offers diplomatic support to POLISARIO Front through its diplomatic missions (Interview with SADR Ambassador to Algeria Mr Abdelkader Taleb Omar, Algiers, 8 May 2023). As the SADR authorities do not control the entire Western Saharan territory and the majority of the governmental institutions are headquartered at Camp Rabouni (one of the Sahrawi refugee camps in Algerian territory), some states have their diplomatic missions in Algiers also accredited to the SADR. The ambassadors of such countries present their credentials to the SADR's President in Tifariti or Bir Lehlu on the Liberated Territories (Sahara Press Service 8.03.2018, Web; Sahara Press Service 21.05.2018, Web).

In the context of the Western Sahara case, an unusual issue is the withdrawal or freezing of its international recognition, as this is incongruent with the still binding Montevideo Convention on the Rights and Duties of States of 26 December 1933, whose Article 6 says: "The recognition of a state merely signifies that the state which recognises it accepts the personality of the other with all the rights and duties determined by international law. Recognition is unconditional and irrevocable" (Montevideo Convention on the Rights and Duties of States 1933). In other words, once a state has recognised the SADR as a sovereign state, then this state cannot revoke their recognition – it may only break their diplomatic relations with the SADR (Centro de Estudos do Sahara Occidendal da USC, Web). "Derecognition" of Western Sahara is encouraged by Morocco, which insists on treating the territory as its province. According to Riccardo Fabiani, project director for North Africa at the International Crisis Group, over the longer term Morocco has been "winning" the diplomatic war in Africa by managing to convince a large number of African countries (around 22) to open consulates in Western Sahara and, most importantly, de facto freezing all discussions on Western Sahara at the African Union (Fabricius 2022).

2.4.3. Jus standi

The concept of jus standi includes the right to incur international responsibility and bring claims in the international arena. The principles relating to liability in public international law have been developed by the UN International Law Commission in the form of the Draft Articles on the Responsibility of States for Internationally Wrongful Acts (International Law Commission 2001). In general, this document refers to the responsibility of states, but it is argued in the literature that there are no reasons to not apply its general provisions to all subjects of international law. It seems that such a possibility does exist as far as international organisations are concerned, as their international subjectivity is uncontroversial today. However, the question of passive and active jus standi capacity arises with regard to those participants in international relations whose statehood, and consequently full international subjectivity, is contested. Their ability to bear international responsibility and to assert claims in international legal transactions would demonstrate a certain degree of international subjectivity. Understood in this way, subjectivity would be detached from statehood and have a limited scope compared to the full subjectivity of states with undisputed status. It seems that this thesis is confirmed by international relations practice. Indeed, it is possible to identify both cases where *de facto states* have attempted to assert their claims and those where international responsibility has been attributed to them for the damage caused. In the context of the partial subjectivity of national liberation movements, they often proclaim the independent existence of their state at an early stage of their struggle, at which time part of the international community may begin to perceive them as *de facto states*. In this situation, Article 10(2) of the Draft Articles on the Responsibility of States for Internationally Wrongful Acts regulates the question of responsibility for the actions of these pre-state forms of organisation in the international arena. Thus, if a national liberation movement forms a new state, "it would be anomalous if the new regime or new State could avoid responsibility for conduct earlier committed by it." According to the principles of public international law, the basis for attributing responsibility for the actions of a national liberation movement that has succeeded in establishing a state to this newly created state is seen in the continuity between the movement and the newly formed government (Article 10, Draft Articles on Responsibility of States for Internationally Wrongful Acts, point 4). The same entity that had the characteristics of an insurrectional or national liberation movement effectively becomes the government of the state it fought to establish. In such a situation, the accepted principle is to require the new state to accept responsibility for the acts committed in order to establish it (Article 10, Draft Articles on Responsibility of States for Internationally Wrongful Acts, point 6). It is worth emphasizing the position of the authors of the Draft Articles who propose not to differentiate such a movement's responsibility on the basis of any international "legitimacy" or of any illegality in respect of their establishment as a government, even if this is relevant for the application of public international law in other contexts (Article 10, Draft Articles on Responsibility of States for Internationally Wrongful Acts, point 11).

As far as the ability of *de facto states* to pursue their claims internationally is concerned, this appears to be limited, in accordance with the extent of recognition of a given entity in the international arena. A *de facto state* will be able to assert its rights more successfully in an environment that recognises its international legal subjectivity. This applies to both bilateral and multilateral relations. In institutionalised multilateral relations, a *de facto state* may benefit from the accepted systemic solutions, which may facilitate effective redress (Zaręba 2020, p. 271). Nevertheless, it should be emphasised that even the possibility of claiming liability for damage suffered by a *de facto state* does not imply the recognition of its statehood. Indeed, the law of international organisations may provide that an entity with an undetermined international legal status may act in a different capacity, e.g. as a customs territory or a fishing entity (Zaręba 2020, p. 271). The possibility of pursuing claims by an organisational entity that is qualified in the doctrine as a *de facto state* has also been considered in disputes before international tribunals. For example, the procedural capacity of POLISARIO Front was considered in the judgment of the General Court of 29 September 2021 in Case T-279/19 POLISARIO Front vs. Council of the European Union (Judgment of the General Court of 29 September 2021 in Case T-279/19 Front populaire pour la libération de la Saguia el-Hamra et du Rio de oro (Front Polisario) v Council of the European Union). The applicant claimed that, being a national liberation movement, it derived its rights and obligations directly from international law, invoking the "separate and distinct status of Western Sahara and the right to self-determination of the Sahrawi people." (Judgment of the General Court of 29 September 2021 in Case T-279/19, para. 81) It argued that, being a subject of international law, it thus fulfilled the condition of having legal personality within the meaning of the fourth paragraph of Article 263 TFEU. The General Court examined, in particular, whether the role played by POLISARIO Front in the self-determination process of Western Sahara could be related to the capacity to bring legal proceedings before the EU courts (Judgment of the General Court of 29 September 2021 in Case T-279/19, para. 90). The General Court found it undisputed that the UN bodies had granted POLISARIO Front the status of the representative of the people of Western Sahara in the self-determination process for that non-self-governing territory (Judgment of the General Court of 29 September 2021 in Case T-279/19, para. 103). It rejected the argument that POLISARIO Front's links with the Sahrawi Arab Democratic Republic deprived it of the independence and liability necessary to act within the context of legal relations. Neither was POLISARIO Front's capacity to bring legal proceedings undermined by the lack of international recognition by the Union itself or its member states (Judgment of the General Court of 29 September 2021 in Case T-279/19, para. 105). The Court also referred to the fact that the EU institutions had already accepted the representativeness of POLISARIO Front and treated it as a legitimate partner on the Western Sahara issue. The General Court also rejected the Commission's argument that by granting POLISARIO Front the capacity to bring legal proceedings, it became a "quasi-international" court, that the Court was trying to replace the institutions managing the EU's external relations and was issuing a "political decision" (Judgment of the General Court of 29 September 2021 in Case T-279/19, para. 109-113). After a detailed analysis of all the arguments outlined above, the General Court recognised POLISARIO Front's capacity to bring legal proceedings and its action against the Council of the EU was heard.

Conclusion

In the contemporary international reality, the functioning of *de facto states*, which suffer from a significant deficit in terms of the recognition of their international legal subjectivity, is full of mutual contradictions. On the one hand, these entities can be characterised by significant functional permanence, which is not necessarily hampered by their unregulated legal status. They have often learnt to use a variety of legal means to function in the global world as customs territories (as Taiwan does as a member of the World Trade Organization), and even use trade representative offices to pursue diplomatic-consular interests. On the other hand, unrecognised states have historically been examples of short-lived entities. In a number of *de facto states*, their level of development and democracy, as well as the stability of their governments, exceed that of various internationally recognised dysfunctional states. This is exemplified by Turkish Northern Cyprus, which has one of the highest levels of citizen participation in direct democracy through referendums in the world, or Somaliland, a stable economic entity in the Horn of Africa, not to mention Taiwan's economic development. On the other hand, this group also includes entities whose situation is much more difficult as they struggle for not only legal but also factual existence (such as Western Sahara). In view of such contrasts, the creation of a unified theory that would situate unrecognised *de facto states* in the "concert of nations" of contemporary international law is far from obvious. Regardless of their potential, they are condemned to function on the periphery of this legal system, although it should be noted that the greater the number of actors recognising a state, the more stable its international legal position appears to be (of which Kosovo is the best example). Indeed, the recognition of a state is a vector that is the product of bilateral relations – the more of them there are, the more stable the vector.

References

Bauman, Zygmunt: *Liquid Modernity*, Polity Press: Cambridge 2000.

Bieleń, Stanisław: "Państwa upadłe". In: Symonides, Janusz (ed.): *Organizacja Narodów Zjednoczonych – bilans i perspektywy*. Scholar: Warsaw 2006.

Bierzanek, Remigiusz / Symonides, Janusz: *Prawo międzynarodowe publiczne*. Wydawnictwo Prawnicze PWN: Warsaw 1998.

Boehme, Olivier: "The Involvement of the Belgian Central Bank in the Katanga Secession, 1960-1963". *African Economic History* 33, 2005.

Bot, Ben: *Nonrecognition and Treaty Relations*. Oceana Publications: Leyden 1968.

Brownlie, Ian: "The Expansion of International Society: the Consequences for the Law of Nations". In: Bull, Hedley / Watson, Adam (eds.): *The Expansion of International Society*. Clarendon Press: Oxford 1984.

Caspersen, Nina: *Unrecognized States. The Struggle for Sovereignty in the Modern International System*. Polity Press: Cambridge, 2012.

Caspersen, Nina / Stansfield, Gareth: *Unrecognized States in the International System*. Routledge: London and New York 2011.

Chen, Ti-Chiang: *The International Law of Recognition*. Frederick A. Preager: New York 1951.

Crawford, James: "The Criteria for Statehood in International Law". *British Year Book of International Law* 48(1) 1976.

Czapliński, Władysław / Wyrozumska, Anna: *Prawo międzynarodowe publiczne. Zagadnienia systemowe*. C. H. Beck: Warsaw 1999.

Dasgupta, Punyapriya: "Derecognition of Western Sahara: Foreign Policy Volte-Face". *Economic and Political Weekly*, 35(33) 2000.

Distefano, Giovanni / Henry, Etienne: "Final Provisions, Including the Martens Clause". In: Clapham, Andrew et al. (eds.): *The 1949 Geneva Conventions: A Commentary*. Oxford University Press: Oxford.

Dudkiewicz, Hubert: "Prawo międzynarodowe w kwestii państwa upadłego". In: Kłosowicz, Robert (ed.): *Problem upadku państw w stosunkach międzynarodowych*. Wydawnictwo Uniwersytetu Jagiellońskiego: Krakow 2012.

Dynia, Elżbieta: *Uznanie państwa w prawie międzynarodowym. Zarys problematyki*, Wydawnictwo Uniwersytetu Rzeszowskiego: Rzeszów 2017.

Economist Intelligence Unit: Kenya Establishes Consul-General's Office in Somaliland, 6.05.2022, retrieved 7.7.2023, from https://country.eiu.com/article.aspx?articleid=1242081307&Country=Kenya&topic=Politics&subtopic=-Forecast&subsubtopic=International+relations.

El Presidente de la República recibe en Tifariti las cartas credenciales del embajador de Zimbabwe, *Sahara Press Service*, 21.05.2018, retrieved 24.09.2023, from https://www.spsrasd.info/news/es/articles/2018/05/21/15538.html

Fabricius, Peter: "SADR Grows Theoretically Stronger but Diplomatically Weaker". Institute for Security Studies, 7.10.2022, retrieved 7.7.2023, from https://issafrica.org/iss-today/sadr-grows-theoretically-stronger-but-diplomatically-weaker.

Fassbender, Bardo / Peters, Anne: *The Oxford Handbook of International Law*. Oxford Academic: Oxford 2013.

Geldenhuys, Deon: *Contested States in World Politics*. Palgrave Macmillan: London 2009.

Graham, Malbone Watson: *The Diplomatic Recognition of the Border States, Part II Estonia*. University of California Press: Berkeley 1939.

Harper, Mary: *Getting Somalia Wrong? Faith, War and Hope in a Shattered State*. Zed Book Ltd: London/New York 2012.

Haskin, Jeanne M.: *The Tragic State of Congo. From Decolonisation to Dictatorship*. Algora Publishing: New York 2005.

Hobsbawm, Eric: *The Age of Extremes*, Abacus: London 1995.

Imeseis, Ardi: "On Membership of the United Nations and the State of Palestine: A critical Account", *Leiden Journal of International Law* 34(4) 2021.

International Court of Justice, Advisory Opinion of 21 June 1971, Legal Consequences for States of the Continued Presence of South Africa in Namibia (South West Africa) Nothwithstanding Security Council Resolution 276 (1970), para. 118, p. 54, retrieved 12.6.2023, from https://www.icj-cij.org/public/files/case-related/53/053-19710621-ADV-01-00-EN.pdf.

International Law Commission: Draft Articles on the Responsibility of International Organizations. 2011, retrieved 19.2.2023, from https://legal.un.org/ilc/texts/instruments/english/draft_articles/9_11_2011.pdf.

International Law Commission: Draft Articles on Responsibility of States for Internationally Wrongful Acts, with Commentaries, 2001, retrieved 19.2.2023, from https://legal.un.org/ilc/texts/instruments/english/commentaries/9_6_2001.pdf.

Jackson, Robert: *Quasi-States: Sovereignty, International Relations and the Third World*. Cambridge University Press: Cambridge 1996.

Jackson, Robert H.: "Quasi-States, Dual Regimes, and Neoclassical Theory: International Jurisprudence and the Third World". *International Organization* 41(4) 1987.

Jackson, Robert / Rosberg, Carl G.: "Why Africa's Weak States Persist: The Empirical and Juridical in Statehood". *World Politics* 35(1) 1982.

Jessup, Philip C.: *A Modern Law of Nations. An Introduction.* Macmillan: New York 1949.

Judgment of the Court of Justice of the EU of 21 December 2016 in Case C-104/16 P, retrieved 19.2.2023, from https://curia.europa.eu/juris/document/document.jsf?text=&docid=186489&pageIndex=0&doclang=PL&mode=lst&dir=&occ=first&part=1&cid=309583.

Judgment of the General Court of 29 September 2021 in Case T-279/19 Front populaire pour la libération de la Saguia el-Hamra et du Rio de oro (Front Polisario) v Council of the European Union, retrieved 12.6.2023, from https://eur-lex.europa.eu/legal-content/en/TXT/?uri=CELEX:62019TJ0279.

Judgment of the General Court of 10 December 2015 in Case T-512/12 Front populaire pour la libération de la saguia-el-hamra et du rio de oro (Front Polisario) v Council of the European Union, retrieved 19.2.2023, from https://eur-lex.europa.eu/legal-content/EN/TXT/?uri=CELEX%3A62012TJ0512.

Kine, Phelim: "On the Horn of Africa, a tiny 'country' has Congress' ear." *Politico*, 21.12.2021, retrieved from 8.11.2022, from https://www.politico.com/news/2021/12/21/somaliland-china-taiwan-congress-525842.

Kłosowicz, Robert: "Policies of the Maghreb Countries Toward Western Sahara: Mauritania's Perspective". *Hungarian Journal of African Studies*, 16(1) 2022.

Kłosowicz, Robert / Mormul, Joanna: *Erytrea i jej wpływ na sytuację polityczną w Rogu Afryki*, Wydawnictwo Uniwersytetu Jagiellońskiego: Kraków 2018.

Kocot, Kazimierz: "Kilka uwag z zakresu prawa narodów o pojęciu 'nowych państw'". *Ruch Prawniczy, Ekonomiczny i Socjologiczny* 4, 1961.

Kolstø, Pål: "The Sustainability and Future of Unrecognized Quasi-States". *Journal of Peace Research*, 43(6) 2006.

Kosidło, Adam: *Sahara Zachodnia. Fiasko dekolonizacji czy sukces podboju? 1975–2011.* Wydawnictwo Uniwersytetu Gdańskiego: Gdańsk 2012.

Koźbiał, Krzysztof: "Państwa nieuznawane jako element dezintegrujący w stosunkach międzynarodowych. Wybrane aspekty". *Rocznik Stowarzyszenia Naukowców Polaków Litwy*, 18 2018.

La embajadora de Namibia para la RASD presenta sus credenciales al Presidente de la República en TT.LL, *Sahara Press Service*, 8.03.2018, retrieved 24.09.2023, from https://www.spsrasd.info/news/es/articles/2018/03/08/14099.html

Lauterpacht, Hersch: *Recognition in International Law.* Cambridge University Press: Cambridge 1947.

Lawrence, Thomas J.: *The Principles of International Law*. D.C. Heath & Co: Boston 1910.

League of Nations: The Covenant of the League of Nations, signed 28 April 1919. Retrieved 12.6.2023, from https://avalon.law.yale.edu/20th_century/leagcov.asp.

Letter addressed to M. Paderewski by the President of the Conference transmitting to him the Treaty to be signed by Poland under Article 93 of Treaty of Peace with Germany. In: Temperley, Harold William (ed.): A History of the Peace Conference of Paris, vol. V. London Oxford University Press, Hodder & Stoughton: London 1921, p. 433.

Lewis, Ioan: *Understanding Somalia and Somaliland*. Hurst Publishers: London 2009.

Lynch, Dov: "Separatist States and Post-Soviet Conflicts". *International Affairs* 4, 2002.

Łoś-Nowak, Teresa: "Państwowy poziom analizy w stosunkach międzynarodowych." In: Haliżak, Edward / Pietraś, Marek (eds.): *Poziomy analizy stosunków międzynarodowych*, Rambler: Warsaw 2013.

Łoś-Nowak, Teresa: *Stosunki międzynarodowe. Teorie-systemy-uczestnicy*, Wydawnictwo Uniwersytetu Wrocławskiego: Wrocław 2006.

Mantoux, Paul / trans. Link, Arthur: *The Deliberations of the Council of Four, March 24-June 28, 1919. Notes of the Official Interpreter*. Princeton University Press: Princeton 1992.

Meservey, Joshua: "The U.S. Should Recognize Somaliland". Backgrounder 3660, 19.10.2021, retrieved 8.11.2022, from https://www.heritage.org/sites/default/files/2021-10/BG3660.pdf.

Middlebush, Frederick A.: "International Affairs: The Effect of the Non-Recognition of Manchukuo". *The American Political Science Review* 28(4) 1934.

Mielus, Kamil: "Legal Implications of Palestine's Enhanced Status in the UN General Assembly". *Polish Review of International and European Law*, 3(1-2) 2014.

Military Occupation of Western Sahara by Morocco. In: Bellal, Annyssa: The War Report. Armed Conflicts in 2016. Geneva Academy of International Humanitarian Law and Human Rights: Geneva 2017, retrieved 25.3.2023, from https://www.rulac.org/browse/conflicts/military-occupation-of-western-sahara-by-morocco#collapse2accord.

Montevideo Convention on the Rights and Duties of States, done at Montevideo, 26.12.1933, retrieved 7.7.2023, from https://www.jus.uio.no/english/services/library/treaties/01/1-02/rights-duties-states.html.

Muszyński, Mariusz: *Siła, norma, idea. Prawo międzynarodowe publiczne w ujęciu historycznym*, vol. 1. Wydawnictwo Naukowe UKSW: Warsaw 2019.

Oppenheim, Lassa: *International Law. A Treatise*. Peace, Green: New York, Bombay-Calcutta-Madras 1920.

Paxson, Frederick L.: *The Independence of the South American Republics: A Study in Recognition and Foreign Policy*. Ferris and Leach: Philadelphia 1916.

Pegg, Scott: *De Facto States in the International System*. Institute of International Relations, The University of British Columbia: Vancouver 1998.

Pegg, Scott: *International Society and the De Facto States*, Routledge: London 1998a.

Pegg, Scott: "Twenty Years of de facto State Studies: Progress, Problems, and Prospects". *Oxford Research Encyclopedia of Politics*, 2017, retrieved 19.2.2023, from https://doi.org/10.1093/acrefore/9780190228637.013.516.

Perkowski, Maciej: *Podmiotowość prawa międzynarodowego współczesnego uniwersalizmu w złożonym modelu klasyfikacyjnym*. Temida 2: Białystok 2008.

Prashad, Vijay: "Morocco Drives a War in Western Sahara for Its Phosphates". *Green Left Weekly* (1331) 25.1.2022, p. 16.

Quigly, John B.: *Consular Law and Practice*. Oxford University Press: Oxford 2008.

Recognition of Somaliland – Claiming our Rightful Place Within the Community of Nations, retrieved 19.2.2023, from https://recognition.somaliland gov.com.

Recognition of Somaliland. The Legal Case, retrieved 20.11.2022, from https://recognition.somalilandgov.com/legal/.

Reno, William: *Warlord Politics and African States*. Lynne Rienner Publishers: Boulder 1999.

Rosner-Merker, Tina: "Why Is Western Sahara Losing Recognitions?". De Facto States Research Unit, 5.4.2021, retrieved 6.12.2023, from https://defactostates. ut.ee/blog/why-western-sahara-losing-recognitions.

Rotberg, Robert: "The Failure and Collapse of Nation-States – Breakdown, Prevention and Repair". In: Rotberg, Robert (ed.): *When States Fail – Causes and Consequences*. Princeton University Press: Princeton 2003.

Rutland, Peter: Frozen Conflicts, Frozen Analysis (paper presented at the International Studies Association, Chicago, 1 March 2007), retrieved 12.6.2023, from https://www.scribd.com/document/253058977/Peter-Rutland-Frozen-Conflicts.

SADR Recognitions, Centro de Estudos do Sahara Occidendal da USC, Universidade de Santiago de Compostela, retrieved 7.7.2023, from https://www.usc. es/en/institutos/ceso/RASD_Reconocimientos.html.

Saganek, Przemysław: "Uznanie jako akt jednostronny państwa a systemowy charakter prawa międzynarodowego". In: Kwiecień, Roman (ed.): *Państwo a prawo międzynarodowe jako system prawa*. Wydawnictwo UMCS: Lublin 2015.

Schwarzenberger, Georg: *A Manual of International Law*. Stevens and Sons: London-New York 1960.

Schwelb, Egon: "The Nuclear Test Ban Treaty and International Law". *American Journal of International Law* 58(4) 1964.

Shelby, Toby: *Endgame in the Western Sahara. What Future for Africa's Last Colony?*, Zed Books: London 2004.

Srogosz, Tomasz: "Podmiotowość prawno-międzynarodowa w świetle Third World Approaches to International Law". In: Cała-Wacinkiewicz, Ewelina et al. *Podmiotowość prawnomiędzynarodowa i jej współczesne aspekty*. Wydawnictwo C. H. Beck: Warsaw 2020.

Srogosz, Tomasz: "Upadłość państwa z perspektywy prawa międzynarodowego". *Sprawy międzynarodowe* 2, 2009.

Stanislawski, Bartosz H.: "Para-States, Quasi-States, and Black Spots". *International Studies Review* 10(2) 2008.

Stiglitz, Joseph: *Making Globalization Work*. WW Norton & Company: New York-London 2006.

Sutor, Julian: *Prawo dyplomatyczne i konsularne*. Wolters Kluwer: Warsaw 2019.

Symonides, Janusz: "Czy 'ogólne zasady prawa uznane przez narody cywilizowane' są źródłem prawa międzynarodowego". *Gdańskie Studia Prawnicze* 2, 2019.

"Taiwan, Somaliland Ties Growing Despite Diplomatic Isolation". *The Diplomat* 10.2.2022, retrieved 22.11.2022, from https://thediplomat.com/2022/02/taiwan-somaliland-ties-growing-despite-diplomatic-isolation/.

The Treaty of November 27, 1912, Between France and Spain Concerning Morocco. *American Journal of International Law* 7(2) 1913.

Walker, Edward: *No Peace, No War in the Caucasus: Secessionist Conflicts in Chechnya, Abkhazia and Nagorno-Karabakh*, Cambridge: Harvard University Center for Science and International Affairs 1998.

Ullendorf, Edward: "The 1897 Treaty Between Great Britain and Ethipia", *Rassegna Di Studi Etiopici* 22, 1966.

United Nations, Charter of the United Nations, 24.10.1945, 1 UNTS XVI.

United Nations General Assembly, Reparation for injuries incurred in the service of the United Nations, 1 December 1949, A/RES/365.

Zajadło, Jerzy: "Prawo międzynarodowe wobec problemu 'państwa upadłego'". *Państwo i Prawo* 2, 2005.

Zajączkowski, Kamil: "Afryka w okresie międzywojennym – Liga Narodów a miejsce i rola Afryki w porządku międzynarodowym." In: Gawrycki, Marcin F. / Bógdał-Brzezińska, Agnieszka (eds.): *Liga Narodów Wybranych*. Wydawnictwo Uniwersytetu Warszawaskiego: Warsaw 2020.

Zaręba, Szymon: *Skutki uznania państwa w świetle prawa międzynarodowego*. Instytut Nauk Prawnych PAN: Warsaw 2020.

Joanna Mormul, Kateřina Ženková Rudincová

Chapter 3. International Relations of *De Facto States*[1]

The chapter examines the international relations of *de facto states*, with a particular emphasis on their pursuit of international recognition. It elucidates the objectives of *de facto states* and the strategies they employ in engaging with diverse actors within the international system. The discussion is illustrated through the case of the Sahrawi Arab Democratic Republic (SADR), distinguished by its origin in unresolved decolonisation. The central argument posits that the SADR must establish and sustain international relations with various actors in the international system, including states and international organisations. This is essential not only to reclaim territory occupied by Morocco and to legitimise its existence but also to foster economic development and ultimately ensure the exercise of the right to self-determination for the Sahrawi people.

Keywords: *de facto states,* unrecognised states, international relations, Western Sahara, SADR, Morocco

Introduction

De facto or unrecognised states resemble "normal" states, but they have not achieved international recognition. A basic political science definition of *de facto states* was proposed by Pål Kolstø (2006). In his understanding, a *de facto state* is a political entity that has control over most of the territory it claims, seeks the international recognition of other states (but is in most cases deprived of it), and has existed for at least two years (Kolstø 2006, pp. 749–50). Different terms have been used to reference these entities, such as *separatist states, de facto states, pseudo-states, quasi-states,* and *unrecognised states* (Kolstø 2006; Pegg 1998; Caspersen 2012). In addition to this terminological plurality causing possible confusion, the concept *"quasi-*state" was used by Robert H. Jackson, in his book *Quasi-States: Sovereignty, International Relations and the Third World,* to refer to those states which, according to current research/knowledge, can be defined as dysfunctional or fragile ones (Jackson 1990, pp. 21–26; Kłosowicz / Mormul 2013, pp. 18–19). Pål Kolstø (2006, pp. 748-49) also draws attention to the

1   This chapter is the result of a research project financed by the National Science Centre (Narodowe Centrum Nauki), Poland, grant ID: 2017/25/B/HS5/00958.

existing terminological chaos in this matter, highlighting that the term "*quasi-states*" itself should be reserved for unrecognised, *de facto states,* also known under the name of "pseudo-states" or "para-states".

In our chapter, to avoid the terminological uncertainty and plurality connected with the study of this phenomenon, we decided to use the term *de facto states* introduced by Scott Pegg (1998). He defines a *de facto state* as "a functioning reality with effective territorial control of a given area that is denied legitimacy by the rest of international society" (Pegg 1998, p. 2). *De facto states* fulfil the criteria of statehood as defined by the 1933 Montevideo convention, namely population, territory, and effective government, and can establish international relations with other actors in the international system (UIO 1933). Generally, they are considered to possess a relatively high degree of internal sovereignty and lack the external dimension (Berg / Kuusk 2010). Due to the lack of international recognition, however, they are perceived to be anomalies and are considered to be isolated by the international community. Their position in the international system is made difficult by the threat from their parent state of being reincorporated (Berg / Toomla 2009). *De facto states* have even been portrayed as puppets in the hands of their patrons with no independent agency in terms of their international politics (Kolstø / Blakkisrud 2017). However, recent literature and empirical evidence show that *de facto states* possess some form of agency in the current international system (Caspersen 2009; von Steinsdorff / Fruhstorfer 2012).

Adrian Florea (2014) distinguishes four pathways through which *de facto states* could have developed: 1. an outcome of internal warfare; 2. contentious interaction between separatists and the parent state; 3. as a consequence of state collapse; and 4. the result of the decolonisation process. The last one fits the situation of the Sahrawi Arab Democratic Republic (SADR), whose case is often described as "unfinished decolonisation" (Florea, 2014, 796). In the same study, Florea (2014, pp. 792-794) presents a dataset in the article "De Facto States in International Politics (1945-2011)", revealing that between 1945 and 2011, there were 34 *de facto states.* Historically, Africa has been the continent most susceptible to "*de facto* separation", while Europe, particularly after the collapse of Yugoslavia in the mid-1990s, has emerged as the region with the highest number of such states.

Different authors recognise various amounts of *de facto states,* i.e., Scott Pegg in 1998 recognised four of them, while Nina Caspersen identified seventeen in 2012 (the SADR was not included in either list). Apart from the time gap and changes in the international system, these differences are often the result of terminological disagreement (Pegg 1998; Caspersen 2012). Hoch and Rudincová

(2015, pp. 37–38), reviewing the state-of-the-art of the research on *de facto states*, indicate only six entities that most scholars could agree added up to *de facto statehood*: Somaliland, Abkhazia, South Ossetia, Nagorno-Karabakh, Transnistria, and Northern Cyprus. All of these were formed as a result of the armed conflicts they had experienced in the second half of the 20th century and in the face of the impossibility of finding any other political solution.

Some additional borderline cases may be identified, such as the SADR, which are designed as *de facto states* according to a wider definition and conceptualisation of these entities even though they are not able to effectively control their whole territories (Toomla 2016; Caspersen 2012, p. 8). Another state identified as a borderline case is Taiwan, which has managed to establish effective relations (especially economic ones) with several states within the international system, including the USA (Berg / Pegg 2016). Another borderline case, Kosovo, may be considered a *de facto state* since it has not been accepted as a member of the UN yet (Caspersen 2012, p. 10). Additionally, there are also historical *de facto states*, e.g., in Africa – Katanga or Biafra, which do not exist anymore since they were reincorporated by their parent states but declared their independence during certain historical periods (Kolstø 2006).

Even though *de facto states* are considered to be isolated, they need to establish relations with states in the international system for several reasons, including economic development, or even ensuring their mere existence. In this respect, they can approach different actors in the international community and promote their interests. The level of connectedness of *de facto states* is a spectrum including a vast variety and quality of relations. On the one hand, there are *de facto states* such as Abkhazia, South Ossetia, or Transnistria, which have patrons guaranteeing their existence by military means and influencing their internal development (Kolstø 2021). On the other hand, there are patronless *de facto states*, such as Somaliland, which must diversify their international relations and seek support from a variety of actors. The relations between *de facto states* and other actors in the international system evolve over time and exhibit different dynamics.

In this chapter, we aim to explain the objectives *de facto states* have and the strategies they apply in engaging with different actors in the international system with a special focus on their goal of achieving international recognition. We understand the term engagement following, e.g., Ker-Lindsay (2015), as "any form of interaction between *de facto states* and recognised states or between *de facto states* and international organisations" (Caspersen 2018, p. 375). Engagement thus may involve different forms and may take place between different actors in *de facto states* and recognised states in the international community. Since the engagement of the international community with *de facto states* is considered to be highly contextual (Ker-Lindsay 2018; Toomla 2016), herein, we are presenting an intrinsic case study (Stake 1995) of the international relations of the Sahrawi Arab Democratic Republic with selected states of the international community. The SADR has been chosen as an illustrative case of this chapter since it is a *de facto state* that can establish and maintain a considerable variety of relations with other actors in the international system and needs them for its survival. We intend to find the answers to the following questions: 1) What are the reasons and motives behind the SADR's aim to diversify its international relations?; 2) What are the benefits for both the SADR and different actors in the international system resulting from common engagement?; 3) What is the quality, dynamic, and sustainability of the relationship between the Sahrawi Arab Democratic Republic and selected partners in the international community and how can this influence the possibility of the SADR achieving international recognition?

We first present a theoretical framework of international relations and different types of external actors engaging with *de facto states*. Next, we identify the motives behind the actions of both *de facto states* and external actors in establishing relations between each other and the benefits they each gain from the relationship. Finally, building on the theoretical framework, we develop a case study of the international relations of Western Sahara with a focus on the most important actors engaging with this *de facto state*.

International relations of *de facto states* – objectives and strategies

The objectives and strategies of de facto states

The emergence of *de facto states* and unilaterally declared independence is usually the result of a preceding civil war between *de facto states* and their parent states. The creation of *de facto states* takes place without permission or even against the will of their parent states. Therefore, they are not welcomed by the international community and in fact, they are rather stigmatised (Ker-Lindsay 2018). Nevertheless, *de facto states* are aware that the support of external actors is needed in their quest for international recognition. In a situation in which international recognition is not guaranteed, *de facto states* have to seek different levels of external support and international cooperation to ensure their survival (Caspersen 2018). The much-needed support is often provided by the patrons (for the elaboration of the patron-client relations, see, e.g., Kosienkowski 2019; Devyatkov 2022; Berg / Vits 2020). However, as patron-client relations are vulnerable and possibly lead to deepening dependence of the *de facto state* on the patron and loss of independent agency, it is in the *de facto states'* interest to diversify their external support (Caspersen 2018, p. 374).

De facto states are motivated in their search for partners (or patrons) by their need to 1) provide for their reconstruction as *de facto states* emerged mostly as a result of destructive civil wars; 2) assure economic development (investments and trade); 3) achieve international recognition; 4) prove the legitimacy of their existence as they are constantly threatened by their parent states (Caspersen 2015a, pp. 185–186). Establishing relations with other states in the international community is also considered a tool for enhancing the internal legitimacy of *de facto states* (Berg and Vits 2018).

Political reasons: The most important political aim of *de facto states* is to achieve international recognition and external sovereignty. The decision on the recognition of new states lies somewhere in between international politics and international law. There is a conviction that recognition is a legal act that pertains to the international sphere; on the other hand, national political leaders often assume that they should be able to decide freely to recognise or not a political entity seeking recognition. In such cases, the fate of a whole nation and its international status could be dependent on arbitrary political decisions. From the legal perspective, there is a longstanding debate between two theories of recognition: constitutive and declaratory (see e.g., Grzybowski 2019; Rossi 2020). According to the first one, an entity becomes a state when it is recognised as such, so only because of the actions of other states (Crawford 2007; Eriksson 2018, p. 40). The declaratory theory identifies statehood with the use of a set of observable constitutive elements of a state that can be found in Article 1 of the 1933 *Montevideo Convention on the Rights and Duties of States*: "The state as a person of international law should possess the following qualifications: (a) a permanent population; (b) a defined territory; (c) government; and (d) capacity to enter into relations with the other states." (UIO 1933). Although it is the declaratory theory that seems to be dominant in international law, the very existence of such entities as *de facto states* proves the importance of the constitutive one as well (Geldenhuys 2009, pp. 20–21).

De facto states seek independence from their parent states and sovereignty is for them non-negotiable in the sense that the former oppose negotiation with parent states which would lead to any form of federation. *De facto states* do not oppose contact with their parent states in general, but these contacts and relations must be voluntary and equal and cannot threaten their achieved sovereignty (Lynch 2002). *De facto states* seek patrons that may influence other states within the international system to support the *de facto state* or its international recognition. The more powerful the patron, the more leverage it can use to promote the *de facto state*'s case (Toomla 2016). Even in cases when international recognition is not a possibility and the *de facto state* does not have any patron, it needs an external partner to articulate its needs and let its voice be heard in an international forum (Berg / Toomla 2009, p. 30). Engagement is thus seen as a tool to increase the chance of international recognition (Caspersen 2018).

It has been assumed that *de facto states* primarily seek international recognition. However, this may not always be the case: the examples of Transnistria, South Ossetia, Abkhazia, or Nagorno-Karabakh show that their goal does not have to be international recognition and that they could content themselves with maintaining the *status quo* or merging with their patron states, even despite official political declarations (Kosienkowski 2013; Seth 2021).

Economic reasons: *De facto states* seek cooperation in terms of trade and investments because they suffer from the "economic cost of non-recognition" (Pegg 1998, p. 43). This means that they have only limited options to apply for funds from international financial institutions. The volume of international trade is also limited, as are foreign investments. Due to the unrecognised status of *de facto states*, international companies are reticent to invest there as a result of uncertainty about the validity of international agreements and the possibility of lack of investment insurance (Pegg / Kolstø 2015, p. 200). In addition, investors may also be worried about the reaction of parent states to their engagement in a *de facto state* (Kolstø 2006, p. 729). *De facto states* need to deal with the lack of economic opportunities as they base their internal legitimacy on their economic performance, which must be perceived as better than that of the parent states (Dembinska / Campana 2017, p. 13).

Social reasons: The population of *de facto states* needs a connection with the outside world, which can be secured through acceptance of travel documents, regular transportation connections, telecommunication, Internet connections, or contacts with the diaspora.

Strategies: Since *de facto states* need to diversify their external partners, they develop different strategies for engagement with the states in the international community. Their main goal is to achieve international recognition; however, when this is not possible, *de facto states* engage with other actors using strategies identified as "engagement without recognition" (see e.g. Cooley / Mitchell 2010; Ker-Lindsay / Berg 2018; Berg / Vits 2018). This strategy is used when 1) the states within the international community consider engagement with *de facto states* a tool to achieve their wider strategic aims; 2) *de facto states* themselves seek to diversify their external relations (Berg / Vits 2018, p. 398). The policy was first articulated by the EU special representative for the South Caucasus,

Peter Semneby, and contained the strategy for interactions with breakaway territories in the Caucasus without compromising Georgia's territorial integrity (Ker-Lindsay / Berg 2018). It was systematically elaborated first by Cooley and Mitchell (2010) and later by, e.g., Berg and Pegg (2016), Ker-Lindsay (2018), and Caspersen (2018). This policy enables breakaway territories to find effective and creative ways to establish contacts with various actors in the international system, but at the same time prevents their quest for independence being used as a tool for geopolitical rivalries in their regions (Berg / Pegg 2016).

In addition to official channels, *de facto states* use their diasporas to influence the level of engagement of a particular state (the one the diaspora is living in) with the *de facto state* (Pegg / Berg 2014). It is not surprising that the representative offices of *de facto states* are situated in states with relevant large diasporas. They fulfil two aims: they connect influential people from the *de facto state* with decision-makers of host countries and serve as an essential channel for gathering resources (Berg / Vits 2018, p. 394). The case of the *de facto state* can be articulated by the commerce offices or individuals, such as honorary consuls or through other para-diplomacy tools (Berg / Vits 2018).

How to deal with de facto states? The approach of different actors in the international system

The international community generally opposes unilateral secession declarations and the emergence of *de facto states*. Instead, it adheres to the principle of the territorial integrity of states (Ó Beacháin / Comai / Tsurtsumia-Zurabashvili 2016). However, a consensus has not been achieved in the academia on how to deal with *de facto states*. On the one hand, Kolstø (2006) claims that any sort of normalisation of relations with *de facto states* leads to the prolonging of conflicts with their parent states. On the other, Lynch (2004, p. 143) argues that *de facto states* have become the reality in the current international system and it is not possible to ignore their existence. Instead, he proposes that "a solution that balances *de facto* with *de jure* sovereignty is the key to achieving a lasting settlement" (Lynch 2004, p. 143). Four general approaches toward *de facto states* may be identified (Berg / Toomla 2009, p. 29): attacking it, embargoing it, engaging with it, and ignoring it. As the SADR has been capable not only of surviving up until now but also of developing a vast variety of relations with several actors in the international system, we will focus mainly on the engagement with this *de facto state*.

Not all *de facto states* are treated equally by the other actors in the international system. On the one hand, some *de facto states* are widely rejected and isolated by the international community, on the other, some of them can engage with states within the international system despite their non-recognition (Ker-Lindsay 2018). As Caspersen (2018) points out, it is necessary to distinguish between two forms of engagement: 1) with the parent state; and 2) with other states of the international community. Engagement with *de facto states* generally takes place around three spheres – political, economic, and public. The political sphere includes international recognition, representation of *de facto states* abroad and that of other countries in *de facto states*, mutual meetings between representatives of *de facto states* and other states, the existence of a patron, and representation in international organisations. The economic sphere includes foreign trade and investments, and the public sphere focuses on the possibilities of the movement of people across borders (Berg / Toomla 2009, p. 30).

Several stages or degrees of engagement with *de facto states* can be identified, ranging from patronage to active opposition to their existence. The degree of engagement with a particular *de facto state* is determined, according to Ker-Lindsay (2018, p. 370), by systemic, contextual, and national factors. As for systemic determinants, it is necessary to consider the approach of the UN and states to unilateral secession and their adherence to the principle of territorial integrity. Contextual and national factors include the behaviour of the *de facto state* after the declaration of independence, the position of the parent state, and the ethnic, historical, and cultural circumstances of the emergence of the *de facto state*. The position of states and powers to the *de facto states* is thus highly contextual and depends on the interests of the states and powers within the international system (Toomla 2016; Pegg / Berg 2014). As Caspersen (2018, p. 385) claims, the international community is unlikely to engage with *de facto states* unless parent states accept engagement as a part of conflict settlement, or they have a strategic interest in the territory of the *de facto states*.

Several types or degrees of engagement with *de facto states* may be identified. The patron-client relationship is the closest relationship between the state and the *de facto state*. Patrons of *de facto states* provide their clients with security and economic guarantees, making the clients dependent on their patrons. Patrons protect their clients through military presence, preventing parent states from reincorporating the secessionist territories (Kolstø 2021, p. 893), providing much-needed financial assistance, and contributing to institution-building in *de facto states* (Ó Beacháin / Comai / Tsurtsumia-Zurabashvili 2016). However, patronage can also take place on the unofficial level (Hoch 2011). This protection means that political forces in the client *de facto state* themselves support retaining strong relations with the patron since its weakening would put the mere existence of client *de facto states* in danger (Kolstø 2021, p. 893). Due to the dependence of a client *de facto state* on its patron, the patron's priority is to promote political stability and prevent social unrest in client *de facto states* as has been apparent in the case of Russian Federation and its client *de facto states* – Transnistria, South Ossetia, and Abkhazia (Kolstø 2021, p. 897). However, the patron-client relationship should not be understood as puppeteering but rather as a mutually beneficial bargaining game (Kolstø / Blakkisrud 2017, p. 507; Berg / Vits 2018), in which clients act as autonomous political entities (Dembinska / Campana 2017). Kolstø (2006) even claims that *de facto states* have an agenda of their own and can promote it in relations with their patron states.

In addition, Kosienkowski and Ženková Rudincová (2022) identify and conceptualise a new actor in the international community as regards the relations with *de facto states*, i.e., quasi-patrons. They resemble patrons in their approach to *de facto states*; however, the difference is that they do not provide security guarantees to *de facto states*. The researchers propose that in the case of Somaliland, Ethiopia may serve as a quasi-patron since it provides Somaliland with appreciated political, economic, and social benefits, and, in return, Somaliland provides Ethiopia with much-needed access to the sea.

Besides patrons and quasi-patrons promoting their geopolitical interests through the (quasi)-patronage of particular *de facto states*, the strategies of recognised states in the international system of engagement with *de facto states* include a continuum ranging from the one 'extreme' of military action to suppress a unilateral bid for statehood to the other 'extreme' of *de jure* recognition (Geldenhuys 2009, p. 46). Recognition of *de facto states* is a matter of politics and is a zero-sum game as recognition of a *de facto state* challenges the sovereignty of its parent state (Berg / Kuusk 2010, p. 46). Therefore, the parent state's potential reaction must be considered before engaging with a particular *de facto state* (Berg / Pegg 2016). Parent states usually seek to isolate *de facto states* by stressing that they originated during a civil war, lack internal support, and are considered illegal in the international system. They endeavour to avoid the engagement of *de facto states* in international organisations and economic development and pursue the socio-political isolation of *de facto states* (Pegg / Berg 2014; Caspersen 2015b; 2018).

Despite their factual illegality in the international system (Caspersen 2012, p. 31; Coppieters 2018), *de facto states* have been rather approached than ignored or suppressed. According to Pegg (1998, p. 177), states in the international system have several possibilities for how to deal with *de facto states*, including 1) actively opposing them with embargoes and sanctions; 2) generally ignoring them, and 3) coming to some sort of limited acceptance of their presence. The last possible approach is similar to the "engagement without recognition strategy" based on the assumption that the engagement with *de facto states* would bring benefits both for the *de facto states* and for other states involved, without compromising adherence to the territorial integrity of parent states (Cooley / Mitchell 2010; Ker-Lindsay / Berg 2018). As proven in the case of Abkhazia, the isolation of *de facto states* may be a harmful tactic leading to the renewal of the conflict, strengthening the patron's position, and the deprivation of the local population (Cooley / Mitchell 2010). The engagement without recognition policy includes both economic and political strategies of engagement. More concretely, this means regular meetings of political representations, the establishment of "liaison offices" resembling embassies in their functions, acceptance of passports, and economic interactions in the form of trade and aid programs (Ker-Lindsay 2018, p. 364). It also includes support from international financial institutions such as the World Bank for funding development projects (Cooley / Mitchell 2010).

Aside from recognised states, other actors in the international system establish and maintain relations with *de facto states*. International organisations, such as the UN, OSCE, and NATO, play an important role in conflicts between *de facto states* and their parent states and engage in the peacekeeping missions deployed to *de facto states* (Kolstø 2006). According to Axyonova and Gawrich (2018, pp. 410–411), international organisations may interact with *de facto states* through several practices, including 1) avoidance (= ignoring their existence), 2) monitoring (= observing the situation on the ground), 3) negotiation (= creating dialogue between conflict parties), 4) cooperation (= mainly in non-political spheres). In this context, it is interesting that the status of *de facto states* as unrecognised entities does not prevent international organisations from interacting with them. Therefore, it is not the status of the entity but rather the quality of its *de facto* authorities that matters regarding an interaction with international organisations (Axyonova / Gawrich 2018).

SADR: A non-self-governing territory and a *de facto state*

The Sahrawi Arab Democratic Republic (SADR) does not constitute a widely respected example of a *de facto state*. It is rather considered to be a border case of such a state (e.g., by Caspersen 2012; Kolstø 2006) or an exception that meets only some criteria of *de facto statehood*, similarly to, for example, Iraqi Kurdistan or the Palestinian Authority, albeit for different reasons (Pegg 1998). The exclusion of the SADR from this imagined *de facto state* set, despite its meeting all the other criteria, is most often caused by its lack of control over the claimed territory (Caspersen 2012). However, a comparison with another *de facto state* located on the African continent is instructive here: Somaliland, despite being in control of practically the whole national territory it claims, has never been recognised by any independent state, while the SADR is recognised by more than forty states around the world (Fernández-Molina / Ojeda-García 2020, pp. 83–84) and by the African Union.

Since 1963, Western Sahara has been listed by the United Nations as a non-self-governing territory. This means that according to the UN, the process of decolonisation of Western Saharan territory has not yet been accomplished. Chapter XI of the Charter of the United Nations defines non-self-governing territories as "territories whose people have not yet attained a full measure of self-government". Currently, there are 17 territories considered by the UN to be non-self-governing territories, inhabited in total by fewer than two million people. Of the territories on this UN list (last updated 4 August 2023), Western Sahara is the only one that is considered (at least by some scholars) to be a *de facto state* and the only one located in Africa (most such entities are islands in the Caribbean and Pacific). It is also the only one of its kind to not have an administering power indicated, albeit with the largest population and territory among such entities (United Nations 2022). Decolonisation continues to be a priority for the UN as it derives from the principle of "equal rights and self-determination of peoples" – as already mentioned in the Charter of the United Nations (Article 1(2)). More details can be found in the three specific chapters of the Charter: Chapter XI 'Declaration Regarding Non-Self-Governing Territories', as well as Chapters XII and XIII devoted to the international trusteeship system and council. The powers administrating non-self-governing territories are obliged under the Chapter XI to pass on the information regarding these territories, while the United Nations monitors their progress towards self-determination. Moreover, in 1960, the UN General Assembly adopted the Declaration on the Granting of Independence to Colonial Countries and Peoples (resolution 1514 (XV)), also known as the Declaration on Decolonisation. That same year another General Assembly resolution (1541 (XV)) specified that a non-self-governing territory can be understood to have attained a full measure of self-government by its emergence as a sovereign independent state, free association with an independent state, or its integration with an independent state (United Nations 2022). Being considered by the United Nations a non-self-governing territory constitutes for the Sahrawi Arab Democratic Republic (the emanation of the Western Saharan state) an additional argument in favour of its existence (as a *de facto state*) and its territorial claims.

The Sahrawi Arab Democratic Republic was established similarly to other *de facto states* as a result of conflict, in this case between Morocco and Mauritania who both claimed this territory on the one side, and the POLISARIO Front, the Sahrawi national liberation movement that initially sought independence from

Spanish colonialism on the other. Following the difficult internal situation in Spain related to the prolonged illness of General Francisco Franco, King Hassan II of Morocco organised at the beginning of November 1975 what is referred to as "Green March", which mobilised approximately 250,000–300,000 Moroccans (mostly civilians) to cross the border in the south and seize the territory of Western Sahara. In consequence, Spain agreed to the division of its former colony between Morocco and Mauritania (referred to as the Madrid Accords, November 14, 1975), which also expressed claims to this area (Fernández-Molina / Ojeda-García 2020, p. 85; Zoubir 1990, p. 226; Kosidło 2012, pp. 42–52). This move was an overt negation of the *uti possidetis* principle that was applied across Africa through the resolution adopted by the Assembly of Heads of State and Government of the Organisation of African Unity in 1964 in Cairo as one of the means of avoiding interstate conflicts after the decolonisation process. The Moroccan policy of *faits accomplis*, involving the occupation of the territory of Western Sahara, and then organising a mass Moroccan settling, while at the same time resettling the Sahrawis, met with an overwhelming response by the POLISARIO Front, which after the ultimate withdrawal of the Spanish colonial troops, on February 27, 1976, unilaterally proclaimed the Sahrawi Arab Democratic Republic, and waged an open war against Morocco and Mauritania. The latter withdrew from the conflict in 1979, but the war with Morocco lasted until September 1991, when the ceasefire agreement, negotiated under the auspices of the United Nations, went into effect (Kosidło 2012, pp. 85–106).

Currently, the armed phases of the conflicts that laid the cornerstone for the emergence of *de facto states* are generally over, however, the Western Saharan case, similar to the situation in Nagorno-Karabakh, contradicts this rule. In November 2020, regular exchanges of fire began between Moroccan forces and the POLISARIO Front troops, first in Guerguerat and then in several other locations along the armistice line separating the territory of Western Sahara between the part controlled by Morocco and the part controlled by the SADR. Consequently, the POLISARIO Front officially broke the 30-year-long ceasefire, blaming Moroccan forces for invading the buffer zone near Guerguerat, a sort of no-man's-land monitored by the United Nations Mission for the Referendum in Western Sahara (*Mission des Nations Unies pour l'Organisation d'un Référendum au Sahara Occidental*). Since then, the conflict, albeit of low intensity, has flared up again (Kłosowicz 2022, pp. 64–65).

Even though the SADR is considered a border case of a *de facto state*, it seems that it fulfils the criteria required to classify a polity as such according to the seven-element definition of a *de facto state* created by Florea (2014, pp. 791–92):

Table 3. Sahrawi Arab Democratic Republic vs. Adrian Florea's definition of a *de facto state* (Authors' own analysis)

Belonging to or administered by a recognised country, but not a colonial possession	Around four-fifths of Western Saharan territory is controlled and administered by Morocco.
Seeking some degree of separation from that country and having declared independence (or having demonstrated its aspirations for independence)	The Sahrawi people have constantly sought independence since November 1975 (the Green March and the beginning of Moroccan presence on Western Saharan territory) and on Feb 27, 1976, they unilaterally proclaimed the independence of the Sahrawi Arab Democratic Republic.
Exerting military control over a territory or portions of territory inhabited by a permanent population	The Sahrawis maintain permanent settlements in what is referred to as Liberated Territories (approx. one-fourth of the claimed territory), where Tifariti, the SADR's *de facto* capital, is located.
Not sanctioned by the government	The Moroccan authorities have never recognised the existence of the Sahrawi Arab Democratic Republic.
Performing basic governance functions (provision of social and political order)	The Sahrawi authorities govern in the Liberated Territories and in the refugee camps in Algeria, where most of the Sahrawi population outside Western Sahara lives; they provide healthcare, access to education, a justice system, etc.
Lacking international legal sovereignty (recognition by a simple majority of UN Security Council permanent members plus recognition by a simple majority of UN members)	At its peak, the Sahrawi Arab Democratic Republic was recognised by 84 UN member states; however, none of them were a UN Security Council permanent member.
Existing for at least two years (24 months)	The Sahrawi Arab Democratic Republic has existed for 47 years.

As indicated above, practically all these features are observable in the *de facto statehood* of the Sahrawi Arab Democratic Republic. However, its inability to exercise control over the entirety of the claimed territory, and thus the challenge in governing the population residing under Moroccan control, may raise concerns regarding the virtual nature of its statehood. Consequently, this could potentially weaken the inclination of other international actors (if they were such) to recognise it. Nevertheless, it appears that in most instances, the matter is considerably more intricate and contingent upon other factors, particularly political considerations, which will be discussed later.

It is also worth mentioning, at the end of this section, that the ambiguous *de facto statehood* of the SADR sometimes leads to a suggestion to consider it an example of a territory administered by exiled governing authorities (government-in-exile), and therefore comparable to other exiled governing bodies, such as the Tibetan Government-in-Exile (TGiE) (Wilson / McConnell 2015, p. 204). Both governments provide services and administer resources intended for the Sahrawi and Tibetan populations, respectively, despite not being situated in Western Sahara or Tibet. The Sahrawi government operates from Algeria, specifically from the administrative refugee camp at Rabouni, while the Tibetan government does so from McLeod Ganj, a suburb of Dharamshala in India. However, both assert strong claims to political legitimacy. Nonetheless, there are some differences. The TGiE does not have any formal contact with the Tibetan population in the claimed national territory, while the SADR administers around 20% of Western Saharan territory and provides some services, such as healthcare, education, and a justice system to the Sahrawi population living there (although it must be emphasised that the majority of the Sahrawi population lives in the refugee camps in Algeria or on the Western Saharan territory controlled by Morocco). Both governments also issue official documentation to the populations they govern (Wilson / McConnell 2015, pp. 203–10). The Tibetan Government-in-Exile does not assert itself as a state and cannot rely on international recognition from other state actors, whereas the Sahrawi Arab Democratic Republic (SADR) has garnered partial recognition from dozens of states and, as we have observed, from the most significant regional organisation in Africa.

The international relations of the SADR: Motivations and strategies

International recognition and political cooperation

In October 1975, the International Court of Justice ruled that the population of Western Sahara (then known as Spanish Sahara) had the right to self-determination; this decision was tantamount to recognising the legitimacy of the actions of the Popular Front for the Liberation of Saguia El Hamra and Rio de Oro (*Frente Popular de Liberación de Saguía el Hamra y Río de Oro*) – the

POLISARIO Front, founded in 1973 and since that time fighting for the creation of an independent state for the indigenous population of the area, the Sahrawis.

Both the International Court of Justice ruling and the already mentioned UN designation of Western Sahara as a non-self-governing territory became legal and rational sources of legitimacy for the SADR and the POLISARIO Front, as well as many ordinary Sahrawis (both in the refugee camps and the territories controlled by Morocco), especially since in the following decades the UN Security Council in its resolutions continued to stress the right to the self-determination of the Sahrawi people. All this combined constitutes the SADR's founding narrative: that it merely wants the Sahrawis' right to be respected to be seen as even more credible (Wilson / McConnell 2015, pp. 207–8).

Unilaterally proclaiming the independence of the SADR did not rule out the need for international recognition. According to Adrian Florea (2017, p. 345), international recognition is a powerful selection mechanism that influences an entity's potential longevity; in other words, it is of key importance for a polity's survival prospects. As mentioned before, there are *de facto states* that lack any kind of recognition (such as Somaliland); others can count only on the recognition of a patron state (i.e., Northern Cyprus), while some – like the Sahrawi Arab Democratic Republic – have been recognised by a dozen entities (Florea 2017, p. 345).

Nevertheless, in the case of the Sahrawi Arab Democratic Republic, since its proclamation in 1976, international recognition has been one of its main goals and one of the pillars of its foreign policy. Hence the great effort the SADR has put into achieving it. Recognition is also an important element in the self-construction of states (Kyris 2022, p. 292).

As put by Fernández-Molina and Ojeda-García (2020, p. 93), Western Sahara's recognition is based on three pillars: 1) the recognition of the POLISARIO Front as a national liberation movement; 2) the recognition of the SADR as a sovereign state; 3) non-recognition of Morocco's claims over Western Saharan territory. The uniqueness of the case of the Sahrawi Arab Democratic Republic is embedded in the fact that its declaration of independence did not originate from a secessionist process but was the result of unsuccessful decolonisation and the foreign occupation that came afterwards. For the issue of international recognition, this is even more important, because the independence of Western Sahara is not in conflict with international law or the principle of *uti possidetis* (in the latter case, in fact, it is in line with this principle) (Fernández-Molina / Ojeda-García 2020, p. 84).

As of December 2022, the Sahrawi Arab Democratic Republic was recognised by 47 UN member states, as well as another *de facto state*, South Ossetia. However,

36 other countries that had previously recognised the SADR have already frozen (i.e., suspended) or withdrawn their recognition, and one country (Yugoslavia) has disappeared (USC 2022). Besides achieving recognition by several states of the international community, the SADR was admitted to the OAU (Organisation of African Unity) in 1982 and is a founding member of the AU (African Union) (Pinto Leite 2015, p. 370). The close relations with this regional international organisation suggest that the SADR is widely recognised by its member states (around 70%); however, they are reluctant to oppose or use force to expel Morocco from Western Saharan territory.

The number of states that recognise Western Sahara is constantly changing and its goal is not only to maintain but also to raise the number of states that recognise it. The withdrawal of recognition itself is not only problematic from a political/geopolitical point of view but also from a legal one. According to the Montevideo Convention on the Rights and Duties of States, one state cannot simply withdraw recognition of another. Article six of the Convention says that:

> the recognition of a state merely signifies that the state which recognizes it accepts the personality of the other with all the rights and duties determined by international law. Recognition is unconditional and irrevocable (UIO 1933).

The SADR, which has witnessed significant fluctuations in recognition, finds itself in a difficult position. George Kyris, who uses the term "de-recognition" for this situation, also points out that apart from Western Sahara, a similar problem (although not on the same scale) is also experienced by Kosovo or Taiwan (Kyris 2022, pp. 288, 294–95, 300–301). Recognition evolves over time and is primarily influenced by politics rather than law; as Jakob Eriksson argues, a compelling example illustrating this correlation is Sweden's recognition of Palestine in 2014 (Eriksson 2018, pp. 39–49).

The international recognition of the SADR since its very foundation has always had "a distinct non-aligned bias" and no Western state has ever recognised it, i.e., the EU member states stick to "a twofold stance of nonrecognition" – they do not recognise the SADR (and in consequence do not maintain any official relations with it) and they do not recognise Moroccan sovereignty over Western Saharan territory either (Fernández-Molina / Ojeda-García 2020, p. 94; Bouris / Fernández-Molina 2018, p. 314). Additionally, not only member states, but also EU institutions are divided on the Western Sahara issue. On the one hand, the European Commission is more willing to cooperate with Morocco, while the European Parliament seems to be more receptive to the agenda and requirements of the Sahrawi people and their organisations and has blocked some of the proposed agreements with Morocco. The EU's Western Sahara policy seems to be incoherent on the level of both member states and EU institutions (Noutcheva 2020, p. 464).

By possibly being granted international recognition, the Sahrawi people seek to exercise their right to self-determination in the decolonial context. They are still being denied such rights as the majority of the Sahrawi population lives either in refugee camps in exile or in the territories occupied by Morocco (Pinto Leite 2015, pp. 361–62).

Economic development

The SADR's options for economic development are quite limited since it controls only one-fifth (20%) of its territory. Furthermore, the so-called Liberated Territories that it does control do not have access to the sea and form part of the Sahara Desert. Due to the harsh climate, very limited access to water, and lack of any known mineral resources that could be extracted (so far), this part of Western Saharan territory is scarcely inhabited (est. 30,000-40,000 people, mostly Sahrawi nomads that during the rainy season use this land to graze their animals) and the development of any viable economy is also difficult (Volpato / Lamin Saleh / Di Nardo 2015, pp. 2–4). The majority of the Sahrawi population over which the SADR authorities have any sort of control live in the refugee camps in Algeria where until the 1990s the economy was also very limited. After the 1991 ceasefire, increasing amounts of money started to flow to the camps, mostly thanks to the remittances from the Sahrawi diaspora, pensions from the Spanish government for former Sahrawi employees, and financial aid from different Spanish solidarity organisations. This situation changed the job market in the refugee camps and introduced cash economy. Sahrawis employed by various NGOs present in the camps started to receive salaries, and others were able to start small businesses, such as grocery stores or hairdressers/barbershops, although most of the camp residents still live off humanitarian aid (Fiddian-Qasmiyeh 2014, pp. 96–97, 110). The SADR's international relations in the economic field are focused on attracting more international humanitarian and development aid, as well as continuing the legal fight against illegal Moroccan extraction of Western Saharan resources and other economic activities on the occupied territories, mostly phosphate mining, fishery, and tourism. There have even been reports regarding the sale of sand from Western Sahara. The emergence of this practice in recent years has sparked considerable controversy in Spain's Canary Islands Autonomous Community, where the sand is utilised for constructing tourist resorts and replenishing pebble beaches. This is against the rulings of the European Court of Justice, according to which the EU-Morocco trade deals exclude any goods from Western Sahara, as they lack the consent of its people, as well as against the legal opinion of the United Nations and the African Union (Abderrahmane 2021; Lundqvist / Bauer 2017; "Western Sahara Resource Watch" 2023).[2] Allan and Ojeda-García (2022) have proposed a very thorough overview of the research (from different fields of study) focusing on natural resource exploitation in Western Sahara, as the problem itself is not new and can be dated back to the second half of the 1970s and the beginning of the Moroccan occupation of this territory.

Social benefits

The Sahrawi population lives under Moroccan occupation, in refugee camps in Algeria, or the territories controlled by the POLISARIO. The Sahrawi diaspora resides mostly in Spain and – together with POLISARIO Front representatives – helps to maintain long-standing relations with Spanish solidarity groups. Their flag program is Holiday in Peace (*Vacaciones en Paz*), which enables Sahrawi children from the refugee camps to spend the hottest summer months in Spain with Spanish families, while at the same time receiving medical treatment (in cases where this is needed), learning Spanish, participating in different holiday activities for children, etc. (Mormul 2021, pp. 176–77). All the social benefits derived from maintaining contact with the outside world can be closely tied to the enhancement of the quality of life of the Sahrawi people residing in the refugee camps. Given that a significant portion of aid originates from Spain and the majority of the Sahrawi diaspora resides there, Spain boasts the most developed and active Sahrawi diplomatic network. This is evidenced by the presence of official delegations of the POLISARIO Front in each of the 17 Spanish autonomous communities (Frente Polisario 2023). Until 2013 and the creation of the University of Tifariti ("Universidad de Tifariti" 2023), located in the Liberated Territories, the Sahrawi youth from the refugee camps had been solely dependent upon the possibilities to study in other countries, mostly in Algeria, Cuba, Libya, Syria (both before the Arab Spring), and Spain (Kłosowicz / Szczepankiewicz-Rudzka 2023, p. 316). The possibility of tertiary education has been a motivational factor for the Sahrawi youth to undertake secondary education in the camps and it seems to be an important social benefit of having maintained some bilateral relations by the SADR, even with countries that have not internationally recognised its statehood (Spain has never recognised the SADR).

---

2   Western Sahara Resource Watch is a network organisation working in solidarity with the Sahrawi people. Since 2005, it has been monitoring the natural resource situation in Western Sahara, raising international awareness of the problem.

The approach taken by foreign powers towards the Western Saharan case

The most important ally of the SADR is Algeria, which has played the role of its patron, providing it with much needed political, economic, and security assistance. Additionally, Algeria is a host of the Sahrawi refugee camps near Tindouf, which is also the headquarters of the SADR's authorities (the temporary capital has been established in Tifariti on the Liberated Territories). Algeria has been motivated in its patronage of the SADR by ideological factors (anticolonial and third-world solidarity) and pragmatic ones (weakening the geopolitical influence of Morocco in the region and balancing the Morocco-Algeria dispute over regional hegemony) (Fernández-Molina / Ojeda-García 2020, p. 89; Joffé 2010, pp. 377, 383).[3]

Morocco's claim over Western Sahara has been an obstacle in its relations with the EU, including trade and economic agreements (see, e.g., Kutz 2021). When it comes to individual EU member states, Spain must balance its relations with Morocco, Algeria, and the Sahrawis and is torn between its desire to secure relations with Morocco and respect the principle of self-determination (Darbouche / Zoubir 2008, p. 101). For half a century, Madrid, the former colonial power in the territory, formally maintained its neutrality in the Western Saharan conflict, having in mind its other flashpoints in the bilateral relations with Rabat, such as Ceuta and Melilla or irregular migration. This position of the Spanish government on the Western Saharan issue was not in line with the majority view of Spanish civil society – generally well-informed and supportive of the Sahrawi claims for independence and the end of the Moroccan occupation. However, the neutrality of the Spanish government ended, when Spain's Prime Minister Pedro Sánchez decided to back the Moroccan autonomy plan for Western Sahara against the backdrop of the scandal with the Pegasus breach, during which a significant amount of data from the mobile phones of members of the Spanish government was obtained, allegedly by Moroccan intelligence (Bartolomé 2022).

Both France and the USA favour Morocco in its claims to Western Saharan territory because "Morocco is more accommodating to Western interests in general and in Africa in particular" (Darbouche / Zoubir 2008, p. 98), and at the

---

3   The Algerian approach to the Western Saharan conflict and Moroccan-Algerian relations in the face of the unresolved Western Saharan problem are analysed in Chapter 6: *The Issue of Western Sahara in the International Relations of States Bordering on Its Territory - Morocco, Algeria, and Mauritania.*

same time, France sought to convince Algeria to lift its support for the Sahrawis in exchange for deliveries of economic and financial aid in the 1990s (Darbouche / Zoubir 2008, p. 99). Paris has officially maintained a neutral stance on the Sahrawi issue; however, it has close political, economic, and strategic ties with Rabat, as well as historical engagement in the Western Saharan conflict (not only did it support the Moroccan invasion, but, between November 1977 and June 1978, French troops directly participated in the conflict on the Mauritanian side). The situation changed slightly during the presidency of the socialist François Mitterand (1981–1995), when France strengthened its relations with Algeria, limited its military aid to Morocco, and allowed the POLISARIO Front to open its office in the French capital. Nevertheless, today, as in the past, Morocco remains France's main ally, and Paris champions Rabat's interests within the EU and on the forum of the UN Security Council, fearing that a weakened Morocco would mean instability and even more serious security issues in the Maghreb region. At the same time, French civil society, unlike the Spanish, is rather ignorant of the Western Saharan question and does not provide much support to the Sahrawis (Benabdallah 2009, pp. 429–30; Zunes 2020).

The USA has offered military and political support to Morocco since the inception of the conflict over Western Sahara. Morocco has been regarded by US policymakers as a crucial ally, initially during the Cold War era and subsequently in the "global war on terror" following the events of 9/11. After 2007, for several years Washington openly opted for the Moroccan autonomy proposal, without much regard for whether it violates the international law. The US approach to Western Sahara has not changed in the past decades, regardless of whether the administration was Republican or Democratic. This support for Morocco led to unexpected recognition of the Moroccan sovereignty over Western Sahara by the Trump administration in December 2020. Both governments reached an agreement according to which the United States would change its position and recognise Moroccan sovereignty over the Western Saharan territory in exchange for Rabat establishing full diplomatic relations with the State of Israel (part of what is referred to as the Abraham Accords). Additionally, the USA was to open its consulate in the occupied territories in the southern city of Dakhla (Zoubir 2018, pp. 58–63; Kutz 2021; White House 2020). After taking Office in January 2021, the new American President Joe Biden was believed, at least by some, to reverse Trump's decision. However, neither has he done so nor has his administration reconfirmed this recognition. The constant refusal of White House officials to answer journalists' questions regarding these issues seems to suggest that the accepted tactic is to avoid the subject at this stage (Zunes 2022).

To highlight the stance of international organizations towards the Sahrawi Arab Democratic Republic, it is noteworthy that the African Union remains neutral. The SADR maintains its membership within the African Union, while Morocco re-entered the AU in 2017, having withdrawn its membership from the Organisation of African Unity (OAU) in response to the admission of the SADR in 1984. Additionally, the SADR fosters positive relations with numerous African countries, notably South Africa, which stands as the most significant Sahrawi ally on the continent, following Algeria (Mirilovic / Siroky 2021, p. 557).

Conclusion

As follows from this chapter, *de facto states*, even though not internationally recognised, can establish and maintain international relations with sovereign states of the international community, international organisations, or other actors in the international system, such as NGOs or other *de facto states*. In their effort, they use official channels through liaison offices, but also various tools of paradiplomacy, such as commerce offices or diaspora. Acquiring support from other states or even patronage is needed in their quest for international recognition. They seek external support not only to ensure their mere existence but also to enhance the economic development and well-being of their citizens.

Western Sahara, which has been selected as an illustrative case for this chapter, is not a typical example of a *de facto state*. It is still on the UN list of non-self-governing territories and its case is unique as it is the result of unfinished decolonisation. The SADR, however, fulfils the criteria of *de facto statehood* as defined by Florea (2014). It has a permanent population, and the Sahrawi administration performs basic governance functions; however, the majority of its territory is claimed and occupied by Morocco. Nevertheless, the SADR has been able to establish relations with several states of the international community and international organisations and even achieved international recognition by tens of sovereign states. The SADR needs international support to enhance its legitimacy and gain control over its territory, which is crucial for the political representation of the SADR and Sahrawi population. By gaining sovereignty, the Sahrawi people would be finally able to achieve self-determination, guaranteed by numerous UN documents and the decision of the International Court of Justice. The SADR also seeks the support of the international community because it needs leverage which would put additional pressure on Morocco to leave Western Saharan territory. Last but not least, it also seeks economic benefits from regaining Sahrawi territory as it would get access to the sea and natural resources, such as phosphates.

To gain support, the SADR approaches different actors within the international community. The most important ally or even patron of the SADR is Algeria, which hosts the Sahrawi population in the refugee camps in Tindouf province and uses the Western Sahara's case as leverage in its competitive relations with Morocco. The relations of the SADR with EU member states may be qualified as "engagement without recognition" as conceptualised by, e.g., Cooley and Mitchell (2010), Ker-Lindsey (2015), and Ker-Lindsay and Berg (2018). In the case of EU states, this means their informal support without compromising relations with Morocco, but at the same time reluctance to provide official international recognition. Spain, for example, needs to balance its relations with Morocco, Algeria, and the Sahrawis and maintain neutrality in political issues. Spanish civil society, however, provides humanitarian aid and development cooperation to the Sahrawi population through a variety of development programmes.

Possible engagement with the SADR is determined by regional and global political dynamics. It has been especially evident in the case of the US approach. Morocco became the key ally of the USA in the region, and therefore, the US supported its claim to Western Sahara. Another supporter of Moroccan policy in Western Sahara is France, despite maintaining an officially neutral stance.

Considering that Western Sahara is a member state of the AU and has been recognised by tens of sovereign states, it is apparent that it uses different tools to enhance its international position, approaches various actors in the international system, and can attract support from them, or even international recognition. For the SADR, the crucial aim is to regain the territory that is occupied by Morocco to legitimise its very existence, but also enhance economic development and, finally, ensure the exercising of the right to self-determination for the Sahrawi people.

References

Abderrahmane, Abdelkader: "Canarian Tourism Industry Built on Western Saharan Sand". *ENACT Observer* 14.9.2021, retrieved 27.8.2023, from https://enactafrica.org/enact-observer/canarian-tourism-industry-built-on-western-saharan-sand.

Allan, Joanna / Ojeda-García, Raquel: "Natural Resource Exploitation in Western Sahara: New Research Directions". *The Journal of North African Studies* 27 (6) 2022, pp. 1107–36, DOI: 10.1080/13629387.2021.1917120.

Axyonova, Vera / Gawrich Andrea: "Regional Organizations and Secessionist Entities: Analysing Practices of the EU and the OSCE in Post-Soviet Protracted

Conflict Areas". *Ethnopolitics* 17 (4) 2018, pp. 408–25, DOI: 10.1080/17449057.2018.1495358.

Bartolomé, Marcos: "Why Is Spain Pandering to Morocco on Western Sahara?". *Foreign Policy* 13.5.2022, retrieved 28.8.2023, from https://foreignpolicy.com/2022/05/13/spain-sanchez-morocco-polisario-western-sahara-algeria/.

Benabdallah, Karima: "The Position of the European Union on the Western Sahara Conflict". *Journal of Contemporary European Studies* 17 (3) 2009, pp. 417–35, DOI: 10.1080/14782800903339362.

Berg, Eiki / Kuusk, Ene: "What Makes Sovereignty a Relative Concept? Empirical Approaches to International Society". *Political Geography* 29 (1) 2010, pp. 40–49, DOI: 10.1016/j.polgeo.2010.01.005.

Berg, Eiki / Pegg, Scott: "Scrutinizing a Policy of 'Engagement Without Recognition': US Requests for Diplomatic Actions With *De Facto* States". *Foreign Policy Analysis*, May 2016, DOI: 10.1093/fpa/orw044.

Berg, Eiki/ Toomla, Raul: "Forms of Normalisation in the Quest for De Facto Statehood". *The International Spectator* 44 (4) 2009, pp. 27–45, DOI: 10.1080/03932720903351104.

Berg, Eiki / Vits, Kristel: "Quest for Survival and Recognition: Insights into the Foreign Policy Endeavours of the Post-Soviet de Facto States". *Ethnopolitics* 17 (4) 2018, pp. 390–407, DOI: 10.1080/17449057.2018.1495359.

———: "Exploring de Facto State Agency: Negotiation Power, International Engagement and Patronage". In: Baldacchino, Godfrey / Wivel, Anders (eds.): *Handbook on the Politics of Small States*. Edward Elgar Publishing: Cheltenham /Northampton MA, 2020, pp. 379–94, DOI: 10.4337/9781788112932.00034.

Bouris, Dimitris / Fernández-Molina, Irene: "Contested States, Hybrid Diplomatic Practices, and the Everyday Quest for Recognition". *International Political Sociology* 12 (3) 2018, pp. 306–24, DOI: 10.1093/ips/oly006.

Caspersen, Nina: "Playing the Recognition Game: External Actors and De Facto States". *The International Spectator* 44 (4) 2009, pp. 47–60 DOI:10.1080/03932720903351146.

———: *Unrecognized States*. Polity Press: Cambridge, UK, 2012.

———: "Degrees of Legitimacy: Ensuring Internal and External Support in the Absence of Recognition". *Geoforum* 66 (November) 2015a, pp. 184–92, DOI: 10.1016/j.geoforum.2014.10.003.

———:"The Pursuit of International Recognition After Kosovo". *Global Governance: A Review of Multilateralism and International Organizations* 21 (3) 2015b, pp. 393–412, DOI: 10.1163/19426720-02103004.

———:"Recognition, Status Quo or Reintegration: Engagement with de Facto States". *Ethnopolitics* 17 (4) 2018, pp. 373–89, DOI: 10.1080/17449057.2018.1495360.

Cooley, Alexander / Mitchell, Lincoln A.: "Engagement without Recognition: A New Strategy toward Abkhazia and Eurasia's Unrecognized States". *The Washington Quarterly* 33 (4) 2010, pp. 59–73, DOI: 10.1080/0163660X.2010.516183.

Coppieters, Bruno: "'Statehood', 'de Facto Authorities' and 'Occupation': Contested Concepts and the EU's Engagement in Its European Neighbourhood". *Ethnopolitics* 17 (4) 2018, pp. 343–61, DOI: 10.1080/17449057.2018.1495361.

Crawford, James: *The Creation of States in International Law*. Clarendon Press: Oxford, 2007.

Darbouche, Hakim / Zoubir, Yahia H.: "Conflicting International Policies and the Western Sahara Stalemate". *The International Spectator* 43 (1) 2008, pp. 91–105, DOI: 10.1080/03932720701880049.

Dembinska, Magdalena / Campana, Aurélie: "Frozen Conflicts and Internal Dynamics of De Facto States: Perspectives and Directions for Research". *International Studies Review* 19 (2) 2017, pp. 254–78, DOI: 10.1093/isr/vix010.

Devyatkov, Andrey: "Russia and Transnistria in a Patron-Client Relationship". *Anuarul Laboratorului Pentru Analiza Conflictului Transnistrean* 1. 2022, pp. 17–22.

Eriksson, Jacob: "Swedish Recognition of Palestine: Politics, Law, and Prospects for Peace". *Global Affairs* 4 (1) 2018, pp. 39–49, DOI: 10.1080/23340460.2018.1507279.

Fernández-Molina, Irene / Ojeda-García, Raquel: "Western Sahara as a Hybrid of a Parastate and a State-in-Exile: (Extra)Territoriality and the Small Print of Sovereignty in a Context of Frozen Conflict". *Nationalities Papers* 48 (1) 2020, pp. 83–99, DOI: 10.1017/nps.2019.34.

Fiddian-Qasmiyeh, Elena: *The Ideal Refugees: Gender, Islam, and the Sahrawi Politics of Survival*. (Gender, Culture, and Politics in the Middle East). Syracuse University Press: Syracuse, New York, 2014.

Florea, Adrian: "De Facto States in International Politics (1945–2011): A New Data Set". *International Interactions* 40 (5) 2014, pp. 788–811, DOI: 10.1080/03050629.2014.915543.

———: "De Facto States: Survival and Disappearance (1945–2011)". *International Studies Quarterly* 61 (2) 2017, pp. 337–351, DOI: 10.1093/isq/sqw049.

Frente Polisario: "Delegación del Frente Polisario en España" 2023, retrieved 29.8.2023, from https://frentepolisario.es/.

Geldenhuys, Deon: *Contested States in World Politics*. Palgrave Macmillan: New York, 2009.

Grzybowski, Janis: "The Paradox of State Identification: De Facto States, Recognition, and the (Re-)Production of the International". *International Theory* 11 (November) 2019, pp. 241–63, DOI: 10.1017/S1752971919000113.

Hoch, Tomáš: "EU Strategy towards Post-Soviet De Facto States". *Contemporary European Studies* 6 (January) 2011, pp. 69–85.

Hoch, Tomáš / Rudincová, Kateřina: "Legitimization of Statehood in de Facto States: A Case Study of Somaliland". *AUC GEOGRAPHICA* 50 (1) 2015, pp. 37–49, DOI: 10.14712/23361980.2015.85.

Jackson, R.H.: *Quasi-States: Sovereignty, International Relations, and the Third World.* (Cambridge Studies in International Relations.) Cambridge University Press: Cambridge, 1990.

Joffé, George: "Sovereignty and the Western Sahara", *The Journal of North African Studies* 15 (3) 2010, pp. 375–84, DOI: 10.1080/13629387.2010.520237.

Ker-Lindsay, James: "Engagement without Recognition: The Limits of Diplomatic Interaction with Contested States". *International Affairs* 91 (2) 2015, pp. 267–85, DOI: 10.1111/1468-2346.12234.

———: "The Stigmatisation of de Facto States: Disapproval and 'Engagement without Recognition'". *Ethnopolitics* 17 (4) 2018, pp. 362–72, DOI: 10.1080/17449057.2018.1495363.

Ker-Lindsay, James / Berg, Eiki: "Introduction: A Conceptual Framework for Engagement with de Facto States". *Ethnopolitics* 17 (4) 2018, pp. 335–42, DOI: 10.1080/17449057.2018.1495362.

Kłosowicz, Robert: "Policies of the Maghreb Countries Toward Western Sahara: Mauritania's Perspective". *Afrika Tanulmányok / Hungarian Journal of African Studies* 16 (1) 2022, pp. 57–70, DOI: 10.15170/AT.2022.16.1.4.

Kłosowicz, Robert/ Mormul, Joanna: "Pojęcie dysfunkcyjności państw: Geneza i definicje". In: Kłosowicz, Robert: *Państwa dysfunkcyjne i ich destabilizujący wpływ na stosunki międzynarodowe,,* pp. 11–36. Wydawnictwo Uniwersytetu Jagiellońskiego: Kraków, 2013.

Kłosowicz, Robert / Szczepankiewicz-Rudzka, Ewa „Między polityką zaangażowania a pozytywną neutralnością. Libia i Tunezja wobec kwestii Sahary Zachodniej". *Politeja* 20 (1(82)) 2023, pp. 309–28, DOI: 10.12797/Politeja.20.2023.82.16.

Kolstø, Pål: "The Sustainability and Future of Unrecognized Quasi-States". *Journal of Peace Research* 43 (6) 2006, pp. 723–40, DOI: 10.1177/0022343306068102.

———: "Authoritarian Diffusion, or the Geopolitics of Self-Interest? Evidence from Russia's Patron–Client Relations with Eurasia's *De Facto* States". *Europe-Asia Studies* 73 (5) 2021, pp. 890–912, DOI: 10.1080/09668136.2020.1806209.

Kolstø, Pål / Blakkisrud, Helge: "Regime Development and Patron–Client Relations: The 2016 Transnistrian Presidential Elections and the 'Russia Factor'". *Demokratizatsiya: The Journal of Post-Soviet Democratization* 25 (4) 2017, pp. 503–28.

Kosidło, Adam: *Sahara Zachodnia. Fiasko Dekolonizacji Czy Sukces Podboju 1975-2011*. Wydawnictwo Uniwersytetu Gdańskiego: Gdańsk, 2012.

Kosienkowski, Marcin: "Is Internationally Recognised Independence the Goal of Quasi-States? The Case of Transnistria". In: Cwicinskaja, Natalia / Oleksy, Piotr (eds.): *Moldova: In Search of Its Own Place in Europe*. Oficyna Wydawnicza Epigram: Bydgoszcz, 2013, pp 55–65..

———: "The Patron Client Relations between Russia and Transnistria". In: Hoch, Tomáš / Kopeček, Vincenc (eds.): *De Facto States in Eurasia* 1st ed.. Routledge: Abingdon, Oxon; New York, NY, 2019, pp. 183–207, DOI: 10.4324/9780429244049.

Kosienkowski, Marcin / Ženková Rudincová, Kateřina: "Client De Facto States and Quasi-Patrons: Insights from the Relationship Between Somaliland and Ethiopia". *Ethnopolitics*, September, 2022, pp. 1–21, DOI: 10.1080/17449057.2022.2121470.

Kutz, William: "Between Dependency and Engagement: Centring Subaltern Geopolitics in Multiperspectival Border Studies. Lessons from the Western Sahara". *Political Geography* 89 (August) 2021, DOI: 10.1016/j.polgeo.2021.102431.

Kyris, George: "State Recognition and Dynamic Sovereignty". *European Journal of International Relations* 28 (2) 2022, pp. 287–311, DOI: 10.1177/13540661221077441.

Lundqvist, Anders / Bauer, Rowan: "Trouble in Paradise: The Canary Island Beach Accused of Illegally Importing Sand". *The Guardian*, 28 July 2017, retrieved 28.8.2023, from https://www.theguardian.com/world/2017/jul/28/trouble-in-paradise-the-canary-island-beach-accused-of-illegally-importing-sand.

Lynch, Dov: *Engaging Eurasia's Separatist States: Unresolved Conflicts and de Facto States*. United States Institute of Peace Press: Washington, D.C, 2004.

Lynch, Dov: "Separatist States and Post–Soviet Conflicts", *International Affairs* 78 (4) 2002, pp. 831–48, DOI: 10.1111/1468-2346.00282.

Mirilovic, Nikola/ Siroky, David S.: "International Recognition, Religion, and the Status of Western Sahara". *Acta Politica* 56 (3) 2021, pp. 548–66, DOI: 10.1057/s41269-020-00166-4.

Mormul, Joanna: "Hijos de las Nubes i 45 lat marzeń: Uchodźcy Saharawi na terytorium Algierii". *Politeja* 18 (6(75)) 2021, pp. 159–82, DOI: 10.12797/Politeja.18.2021.75.08.

Noutcheva, Gergana: "Contested Statehood and EU Actorness in Kosovo, Abkhazia and Western Sahara". *Geopolitics* 25 (2) 2020, pp. 449–71, DOI: 10.1080/14650045.2018.1556641.

Ó Beacháin, Donnacha / Comai, Giorgio / Tsurtsumia-Zurabashvili, Ann: "The Secret Lives of Unrecognised States: Internal Dynamics, External Relations, and Counter-Recognition Strategies". *Small Wars & Insurgencies* 27 (3) 2016, pp. 440–66, DOI: 10.1080/09592318.2016.1151654.

Pegg, Scott: *International Society and the De Facto State*. Routledge: London, 1998.

Pegg, Scott / Berg, Eiki: "Lost and Found: The WikiLeaks of *De Facto* State-Great Power Relations". *International Studies Perspectives*, May, 2014, pp. 267–86, DOI: 10.1111/insp.12078.

Pegg, Scott / Kolstø, Pål: "Somaliland: Dynamics of Internal Legitimacy and (Lack of) External Sovereignty". *Geoforum* 66, 2015, pp. 193–202, DOI: 10.1016/j.geoforum.2014.09.001.

Pinto Leite, Pedro: "Independence by Fiat: A Way out of the Impasse – the Self-Determination of Western Sahara, with Lessons from Timor-Leste". *Global Change, Peace & Security* 27 (3) 2015, pp. 361–76, DOI: 10.1080/14781158.2015.1083542.

Rossi, Michael: "The Durability of Parastates: Declarative Statehood in the Absence of Constitutive Sovereignty". *Nationalities Papers* 48 (1) 2020, pp. 24–41, DOI: 10.1017/nps.2019.59.

Seth, Michael J.: *Not on the Map: The Peculiar Histories of De Facto States*. Lexington Books: Lanham, 2021.

Stake, Robert E.: *The Art of Case Study Research*. Sage Publications: Thousand Oaks, 1995.

Steinsdorff, Silvia von/ Fruhstorfer, Anna: "Post-Soviet de Facto States in Search of Internal and External Legitimacy. Introduction". *Communist and Post-Communist Studies* 45 (1–2) 2012, pp. 117–21, DOI: 10.1016/j.postcomstud.2012.03.009.

Toomla, Raul: "Charting Informal Engagement between de Facto States: A Quantitative Analysis". *Space and Polity* 20 (3) 2016, pp. 330–45, DOI: 10.1080/13562576.2016.1243037.

United Nations "Non-Self-Governing Territories". *The United Nations and Decolonization* 2022, retrieved 22.11.2022, from https://www.un.org/dppa/decolonization/en/nsgt.

Universidad de Tifariti. 2023, retrieved 29.8.2023, from https://universidadtifariti.org/.

UIO: "Montevideo Convention on the Rights and Duties of States", *University of Oslo* 1933, retrieved 27.11.2022, from https://www.jus.uio.no/english/servi ces/library/treaties/01/1-02/rights-duties-states.xml.

USC: "Centro de Estudios Del Sahara Occidental de la USC" 2022, retrieved 27.8.2023, from. https://www.usc.es/es/institutos/ceso/.

Volpato, Gabriele / Saleh Mohamed Lamin Saleh / Di Nardo, Antonello: "Ethnoveterinary of Sahrawi Pastoralists of Western Sahara: Camel Diseases and Remedies". *Journal of Ethnobiology and Ethnomedicine* 11 (1) 2015, p. 54, DOI: 10.1186/s13002-015-0040-4.

Western Sahara Resource Watch 2023, retrieved 30.8.2023, from https://wsrw.org.

White House: "Proclamation on Recognizing the Sovereignty of the Kingdom of Morocco over the Western Sahara", 10 December 2020, retrieved 28.11.2022, from https://trumpwhitehouse.archives.gov/presidential-actions/proclamat ion-recognizing-sovereignty-kingdom-morocco-western-sahara/.

Wilson, Alice / McConnell, Fiona: "Constructing Legitimacy without Legality in Long Term Exile: Comparing Western Sahara and Tibet". *Geoforum* 66 (November) 2015, pp. 203–14, DOI: 10.1016/j.geoforum.2014.11.008.

Zoubir, Yahia H.: "The Western Sahara Conflict: Regional and International Dimensions". *The Journal of Modern African Studies* 28 (2) 1990, pp. 225–43.

Zoubir, Yahia H.: "The United States and the Question of Western Sahara: A Low Priority in US Foreign Policy". *Africana Studia: Revista Internacional de Estudos Africanos* 29, 2018, pp. 53–64.

Zunes, Stephen: "East Timor's Independence from Indonesia Is a Model for Western Sahara and Morocco". *Foreign Policy*, 9 December 2020, retrieved 14.8.2023, from https://foreignpolicy.com/2020/12/09/east-timor-western-sahara-morocco/.

———: "Biden's Dangerous Refusal to Reverse Trump's Western Sahara Policy". *Foreign Policy in Focus*, 21 January 2022, retrieved 28.8.2023, from https://fpif. org/bidens-dangerous-refusal-to-reverse-trumps-western-sahara-policy/.

Joanna Mormul

Chapter 4. The Foreign Policy of a *De Facto State* – the Sahrawi Arab Democratic Republic and Its Diplomatic Struggle[1]

The Sahrawi Arab Democratic Republic (SADR) was unilaterally proclaimed by the PO-LISARIO Front in February 1976 in the territory of the former Spanish Sahara. Despite enjoying recognition from several dozen UN member states, as well as from the African Union, the Sahrawi government controls only about 20% of the territory it claims rights to. Therefore, the SADR's foreign policy constitutes an ongoing struggle for international recognition within the protracted conflict over Western Sahara. However, achieving this goal appears increasingly remote due to recent events: the Guerguerat crisis, which terminated the 1991 ceasefire with Morocco; the decision by the administration of President Donald Trump to recognise Moroccan sovereignty over the disputed Western Sahara territory; the shift in stance by the Spanish government, currently expressing support for Morocco's autonomy plan; and, significantly, Morocco's accession to the African Union in January 2017. The chapter aims to analyse the foreign policy of the SADR within the context of its limited financial resources and the prevailing international conditions in the Maghreb region. It relies heavily on qualitative data gathered during field research conducted between 2016 and 2023, comprising several research visits to Algeria and Spain.

Keywords: Sahrawi Arab Democratic Republic, POLISARIO Front, foreign policy, *de facto state*, diplomacy

Introduction

The Sahrawi Arab Democratic Republic (SADR) was established on 27 February 1976 in Bir Lehlu[2] during a months-long conflict between the forces of Morocco and Mauritania and the POLISARIO Front – the representative of the Sahrawi people[3] living in the territory of the former Spanish colony – Spanish

---

1   This chapter is the result of a research project financed by the National Science Centre (Narodowe Centrum Nauki), Poland, grant ID: 2017/25/B/HS5/00958.
2   A town in Western Sahara, in the area under the control of the POLISARIO Front.
3   The POLISARIO Front (*Frente Popular por la Liberación de Saguía el Hamra y Río de Oro*) was created on 10 May 1973. At the beginning, its main goal was the armed struggle against the Spanish coloniser. Due to the passivity of the Spanish troops remaining in the territory of Western Sahara, the POLISARIO Front took up arms, thus

Sahara (*Sáhara Español*).[4] The conflict began on 6 November 1975 as a result of thousands of Moroccans (mainly civilians accompanied by Moroccan troops) entering the territory of Spanish Sahara, which had not yet been decolonised at that time. This is referred to as the Green March (known as the Black March by the Sahrawis). The Green March, announced by King Hassan II of Morocco in October 1975, lasted only four days, but its effects are still felt today. Its consequence was the signing of the Madrid Accords on 14 November 1975, which *de facto* ended Spanish administration over the territory of Western Sahara, consequently transferred to Morocco and Mauritania. The active phase of the armed conflict that broke out because of these decisions was ended by the ceasefire agreement signed by Morocco and the POLISARIO Front,[5] which entered into force on 6 September 1991 (Kosidło 2012, pp. 45-48, 102-103). However, it did not resolve the Western Saharan issue or the conflict itself. Currently, the territory of Western Sahara is recognised by the United Nations as a non-self-governing territory, i.e., it is subject to decolonisation under Article XI of the United Nations Charter. The UN has kept a list of non-self-governing territories since 1946, with Western Sahara on it since 1963, as the largest non-self-governing territory in terms of the area it covers (United Nations: Web). Currently, the part controlled by the POLISARIO forces (Free Zone / Liberated Territories) and the one occupied by Morocco are separated by a 2,720-km-long sand wall (berm) with fortifications, built by Morocco in several stages in the 1980s, during the conflict. The eastern part of the territory of Western Sahara (approx. 20%) controlled by the SADR consists mainly of desert areas, which are characterised by very difficult natural conditions and pose a significant challenge to permanent settlement. In turn, the area controlled by Morocco not only includes the entire coastline (1,100 km) with access to the Atlantic Ocean, including attractive seaside beaches and waters rich in various species of fish, but also areas rich in mineral resources, including one of the world's largest deposits of phosphate rock, necessary to produce fertilisers (Chograni 2021). It is also worth mentioning that due to the prolonged unresolved conflict over Western Sahara, over

---

becoming the only force fighting the Moroccan and Mauritanian armies. Since 1975, it has been recognised by the UN as the sole representative of the Sahrawi people (Kosidło 2012, pp. 37-53; Chograni 2021).

4   Between 1884 and 1958, it was a Spanish overseas colony, while from 1958 to 1976 – one of the provinces of Spain.

5   Mauritania withdrew from the conflict earlier – in 1979, after having signed a peace agreement with the POLISARIO Front.

170,000 Sahrawis[6] are currently living in exile in southwestern Algeria – in ref-ugee camps near the city of Tindouf, which also became the centre of political life of the Sahrawi Arab Democratic Republic.[7]

Starting in 2017, the protracted Western Saharan conflict began to gain a little more attention in the global media. This was caused primarily by the fact that in January of that year Morocco joined the African Union (AU) – the only re-gional organisation bringing together (after Morocco's admission) all the states on the African continent. In November 1984, Morocco left the Organisation of African Unity (OAU), the progenitor of the AU, in protest against the SADR's membership. In turn, in November 2020, the unresolved problem of Western Sahara manifested itself once again when regular exchanges of fire began to occur between Moroccan forces and POLISARIO Front troops, first in Guer-guerat, and then in several other places along the armistice line dividing the territory of Western Sahara into the part controlled by Morocco and the one controlled by the SADR (Reuters 2020, Web). As a result of these incidents, the POLISARIO Front officially broke the ceasefire that had been going on for over 30 years, blaming Moroccan forces for the incursion into the buffer zone near Guerguerat, a kind of no man's land supervised by the United Nations Mission for the Referendum in Western Sahara (*Mission des Nations Unies pour l'Organi-sation d'un Référendum au Sahara Occidental*, MINURSO).[8] Since then, the con-flict, although of low intensity, has flared up on multiple occasions. While the

---

6   Based on the research results of the UNHCR expert mission that stayed in the camps in January 2018, the Sahrawi population was estimated at 173,600 people. This number does not include Sahrawis living outside the camps, including Sahrawi students over 18 years of age who are studying abroad (UNHCR 2018).

7   On Sahrawi refugees in Algeria, see more in Chapter 5: *The population of a de facto state – the case of the Sahrawi people in the protracted refugee situation.*

8   The Moroccans were carrying out an operation there to remove Sahrawi protesters who were blocking the main land route leading from Morocco through Western Sahara to Mauritania, thus opposing the expansion of a very important communication route from the economic point of view (land connection between Morocco and Mauritania), running through the buffer zone, which under the 1997 military agreement between the Royal Moroccan Armed Forces, the Armed Forces of the POLISARIO Front, and MINURSO was under the control of international forces ("Military Agreement no. 1 between the Royal Moroccan Army and MINURSO on the one side, and the Frente POLISARIO Military Forces and the MINURSO on the other side, December 1997 [Not published by the United Nations, but mentioned in paragraph 18 of the Report of the Secretary-General to the Security Council S/1998/35]", see CESO USC: "Military Agreement").

Moroccan forces' incursion into the buffer zone and the initiation of military/po-lice actions there can be viewed as the direct catalyst for the POLISARIO Front's ending of the ceasefire, the prevailing sentiment among the Sahrawis themselves, particularly the youth, likely played (and continues to play) a significant role. For a long time, the SADR authorities have had to deal with the growing frustration of people who have been living in refugee camps since birth, disappointed with the lack of results of the peace process conducted under the aegis of the UN and interested in seeking a military solution to the conflict, or at least taking actions that would provide a prospect for any change in the situation (Dworkin 2022; Fabiani 2022).[9]

This chapter attempts to analyse the foreign policy of the Sahrawi Arab Dem-ocratic Republic (SADR) in the context of its limited financial resources and international conditions in the Maghreb region. It further intends to verify the hypothesis that the foreign policy goals of the SADR outlined in its constitu-tion are, in fact, significantly limited due to external (international) conditions. For the purposes of the chapter, it is assumed that the foreign policy of a non-recognised state can be analysed in a similar way (with some differences) as the foreign policy of a (recognised) state.[10]

The chapter is largely based on qualitative data collected during field research conducted between 2016 and 2023, comprising several research visits to Algeria (mainly to the capital of the country – Algiers and to the refugee camps for Sah-rawi refugees in the province of Tindouf, but also in Oran and Annaba) and Spain: Madrid; Salamanca, Valladolid (Castile and León), Vitoria-Gasteiz and Bilbao (the Basque Country); and Las Palmas de Gran Canaria (the Canary Is-lands). The conversations and interviews were conducted in Spanish, French, and (to a lesser extent) in English. Some of the interviewees asked to remain anonymous. Primarily, qualitative research methods were used (in-depth inter-views – semi-structured, informal conversations, observations – both open and covert, participating and non-participating). In addition, a critical qualitative analysis of the literature of the subject, official documents, and media materials (mainly press) was carried out; the historical method and elements of discourse

---

9   Similar information was provided to the Author during a visit to the Sahrawi Min-istry of Foreign Affairs in the Rabouni camp in 2016 (Interview with Hamdi Bueha, May 2016).

10   More about the international relations of de facto states can be found in Chapter 3: *In-ternational Relations of De Facto States.*

analysis were also applied. Where possible, information was verified in more than one source.

Sahrawi foreign policy objectives

In this part of the chapter, it is necessary to begin with some controversies related to the political system of the Sahrawi Arab Democratic Republic. The SADR political system, as the Sahrawis themselves emphasise, is a transitional system put in place as a result of the specific situation of the Sahrawi statehood.[11] It is expected to change when the SADR regains control over the entire state territory and obtains international recognition. Its current form can be best described as a participatory democracy. As such, it is interpreted in various ways, and there have long been critical voices (not necessarily Moroccan ones) that in its current form the SADR does not meet the standards of a democratic system. Although the POLISARIO Front is formally not a political party but a national liberation movement (and as such it is internationally recognised as the representative of the Sahrawi population), in the SADR state system it functions as a political party, while the political system itself as a one-party system (Wilson 2010, pp. 423-438). The SADR is headed by the president, and this function is exercised, in accordance with the Constitution of the Sahrawi Arab Democratic Republic of 2015,[12] *ex officio* by the Secretary-General of the POLISARIO Front, elected during the general congress of the POLISARIO Front in a secret and direct vote for a three-year term (Article 51 of the SADR Constitution) (ICT Policy Africa: "The Constitution of the Sahrawi Arab Democratic Republic" 2015). Since July 2016, the president of SADR is Brahim Ghali, who previously served as the SADR ambassador in Algeria and Spain. He was re-elected to this position in January 2023 (Sahara Press Service 2023, Web).

The foreign policy objectives of the Sahrawi Arab Democratic Republic are defined in full in Article 24 of the SADR Constitution of 2015, which is in its entirety dedicated to this issue. It identifies five goals that should guide the foreign policy of the Sahrawi state. In the order they appear in the text (without numeration), these are as follows: "*1. Defend the legitimate rights of the Sahrawi people to independence and the recovery of their national sovereignty over*

---

11 This does not change the fact that this "temporary political system" has been in place for several dozen years.

12 The latest version of the Sahrawi constitution was adopted at the 14th Congress of the POLISARIO Front, which took place on 16-20 December 2015.

the entire national territory; 2. Support the peoples' right to self-determination; 3. Contribute to concretising the unity of the Maghreb where the SADR shall have its own rightful place; 4. Support the African Union in its efforts to consolidate political stability in Africa and achieve economic complementarity among its Member States; 5. Establish international peace and stability and contribute towards economic and social development of the peoples of the world on the basis of justice and equity" (ICT Policy Africa: "The Constitution of the Sahrawi Arab Democratic Republic" 2015). These goals, apart from the first one, are, as easily noticeable, quite general in their tone. Although they result directly from the text of the Constitution, it seems that they constitute a specific political projection of the SADR leadership combined with an outline of the possible role of Western Sahara in the region and, more broadly speaking, in the international environment. They are also axiological in their nature, as it is possible to deduce what values guide not only Sahrawi foreign policy, but also Sahrawi statehood itself. Nevertheless, a rather cursory reflection on the political practice of the SADR in the international arena indicates that the three basic goals of its foreign policy include: 1. efforts to obtain international recognition, including – in the first place – maintaining the number of countries that already recognise the SADR, and – in the second – enlarging their number;[13] 2. resolving the conflict over Western Sahara through an independence referendum; 3. independence of the Sahrawi Arab Democratic Republic within the borders of the former Spanish colony – Spanish Sahara, i.e., sovereignty over the entire state territory to which the SADR claims rights. The last of these can be considered the primary goal declared by the SADR leadership, to which the first and second goals are in fact complementary. It also predominantly reflects the first foreign policy goal outlined in the Constitution of the Republic. Additionally, it is noteworthy to consider the fourth objective specified in Article 24, pertaining to the African Union. Membership and active participation in the work of this organisation, like its predecessor – the OAU, even though not all AU member states recognise Western Saharan statehood, is one of the greatest international successes of the POLISARIO Front and constitutes great support for all diplomatic efforts of the

---

13 At the end of 2022, the Sahrawi Arab Democratic Republic was recognised by 47 of the world's 193 countries, another 36 had recognised the SADR in the past, but had since frozen or withdrawn their recognition (formally, such a step is contrary to international law, which states that recognition once expressed cannot be withdrawn), one country recognised the SADR but has since ceased to exist (Yugoslavia) (CESO USC 2023, Web).

SADR on the African continent. This seems to be even more worth emphasising, since limiting the foreign policy goals pursued by the SADR only to efforts aimed at enforcing the rights of the Sahrawi people to self-determination, through international recognition of the Sahrawi statehood within colonial borders, is in principle dictated by the weak international position of the SADR – obvious in the situation of having only partial recognition of its statehood. Membership in the most important regional international organisation on the African continent undoubtedly provides enormous support for the diplomatic efforts of the POLISARIO Front, even if, after Morocco's admission to the African Union, there are more or less official attempts to weaken or prevent such activity.

In this scenario, the primary Sahrawi voice in the international arena is the authorities in Algiers. In practice, since the establishment of the Sahrawi Arab Democratic Republic, Algeria has been perceived as the patron state of *de facto* Sahrawi statehood. As Mohamed Larbi Ould Khelifa, president of the Algerian People's National Assembly (*Assemblée populaire nationale*), put it, "Algeria's support for the Sahrawi issue is based on the principles underlying its foreign policy" (Sahara Press Service 2015).[14] Since the Algerian War of Independence, it has been guided by two principles: defence of territorial integrity and sovereignty, and defence of the right of nations to self-determination. Consequently, Algiers has always viewed the Western Sahara problem as a decolonisation conflict whose resolution is the responsibility of the international community. In official statements by Algerian politicians, as well as in conversations with Algerian researchers, it is also emphasised that the support given to the Western Saharan issue has never had any expansionist basis for Algeria (Interview with Dr. Saïd Ayachi, May 2023). In relation to this line of argument, the late Algerian president Abdelaziz Bouteflika's in 2007 made the following famous statement, "if the Sahrawi people decide that Western Sahara is to be controlled by Morocco, the first messages of congratulations will come from Algeria" (Thieux 2017, pp. 122-123). However, Algeria's political involvement in the Western Saharan conflict, including its rather unambiguous attitude, invariably has major consequences for its foreign policy. During the Cold War, Algiers enjoyed the reputation of a mecca for anti-colonial revolutionaries, and Algeria itself, despite its newly

---

14 "*Le soutien de l'Algérie à la lutte du peuple sahraoui repose sur les principes de sa politique extérieure*" – author's translation. Source also obtained together with other materials received from the Sahrawi Mission in Algiers – Information Centre Martyr Mohamed Fadel Ismael, Algiers, May 2017.

.

gained independence, was considered one of the most important from among what is referred to as the non-aligned countries, supporting many of the national liberation and revolutionary movements in Africa and Latin America at the time (Szeptycki 2015, pp. 209-232). In the post-Cold War reality and in the face of serious internal problems (the civil war in Algeria in 1991-2001, referred to as the "Black Decade"), supporting the Sahrawi cause did not make it easier to establish relations with the strongest of Algeria's neighbours, i.e., Morocco, which even today are, to put it mildly, very complicated (Dworkin 2022). Additionally, Algeria's involvement in the Western Sahara issue gives Morocco the basis to use one of the main arguments in its narrative against the recognition of Western Sahara statehood – namely, the accusations that the SADR is just a puppet in Algerian hands, whose decision-making centre is actually in Algiers, which in turn encourages Rabat to promote the thesis that resolving the dispute over Western Sahara is possible only through direct Moroccan-Algerian negotiations. Such arguments are categorically rejected by both the Algerian authorities and the POLISARIO Front (Interview with Prof. Smail Debeche, May 2023; de Orellana 2015, p. 483).[15] However, this does not change the fact that in the context of the SADR's foreign policy, the most important Sahrawi diplomatic mission (with the status of an embassy) is located in Algiers, in a representative villa on one of the main streets in the centre of the Algerian capital – rue Franklin Roosevelt.[16] A short distance from it, on rue Didouche Mourad, there is also the Sahrawi Mission in Algiers – Information Centre (Mission Sahraouie – Alger – Center d'Information Martyr Mohamed Fadel Ismael). It has been located there since 2004 and was named after Mohamed Fadel Ismael – a Sahrawi politician, member of the POLISARIO Front and a long-time employee of the Sahrawi diplomatic service, including serving as the SADR representative in France and Sweden, as the SADR ambassador in Addis Ababa, and also as permanent representative to the African Union. This institution is a kind of Sahrawi press and cultural center in the capital of Algeria, and its employees are also involved in archiving

---

15 The second key argument used by the authorities in Rabat against the SADR and the POLISARIO Front involves accusations of maintaining relations with a number of terrorist organisations operating in the Maghreb region and in the Middle East. According to Pablo de Orellana, Rabat achieved partial success in this matter, using this argument in the context of the war on terrorism and Morocco's relations with the United States and France. See: de Orellana 2015, pp. 477-499.

16 The author had the opportunity to visit the SADR Embassy in Algiers twice – in April 2016 and in May 2023.

information about the SADR, the POLISARIO Front and the Sahrawi people, which appears in Algerian and foreign media.[17]

Scarce resources – ambitious diplomacy

In accordance with Articles 57 and 58 of the SADR Constitution, the most important role in conducting the foreign policy of the Republic is exercised by its President, who is responsible for foreign policy and deciding on its programs of action, accepting the credentials of ambassadors accredited to the SADR and signing international treaties and conventions. The President of the Republic also nominates ambassadors and heads of diplomatic missions (ICT Policy Africa: "The Constitution of the Sahrawi Arab Democratic Republic" 2015). To achieve the SADR's foreign policy goals, the Sahrawi foreign service is used directly, but also, indirectly, through contacts and lobbying within less official channels, such as friendship/solidarity associations with the Sahrawi people existing in Western European countries – primarily in Spain, but also elsewhere in the world, e.g., in North Africa – Algeria, Egypt.[18] As a result of these activities, the position of the SADR authorities in the conflict over Western Sahara is spread and the conflict itself is not forgotten, pressure is also exerted, as far as possible, on the authorities of the country in which a given association operates in order to enforce a certain position or take specific actions. Interestingly, the Moroccan independence movement in the 1940s and 1950s used practically the same methods and practices of raising awareness among the international

---

17 Information obtained during a visit to the Sahrawi Mission in Algiers – Information Centre named after Martyr Mohamed Fadel Ismael, Algiers, May 2017.

18 While Algeria's stance aligns with the government's official approach, Egypt's position appears somewhat divergent from Cairo's policy, which tends to adopt a conservative stance on the Western Sahara matter, akin to the prevailing sentiment in most Arab nations, excluding Algeria and, to a lesser extent, Mauritania. Dr. Saïd Ayachi explicates this discrepancy, attributing it to political dynamics: Arab monarchies predominantly favour Morocco's standpoint, given its monarchical system (a caveat, however, is warranted for Egypt, having transitioned away from monarchy in 1952). Consequently, the Algerian discourse seeks to juxtapose support for the Sahrawi Arab Democratic Republic (SADR) as an endorsement of democracy against backing Morocco as tacit support for dictatorship. Nevertheless, this portrayal oversimplifies the complexities of the situation, suggesting a nuanced examination, incorporating geopolitical considerations relevant to the Middle East landscape. For instance, Egyptian authorities may seek to avoid antagonizing Morocco, given its historically amicable relations with Persian Gulf states (Interview with Dr. Saïd Ayachi, May 2023).

community. By creating, quite innovatively for that time, an international network of supporters of the Moroccan independence cause, including well-known names such as Eleanor Roosevelt, not only were independence slogans propagated, but also "globalising the Moroccan question" was possible (in an era before the Internet and social media). Allies and sympathisers from other cultural circles "were translating" Moroccan demands for independence so that they were understandable in the environment and culture from which they came, and, moreover, to a certain extent, they were legitimising them among wider circles of the international community (Stenner 2019, pp. 2-10, 147). What put Moroccan nationalists in the vanguard of the anti-colonial struggle during the independence struggle has actually been exploited by the Sahrawi people from the very beginning of their struggle for independence, not only through contacts with non-governmental organisations in solidarity with their struggle, but also by enabling (and often organising) visits and stays in the Sahrawi refugee camps of hundreds (maybe thousands) of foreigners: journalists, politicians, volunteers, scientists, representatives and employees of various types of international organisations (governmental and non-governmental).[19]

In the context of Sahrawi diplomatic efforts, the fact that SADR diplomats are very active, while having very limited financial resources, deserves special attention. Based on publicly available data, R. Joseph Huddleston prepared a list of official meetings of SADR diplomatic employees or representatives of the PO-LISARIO Front with representatives of third countries in the years 2014-2018, showing that such meetings took place 250 times. This number may be higher if we assume that various types of unofficial meetings were also held, which were not made public. Huddleston points out that due to limited financial resources (in most cases, foreign SADR representative offices do not have impressive

---

19 Based on the author's observations during a visit to Sahrawi refugee camps in May 2016. It is also worth remembering something that has largely been ignored in scientific research so far, namely that currently, due to the ubiquity of social media, part of these activities of informing and sensitising about the problem of Western Sahara, as well as organising grassroots forms of assistance, have been taken over by committed individuals, not necessarily associated with the above-mentioned solidarity associations, but having a group of permanent followers. This is especially visible in countries where such an association base is very limited or non-existent, such as in Poland. In the Polish Internet space, such a pro-Sahrawi voice is blogger and Instagrammer Lena Khalid – on the one hand, informing about the Sahrawi issue and the life of ordinary Sahrawis, both in the refugee camps and in the occupied territories, on the other – organising help (https://www.instagram.com/polkanapustyni/).

offices[20]) these are often one-person "operations", and Sahrawi diplomats often work from an office that serves as their apartment. Most of them have families living in the refugee camps, and they are transferred from one facility to another relatively often. In his article from 2019, Huddleston also recalls information obtained during interviews, according to which the monthly budget of a SADR representative in Washington was 6,000 USD, while a Sahrawi diplomat in London had to organise his work for the equivalent of 4,500 USD. With this amount, they had to pay for their office/apartment from which they worked, business trips and any other minor work-related expenses (Huddleston 2019).[21] Dimitris Bouris and Irene Fernández-Molina describe the activities of SADR diplomats as "hybrid diplomatic practices", in which, in the face of only partial recognition of the SADR in the international arena, they use their *de facto statehood* and in situations where it is easier for them to achieve their goals or take part in an event they act as representatives of the national liberation movement or even as a lobbying group.[22] As an example, they cite the actions of Sahrawi diplomats in Brussels, where formally there is no official representative of the SADR to the EU, but the contacts with EU institutions and member states are the responsibility of a representative of the POLISARIO Front with the title of minister-delegate for European affairs, and there is also a single-person office in the capital of Belgium representative offices of the POLISARIO Front. These delegates use different titles depending on the possibilities and adequacy of the situation, sometimes accepting the label of lobbying groups – if it allows them to enter a specific EU institution and participate in its deliberations. It can be said that they are very flexible and purposeful in their diplomatic efforts by using the resources and opportunities at their disposal (Bouris / Fernández-Molina 2018, pp. 306-324).

The Sahrawi Arab Democratic Republic maintains embassies in 22 countries: 12 African countries (in four cases, SADR ambassadors are dually accredited), 9 Latin American countries (one dually accredited ambassador) and one

---

20 The exception is the already mentioned embassy in Algiers, the maintenance of which, according to the information obtained by the author, is financed by the Algerian government.

21 Huddleston describes it as a *shoestring budget*.

22 The POLISARIO Front as a national liberation movement enjoys much wider recognition than the SADR as a state. The POLISARIO Front's status as a national liberation movement was confirmed in 1979 by the UN General Assembly, which recognised it as the "representative of the Sahrawi people".

Asian country (dually accredited).[23] In addition, the SADR has numerous diplomatic representations (most often called official representations or delegations)[24] in many other countries (also those that do not recognise the Sahrawi Arab Democratic Republic), including permanent representations in a number of EU countries, as well as in the United States, Australia and the Russian Federation. Such high activity of SADR diplomacy is very mobilising for the authorities in Rabat, a great example of which is the case of Australia. After opening a Sahrawi representative office there, Morocco decided to open an embassy in Canberra, even though it had previously relied on its ambassador accredited in Indonesia (Huddleston 2019).

Spain is a special case, where the SADR or POLISARIO Front representations are also present outside the capital – in all Spanish autonomous communities, even those less important in terms of political or economic power, such as Castile and León (Delegación Saharaui en Castilla y León).[25] In addition, the SADR is represented (even if it is not, as already mentioned, an official representation) at the most important international organisations: the UN, the European Union, and the African Union (of which it is, as already mentioned, a full member). In order to achieve the goals of its foreign policy, the SADR must first of all make sure that the Western Saharan issue is not forgotten and is constantly present in international space, so it uses every opportunity to present its arguments in the media and in different institutions (international, governmental, non-governmental, educational), or in a specific country or even its region (this is especially visible in the above-mentioned Spanish example).

---

23 On the African continent, these are: Algeria, Angola (accredited in Namibia), Botswana, Ethiopia, Ghana, Kenya, Mozambique, Nigeria, South Africa (accredited in Lesotho), Tanzania (accredited in Mauritius), Uganda (accredited in Rwanda) and Zimbabwe. In turn, Latin American countries hosting the SADR embassies on their territory include Ecuador, Colombia, Cuba, Mexico, Nicaragua (accredited in Belize), Panama, Peru, Uruguay, Venezuela. On the Asian continent, the only SADR representative office with embassy status is located in East Timor (the ambassador is also accredited in Vanuatu). Author's own study based on internet sources.

24 In some cases, these are official representations of the POLISARIO Front – since it enjoys international recognition by the UN as the official representation of the Sahrawi people and often such a formula is more acceptable to the host party.

25 A list of all POLISARIO Front / SADR representations in Spain – in each of the 17 autonomous communities – is available on the website of the POLISARIO Front Delegation to Spain (Frente Polisario, Web).

The most important event of the year from the perspective of less official activities of the SADR related to the cooperation with solidarity groups is the European Conference for Support and Solidarity with the Sahrawi people (*Conferencia Europea de Apoyo al Pueblo Saharaui*, EUCOCO), organised cyclically every year in November or December (the exception was year 2020, when it was cancelled due to the ongoing COVID-19 pandemic). It is usually organised in one of the Spanish cities[26] by a local solidarity association in cooperation with the local government – the authorities of a given city, province, or autonomous community, as well as the POLISARIO Front. During the plenary session, the deliberations are more about expressing support for the Sahrawi cause, with representatives of the governments that have recognised the SADR, various solidarity associations from other countries, NGOs, local politicians, the media present. Current information on the broadly understood Western Sahara issue and its population, as well as the efforts of non-governmental organisations to improve life in the refugee camps and calls for the release of Sahrawi political prisoners in Morocco are also presented. Panel discussions (usually four thematic panels) are of a workshop nature, during which an attempt is made to develop certain solutions or good practices that can provide solutions for the broadly understood "Western Sahara issue", e.g., through a wider presence of the Sahrawi problem in the media, pressure on administrative bodies or the government of the countries of origin of the conference participants in order to force certain pro-Western Saharan political decisions or other actions. After the conference, quite extensive reports of its proceedings are published in the media – especially the Sahrawi media, but also Spanish and Algerian.[27]

International determinants of Sahrawi foreign policy

Of course, the question arises whether the SADR can achieve its goals through diplomatic means, and if not, what external factors, assuming favourable internal conditions, will stand in its way. It seems that the Sahrawi Arab Democratic Republic's international position is rather weak and is based mainly on its membership in the African Union, the support of Algeria (and, on the African

---

26 However, in 2022, the 46th EUCOCO conference was organized in Berlin. The next 47th conference will be held in December 2023 in Toledo (47a EUCOCO – Conferencia Europea de Apoyo y Solidaridad con el Pueblo Saharaui, Web).

27 Observations and conversations conducted by the author during the 44th EUCOCO Conference in Vitoria-Gasteiz (22-23 November 2019) and the 45th EUCOCO Conference in Las Palmas de Gran Canaria (10-11 December 2021).

continent, also of another important regional player – South Africa), as well as Spanish solidarity associations. On the one hand, undoubtedly the SADR's international connections, even though they often do not go hand in hand with international recognition, have a very large impact on the effectiveness of its foreign policy, an example of which is the fact that Spain does not recognise the SADR, with which it does not maintain official diplomatic relations, but support is provided through the very active Spanish solidarity associations, often described as crucial when it comes to helping the Sahrawi population living in refugee camps on Algerian territory.[28]

By analysing the current international situation of the SADR and taking into account the very dynamically changing international environment close to this unrecognised state, it was possible to isolate six changes/trends in the international environment that have the greatest impact and will most likely influence the shape of Sahrawi foreign policy in the future and the possible implementation of its constitutional and actual goals.

Further deterioration of Moroccan-Algerian relations. The escalating situation between Rabat and Algiers is unconducive not only to solving the problem of Western Sahara, which is probably a long way off, but even to maintaining the current *status quo*. Officially, in the opinion of the Algerian side, bad relations with Morocco are not purely the result of Algeria's support for the POLISARIO Front, but rather the result of Morocco's expansionist tendencies, which, after Western Sahara gains independence, will supposedly accumulate like in a lens in the concept of what is referred to as the Greater Morocco (*Al-Maghrib al-Kabir*). However, the Western Saharan problem has been present in mutual relations for several decades and it does not seem that this will change soon. Moroccan-Algerian tensions from time to time find an outlet in serious border incidents, resulting in fatalities, such as in 2014, when an Algerian border guard opened fire on a group of Moroccans on the border near the north-eastern city

---

28 According to Elena Fiddian-Qasmiyeh, it is crucial that the POLISARIO Front partly created a certain secular and egalitarian image of life in the refugee camps. Fiddian-Qasmiyeh also believes that aid provided by various international organisations (e.g., UNHCR, UNICEF, WFP) is less appreciated by Sahrawis (unfairly, in her opinion). For more, see: Fiddian-Qasmiyeh 2014. Indeed, the Author's interlocutors in the Sahrawi refugee camps often referred to the humanitarian activities of Spanish solidarity associations, and one could get the impression that they appreciated them very much. They also proudly showed its tangible manifestations (e.g., libraries, outpatient clinics, ambulances). Author's observations made during a visit to the Sahrawi refugee camps in Algeria (Boujdour, Rabouni, Smara), May 2016.

of Oujda. According to the authorities in Rabat, these were unarmed civilians, and according to the Algerian side, they were smugglers who threw stones at the border guards (Al Arabiya News 2014). In November 2021, three Algerian drivers died when Moroccan forces bombed a truck convoy that was moving through the POLISARIO-controlled part of Western Sahara (Dworkin 2022). In turn, at the end of August 2023, the Algerian coast guard shot two Moroccans who, in a group of four on jet skis, entered Algerian territorial waters (the third Moroccan was detained by the Algerian services, one managed to escape). According to media reports, these were tourists who had lost their orientation and crossed the sea border with Algeria accidentally. In an official statement after the incident, the Algerian Ministry of Defence pointed out that these men had secretly entered Algerian territorial waters in an area where the activities of various smuggling groups are intensifying (Al Jazeera "Morocco protests...", 2023). The land border between Algeria and Morocco has been closed since 1994. At that time, Algeria was embroiled in civil war and struggling with radical Islamism. However, despite the end of the conflict in 2002, due to the still tense relations between the two countries, it has never been re-opened. While it is often stated, e.g., in media reports, that the border remains closed due to Algeria's involvement in the Western Saharan conflict, this is a certain simplification. The problem of smuggling appears most often in the narrative on the Algerian side. According to Algiers, it would of course be better if the border with Morocco was open – this would allow the development of mutual relations as well as broader regional cooperation. On the other hand, the Algerian authorities point out that Rabat is reluctant to engage in an in-depth dialogue on the border issue and, above all, on how to fight smugglers, mainly smuggling drugs,[29] but also on the protection of the Algerian market of basic food products and gasoline, which are heavily subsidised by the state, thus very cheap (Interview with Dr. Saïd Ayachi, May 2023). The situation is not helped by the fact that both countries are unofficially involved in an arms race, which has intensified in recent years, with the authorities in Rabat announcing in 2020 a plan to build a military base in Jerada province, approximately 38 km from the border with Algeria. According to Algiers, it is to be packed with modern electronic systems provided to Morocco by Israel (Hernández 2020). The normalisation of Moroccan-Israeli relations (more on this later), which took place at the end of 2020, became another flashpoint

---

29 In the past, it was mainly marijuana and hashish, now also other drugs, e.g., cocaine. The problem of Morocco as a hub on the drug transport route to Europe and beyond, is also noticeable outside Algeria (ENACT Africa 2023).

in mutual relations, just like Morocco's vote of support for the independence of Algerian Kabylia expressed by the Morocco's Permanent Representative to the United Nations in New York, Omar Hilale, in July 2021. In 2021, a scandal also broke out involving Pegasus software, probably used by the Moroccan services to eavesdrop and spy on Algerian politicians. As a result, in August 2021, Algeria broke off diplomatic relations with Morocco, and in November it suspended gas exports to Europe via the gas pipeline running through Moroccan territory (it did not extend the transit agreement with Rabat) (Dworkin 2022).

The political situation in Algeria. In December 2019, presidential elections took place in Algeria. The elections were associated with high hopes in the context of calming and stabilising the situation in the country after the Hirak social protests (February-December 2019),[30] aimed at introducing political and systemic changes. The political situation in Algeria was closely monitored by the POLISARIO Front, which can be confirmed by the fact that its annual convention was scheduled only a week after the Algerian presidential elections. They were won by former Prime Minister Abdelmadjid Tebboune, who comes from the political elite that previously ruled Algeria, i.e., the circle of President Abdelaziz Bouteflika, who resigned from his position in April 2019 as a result of protests. Nevertheless, Tebboune was considered to be in conflict with the oligarchs from the immediate circle of the former president. Regarding the attitude towards the Western Saharan issue, no sudden changes were expected, which was confirmed in the first days after the elections. President Tebboune's statements were consistent with the previously propagated narrative presenting the problem of Western Sahara as a matter of decolonisation that should be resolved under the auspices of international organizations – the UN and the AU, while Algeria's involvement was defined in terms of helping a nation struggling to exercise its right to self-determination (Al Jazeera 2019). Nevertheless, in the context of domestic politics, after the new president's power and the worst months of the pandemic were stabilised, the authorities in Algiers began to crack down on what was left of the Hirak movement, independent journalists and non-governmental organisations. One such example was the dissolution in early 2023 of the Algerian League for the Defence of Human Rights (*Ligue Algérienne pour la Défense des Droits de l'Homme*, LADDH), operating since 1985, the most recognised and distinguished organisation in this field in Algeria (Ghebouli 2022; Bobin 2023). At the moment, it is difficult to say whether the actions taken by the Algerian authorities will ultimately bring further years of internal peace, and whether the

---

30 Protests referred to as Hirak also took place again in 2020 and 2021.

divided Algerian opposition will give up and will not be able to bring about further democratic changes, or whether more social upheaval will occur. Of course, during these Algerian social protests against the government, there were no slogans regarding Western Sahara or stopping aid to refugees; however, deep political changes and their possible consequences (e.g., economic ones) may weaken Algerian aid for the SADR. This is probably what politicians and activists of the POLISARIO Front fear the most, as it must not be forgotten that they have long had good and close relations with the political and military regime ruling in Algeria.

Active Moroccan politics on the African continent. In the new Moroccan constitution adopted in 2011, which was King Mohammed VI's response to the protests of the February 20 Movement (*Mouvement du 20 Février*) – part of the Arab Spring then taking place in the region, the emphasis was placed primarily on changes and legal guarantees regarding the state's internal policy and social life of its citizens. However, it is worth noting that the direction of the development of Moroccan foreign policy was also indicated, as in the preamble of the Basic Law, where we can find declarations obliging Morocco "to consolidate relations of cooperation and of solidarity with the peoples and the countries of Africa, notably the Sub-Saharan countries and [the countries] of the Sahel" and "to reinforce South-South cooperation" (Constitute Project: "Morocco's Constitution of 2011", p. 3). The culmination of the new Moroccan foreign policy on the African continent was the already mentioned admission of Morocco to the African Union and the famous words uttered by Mohammed VI in his speech at the 28th Summit of the African Union in Addis Ababa on January 31, 2017, where it was decided to let Morocco into the AU: "*It is so good to be back home, after having been away for too long! It is a good day when you can show your affection for your beloved home! Africa is my continent, and my home*" (Kingdom of Morocco: "Full Speech..." 2017).[31] The following years will see Morocco's even greater openness to developing political and economic relations with other African countries, especially from Sub-Saharan Africa, and within the framework of the above-mentioned South-South cooperation with Latin American countries.[32] Morocco's foreign

---

31 Interestingly, on the same government website you can find the tab "The African dimension of Morocco", which redirects to an album with photos commemorating various events (e.g., foreign visits) related to African countries throughout the history of independent Morocco (i.e., since 1956).

32 Although efforts to strengthen ties with Russia, India, and China have also been pursued, it appears that Sub-Saharan Africa currently holds precedence for Rabat. Between 2003 and 2017, 60% of Moroccan foreign direct investments (FDI) were directed

policy has definitely shifted its focus primarily to Sub-Saharan countries, while in the first decades after gaining independence it was rather targeted at the Arab world and then developing relations within the Mediterranean basin. Although at first glance it seems that pragmatic arguments have come to the fore, and according to some analysts, Morocco has stopped conditioning its foreign policy on the issue of Western Sahara, because the development of economic relations, business and direct investments have become more important. It is with more careful observation that one may get the impression that only the Moroccan tactics have changed and the Western Saharan issue is being introduced through the "back door", e.g., when a number of African or Latin American countries, as a result of the offensive of Moroccan diplomacy and in the face of newly opening economic opportunities, begin to adopt Moroccan narrative towards Western Sahara and withdraw the recognition previously granted to the SADR (Messari 2020). Nowadays, there is more and more talk about Morocco's "fertiliser diplomacy". After the Russian invasion in Ukraine, African countries began to experience shortages of fertilisers, the production of which uses phosphates extracted both in Russia and Ukraine, but also, as mentioned, in Western Sahara (in the part of the territory controlled by Morocco). Rabat is probably increasingly using the issue of the availability of phosphate fertilisers in its lobbying against the Western Saharan issue on the African continent. It is possible that the newly elected Kenyan President William Ruto fell victim to this strategy, when, without consulting the government and after talks with the envoy of King Mohammed VI, he wrote on Twitter that Kenya was withdrawing its recognition of the SADR. During the election campaign, Ruto promised to help farmers solve the problem of the lack of fertilisers. After protests from politicians from the ruling coalition, the tweet was quickly deleted, and Kenya confirmed its recognition of the SADR (Fabricius 2022). This does not change the fact that Morocco's foreign policy on the African continent is bringing the intended results. In the years 2019-2022, several African countries decided to open their consulates in

---

towards the African continent. In February 2017, Morocco even expressed its intent to join the Economic Community of West African States (ECOWAS) and formally submitted an application for membership. However, this application remains unanswered, likely due to Nigeria's predominant role within the organisation, which fears potential competition for its economic influence in the region. Furthermore, Nigeria, a country that recognises the Sahrawi Arab Democratic Republic and hosts a Sahrawi embassy, perceives Morocco's de facto control over much of the Western Saharan territory as a vestige of colonialism (Al Qays Talha Jebril 2023).

the Morocco-occupied areas of Western Sahara – in El Aaiún (Laâyoune) and Dakhla: Burundi, Central African Republic, Comoros, Gabon, Côte d'Ivoire, Senegal, São Tomé and Príncipe, Liberia, Djibouti, Guinea, Gambia, Equatorial Guinea, Cabo Verde, Burkina Faso, Eswatini. This is undoubtedly a great success of Moroccan foreign policy. Researchers, such as Yahia Zoubir and Alex Vines, agree that this is an attempt to legalise the occupation of Western Sahara and the presence of Moroccan state institutions in this territory through the "back door" (Schwikowski / Flotat-Talon 2020).[33]

Donald Trump's decision to recognize Morocco's sovereignty over the territory of Western Sahara. Back in May 2019, R. Joseph Huddelston wrote in *Foreign Policy* that the SADR authorities see the Trump administration as the greatest chance in years to change their situation and gain independence. These hopes were placed in John Bolton, the US President's security adviser, who had personal ties to Western Sahara and was well-informed about the trajectory of the conflict itself. In the years 1997-2000, Bolton worked *pro bono* as the deputy of James Baker – the UN special envoy for Western Sahara (1997-2004); thus, he knew the complex Western Sahara peace process from the inside out. In 2006, when he served as the United States ambassador to the United Nations, he threatened to disband MINURSO; thus, signalling an impasse and a certain pointlessness of the further activities of this mission in its current form. Moreover, he was one of the few Western diplomats to personally visit the Sahrawi refugee camps in Algeria. In 2019, Bolton continued to maintain his position regarding the MINURSO mission – either it should fulfil its mandate related to the referendum on the future of Western Sahara or it should be disbanded. Most likely, he was responsible for the change in the extension period of the MINURSO mission, which was shortened from 12 to 6 months (Huddleston 2019). However, Sahrawi politicians could not have known that in 2020 he would lose his position and the United States would decide to recognise the *de facto* Moroccan occupation of Western Sahara and establish an American consulate in the coastal city of Dakhla in the occupied territories. On 10 December 2020, President Donald Trump, in his typical style, announced on Twitter that the United States recognises Moroccan sovereignty over the territory of Western Sahara. In return, Morocco decided to normalise relations with the State of Israel and

---

33 List of countries that have opened consulates in the territories occupied by Morocco compiled based on information available on the Internet.

it became part of what is referred to as the *Abraham Accords*.[34] This decision, apart from many other aspects and potential consequences, was made at a very unfortunate time for the development of the Western Saharan conflict, since, less than a month earlier, as already mentioned, in November 2020, the ceasefire, on which the entire peace process was in practice based, was broken (Huddleston / Ghoorhoo / Maquera Sardon 2021). Regular observers of the Western Sahara issue expected a clear change after Joe Biden's victory in the elections. Nevertheless, despite taking office in January 2021, the topic of changing his predecessor's decision regarding the recognition of Moroccan sovereignty over Western Sahara has not been included in Biden's political agenda. The tactic of remaining silent on the Sahrawi problem was adopted, Trump's decision was not reversed; however, it has also not been referred to or confirmed in any way. The opening of the American consulate in Dakhla also did not take place, although its potential location is guarded by Moroccan soldiers, and the Secretary of State Antony Blinken, during his trip to the Middle East and North Africa in March 2022, was subjected to quite a lot of pressure regarding the opening of American consulates in Dakhla and Jerusalem (Zunes 2022; Jakes / Alami 2022). Despite the passage of time, the consequences of Donald Trump's decisions are still felt. On 17 July 2023, following the United States, Israel recognised Morocco's sovereignty over Western Sahara, most likely also taking into account the successfully developing relations with Rabat. In official information provided by Rabat, the Israeli government is considering opening a consulate in Dakhla. In turn, Israeli Foreign Minister Eli Cohen said that recognising Western Sahara as part of Morocco will strengthen Israeli-Moroccan relations and contribute to greater stability in the region. By July 2023, 28 countries had decided to open consulates in the occupied territories, in the cities of Laâyoune or Dakhla (Al Jazeera, "Israel recognises Western Sahara as part of Morocco" 2023).

Spanish support for the Moroccan autonomy project for Western Sahara. Another setback to the Western Saharan issue occurred with the shift in Spain's stance, as Madrid departed from several decades of neutrality on the conflict. In April 2022, Spanish Prime Minister Pedro Sánchez, representing the Spanish Socialist Workers' Party (Partido Socialista Obrero Español, PSOE), unexpectedly lent support to Morocco's autonomy proposal for Western Sahara from 2007—a proposition categorically rejected by the POLISARIO Front. Simultaneously, this

---

34 A series of agreements normalising Israel's relations with Arab states brokered by the United States. In addition to Morocco, such agreements have also been signed by the United Arab Emirates, Bahrain, and Sudan.

move de facto acknowledged the Western Saharan issue as Morocco's internal affair. Behind this unexpected manoeuvre, which faced unanimous opposition from representatives of various Spanish political factions (ranging from PSOE's coalition partner Podemos to the far-right VOX), a rarity in Spanish politics, lay the Pegasus software scandal. In 2021, this scandal involved the alleged use of Pegasus software to spy on the Spanish Prime Minister and some members of his cabinet, with Moroccan involvement being the likely culprit (Bartolomé, 2022). Furthermore, the ongoing context of Moroccan-Spanish relations must be considered, notably Morocco's migration-related pressures on Spain, alongside Rabat's territorial claims concerning the Spanish autonomous cities bordering Morocco: Ceuta and Melilla.[35] Both issues have been present in the bilateral relations of these two countries for years. However, the "honeymoon period", as the Spanish media put it, did not last long in relations between Rabat and Madrid. In May 2023, during the regional election campaign, journalists from *El Mundo* uncovered an electoral fraud scheme involving postal voting in Melilla. The scheme implicated local politicians of Arab descent affiliated with the Coalición por Melilla party, who were found to have travelled to Morocco to meet with agents of the Moroccan secret services[36]. Subsequently, in August 2023, the Moroccan embassy in Madrid published a map of Morocco on its website, depicting Ceuta and Melilla as part of the Moroccan state. This action was perceived as yet another provocation by Rabat (El Faro de Melilla, 2023).

The War in Ukraine and relations with the Russian Federation. The Russian invasion of Ukraine, which began on 24 February 2022 and continues to this day, has huge consequences not only for European countries, but also for North Africa. As a result, a number of economic sanctions were imposed on Russian Federation on an unprecedented scale, the tangible result of which was the need for European countries to become independent from Russian energy resources. In this scenario, the European Union, particularly countries in the southern region of the continent, directed their attention towards Algeria. However, owing to the tense regional circumstances and the aforementioned strained relations between Algeria and Morocco, Algiers suspended gas transportation to Europe via Morocco in November 2021. The situation was supposed to be alleviated by

---

35　They function like Spanish autonomous communities, i.e., they are simply smaller territorial units.

36　All Spanish dailies, including the local ones, wrote about the case for a long time, but the whole scheme was presented in the most detail by *El Mundo*, see, e.g., Peñalosa, 2023; Madueño / Carvajal, 2023.

the visit of US Secretary of State Antony Blinken to Algiers on 30 March 2022, during the already mentioned Middle East and North African diplomatic tour. It was the first visit by a high-ranking American politician after Washington recognised Moroccan sovereignty over Western Sahara, but it achieved little. Blinken, trying to convince the Algerians to change their position on the gas pipeline, did not have much to offer politically. When asked about Western Sahara at a press conference, he gave a general answer about focusing on diplomatic efforts and supporting the peace process within the UN. Considering the traditionally good Algerian-Russian relations and Moscow's growing interest in the African continent, long before the start of full-scale aggression in Ukraine, this is not enough (Hill 2022; Rousselier 2018). In November 2022, the Algerian authorities announced that they were applying for BRICS membership and were guaranteed the support of China and Russian Federation in this matter. At the UN forum, Algerian representatives refrained from voting against Moscow's interests, which they explain as not indicating unconditional support for Russia, thereby rejecting the attitude of countries such as North Korea, Syria, Belarus, and Eritrea, which vote against UN resolutions condemning Russian aggression. Moreover, there appears to be a lack of comprehension on the Algerian side regarding the nature of the conflict, which is perceived through the lens of proxy wars between major powers reminiscent of the Cold War era. Even though there is a "humane" sense of sympathy for the Ukrainian nation, Algerians deny it agency. The Algerian narrative closely aligns with that of the Sahrawi people. After all, Algeria maintains the closest relations and cooperation with the Sahrawi Arab Democratic Republic. The conflict itself among diplomats and politicians of the POLISARIO Front raises concerns as well as some uncertainty. Despite the passage of several months since the conflict began, it remains unclear how to navigate diplomatic relations without risking loss of face in the international arena or jeopardizing diplomatic efforts in the West. Defending Russian aggression and the atrocities committed against Ukrainian civilians proves challenging in diplomatic exchanges with Western nations. In the meantime, the authorities in Rabat are not remaining idle and are trying to strengthen their image as a reliable ally of Western countries, taking advantage of the conflict in Ukraine, for example, by being the first African country to send military aid to Kyiv (T-72 tanks with parts) (Belkaïd 2023; Interview with Dr. Saïd Ayachi, Interview with Prof. Smail Debeche, Interview with the SADR Ambassador in Algeria and member of the National Secretariat of the POLISARIO Front, Abdelkader Taleb Omar, May 2023).

Conclusions

The specificity of the foreign policy of the Sahrawi Arab Democratic Republic is related to its problematic status as an unrecognised state. Moreover, there is no indication that the conflict underlying this situation can be permanently resolved soon. The SADR's unrecognised statehood is particularly problematic in its relations with Western countries, none of which recognise it. Sahrawi diplomats thus resort to quite flexible solutions, described in the literature as "hybrid diplomatic practices" (Bouris, Fernández-Molina 2018). The specific functioning of the SADR, whose main political centre is located in the refugee camps on the territory of Algeria, as well as the fact that in November 2020 the conflict with Morocco returned to its active phase, makes it difficult to conduct any effective foreign policy, as well as depriving the Sahrawi authorities of the argument, frequently used in previous decades, for a peaceful struggle for independence and trust in the peace process under the auspices of the UN. The constitutional goals of the SADR's foreign policy are very broadly outlined and they also contain a certain projection as to the future active role of the Sahrawi state in shaping international relations on the African continent. The reality, however, is much more pragmatic. Sahrawi activities, also in the area of international politics, depend to a large extent on the aid provided by Algeria, which plays the role of a patron state for Sahrawi statehood. Algiers not only provides material assistance, a particular example of which are the refugee camps around Tindouf, but also serves as a "window to the world", through which the Sahrawi population living in the refugee camps, as well as the SADR authorities, can travel and contact the outside world. Moreover, and perhaps even more importantly, Algeria supports the SADR's demands in the African Union and other international forums and tries to multiply the Sahrawi voice in those bodies where the Sahrawis are not represented. Good relations with the authorities in Algiers are crucial for the POLISARIO Front, and in this case, it is difficult to talk about any possibility of diversification and finding a counterweight to the patron state. At the same time, the support given to Algeria itself by the SADR, which, at least officially, is ideological and based on values dating back to colonial times and then the Cold War, costs a lot in the international arena, especially in the context of regional relations in the Maghreb region.

The determinants of Sahrawi foreign policy that have the greatest impact on its shape are international in nature and are related to trends and changes in the international environment closest to the SADR, i.e., primarily the Maghreb region and, more broadly, on the African continent, where Morocco's diplomatic offensive brings, at least partially, the intended effects. The country has sufficient material resources and a strong enough position in the region to effectively influence the weaker and less politically and economically significant states of the global South, primarily in Sub-Saharan Africa. Undoubtedly, due to the decisions made by the Donald Trump administration and the Spanish Prime Minister Pedro Sánchez, the problem for the POLISARIO Front lies in the fact that in the face of the ongoing Russian aggression in Ukraine, Sahrawi diplomatic efforts in Western countries are unlikely to be successful. Therefore, the countries of the global South, primarily in Sub-Saharan Africa and Latin America, are a somewhat natural geographical area of operations and activities for the SADR diplomacy. Thus, this leads to a bizarre situation that opens another front of the Moroccan-Saharan conflict – a diplomatic one, in which the main stake is the fight for the recognition of Moroccan sovereignty over the territory of Western Sahara or the international recognition of the Sahrawi Arab Democratic Republic.

References

Al Arabiya News: "Algeria-Morocco tensions flare over border shooting", *Al Arabiya News* 20.10.2014, retrieved 27.6.2023, from https://english.alarabiya. net/News/africa/2014/10/20/Algeria-Morocco-tensions-flare-over-border-shooting.

Al Jazeera: "Abdelmadjid Tebboune: Who is Algeria's new president?", *Al Jazeera* 13.12.2019, retrieved 2.4.2023, from https://www.aljazeera.com/news/2019/12/abdelmadjid-tebboune-algeria-president-191213161923647.html.

Al Jazeera: "Israel recognises Western Sahara as part of Morocco", *Al Jazeera*, 17.7.2023, retrieved 14.8.2023, from https://www.aljazeera.com/news/2023/7/17/israel-recognises-western-sahara-as-part-of-morocco.

Al Jazeera: "Morocco protests over killed jet ski tourists in Algeria", *Al Jazeera*, 4.9.2023, retrieved 5.9.2023, from https://www.aljazeera.com/news/2023/9/4/morocco-protests-over-killed-jet-ski-tourists-in-algeria.

Al Qays Talha Jebril, Imru: "Morocco-ECOWAS: Good intentions are not enough", *MIPA Institute* 9.9.2023, retrieved 11.6.2023, from https://mipa.institute/en/7323.

Bartolomé, Marcos: "Why is Madrid Pandering to Morocco?", *Foreign Policy* 13.5.2022, retrieved 29.6.2023, from https://foreignpolicy.com/2022/05/13/spain-sanchez-morocco-polisario-western-sahara-algeria/.

Belkaïd, Akram: "Algeria and Morocco vie to keep Russia onside", *Le Monde diplomatique* 6.2. 2023, retrieved 28.8.2023, from https://mondediplo.com/2023/02/06maghreb-ukraine.

Bobin, Frédéric: "En Algérie, la dissolution de la Ligue des droits de l'homme illustre l'escalade répressive du régime", *Le Monde* 1.2.2023, retrieved 4.9.2023, from https://www.lemonde.fr/afrique/article/2023/02/01/en-algerie-la-diss olution-de-la-ligue-des-droits-de-l-homme-illustre-l-escalade-repressive-du-regime_6160088_3212.html.

Bouris, Dimitris / Fernández-Molina, Irene: "Contested States, Hybrid Diplomatic Practices, and the Everyday Quest for Recognition", *International Political Sociology*, 12 (2018), pp. 306-324.

Chograni, Houda: "The Polisario Front, Morocco, and the Western Sahara Conflict", *Arab Center Washington DC,* 22.6.2021, retrieved 2.9.2023, from https://arabcenterdc.org/resource/the-polisario-front-morocco-and-the-western-sahara-conflict/.

CESO USC: "Military Agreement no. 1 between the Royal Moroccan Army and MINURSO on the one side and the Frente POLISARIO Military Forces and the MINURSO on the other side", December 1997 [Not published by the United Nations, but mentioned in paragraph 18 of the Report of the Secretary-General to the Security Council S/1998/35], *Centro de Estudos do Sahara Occidental da USC,* retrieved 26.6.2023, from https://www.usc.es/export9/sites/webinstitucional/gl/institutos/ceso/descargas/Military-Agreement-1.pdf.

CESO USC: "SADR Recognitions", *Centro de Estudos do Sahara Occidental da USC,* retrieved 5.9.2023, from https://www.usc.es/en/institutos/ceso/RASD_Reconocimientos.html.

Constitute Project: "Morocco's Constitution of 2011", *Constitute Project,* retrieved 26.8.2023, from https://www.constituteproject.org/constitution/Morocco_2011.

Frente Polisario: "Delegación del Frente Polisario para España", retrieved 2.9.2023, from https://frentepolisario.es

Dworkin, Anthony: "North African standoff: How the Western Sahara conflict is fuelling new tensions between Morocco and Algeria", *European Council on Foreign Relations,* 8.6.2022, retrieved 30.6.2023, from https://ecfr.eu/publication/north-african-standoff-how-the-western-sahara-conflict-is-fuelling-new-tensions-between-morocco-and-algeria/.

de Orellana, Pablo: "Struggles over identity in diplomacy: 'Commie terrorists' contra 'imperialists' in Western Sahara", *International Relations* 29 (4) 2015, pp. 477-499.

El Faro de Melilla: "Otra vez un mapa de Marruecos que incluye a Melilla y Ceuta", *El Faro de Melilla,* 19.8.2023, retrieved 20.8.2023, from https://elfarodemelilla.es/otra-vez-un-mapa-de-marruecos-que-incluye-a-melilla-y-ceuta/.

ENACT Africa: "Morocco: a critical link in the Latin America-Europe cocaine chain", *ENACT Africa*, 27.1.2023, retrieved 10.7.2023, from https://enactafrica.org/enact-observer/morocco-a-critical-link-in-the-latin-america-europe-cocaine-chain.

EUCOCO: "47a EUCOCO: Conferencia Europea de Apoyo y Solidaridad con el Pueblo Saharaui", retrieved 2.04.2023, from https://aapstoledo.org/eucoco/inscripcion/.

Fabiani, Riccardo: "Getting Diplomacy Back on Track in Western Sahara", *International Crisis Group*, 5.11.2021, retrieved 22.6.2023, from https://www.crisisgroup.org/middle-east-north-africa/north-africa/western-sahara/getting-diplomacy-back-track-western-sahara.

Fabricius, Peter: "SADR grows theoretically stronger but diplomatically weaker", *ISS. Institute for Security Studies*, 7.10.2022, retrieved 27.6.2023, from https://issafrica.org/iss-today/sadr-grows-theoretically-stronger-but-diplomatically-weaker.

Fiddian-Qasmiyeh, Elena: *The Ideal Refugees: Gender, Islam, and the Sahrawi Politics of Survival*. Syracuse University Press: Syracuse, NY, 2014.

Ghebouli, Zine Labidine: "Algeria's opposition after the Hirak: Limitations and divisions", *Middle East Institute*, 22.2.2022, retrieved 26.8.2023, from https://www.mei.edu/publications/algerias-opposition-after-hirak-limitations-and-divisions.

Hernández, Henar: "Algeria to build a military base near the border with Morocco", *Atalayar*, 26.6.2020, retrieved 30.6.2023, from https://atalayar.com/en/content/algeria-build-military-base-near-border-morocco.

Hill, Thomas M.: "Ukraine War Puts New Focus on Conflict in Western Sahara. Amid new tensions, can diplomacy unstick a long-stalled peace process with Morocco and Algeria?", *United States Institute of Peace*, 14.4.2022, retrieved 30.6.2023, from https://www.usip.org/publications/2022/04/ukraine-war-puts-new-focus-conflict-western-sahara.

Huddleston, R. Joseph: "Can John Bolton Thaw Western Sahara's Long-Frozen Conflict?", *Foreign Policy*, 9.5.2019, retrieved 5.6.2023, from https://foreignpolicy.com/2019/05/09/can-john-bolton-thaw-western-saharas-long-frozen-conflict-morocco-western-sahara-polisario-minurso-sahrawi-republic/.

Huddleston, R. Joseph / Ghoorhoo, Harshana / Maquera Sardon, Daniela A.: "Biden Can Backtrack on Trump's Move in Western Sahara", *Foreign Policy*, 9.1.2021, retrieved 20.7.2022, from https://foreignpolicy.com/2021/01/09/biden-can-backtrack-on-trumps-move-in-western-sahara/.

ICT Policy Africa: "The Constitution of the Sahrawi Arab Democratic Republic". Adopted by the 14th Congress of the Frente POLISARIO, 16-20 December

2015, *ICT Policy Africa*, retrieved 14.8.2023, from https://ictpolicyafrica.org/en/document/iynr7udq57b?page=1.

Information gathered during a visit to Mission Sahraouie – Alger – Centre d'Information Martir Mohamed Fadel Ismael, Algier, May 2017.

Interview with the Ambassador of the Sahrawi Arab Democratic Republic in Algeria and member of the National Secretariat of the POLISARIO Front Abdelkader Taleb Omar, Algiers, May 2023.

Interview with Dr. Saïd Ayachi, Chair of the Algerian National Solidarity Committee (*Le Comité national algérien de solidarité avec le peuple sahraoui*), Algiers, Algeria, Myj 2023.

Interview with Hamdi Bueha, Secretary-General of the SARD Ministry of Foreign Affairs and Mohamed Hammadi from the Department of Europe and the Arab World at the SADR Ministry of Foreign Affairs, Rabouni Camp, Algeria, May 2016.

Interview with Prof. Smail Debeche, Université d'Alger 3, Algiers, May 2023.

Jakes, Lara / Alami, Aida: "U.S. Pressured to Open Consulates in Jerusalem and Western Sahara", *New York Times*, 30.3.2022, retrieved 28.8.2023, from https://www.nytimes.com/2022/03/30/world/africa/jerusalem-western-sahara-us-consulates.html.

Kingdom of Morocco: "Full Speech of HM the King at 28th African Union Summit", *Kingdom of Morocco* – official web page, 31.1.2017, retrieved 19.9.2023, from https://www.maroc.ma/en/royal-activities/full-speech-hm-king-28th-african-union-summit.Kosidło, Adam: *Sahara Zachodnia. Fiasko dekolonizacji czy sukces podboju 1975-2011*. Wydawnictwo Uniwersytetu Gdańskiego: Gdańsk, 2012.

Madueño, Juan Diego / Carvajal, Álvaro: "El 'lejano oeste' del yerno del líder de Coalición por Melilla", *El Mundo*, 24.5.2023, p. 9.

Messari, Nizar: "Moroccan Foreign Policy Under Mohammed VI: Balancing Diversity and Respect", *Istituto Affari Internazionali*, 28.10.2020, retrieved 18.6.2023, from https://www.iai.it/it/pubblicazioni/moroccan-foreign-policy-under-mohammed-vi-balancing-diversity-and-respect.

Mormul, Joanna: "Hijos de las nubes i 45 lat marzeń: uchodźcy Saharawi na terytorium Algierii", *Politeja*, 18 (6) 75, 2021, retrieved from: https://doi.org/10.12797/Politeja.18.2021.75.08

Peñalosa, Gema: "Afines a Aberchán se vieron con agentes de Rabat antes del fraude", *El Mundo*, 24.5.2023, p. 8.

Reuters: "Fears grow of new Western Sahara war between Morocco and Polisario Front", *Reuters*, 13.9.2020, retrieved 25.6.2023, from https://www.reuters.com/article/us-morocco-westernsahara-idUSKBN27T15S.

Roussellier, Jacques: "A Role for Russia in the Western Sahara?", *Carnegie Endowment for International Peace*, 5.6.2018, retrieved 2.5.2023, from https://carnegieendowment.org/sada/76532.

Sahara Press Service: "Le soutien de l'Algérie à la lutte du peuple sahraoui repose sur les principes de sa politique extérieure (Ould Khelifa)", *Sahara Press Service*, 3.8.2015, retrieved 31.5.2022, from https://www.spsrasd.info/news/sps archive/fr/node/4274.

Sahara Press Service: "Re-election of Brahim Ghali as Secretary General of the Polisario Front", *Sahara Press Service*, 20.1.2023, retrieved 20.4.2023, from https://www.spsrasd.info/news/en/articles/2023/01/20/43745.html.

Schwikowski, Martina / Flotat-Talon, Hugo: ""New African consulates cause trouble for Western Sahara", *DW*, 31.3. 2020, retrieved 5.9.2023, from https://www.dw.com/en/new-african-consulates-cause-trouble-for-western-sahara/a-52967857.

Stenner, David: *Globalizing Morocco. Transnational Activism and the Postcolonial State*. Stanford University Press: Stanford, California, 2019.

Szeptycki, Andrzej: "Algieria: wrota do Afryki". In: Gawrycki, Marcin F. / Lizak, Wiesław (eds.): *Kuba i Afryka. Sojusz dla rewolucji*. ASPRA JR: Warszawa, 2006.

Thieux, Laurence: "Algerian Foreign Policy towards Western Sahara". In: Ojeda-García, Raquel / Fernández-Molina, Irene / Veguilla, Victoria (eds.): *Global, Regional and Local Dimensions of Western Sahara's Protracted Decolonization: When a Conflict Gets Old*. New York, 2017.

United Nations: "The United Nations and Decolonization. Non-Self-Governing Territories", *United Nations*, 4.8.2023 (updated), retrieved 14.8.2023, from https://www.un.org/dppa/decolonization/en/nsgt.

UNHCR: "Saharawi Refugees in Tindouf, Algeria: Total In- Camp Population. Official Report", *UNHCR*, March 2018, Centro de Estudos do Sahara Occidental da USC, retrieved 5.10.2021, from https://www.usc.gal/export9/sites/webinstitucional/gl/institutos/ceso/descargas/UNHCR_Tindouf-Total-In-Camp-Population_March-2018.pdf.

Wilson, Alice: "Democratising elections without parties: reflections on the case of the Sahrawi Arab Democratic Republic", *The Journal of North African Studies* 15 (4) 2010, pp. 423-438. Retrieved from https://doi.org/10.1080/13629380903424380.

Zunes, Stephen: "Biden's dangerous refusal to reverse Trump's Western Sahara policy", *Foreign Policy in Focus*, 21.1.2022, retrieved 30.3.2023, from https://fpif.org/bidens-dangerous-refusal-to-reverse-trumps-western-sahara-policy/.

Joanna Mormul

Chapter 5. The Population of a *De Facto State* – the Case of the Sahrawi People in the Protracted Refugee Situation[1]

The Sahrawi refugee situation in Algeria, which originated in 1975 and has since evolved into one of the most protracted refugee crises globally, is frequently likened to the issue of Palestinian refugees in Middle Eastern countries or Afghan refugees in Iran. Over time, it has also become a highly politicised matter. The impasse and the absence of clear prospects for a referendum to definitively resolve the conflict cast doubt on the likelihood of the Sahrawi refugee crisis coming to an end anytime soon. This chapter seeks to analyse the refugee plight of the Sahrawi people, who are considered citizens of a *de facto state* – the Sahrawi Arab Democratic Republic (SADR) – given the unique circumstances of the Sahrawi refugee camps in Algeria and their relevance to the Western Sahara issue. The analysis draws primarily from qualitative data gathered during fieldwork in Algeria, including visits to Sahrawi refugee camps, as well as interviews conducted with representatives of Spanish NGOs engaged in assisting Sahrawi refugees and with Sahrawi individuals residing or temporarily staying in Spain.

Keywords: Western Sahara, *de facto state*, Sahrawi people, protracted refugee situation, Sahrawi Arab Democratic Republic (SADR), Algeria

Introduction

Since 1975, successive generations of Sahrawis, the indigenous inhabitants of Western Sahara, a former Spanish colony in North Africa,[2] have been living in refugee camps in southwestern Algeria, near the city of Tindouf, struggling with difficult living conditions and a hot and dry desert climate. Over the years, the issue of the prolonged refugee status of Sahrawis, a direct consequence of the unresolved conflict over Western Sahara, has become a highly politicised one, especially in the context of the number of Sahrawi refugees and its possible impact on the planned referendum which should decide the future of Western Sahara and finally put an end to the conflict. The inability to organise the referendum

1   This chapter is the result of a research project financed by the National Science Centre (Narodowe Centrum Nauki), Poland, grant ID: 2017/25/B/HS5/00958.
2   Until 1975, known as the Spanish Sahara (*Sáhara Español*).

long awaited by the Sahrawis, despite three decades that have passed since the decision to hold it, has become a symbol of the impasse and helplessness of the international community regarding the Western Sahara issue. As a result, the Sahrawi refugee situation, which was initially supposed to be a temporary so-lution, has turned into one of the most long-lasting refugee crises in the world, most often compared to the problem of Palestinian refugees in Middle Eastern countries (see Farah 2008; Fiddian-Qasmiyeh 2012)[3] or Afghan refugees in Iran (see Chatty 2012).

A protracted refugee situation is, according to the definition used by the office of the United Nations High Commissioner for Refugees (UNHCR), a situation in which:

> ...refugees find themselves in a long-lasting and intractable state of limbo. Their lives may not be at risk, but their basic rights and essential economic, social and psychological needs remain unfulfilled after years in exile. A refugee in this situation is often unable to break free from enforced reliance on external assistance (UNHCR 2004, p. 1).

According to the UNHCR, a protracted refugee situation refers to populations that have been living in exile in the territory of a developing country for a period of five years or longer, with no visible signs of resolution or improvement of the situation that gave rise to their refugee status. An additional criterion is the size of the refugee population in a situation of prolonged refugeedom, defined by the UNHCR as a minimum of 25,000 people (UNHCR 2004, p. 2).[4] At the same time, in the case of Sahrawi refugees, it does not seem necessary to reflect on the question whether they are refugees, as their situation falls within the definition of a refugee contained in the Article 1A(2) of the Geneva Convention of 28 July 1951 (Convention Relating to the Status of Refugees). According to it, a refugee is a person who:

> (...) owing to well-founded fear of being persecuted for reasons of race, religion, nation-ality, membership of a particular social group or political opinion, is outside the country of his nationality and is unable or, owing to such fear, is unwilling to avail himself of the

---

3   It is worth emphasising that the POLISARIO Front was, to some extent, inspired by the Palestinian resistance movement, and the intentional similarity between the flags of the Sahrawi Arab Democratic Republic and Palestine (differing only in the pres-ence of a red crescent and a star on a white stripe in the Sahrawi flag) underscores this connection (Farah, 2008, p. 77).

4   At the same time, UNHCR publications emphasise that the size of the refugee pop-ulation should not constitute a rigid exclusion barrier for refugee populations that otherwise qualify as experiencing a protracted refugee situation.

protection of that country; or who, not having a nationality and being outside the country of his former habitual residence as a result of such events, is unable or, owing to such fear, is unwilling to return to it (UNHCR 1951).

It is worth noting that the over the forty-five-year presence of Sahrawi refugees in refugee camps in Algeria, a meeting space has been created for various types of actors involved in helping the population living there. This includes the Sahrawi camp administration (dominated by the POLISARIO Front), foreign non-governmental organisations, Algerian authorities, international organisations providing humanitarian aid, as well as representatives of the host society – Algerians, who have shown support and solidarity with the Sahrawi people over the years. Moreover, the camps themselves appear to serve a variety of purposes, from protecting and caring for the refugee population within them to testing in practice the functionality of the Sahrawi state.

This chapter is based largely on qualitative data collected during fieldwork in Algeria, including Sahrawi refugee camps (2016, 2017, 2023), Morocco and the Morocco-controlled territory of Western Sahara (2013, 2019, 2020), as well as in Mauritania (2019). This also includes interviews and conversations with representatives of Spanish non-governmental organisations involved in helping Sahrawi refugees, Sahrawis living or staying temporarily in Spain (including activists of the POLISARIO Front), conducted in 2019, 2022 and 2023 in Madrid, Salamanca, Vitoria-Gasteiz, Bilbao, Las Palmas de Gran Canaria, and Santiago de Compostela. The conversations and interviews were conducted in Spanish, French, and (to a lesser extent) English. While gathering data, qualitative research methods were mainly used (in-depth interviews, informal conversations, observations – both open and covert, participating and non-participating), as well as elements of ethnographic research, including multi-sited ethnography that does not limit itself to one specific location. In addition, a critical analysis of the literature on the subject, official documents and the press has been carried out, in which the historical method and elements of discourse analysis have been applied.

Children of the Clouds

The Sahrawis, or "people of the desert", "children of the clouds"[5] – as they are sometimes called, were traditionally nomads and mainly camel herders

---

5 A term popular especially in Spanish - *Hijos de las nubes*. The Sahrawi nomads, traveling with their herds of animals, followed the clouds in search of rain. *Hijos de las nubes, la última colonia* (2012) – "Children of the Clouds, the Last Colony" - is also

(sometimes also sheep and goats), of mixed Berber-Arab origin. Their lineage comes from the Berbers from the Sanhaja confederation, who adopted Islam at the turn of the 8th and 9th centuries. Around the 13th century, Arabs arrived in these areas, probably from the area of today's Yemen. The process of the mixing of both groups, including the Arabisation of the Berbers, lasted until the 16th century, resulting in a group professing Sunni Islam and speaking Hassaniya Arabic, which contains many words of Berber origin (Kosidło 2012, p. 15-16; Broglia / Volpato 2008, p. 106). It is also used by the people of Mauritania. Mauritanians (especially what is referred to as the White Moors / Bidan Moors) are definitely closest to the Sahrawi people, not only in terms of language, but also wider culture, including their clothes,[6] customs and traditions.[7]

According to the UNHCR's understanding of protracted refugee situations, they are the result of a political impasse, but they are not inevitable, as they stem from political action or lack thereof (UNHCR 2004). This was also the case of Sahrawi refugees, most often perceived as the consequence of the unfinished (or, if one prefers, failed) decolonisation of Western Sahara, which took place in the mid-1970s. The difficult internal situation in Spain related to the serious illness of General Francisco Franco, as well as the internal problems of Morocco in the first two decades after gaining independence, prompted Hassan II, then head of the Sharifian monarchy, to take radical actions to implement his foreign policy. At the beginning of November 1975, at his initiative, what is referred to as the Green March took place,[8] during which 250,000–300,000 Moroccans (mainly civilian volunteers) marched into the territory of the then Spanish Sahara, thus

---

the title of a documentary film about the situation of the Sahrawi population and the conflict over Western Sahara with the participation of Javier Bardem.

6 Traditional Sahrawi clothing includes *melfha/melafa/meulfeu* for women and *daraa/drâa* for men (in Mauritania more commonly known as *boubou*).

7 This was repeatedly emphasised by Sahrawi interlocutors living both inside and outside the refugee camps. Moreover, Mauritania is the only country, next to Algeria, to which Sahrawis living in refugee camps can travel without major problems. In the case of Algeria – mainly by bus or air transport via Tindouf airport, using identity cards issued by the SADR authorities. As for Mauritania, travel takes place mainly by land through the desert. Crossing the border often takes place in an area where there are no border posts or any control, so it may not be entirely legal, but according to the Author's interlocutors, such people do not have any problems in Mauritania (Information based on interviews during fieldwork in April and May 2016, Boujdour camp, Tindouf province, Algeria and in Salamanca, Castille and León, Spain in July 2019).

8 In Western Saharan historiography, it is referred to as the "Black March".

embodying Moroccan claims to the area and attempting to realise the idea of Greater Morocco (Al-Maghrib Al-Kabir), whose historical territory was to extend from Gibraltar in the north to the Senegal River in the south, while in the west the border was to be the coast of the Atlantic Ocean, and in the east – the western Sahara from Béchar to Tindouf. In other words, Greater Morocco was to include not only Western Sahara (and former Spanish possessions in North Africa), but also western Algeria, most of Mauritania, part of Mali, and even pieces of Senegal (Kosidło 2012, p. 30). As a consequence of the Moroccan incursion and the withdrawal of Spain, an armed conflict occurred (1975-1991), in which Morocco and its ally Mauritania fought against the POLISARIO Front – a political and military organisation representing the Sahrawis. The POLISARIO Front (*Frente Popular por la Liberación de Saguía el Hamra y Río de Oro*) was created on 10 May 1973 and its main goal was the armed struggle against the Spanish colonizer. However, as the second congress of the POLISARIO in 1974 showed, it was guided by a whole range of socialist slogans and democratic ideas, as well as anti-colonialism, anti-tribalism (after all, the Sahrawis belonged to different tribes), anti-feudalism, women's equality, and pan-Arabism. Their struggle was to include, on the one hand, social modernisation, as well as mass public participation in political life, and – on the other – nationalisation of the natural resources of Western Sahara and even support for Islamic institutions. Inspired by the views of Frantz Fanon, Ernest Che Guevara, and Amílcar Cabral, they wanted independence and revolution. It was the POLISARIO Front that took up arms in the face of the passivity of the Spanish troops remaining in the territory of Western Sahara, and following their withdrawal, it became the only force fighting the Moroccan and Mauritanian troops. On 27 February 1976, the Sahrawi Arab Democratic Republic was proclaimed in Bir Lehlu (Kosidło 2012, pp. 37-53). Three years later, in 1979, Mauritania withdrew from the conflict, unable to cope with the attacks of POLISARIO troops despite the military support of France (Operation *Lamantin*, 1977-1978). The war with Morocco lasted until 6 September 1991, when the signed ceasefire came into force, under which the final solution to the conflict was to be a referendum deciding on the future of the disputed territory (independence or incorporation into the Moroccan state), the course and organisation of which was to be supervised by the United Nations Mission for the Referendum in Western Sahara (*Mission des Nations Unies pour l'Organisation d'un Référendum au Sahara Occidental*, MINURSO) (Mundy 2006, pp. 276-277).

Over time, Algeria became the main antagonist of the Moroccan state in the Western Saharan conflict. Houari Boumédiène, president of Algeria in the years 1965-1978, supported the POLISARIO Front at the beginning of the clashes, considering it a representative of the Sahrawi population. He believed that the inhabitants of Western Sahara should decide for themselves about their future, and the Algerian state did not make any territorial claims to the Western Sahara territory, although it made plans for future economic interests with an independent Western Sahara (Kosidło 2012, p. 40). Moreover, the Madrid Accords of 14 November 1975, signed by Spain, Morocco and Mauritania, which purported to establish the division of the Western Saharan territory between the latter two states, were in contradiction with the arrangements adopted at the meeting of the leaders of Algeria, Morocco and Mauritania, which took place in 1970 in the Mauritanian city of Nouadhibou, and the resolutions of which were repeated in 1973 at a meeting in Agadir. A common opinion was then expressed that Western Sahara should gain independence in accordance with the UN General Assembly resolution of 14 December 1960 (Declaration on the Granting of Independence to Colonial Countries and Peoples) (Kasznik-Christian 2006, pp. 422-424; Mundy 2006, p. 281). However, the Madrid Accords were in fact only a confirmation of a certain existing state of affairs, a process that had already started over a week earlier with the Green March of Hassan II. In the following decades, the SADR authorities, but also some researchers of the Western Saharan issue, such as the Spanish historian Pablo San Martín (2010, pp.105-106), have questioned the Madrid Accords and their validity. Sahrawi politicians to this day also argue that Morocco's annexation of the Spanish Sahara was a violation of the principle of *uti possidetis*, which was already in force on the African continent at the beginning of the conflict in 1975. Moreover, in their assessment of the illegality of Moroccan actions, they refer to documents published in October 1975: the report of the UN Visiting Mission and the subsidiary opinion of the International Court of Justice, as well as to the fact that in November 1979 the UN General Assembly adopted resolution 34/37, in which the right to self-determination of the inhabitants of Western Sahara was recognised as inalienable (Interview with Hamdi Bueha 2016; Kłosowicz 2017, pp. 148, 181).[9]

In the context of Algeria's involvement in the Western Saharan independence process, it should also be noted that for the authorities in Algiers, the support provided to the Sahrawis and the SADR was also an element of a policy aimed at securing their own state territory against possible new Moroccan attempts

---

9 Interestingly, the ICJ's subsidiary opinion, containing some ambiguities, was used by Hassan II as a propaganda element allegedly confirming Morocco's rights to the territory of Western Sahara (which was probably more than a positive over-interpretation of the ICJ's opinion – Author's note) (Kosidło 2012, pp. 43-44).

to take over parts of Algerian territory (this concerns the southwestern part of Algeria, which, according to the idea of Greater Morocco, was to be part of the Moroccan state). Thus, independent Western Sahara would in this case play the role of a buffer state. After the conflict over Western Sahara began, Algiers was afraid of Rabat attempting further territorial conquests, so it decided to group its troops in the border territory, near Tindouf. At that time, there were even direct clashes between the two armies: in 1976, the Algerians lost a battle against Moroccan troops near Amgala, after which diplomatic relations between Morocco and Algeria were severed until 1988 (Kasznik-Christian 2006, pp. 422-424). Even today, bilateral relations are not the best (the land border between the two countries has been closed since 1994), although many hopes were associated with Morocco's accession to the African Union in January 2017 and evident attempts by the Kingdom to become more involved in the affairs of the African continent[10]. The earlier absence of Morocco in this body was also related to the Western Saharan issue and the fact that, as a result of Algiers' efforts, in 1982, the SADR was admitted to the AU's progenitor – the Organisation of African Unity (OAU), which led to Morocco leaving the body two years later. Some commentators of international relations in the Maghreb hoped that Morocco's return to African politics under the rule of Mohammed VI would also revive the Arab Maghreb Union – a regional integration organisation established in 1989, which until now, due to strained relations between Morocco and Algerian, has not been very active (Kłosowicz 2017, p. 148).

In discussions on the current situation of Sahrawi refugees, the issue of the responsibility of the Spanish state also appears, not only as an entity that, in principle, should have decolonised the territory, but also in terms of its responsibility for the fate of its own citizens. After all, many Sahrawis who found themselves in the refugee camps in Algeria, had Spanish identity cards and, therefore, Spanish citizenship. In 2023, the coalition of Spanish left-wing parties Sumar proposed in Congress a new naturalisation law for the Sahrawis that would enable them to obtain Spanish citizenship after two years of residency in the country under the condition that they were born in Spanish Sahara before 1976 or that they are the children of parents born in the territory before this date (Sánchez / Ortiz 2023).[11] Up until today, this has been possible, but much more difficult. Possessing

---

10 More on Moroccan-Algerian relations see: Chapter 4 and Chapter 6 of this book.

11 In 2015, the Spanish government approved granting Spanish citizenship in this way to the Sephardi Jews originating from Spain, specifically to the descendants of the communities expelled by the Edict of Granada of 1492.

Spanish passports allows Sahrawis to travel freely, for example, to the territory of Western Sahara controlled by Morocco.[12] The above-mentioned responsibility of Spain for its own stranded citizens of Sahrawi origin and the failure to ensure the actual decolonisation of the territory of the Spanish Sahara are also often raised by Spanish civil society, including multitudes of Spanish citizens (Spaniards, as well as Basques, Catalans or Galicians) involved in helping Sahrawi refugees living in Algeria, mainly through dozens of associations of friendship or solidarity with the Sahrawi people.[13]

As a result of the unfinished decolonisation, most of the territory of Western Sahara (approx. 80%) is under Moroccan control, including rich deposits of phosphates and other natural resources, as well as access to sea fishing grounds, while the rest – entirely desert areas (approx. 20%) – is administered by the SADR, referred to as the Liberated Territories (*Territorios Liberados*) or Free Zone (*Zona Libre*). This division was stabilised in the 1980s by the construction of the Moroccan Western Sahara Wall (the Berm), i.e., a sandy and well-fortified embankment dividing the territory of Western Sahara into two parts. Year-round settlement in the Liberated Territories is a big challenge for the Sahrawis since these are desert areas where access to water is difficult. Moreover, transport connections are very limited. Nevertheless, the SADR maintains several permanent settlements there, the most important of which include Bir Lehlu, formally the administrative capital of the SADR,[14] and Tifariti, the seat of the parliament of the Sahrawi Arab Democratic Republic – the Sahrawi National Council (*Concejo Nacional Saharaui*), and of the only Sahrawi university, founded in 2013,

---

12 Interviews conducted with Sahrawis living in the Boujdour refugee camp during fieldwork in April and May 2016, Tindouf Province, Algeria.

13 The Author's conversations with representatives of Spanish associations of solidarity with the Sahrawi people from various autonomous communities during the 44th EUCOCO in Vitoria-Gasteiz (22-23 November 2019). The story of one of the members of such an association from Castile and León Autonomous Community seems emblematic in this context. He admitted that his involvement in helping the Sahrawis initially stemmed from a certain sense of guilt, felt because of Spanish policy regarding Western Saharan issue and leaving the Sahrawis "at the mercy of Morocco". This man, in his youth (during the rule of General Franco), completed compulsory military service in the Spanish Sahara, which made him feel even more obliged to later support Sahrawi cause.

14 The historical (and only official – in accordance with Article 4 of the Sahrawi Constitution) capital of the SADR is the city of El Aaiún (Laâyoune), which is located on the territory controlled by Morocco (ICT Policy Africa 2015).

the University of Tifariti (*Universidad de Tifariti*). Currently, it is estimated that about 30,000-40,000 people live in the Liberated Territories. This area helps the Sahrawis to maintain at least partial contact with their former nomadic life. Camels, as already mentioned, have traditionally been a key element of the existence of Sahrawi nomadic herders and the basis of their cultural identity. Due to the conflict over Western Sahara and the subsequent need to live in refugee camps in Algeria, many Sahrawis who had led a nomadic lifestyle before the outbreak of the conflict were forced to change their way of life.[15] The Liberated Territories make it possible, to some extent, to maintain the traditions of pastoral nomads also for part of the population living in refugee camps by leading a semi-sedentary lifestyle; i.e., living in refugee camps with their animals and moving to the Liberated Territories during the rainy season (February-June). There, Sahrawi herders lead their herds towards wadis (oued), i.e., dry valley forms that fill with water during the rainy season, thanks to which yerbia[16] vegetation appears.

Citizens of the Sahrawi Arab Democratic Republic

After signing the Madrid Accords, Moroccan and Mauritanian troops quickly began to occupy Western Sahara territory, brutally cracking down on the local population. Sahrawis who were trying to escape from urban settlements, mostly located on the coast or not far from it, towards the east into the desert, were attacked by Moroccan aircraft using napalm, white phosphorus, and cluster bombs. This was accompanied by arbitrary arrests and murders (mainly of men suspected of supporting the POLISARIO Front), as well as robberies and illegal occupation of Sahrawi homes. The goal was to eliminate the rebellious Sahrawis or at least get rid of them from the occupied territory. There were also reports of arbitrary arrests due to reluctance to display the Moroccan flag. The scale and brutality of the Moroccan attacks were so great that even representatives of the retreating Spanish army protested against them. However, in reality, the refugees could only count on the POLISARIO Front, for which, in the face of the Moroccan and Mauritanian invasion, the main goal, apart from repelling attacks by foreign troops, was the evacuation of the civilian population. Most of the

---

15 At the same time, it should not be forgotten that during colonial times, a large part of the Sahrawis permanently settled in the cities, leading a sedentary lifestyle long before the outbreak of the conflict.

16 This term refers to the vegetation that appears with the rain (Broglia / Volpato, 2008, pp. 108-116; Interviews and observations during field research in the Sahrawi refugee camps in Algeria, April-May 2016).

refugees were women, children, and elderly people (young men and those in their prime fought in the ranks of the POLISARIO), so the attacks had no military justification, and their goal was to intimidate the Sahrawi population and expel them from the disputed territory. Escaping into the desert is often interpreted as a natural reaction, innate to the Sahrawis, to imminent danger. It was not fully thought out, and its future consequences were certainly not predicted. As a result of the ongoing conflict and Moroccan attacks, the Sahrawi society was divided into refugees gathered in the Algerian desert near Tindouf and those who, for various reasons, failed to escape from the areas occupied by Moroccan or Mauritanian troops. It is worth emphasising that this division often took place within individual families. During conversations with Sahrawis in refugee camps in Algeria, the Author listened to at least several such stories in which, for example, the mother of a family had fled into the desert together with most of her children, while the husband fought in the ranks of the POLISARIO Front and her sick parents had stayed in the territories occupied by Moroccan troops with their granddaughter taking care of them. These people most often did not realise at the time that they might never see each other again or that it would be several decades before they could meet again (Kosidło 2012, pp. 51, 107-108; Dubois Migoya / Guiridi Aldanondo / López Belloso 2011, pp. 130-131).[17]

The Sahrawis seeking refuge in the desert (about half of the Sahrawi population at the time) first organised makeshift refugee camps in the part of Western Sahara controlled by the POLISARIO Front; i.e., in Guelta, Oum Dreyga and Al Mahbes. However, the possibilities of these camps, even in terms of basic provisions, quickly turned out to be insufficient. In addition, there are four known cases in which the Moroccan air force bombed the camps in Guelta and Oum Dreyga, using napalm and white phosphorus. Sahrawi refugees fled in panic even further east, guided and protected by POLISARIO fighters and, after crossing the border, Algerian troops. They moved onwards to settle in the vicinity of the Algerian city of Tindouf, located in southwestern Algeria, relatively close to the border, but beyond the range of operations of Moroccan troops. Additionally,

---

17 Also based on the Author's conversations with Sahrawis living in the Boujdour refugee camp, Tindouf province, Algeria, April-May 2016. Over the years 2004-2014, as part of the UNHCR "Confidence Building Measures" program, family visits took place (with interruptions), thanks to which Sahrawis from refugee camps in Algeria and Sahrawis from the areas occupied by Morocco could visit their loved ones. During the decade of the program, over 20,000 people benefited from it. For most of these people, it was the first time in 25 years that they could see their loved ones (Jacobsen 2017, pp. 9-12).

and significantly, the area boasted drinking water reservoirs. Moreover, it was noteworthy that the Tindouf region was already home to numerous Sahrawis, some of whom had sought refuge in the area during the Ifni War (1957-1958), while others had resided there for over a century. Interestingly, the majority were members of two confederations of the Reguibat tribe that prided itself on never paying homage to the Sultan of Morocco.[18] Therefore, sending Sahrawi refugees to the area of Tindouf was a conscious step taken by the Algerian authorities not only due to the above arguments, but also because of the already mentioned desire of Algiers to stop Morocco's territorial expansionism (Kosidło 2012, pp. 107-108; Dubois Migoya / Guiridi Aldanondo / López Belloso 2011, pp. 130-131)[19].

According to the census conducted by the Spanish colonial authorities in 1974, the territory of the Spanish Sahara was inhabited by 73,497 Sahrawis[20] and 26,126 Europeans. This census, obviously – considering the area in which it was conducted – did not include the Sahrawis living in southern Morocco, western Algeria or northern Mauritania, even though some Sahrawi tribes had long lived outside Western Sahara (or on the so-called borderland). As a result of conflicts with the colonial authorities that had been going on for some time or the desire to emigrate for work, many Sahrawis had left for neighbouring territories. Most likely, those who were still leading a nomadic lifestyle in the first half of the 1970s were also not included. For the reasons above, this number was questioned by representatives of the Sahrawi population in later years in the context of the debate concerning who is considered eligible to take part in the planned independence referendum (Kosidło 2012, pp. 41, 104). The issue of the size of the Sahrawi population, especially those living in refugee camps, is problematic to this day. At the end of 2004, according to data published by the

---

18 Members of the Reguibat tribe also constituted the majority of the POLISARIO Front.
19 The most complete compendium published so far about the repressions of the Moroccan authorities against the Sahrawi population from the beginning of the conflict in 1975 until 2010 and the suppression of the Sahrawi protests in Gdeim Izik, was prepared by two researchers: Carlos Martín Berestain and Eloisa González Hidalgo (2012). The report is almost 1,000 pages long and was published in two volumes in Spanish with a summary in English of over a hundred pages for each volume. It was published by the Institute for International Cooperation and Development Studies (Instituto de Estudios sobre Desarrollo y Cooperación Internacional, HEGOA) of the University of the Basque Country (Universidad del País Vasco) in Bilbao. The author had the opportunity to conduct conversations about the said report during her visit to HEGOA on 25-26 November 2019. For more, see: Martín Berestain / González Hidalgo 2012.
20 Only 32,516 of them received Spanish identity cards.

UNHCR, the Sahrawi refugee population in Algeria amounted to 165,000 people (UNHCR 2004, p. 107). Over the last two decades, the numbers of Sahrawi refugees provided by different sources have varied significantly. At one point, the most frequently cited discrepancies were between the data presented by the UN, putting the number of refugees at around 91,000, while the Sahrawis themselves claimed that it amounted to around 200,000 people. In order to put an end to these doubts, in 2018, an official UNHCR report was published on the size of the Sahrawi refugee population in Algeria. Based on the research results of the UNHCR expert mission that stayed in the camps in January 2018, the Sahrawi population was estimated at 173,600 people. This number does not include Sahrawis living outside the camps, such as Sahrawi students over the age of 18 who are studying abroad. The discrepancies in the number of refugees so far resulted from the fact that most of the published data were estimates from various sources (the Algerian government, non-governmental organisations, the UNHCR, the World Food Program), with divergent and often not entirely clear methodology. Moreover, the figure of approximately 90,000 refugees often appeared in the data published by the UNHCR; which in fact was the number of the most *vulnerable* people, while it was later repeated many times as the number of all Sahrawi refugees (UNHCR 2018, pp. 3-4, 8-10, 16-17).

After arriving at the Algerian hamada near Tindouf, Sahrawi refugees (mainly women, because the men fought in the ranks of the POLISARIO) organised three large camps: Laâyoune (El Aaiún), Smara (Esmara) and Dakhla (Dajla). In 1985, due to the increase in the number of refugees, a fourth camp was established, i.e., Ausserd (Auserd). The newest and fifth of the Sahrawi refugee camps existing today – Boujdour (El Bojador) – was established as a result of increased settlement in the vicinity of the sub-camp of 27 February (27 de febrero),[21] which functioned primarily as a girls' vocational boarding school.[22] The distances between individual camps vary from 20 to 100 km (with Dakhla being the furthest from the other camps), a deliberate choice by their founders. Given the ongoing conflict and past experiences of aerial attacks, there were concerns that the Moroccan air force might conduct bombings within Algerian territory. By maintaining large distances between the camps, it was hoped that the losses would not affect the entire Sahrawi refugee population. Moreover, at the beginning of the

---

21 Named to commemorate the day the Sahrawi Arab Democratic Republic was proclaimed.

22 The Laâyoune and Smara camps have the largest population, according to UNHCR data, each with over 50,000 inhabitants (UNHCR 2018, p. 5).

refugee camps' existence, when the health care system was just being organized, epidemics were a common problem. The distance between the camps can also be seen as an attempt to limit the spread of infectious diseases. Each refugee camp was named after one of the cities left in the occupied territory. After the creation of the first four camps, it was decided to establish a camp that was to be the administrative centre of the SADR – Rabouni,[23] thus serving as an informal capital where the SADR ministries, state television, two largest hospitals (the main hospital and a military hospital) are based, as well as the offices of humanitarian organisations operating in the camps (Dubois Migoya / Guiridi Aldanondo / López Belloso 2011, pp. 131-132).

The administrative structure of the camps is intended to reflect the territorial division of the Sahrawi state established in Article 16 of the SADR Constitution. This division has three levels: provinces (*wilayat*), municipalities (*dawair*) and districts (*baladiat*). Each camp is considered one province (*wilaya*), headed by a governor (*wali*). Each *wilaya* is divided into several communes, which are governed by mayors. In turn, each commune (*daira*) is divided into four districts (*hays*, in Spanish called *barrios*), corresponding to the districts mentioned in the SADR constitution (Dubois Migoya / Guiridi Aldanondo / López Belloso 2011, pp. 132, 138-139; Kosidło 2012, p. 110; ICT Policy Africa: "The Constitution of the Sahrawi Arab Democratic Republic" 2015). According to the UNHCR report from January 2018, the governors of two of the five camps were women, while at the *dawair* level they held 100% of the mayor positions (116 out of 116) (UNHCR 2018). This proves the high position of women in Sahrawi society. Moreover, in the refugee camps, due to the history of their establishment, they also enjoy the status of founding mothers, who enabled the Sahrawi people to survive at a difficult moment in their history. Additionally, in each camp, apart from the Governor, there is also the institution of the Chief of Protocol (*Director de Protocolo*),[24] who is responsible, e.g., for: organising the stay of foreigners, such as workers of humanitarian organisations, volunteers, scientists

---

23 This decision was dictated, e.g., by much better transport connections with the outside world (the proximity of the Tindouf airport) than in the case of the previously mentioned temporary capital of the SADR in Bir Lehlu located in the Liberated Territories. Moreover, with the increasing presence of foreign employees of international organisations and NGOs, an administrative centre seemed to be a necessity.

24 There is also the institution of the *Director Nacional de Protocolo*, which consents to the stay of foreigners in the refugee camps and may also, in some cases, take over some of the responsibilities of the Heads of Protocol of individual *wilayas*.

(Observations from field research in the Sahrawi refugee camps, Tindouf Province, Algeria, April-May 2016).

The main problems of Sahrawi refugees in Algeria include: the hot and dry desert climate (in summer, temperatures can reach over 50 degrees Celsius), limited access to water (water is delivered by water wagons), difficult living conditions (not all camps are electrified, there is no water sewage system), insufficient amounts of fresh and diversified food (particularly experienced by children and pregnant women, which often leads to their anaemia), inadequate educational and health infrastructure, lack of employment opportunities related to a very limited labour market. Nevertheless, despite unfavourable natural conditions and limited access to financial and material resources (especially in the initial period of the existence of the refugee camps), the Sahrawis (or rather: Sahrawi women) managed to create a quite well-functioning health service and an education system (primary and secondary education, as well as pre-school). This is quite an achievement, considering that during Spanish colonial rule, only 10% of Sahrawi women could read and write. Today, illiteracy among the Sahrawis is practically non-existent, and the SADR's achievements in the field of education are so well known that the widespread opinion is that they are the best educated nation in North Africa. Each *daira* has at least one school, a kindergarten (or kindergarten class) and a nursery. Education is free and compulsory for both boys and girls. The schools are coeducational, classes are taught in the Hassaniya dialect, and from the third grade of primary school, children begin to learn Spanish quite intensively. Secondary schools also have dormitories. Some of the teachers are volunteers, e.g., from Cuba or Spain. The best students leave the refugee camps to continue their studies abroad[25] in Algeria, Spain, Cuba, and in the past (before the outbreak of conflicts resulting from what is referred to as the Arab Spring) – also to Libya or Syria (Chatty / Fiddian-Qasmiyeh / Crivello 2012, pp. 53-62). According to one of the slogans proclaimed at the beginning of the POLISARIO Front's activity – "First education, then liberation" (San Martín 2010, p. 136), building statehood and the future society of an independent Western Sahara is to be primarily served by education. Representatives of the SADR administrative apparatus, in conversations with the Author, very often

---

25 They also often attend secondary school in Algeria. In the past, many Sahrawi children were sent to Cuba, where they finished high school and then college. Currently, this percentage has decreased (such a trip was most often associated with the child's absence from the camps for several years, which is why closer locations are now preferred – Algeria or Spain).

emphasised the priority importance of two areas: health care and education. Investments made in these areas are visible, e.g., new outpatient clinics, modern ambulances, computer rooms in schools, libraries, of which most are funded by Spanish associations of solidarity with the Sahrawi people or humanitarian organisations (Interview with Mohamed Bani and the Author's observations during her visit to the camps; Kosidło 2012, p. 116). In addition, there are also art schools in the camps: *Escuela de Formación Audiovisual Abidin Kaid Saleh* and *Escuela Saharaui de Artes Salek Mulud Sidi Abdala*. In both cases, part of the professorial staff are foreigners (often well-known names in the world of film or fine arts), who come for longer or shorter stays in the refugee camps, during which they conduct classes with young Sahrawis and carry out film and artistic projects, some of which can be seen at events organized in the refugee camps, i.e., at the FiSahara international film festival (*Festival Internacional de Cine de Sáhara Occidental*) or at the ARTifariti art festival (*Encuentros Internacionales de Arte y Derechos Humanos del Sahara Occidental*), organised in the Liberated Territories (Interview with Omar Ahmed; observations made by the Author during a visit to both schools, Tindouf province, May 2016).[26]

It is also worth mentioning that there are also three museums in the refugee camps: the National Museum of Resistance (*Museo Nacional de la Resistencia*), the Museum of the People's Liberation Army (*Museo del Ejército de Liberación Popular*),[27] and the National Museum of the Sahrawi People (*Museo Nacional del Pueblo Saharaui*). These institutions are further elements in the process of nation-building and Sahrawi statehood – projects carried out by the Sahrawi Arab Democratic Republic since its founding in 1976. In this process, the refugee camps are not only, as Randa Farah (2008) puts it, "incubators of political organization", but they also constitute "repositories of collective memory".[28]

---

26 The FiSahara Festival, which was created with the help and involvement of representatives of Spanish civil society, enjoys quite a popularity. Since 2008, Javier Bardem, who is its great advocate, has regularly participated in the event, and thanks to his support, other stars of world cinema also visit the camps (FiSahara, Web; ARTifariti, Web).

27 This was the name of the armed branch of the POLISARIO Front.

28 It is hard to disagree with R. Farah. It seems that the POLISARIO Front has managed to some extent to overcome the strong clan and tribal loyalties, present among the Sahrawis before the outbreak of the conflict. Residents of refugee camps most often emphasise that the only and final goal is an independent Sahrawi state (Farah 2008, pp. 76-81, 84). During the conversations with Sahrawis in the refugee camps, the Author heard such wishes many times, and the slogan *¡Viva el Sáhara Libre!* ("Long live the free Sahara!") is repeated like a spell by children, young people, women, men, old people, former and current POLISARIO fighters, wedding party participants, schoolteachers,

The Algerian authorities do not interfere in the management of the Sahrawi refugee camps, which is entirely the responsibility of the SADR administration, but they nevertheless provide access to basic services, such as water and electricity supplies.[29] The issue of security in the refugee camps also rests with the Sahrawi administration, even though the city of Tindouf is a large military garrison and the Algerian army is stationed not far from the refugee camps. In front of each of the camps, there is a post of the Sahrawi National Police (*Policía Nacional Saharaui*), which also maintains order in the camps themselves. The only exception is Rabouni, which, like the access roads to the camps and the Liberated Territories, is patrolled by the Sahrawi National Gendarmerie *(Gendermería Nacional Saharaui)*. It is worth mentioning that after the events of October 2011, when three foreigners (two Spaniards and one Italian), employees of non-governmental organisations providing humanitarian aid,[30] were kidnapped from Rabouni camp, the Sahrawi security services are quite oversensitive to the security of foreigners, who are subject to a curfew from 7 p.m. to 7 a.m., during which they cannot move between camps unless with police or military escort (Observations during field research in Sahrawi refugee camps, Tindouf province, April-May 2016; Kosidło 2012, pp. 110-111).

Finally, it is also worth discussing the initiatives related to the education of young Sahrawis, but also the humanitarian aid provided to refugees by Spanish civil society. Every year, during the hottest summer months, several thousand Saharan children, aged 7 to 12, go to Spain as part of the *Vacaciones en Paz*

---

and others (Observations during field research in Sahrawi refugee camps in Tindouf area, Algeria, April-May 2016).

29 During the Author's stay in the Sahrawi refugee camps, Algerians gave another expression of support for the Western Sahara cause. 1 May 2016 was proclaimed the Day of Solidarity with the Sahrawi Nation in Algeria. A large celebration was organised in Oran, attended by hundreds of Sahrawis from the refugee camps, most of them women. The event was broadcast live on Algerian and Sahrawi television (Observations from field research in the Sahrawi refugee camps, Tindouf Province, Algeria, April-May 2016).

30 All those kidnapped were released a few months later in northern Mali. A newly established terrorist organisation with links to Al-Qaeda in the Islamic Maghreb, the Movement for Oneness and Jihad in West Africa (*Mouvement pour l'unicité et le jihad en Afrique de l'Ouest*, MUJAO), claimed responsibility for the kidnapping (González 2012). Representatives of the SADR's Ministry of Foreign Affairs claim that the Moroccan services were behind the kidnapping, and that Moroccan agents are still trying to penetrate their structures (Interview with Hamdi Bueha).

("Holidays in Peace") program,[31] organised and financed by the associations of friendship and solidarity with the Sahrawi people (and by the people involved in their activities), as well as sometimes being co-funded by the Spanish Agency for International Development Cooperation (*Agencia Española de Cooperación Internacional para el Desarrollo*) or local regional authorities. The Spanish government, for its part, legalises the stay of children qualified for the program. Children live with local families, learn the Spanish language, go sightseeing, take part in various sports and cultural activities, and are also provided with medical and dental care. Children are qualified for the program based on their academic performance or health problems that require treatment that cannot be obtained in the refugee camps.[32] It has sometimes happened in the past that the receiving family later adopted the child they were taking care of (this is especially the case when these children required constant specialised medical care, to which they did not have access in the camps), or offered care as a kind of foster family, enabling the child to get an education in a Spanish high school and later even at university. However, it should be emphasised that the adoption of Sahrawi children is not promoted either by the POLISARIO Front or by the activists from solidarity associations, so such situations are exceptions rather than the rule.[33] It is worth adding that most often the help of Spanish families does not end after the summer months. The Sahrawi children frequently return to the camps with various types of gifts for their siblings and parents, often additionally equipped with small (from the perspective of the Spanish, but not necessarily the Sahrawis) financial resources. Financial support is sometimes provided year-round.[34]

---

31 On a smaller scale, versions of this program (for a dozen to several dozen people) also took place in Italy, France, and the United States.

32 In the past, priority was also given to children whose parent or parents had died during the war.

33 Sometimes against the wishes of Spanish "foster" parents, who often establish deep emotional bonds with the children they take care of, as the Author could see during conversations with Spanish families receiving Sahrawi children in Madrid (14 July 2019) and in Vitoria-Gasteiz (22-23 November 2019).

34 Interview with Fatma Mehdi Hassam – Secretary General of the National Union of Sahrawi Women (*Unión Nacional de Mujeres Saharauis*), Boujdour camp, Tinduf province, Algeria, 30 April 2016; Conversation (and electronic correspondence) of the Author with Pepe Taboada (14 July 2019, Madrid) – until February 2021, president (currently honorary president) of the pan-Spanish organization coordinating the activities of solidarity associations supporting the Sahrawis - *Coordinadora Estatal de Asociaciones Solidarias con el Sáhara*. Pepe Taboada has been involved in the *Vacaciones en Paz* program since its inception. Like the previously mentioned member of the solidarity

Interestingly, with the intensification of the *Vacaciones en Paz* program in the 1990s, and the resulting increase in financial resources brought by children, with the simultaneous inflow of money sent by the Sahrawi diaspora in Europe, the economy in the refugee camps changed and small businesses began to emerge (shops, hairdressers, eateries). The availability of some food and industrial products has also increased. On the other hand, these changes contributed to deepening economic inequality among different members of the population living in the camps.[35]

Conclusions

The protracted exile of Sahrawis in Algeria has continued for almost five decades. The three refugee camps they founded have become six, some of which have turned into medium-sized cities with a population of over fifty thousand, where subsequent generations are born and die. When proclaiming the Sahrawi Arab Democratic Republic on 27 February 1976, the leaders of the POLISARIO Front did not expect that over the next decades they would have to build a state whose territory would be limited to refugee camps in the Algerian hamada and a desert patch of their native land, practically isolated from the outside world. However, for the Sahrawis, who have few other choices, the refugee camps in the Tindouf province in Algeria have become a substitute for their own statehood, a kind of test of perseverance for both the rulers and the ruled, and – at the same time – an expression of the durability of the idea of Western Saharan independence, an act of courage and persistence, perhaps surprising even to the Sahrawis themselves.

The purpose of establishing the refugee camps was obvious: to provide care and shelter for the Sahrawi population. Additionally, Algeria, fearing Morocco's territorial expansionism, secured its southwestern borders and the territorial integrity of the state thanks to the presence of the Sahrawis (and, above all, POLISARIO fighters). What or who is benefitting from the prolonged exile of

---

association from Castile and León, Pepe Taboada also performed military service in the Spanish Sahara. What is more, he witnessed Operation *Golondrina* (Swallow), i.e. the withdrawal of the Spanish troops from the colony, (Crivello / Fiddian-Qasmiyeh 2012, pp. 85-118).

35 Interview with a young Sahrawi woman studying at one of the universities in Castile and León, former participant of the *Vacaciones en Paz* program, Salamanca, 12 July 2019. Another interesting issue is the emergence of cultural changes that are taking place in the camps because of the program - e.g. children's food preferences are changing. For more, see: Cozza 2012, pp. 119-141.

Sahrawis today? Despite the hardships of refugee life and their dependence on humanitarian aid,[36] which must not be forgotten, the Sahrawis are not passive in their refugee life, they are not just victims. They consider themselves a "nation in exile" rather than refugees. They have organised the camps and their life in them on the model of the state and society they want to create after returning to the territory of Western Sahara, and – as should be emphasised – they have several successes in this field, which they are very skilful in boasting about. From the axiological point of view, life in the camps can be perceived as an act of resistance, an expression of opposition to the still unresolved conflict and one of the few peaceful possibilities to draw the attention of the international community to the problem of Western Sahara. On the other hand, Sahrawi refugees do not have many other options at the moment. Theoretically, they could move to the Liberated Territories, but in practice, despite the loud announcements of the SADR authorities, it is impossible, because this area does not have the conditions (and will not have them anytime soon) to accommodate an additional 170-180 thousand people. Moreover, after relocating to the Liberated Territories, Sahrawis would formally cease to be refugees and would become internally displaced persons (IDPs). Thus, they would no longer be eligible for the international assistance currently provided to them. The issue of maintaining security in and around refugee camps in the face of threats emanating from the still troubled Sahel region also remains open. In addition, one significant problem, which is perhaps too rarely mentioned, are the high intergenerational tensions, including the younger generation's increasingly expressed lack of consent to continue the fight for independence in a peaceful way, which was visible in their support for resuming military actions in November 2020.

The Sahrawis are sometimes referred to as "the most extraordinary refugees". Over the years, the SADR authorities have skilfully disseminated this opinion despite subsequent attacks by the Moroccan propaganda machine trying to deprecate the Sahrawi achievements in the camps. Nevertheless, there are also cracks in this image. One of the allegations raised in scientific literature concerns the

---

36 The COVID-19 pandemic, which has limited the mobility of Sahrawis (including Sahrawi children under the *Vacaciones en Paz* program), has additionally increased dependence on humanitarian aid, including in the context of the fight against the coronavirus. In 2020, the EU allocated EUR 500,000 to support the Sahrawi health system in the fight against the pandemic. In 2021, an additional million euro was provided to support the vaccination campaign in the camps. Moreover, that same year, EUR 10 million was given in humanitarian aid, and these are funds coming from only one source (European Commission 2021).

instrumentalisation of the image of Sahrawi refugees by the POLISARIO Front to achieve the greatest possible benefits both inside and outside the camps. In this case, disseminating the ideal image of Sahrawi refugees is supposed to be a kind of performative act, not entirely consistent with the reality of the refugee camps. One of its elements is the presentation of refugee camps as "ideal secular spaces", as if in opposition to other Muslim communities, which is meant to prove the uniqueness of Sahrawi society. Among researchers dealing with Western Sahara, such a view is presented, for example, by Elena Fiddian-Qasmiyeh (2011; 2014), who is of the opinion that such a conscious strategy of political representation of the Sahrawis, i.e. the POLISARIO Front, denies the voice of people or groups breaking away from its framework, excluded from the officially promoted image of the camps (i.e. such examples would be conservative Muslims or the limitation of the visibility of Islam among the Sahrawis). Fiddian-Qasmiyeh believes that the concepts of secularism and religious tolerance were often raised by the POLISARIO Front, especially in contact with non-Sahrawis, to demonstrate the ideal nature of the Sahrawi refugee camps. She similarly perceives the image of strong and independent Sahrawi women, reinforced by the POLISARIO Front, as a means of strengthening support from various types of state and non-state actors in the Western world. Nevertheless, even if that is the case, in the context of the complete dependence of the Sahrawi refugees' existence on foreign aid, this seems hardly surprising. According to the data published by the European Commission (2023), nearly 80% of the Sahrawi refugees in Algeria rely on humanitarian assistance for their minimum daily food intake, while the dependence of the refugee population on humanitarian aid in the sector of health or education is no less.

References

ARTifariti: "Artifariti. Encuentros Internacionales de Arte y Derechos Humanos del Sahara Occidental", retrieved 23.12.2022, from http://www.artifariti.org.

Broglia, Alessandro / Volpato, Gabriele: "Pastoralism and Displacement: Strategies and Limitations in Livestock Raising by Sahrawi Refugees after Thirty Years of Exile", *Journal of Agriculture and Environment for International Development* 102 (1-2) 2008, pp. 105-122.

Chatty, Dawn (ed.): *Deterritorialized Youth. Sahrawi and Afghan Refugees at the Margins of the Middle East*. (Series: *Forced Migration*). Berghahn Books: New York–Oxford, 2012.

Chatty, Dawn / Fiddian-Qasmiyeh, Elena / Crivello, Gina: "Identity with/out Territory: Sahrawi Refugee Youth in Transnational Space". In: Chatty, Dawn (ed.): *Deterritorialized Youth. Sahrawi and Afghan Refugees at the Margins of the Middle East.* (Series: *Forced Migration*). Berghahn Books: New York–Oxford, 2012, pp. 37-84.

Conversation (and electronic correspondence) of the Author with Pepe Taboada, 2019.

Conversations with Spanish families receiving Sahrawi children in Madrid (14 July 2019) and in Vitoria-Gasteiz (22-23 November 2019).

Cozza, Nicola: "Food and Identity among Sahrawi Refugee Young People". In: Chatty, Dawn (ed.): *Deterritorialized Youth. Sahrawi and Afghan Refugees at the Margins of the Middle East.* (Series: *Forced Migration*). Berghahn Books: New York–Oxford 2012, pp. 119-142.

Crivello, Gina / Fiddian-Qasmiyeh, Elena: "The Ties that Bind: Sahrawi Children and the Mediation of Aid in Exile". In: Chatty, Dawn (ed.): *Deterritorialized Youth. Sahrawi and Afghan Refugees at the Margins of the Middle East.* (Series: *Forced Migration*). Berghahn Books: New York–Oxford, 2012, pp. 85-118.

Dubois Migoya, Alfonso / Guiridi Aldanondo, Luis / López Belloso, Maria: *Desarrollo Humano Local: de la teoría a la práctica. Los casos de la reconversión azucarera en Holguín (Cuba) y de los campamentos saharauis de Tinduf.* Hegoa: Bilbao, 2011.

European Commission: European Civil Protection and Humanitarian Aid Operations, 2021, *Algeria*, retrieved 29.10.2023, from https://ec.europa.eu/echo/where/africa/algeria_en.

European Commission. European Civil Protection and Humanitarian Aid Operations, 2023, *Algeria*, retrieved 23.10.2023, from https://civil-protection-humanitarian-aid.ec.europa.eu/where/middle-east-and-northern-africa/algeria_en.

Farah, Randa: "Refugee Camps in the Palestinian and Sahrawi National Liberation Movements: A Comparative Perspective", *Journal of Palestine Studies* 38 (2) 2008, pp. 76-93.

Fiddian-Qasmiyeh, Elena: *Conflicting Missions? The Politics of Evangelical Humanitarianism in the Sahrawi and Palestinian Protracted Refugee Situations,* MMG Working Paper 12-06, Göttingen 2012.

Fiddian-Qasmiyeh, Elena: *The Ideal Refugees. Gender, Islam, and the Sahrawi Politics of Survival.* Syracuse University Press: Syracuse, 2014.

Fiddian-Qasmiyeh, Elena: "The Pragmatics of Performance: Putting 'Faith' in Aid in the Sahrawi Refugee Camps", *Journal of Refugee Studies* 24 (3) 2011, pp. 533-547.

FiSahara: "FiSahara. Festival Internacional de Cine", retrieved 21.02.2021, from https://fisahara.es.

González, Miguel: "Exteriores confirma que los dos cooperantes liberados están bien", *El País* 18.7.2012, retrieved 24.6.2023, from https://elpais.com/politica/2012/07/18/actualidad/1342619563_870767.html.

ICT Policy Africa: "The Constitution of the Sahrawi Arab Democratic Republic". Adopted by the 14th Congress of the Frente POLISARIO, 16-20 December 2015, *ICT Policy Africa*, retrieved 14.8.2023, from https://ictpolicyafrica.org/en/document/iynr7udq57b?page=1.

Jacobsen, Karen: *"A Frozen Conflict and a Humanitarian Program that Works: UNHCR's Confidence Building Measures in Western Sahara.* Feinstein International Center, Tufts University: Boston, 2017. Retrieved, 12.6.2022 from https://reliefweb.int/sites/reliefweb.int/files/resources/CBM-in-Western-Sahara-Jacobsen-1.pdf.

Interview with a young Sahrawi woman studying at one of the universities in Castile and León, former participant of the *Vacaciones en Paz* program, Salamanca, 12 July 2019.

Interview with Fatma Mehdi Hassam – Secretary General of the National Union of Sahrawi Women (Unión Nacional de Mujeres Saharauis), Boujdour camp, Tinduf province, Algeria, 30 April 2016.

Kasznik-Christian, Aleksandra: *Algieria.* (Series: *Historia państw świata XX i XXI wieku*). Trio: Warszawa 2006.

Kłosowicz, Robert: *Konteksty dysfunkcyjności państw Afryki Subsaharyjskiej.* (Series: *Studia nad rozwojem*). Wydawnictwo Uniwersytetu Jagiellońskiego: Kraków, 2017.

Kosidło, Adam: *Sahara Zachodnia. Fiasko dekolonizacji czy sukces podboju 1975-2011.* Wydawnictwo Uniwersytetu Gdańskiego: Gdańsk, 2012.

Martín Berestain, Carlos / González Hidalgo, Eloisa: *El Oasis de la Memoria: Memoria Histórica y Violaciones de Derechos en el Sáhara Occidental: Tomo I, II.* Hegoa: Bilbao, 2012a. Retrieved 4.04.2023, from https://publicaciones.hegoa.ehu.eus/publications/281.

Martín Berestain, Carlos / González Hidalgo Eloisa: *The Oasis of Memory. Historical Memory and Human Rights Violations in Western Sahara.* Hegoa: Bilbao, 2012b.

Martín Berestain, Carlos / González Hidalgo, Eloisa:, *Truth, Justice and Reparation in the Western Sahara. The Oasis of Memory.* Hegoa: Bilbao, 2012c.

Mormul, Joanna: "Hijos de las nubes i 45 lat marzeń: uchodźcy Saharawi na terytorium Algierii", *Politeja*, 18 6(75) 2021, pp. 159-182, DOI: https://doi.org/10.12797/Politeja.18.2021.75.08.

Mundy, Jacob: "Neutrality or Complicity? The United States and the 1975 Moroccan Takeover of the Spanish Sahara", *The Journal of North African Studies*, 11 (3) 2006, pp. 275-306.

Observations during field research in Sahrawi refugee camps, Tindouf province, April-May 2016.

The Author's conversations with representatives of Spanish associations of solidarity with the Sahrawi people from various autonomous communities during the 44th EUCOCO in Vitoria-Gasteiz (22-23 November 2019).

The Author's conversations with Sahrawis living in the Boujdour refugee camp, Tindouf province, Algeria, April-May 2016.

San Martín, Pablo: *Western Sahara: The Refugee Nation*. (Series: Iberian and Latin American Studies). University of Wales Press: Cardiff, 2010.

Sánchez, Gabriela / Ortiz, Alberto: "Sumar propone en el Congreso dar la nacionalidad por carta de naturaleza a los saharauis nacidos bajo la administración Española", *elDiario.es*, 30.11.2023, retrieved 2.12.2023, from https://www.eldia rio.es/desalambre/sumar-propone-congreso-conceder-nacionalidad-carta-naturaleza-saharauis-nacidos-administracion-espanola_1_10731378.html.

UNHCR: "Convention and Protocol Relating to the Status of Refugees", 1951 [Convention], 1967 [Protocol], UNHCR. The UN Refugee Agency, retrieved 20.10.2022, from https://www.unhcr.org/media/convention-and-protocol-relating-status-refugees.

UNHCR: "Protracted Refugee Situations", Executive Committee of the High Commissioner's Programme, Standing Committee, 30th Meeting, UN Doc. EC/54/SC/CRP.14, 10.6.2004, retrieved 29.9.2023, from https://www.unhcr.org/statistics/unhcrstats/40ed5b384/protracted-refugee-situations.html?query=protracted%20refugee%20situation.

UNHCR: "Saharawi Refugees in Tindouf, Algeria: Total In-Camp Population. Official Report", March 2018, retrieved 22.12.2022, from https://www.usc.gal/export9/sites/webinstitucional/gl/institutos/ceso/descargas/UNHCR_Tindouf-Total-In-Camp-Population_March-2018.pdf.

UNHCR: "The State of the World's Refugees 2004, chapter 5: Protracted refugee situations: the search for practical solutions", 1.1.2005, retrieved 22.12.2022, from https://www.unhcr.org/4444afcb0.pdf.

Volpato, Gabriele / Waldstein, Anna: "Eghindi among Sahrawi Refugees of Western Sahara", *Medical Anthropology*, 33 (2) 2014, pp. 160-177.

Robert Kłosowicz, Joanna Mormul

Chapter 6. The Issue of Western Sahara in the International Relations of States Bordering on Its Territory - Morocco, Algeria, and Mauritania[1]

For over 45 years, the Western Sahara issue has remained a significant matter in international relations within the Maghreb region, leading not only to strained relations between Morocco and neighbouring states but also to Morocco's prolonged absence from the Organisation of African Unity and its successor, the African Union, until January 2017. This chapter examines the importance of the Western Sahara issue in the international relations of states bordering the Western Saharan territory, particularly focusing on Morocco and Algeria. Mauritania, historically, linguistically, and culturally close to the region, finds itself in a challenging position as it seeks to maintain neutrality amidst its powerful neighbours, both vying for leadership in the region. Furthermore, the chapter analyses the historical dimensions of the problem alongside its current state of development. It contextualises the issue within the post-colonial history of the Maghreb region and the broader international context to illustrate that the Western Sahara problem extends beyond the Maghreb, holding extra-regional implications. The research relies on qualitative analysis of existing sources such as official documents and the press, alongside a critical examination of literature pertaining to the subject. Additionally, qualitative data gathered during research visits in Algeria, Morocco, and Mauritania is incorporated into the study.

Keywords: Western Sahara, Morocco, Algeria, Mauritania, international relations, *de facto state*

Introduction

The Western Sahara issue, which has become a matter of international peace and security since the mid-1970s, continues to be a significant problem within

1   This chapter is the result of a research project financed by the National Science Centre (Narodowe Centrum Nauki), Poland, grant ID: 2017/25/B/HS5/00958. Certain sections of this chapter, pertaining to Mauritania's position on the Western Saharan conflict, have been derived from the revised segments of the previously published article titled *Policies of the Maghreb Countries Toward Western Sahara: Mauritania's Perspective* (Kłosowicz, 2022).

the Maghreb region, as well as on the entire African continent, causing tensions in the relations between Morocco and its closest and more distant neighbours. In recent years, this has been somewhat forgotten as a result of a certain state of political limbo related to the failure to implement the United Nations Security Council's stipulation that a referendum should be held in the Western Saharan territory of the former Spanish Sahara (*Sáhara Español*). Since 2017, however, the Western Sahara issue has again become a prominent focus of the media, which is undoubtedly linked to Morocco joining the African Union (AU), an organisation that brings together the African states. Morocco left the Organisation of African Unity (OAU), the AU's predecessor, on 12 November 1984 during the summit in Addis Ababa, in protest against inviting the state formed by the POLISARIO Front, the Sahrawi Arab Democratic Republic (SADR), to join the organisation. The issue of Western Sahara garnered even greater attention following the events of November 2020, when Moroccan and POLISARIO troops engaged in exchanges of fire, initially at Guerguerat and subsequently at various other locations along the truce line dividing Western Sahara between the Moroccan-occupied and POLISARIO-controlled sectors. (Reuters 2020, Web). The POLISARIO Front officially declared the end of the ceasefire, attributing the blame to Moroccan forces for crossing into the UN-patrolled buffered zone near Guerguerat. There, they conducted an operation to disperse Sahrawi protesters who had blocked the main road from Morocco through Western Sahara to Mauritania. Subsequently, the conflict has persisted as a low-intensity war. While the Moroccan incursion into the buffer zone is cited as the immediate cause of the POLISARIO decision, it is likely not without significance that the authorities of the Sahrawi Arab Democratic Republic (SADR) had long grappled with disenchanted youth. These youth, disillusioned with the lack of progress in the UN peace process, were eager to pursue a military solution to the conflict (Dworkin 2022)[2].

---

2   This explanation seems to be in accordance with the information obtained by the authors during their visit in the Sahrawi Arab Democratic Republic Ministry of Foreign Affairs in the Rabouni refugee camp in 2016. The Sahrawi population already seemed to be disappointed with the UN peace process and the lack of progress, with the Sahrawi youth being the most reactive and tired of waiting, while the elder generations much more restrained. Interview with Mr. Hamdi Bueha, Secretary-General of the Ministry of Foreign Affairs of the Sahrawi Arab Democratic Republic, and Mr. Mohamed Hammadi from the Department of Europe and the Arab World of the MFA of the SADR, Rabouni refugee camp, Algeria, May 2016.

According to some scholars and observers of the Sahrawi situation, Rabat's return to the AU in January 2017 might signal a change in Moroccan policy and a more compromising approach to resolving the issue (Interview with Prof. Smail Debeche, May 2017). According to others, Morocco's readmission to the AU (without any preconditions or concessions) puts an end to the Sahrawis' hopes for independence as the Moroccan authorities would probably hope to achieve, over time, if not the expulsion of the SADR, then at least its isolation (Amirah Fernández 2017). Regardless of the direction the issue of Western Sahara's independence takes, the problem itself affects relations between the countries in the region. The status of Western Sahara is still officially unresolved. Approximately 80% of the territory is occupied by Morocco[3], the rest is under the control of the POLISARIO Front. Western Sahara is officially recognised as a non-self-governing territory by the UN, which has been attempting unsuccessfully to resolve the issue of the area's political status since the mid-1980s. This problem is particularly challenging due to the overlapping interests of regional actors, namely Algeria and Morocco, as well as those of various international powers, notably the USA and France. The Sahrawi Arab Democratic Republic, whose authorities are based in the Sahrawi refugee camps near the city of Tindouf in Algeria, is recognised by over 40 countries worldwide and by the African Union.[4]

The chapter reflects on the significance of Western Sahara issue in the international relations of states bordering on Western Sahara and analyses the historical aspects of the problem, as well as its current state of development. The problem is contextualised within the history of the Maghreb region after decolonisation and in the wider international context to demonstrate that the Western Sahara issue is not only a regional Maghrebi problem, but that it has also extra-regional implications. The main research questions are: Why the Western Sahara issue still forms an obstacle in good neighbourly relations between Morocco and Algeria, as well as Morocco and Mauritania? (1); What historical factors contributed the most to the rise of the Western Saharan problem in the international relations of Morocco, Algeria, and Mauritania? (2). The chapter also attempts to make an argument on the challenges to the Western Sahara conflict resolution,

---

3   The Kingdom would dispute the term 'occupation', even if the Moroccan control of the territory is illegal under the international law and meets the characteristics of a military occupation, see more: Ferrer Lloret 2022, pp. 197-246.

4   In the end of 2022, the Sahrawi Arab Democratic Republic was still acknowledged by 47 countries out of 193, while another 36 countries had previously frozen or revoked their acknowledgement.

which could open a new chapter in international relations in the Maghreb region and beyond. It argues that although Morocco's readmission to the AU can be perceived as an important change, it may still be difficult to predict the further course of the Western Saharan conflict and its influence on Moroccan-Algerian relations in the face of the current global situation impacted by serious political and economic difficulties caused by the COVID-19 pandemic and the Russian invasion of Ukraine. The research is based on the qualitative analysis of the already existing sources (official documents, the press) and a critical reading of the literature on the subject, as well as qualitative data gathered during research visits to Algeria (2016, 2017, 2019, 2023), Morocco (2013, 2019, 2020) and Mauritania (2019) in the form of participant observation, in-depth interviews, and informal talks with the subjects of ethnographic study.

Problematic Borderland

From the beginning of Morocco's occupation of Western Sahara, this issue was strongly linked to the internal situation in the country and this connection is still very visible. It is widely believed that the conflict over Western Sahara is a consequence of its late or – if one prefers such terminology – 'unfinished' decolonisation. In this case, additionally, the principle of *uti possidetis* was broken, which up until then had been consistently applied within the process of the decolonisation of Africa (Kłosowicz 2017, pp. 174-5). It so happened that this principle was first used by the OAU during the border conflict between Algeria and Morocco known as the "Sand War" (8 October – 2 November 1963). This conflict was more than just a border dispute, as it was linked to the Tindouf area which neighbours Western Sahara. Even though Western Sahara was a territory under Spanish control when the conflict arose, according to Rabat's long-term plans it was foreseen that Algeria's border with the Spanish Sahara would in the future be a serious obstacle to the incorporation of the territory of the Spanish colony into Morocco. Rabat's claims against Algeria were connected to lands which, according to the Moroccans, were lawlessly occupied by the French during the colonial period. This referred to the borderland regions of Béchar, as well as the above-mentioned area around Tindouf, at the confluence of the borders of Morocco, Algeria, Mauritania, and Western Sahara. For Rabat, the desert area around Tindouf was primarily of strategic importance, as its borders with Western Sahara are 41-km long, which – as it later turned out – had fundamental significance in the context of the conflict surrounding the Western Sahara and the aid Algeria's provided to the Sahrawi. During the liberation struggle led by the Algerians against France, the Moroccan authorities attempted to force the

Algerian insurrectionary government to promise it would introduce territorial modifications that would be to their advantage. On 5 July 1961 an agreement was even signed between the King of Morocco Hassan II and the head of the Provisional Government of the Algerian Republic (*Gouvernement provisoire de la République algérienne*, GPRA), Ferhat Abbas, in which Algeria acknowledged the existence of the problem of the Moroccan-Algerian border as marked out by France during colonial times (Daoudi 2015, p. 20).[5] However, as long as the war continued, it would have been quite awkward for those in power in Rabat to attack the western part of Algeria, because this would have placed Morocco in an uncomfortable position on the international scene, as a country supporting the colonisers – in this case France – and also as a country violating the solidarity of African countries fighting for their independence. However, as soon as Algeria gained independence, the King of Morocco, Hassan II, contacted the newly formed Algerian authorities to resolve the border issues surrounding the towns of Béchar and Tindouf, to which Rabat laid claim. The president of Algeria, Ahmed Ben Bella, initially requested that the king give him more time to reach a decision, arguing that he needed the approval of the political bureau of the National Liberation Front (*Front de libération nationale*, FLN) to tackle the issue. In the autumn of 1963, the vice-president and minister of defence, Colonel Houari Boumédiène, argued that it was "inconceivable to concede any parcel of territory given the suffering of the population to acquire its independence", contrasting "the price of blood of the martyrs" with the Moroccan claims based on historical grounds. Instead, Algiers endorsed the Charter of the African Union (AU), which stipulated that the borders established during the colonial era could not be altered unless both parties agreed to the change (Lounnas and Messari 2020, p. 6).

As a result, Morocco attempted to annex the border territories it had claimed rights to, leading to the outbreak of an armed conflict in 1963 known as the Sand War, as previously mentioned. During the conflict, Algiers was supported by Cuba and the United Arab Republic[6], while Morocco received support from the

---

5   This document seems significant in the later Moroccan narrative, in which there was a certain expectation of Algeria's consent to the resolution of the border issue after independence (Jajili 2018, pp. 141-142; Bardonnet 1990, pp. 115-116).

6   United Arab Republic (1958-1961) was a state in the Middle East, created at first as a political union between Egypt (including the occupied Gaza Strip) and Syria (until 1961). Over the years 1961-1971 Egypt continued to be known as the United Arab Republic.

USA and France. The deployment of Cuban troops to Algeria in October 1963 marked the country's initial military involvement on the African continent. The Cuban forces were of relatively modest size, consisting of 686 soldiers equipped with 22 T-34S tanks, 18 122 mm guns, 18 120 mm mortars, and 18 anti-aircraft guns. They refrained from direct participation in the conflict and were not the largest contingent, particularly when compared to the substantial Cuban deployments in Angola and Ethiopia during the 1980s (approximately 20,000-30,000 and 15,000-18,000 troops, respectively). Nonetheless, their swift deployment to Algeria was officially presented as influencing Morocco towards a more conciliatory stance. Furthermore, it fostered strong Cuban-Algerian relations for many years, which later extended to the establishment of favourable Cuban-Sahrawi relations (Cuba formally recognised the Sahrawi Arab Democratic Republic in January 1980) (Szeptycki 2006, pp. 217-223; Riedel 2021)[7]. The intermediation of the then-influential and highly authoritative Ethiopian emperor Haile Selassie and Malian President Modibo Keïta played a major role in the peace negotiations. Aside from the sympathy the Ethiopian emperor had garnered while in exile in Great Britain during the occupation of his homeland by fascist Italy, he was also backed by serious political support from Washington, as the USA considered him an ally and Africa's most influential politician at the time. This was reflected, for example, in the emperor's October 1963 meeting with President John F. Kennedy in Washington (Kłosowicz, Mormul 2018, pp. 39, 56). The final factor influencing the peace negotiations between Algeria and Morocco was

---

7   In this context the authorities in Rabat accused Algiers that over the years it had forcibly sent between 1,300-1,700 Sahrawi children from the refugee camps to Cuba, where, separated from their parents, they had been brainwashed into hating Morocco (Szeptycki 2006, p. 223). The fact that Sahrawi youth from the camps were sent to Cuba (as well as to Libya, Syria, not mentioning Algeria) to continue their education in high schools and universities was often mentioned by Sahrawis from the refugee camps in our conversations. The authors also had the opportunity to talk to Sahrawis (now in their fifties) who went through such an educational path, none of them perceived it as harm. Currently, however, the preferred destination is Algeria, since studying in Cuba was associated with a long (often up to ten years) separation from their families, many Sahrawi families feared that their children would lose contact with the Sahrawi culture and language. In 2013, the first Sahrawi university was established - the University of Tifariti, located in the Western Saharan territories controlled by the SADR (Interview with Mrs. Fatma Mehdi Hassam, Secretary-General of the National Union of the Sahrawi Women, Boujdour refugee camp, Algeria, April 2016; informal talks with the participants of the 44th European Conference of Support and Solidarity with the Sahrawi People (EUCOCO), Vitoria-Gasteiz, Spain, 22-23 November 2019).

the founding conference of the Organisation of African Unity in Addis Ababa, which took place during the conflict between the two countries. This event further bolstered Haile Selassie's international standing and exerted pressure on the conflicting states to swiftly resolve the ongoing dispute in the interest of future pan-African cooperation. These various aspects played a pivotal role in bringing the conflict to a close and reinstating the pre-war situation. However, this resolution had additional consequences, notably the OAU's adoption of a stance affirming the inviolability of post-colonial borders. Consequently, Algiers would later invoke this principle to support POLISARIO's endeavours to achieve the independence of Western Sahara. It is not coincidental, therefore, that Morocco did not agree to accept the principle of *uti possidetis*, which conflicted with its territorial claims to the Spanish Sahara region, French Mauritania, and Mali (Farsoun and Paul, 1976, pp. 13-16). As history has shown, the retention of territory in the Tindouf province later became crucial for Algeria's support of the Sahrawi cause.

Claims to Western Saharan Territory

It is worth noting that claims to Western Sahara were put forward by Morocco basically from the moment the country gained independence in 1956. Spain recognised Morocco's independence and handed over its protectorate in the north of the country (with the exception of Ceuta and Melilla) in hopes of developing good neighbourly relations. However, these steps did not satisfy Morocco's claims, because as early as a year later, on 12th October 1957 at the United Nations, the country put forward claims against Spain and France. These included Ifni, Western Sahara, and Mauritania. At the same time, Rabat began playing a two-faced game. On the one hand, it secretly supported militants fighting against the Spanish in the Western Sahara territory and the French in Algeria; on the other, it officially supported Paris and Madrid, as evidenced by allowing their troops to use the Agadir airport, but also with the disarmament of Sahrawi militias inside Morocco by Moroccan security forces (Shelley 2004, p. 189). Morocco's actions paid off, as soon after the Sahrawi troops were broken up Madrid handed over the Tarfaya district, also known as Cabo Juby (1958), to Rabat in gratitude for Moroccan assistance. Ten years later, as a result of Rabat's intensive efforts, Morocco regained the enclave of Sidi Ifni from Spain under the Treaty of Fez (1969), in return for which Spain received special fishing privileges off the coast (Jensen 2013, p. 10; Kosidło 2012, p. 30).

King Hassan II, who began his reign in 1961, wove nationalist concepts into the narrative construct of the state and society, an important part of which was the idea of "Greater Morocco" (*al-Maghrib al-Kabir*), intended to consolidate Arab and Berber societies around the throne. Greater Morocco was to extend from Gibraltar in the north to the Senegal River in the south. In the east, it was to include parts of the Sahara, extending from Tindouf Province to Béchar Province in Algeria. In practice, this meant taking over Spanish Sahara and most of Mauritania, part of Mali and the western part of Algeria. However, no ruler in Moroccan history had ever controlled such a large territory (Kosidło 2012, p. 30). As already mentioned, from the moment it gained independence from France, Morocco made claims of sovereignty over the Western Sahara area, which at the time had the status of an overseas Spanish province. In addition, Rabat did not recognise the independence of Mauritania (1960) on historical grounds and made claims to these territories. Similarly, from the beginning of the creation of Algeria (1962) and Mali (1960), the Moroccan authorities maintained that these were artificial constructs – states created by French colonialism (Ożarowski 2012, p. 210; Kłosowicz 2021, pp. 145-146). The claims on the north-western lands of Mali lacked a solid basis and were regarded as circumstantial. However, the situation regarding Mauritania was notably different. One indication of this was the establishment of the Mauritania and Sahara Department in 1957, which initially operated under the Ministry of Internal Affairs. Subsequently, in 1963, the department was elevated to a separate ministry (Kłosowicz, 2022, p. 58). Another illustrative example is the activities of the Army of Liberation (Jish Ettehrir), influenced by Moroccan authorities, which aimed to employ military means to reclaim territories not included in Morocco in 1956. These units engaged in conflict against both Spanish forces in the Spanish Sahara and French forces in northern Mauritania. Notably, many nomads from the Spanish Sahara and Mauritania were among these insurgent units. In 1958, the Army of Liberation penetrated the Adrar region through the Spanish Sahara, advancing as far as the town of Atar. The objective of this expedition was to proclaim the king of Morocco as the ruler of Mauritania and to incorporate this region into the Moroccan state, despite it being under French control at the time. These aspirations garnered support from certain prominent Mauritanian politicians and tribal leaders. Although the Army of Liberation units were ultimately defeated by the French military and forced to withdraw from Mauritanian territory, Morocco viewed their actions in the Western Sahara and Mauritania, alongside the efforts of Sahrawi fighters under the Moroccan flag, as evidence of the loyalty of the inhabitants of present-day Western Sahara and Mauritania to the Moroccan crown (Isidoros, 2018, pp. 21-22; Kłosowicz, 2022, pp. 58-59).

Undoubtedly, Mauritania shares the closest historical and cultural ties with the inhabitants of Western Sahara. These ties are primarily evident in the connections between the populations of Mauritania, particularly the White Moors (Bidan Moors), and the people of Western Sahara. They are bound together by a common language, namely a dialect of Arabic known as Hassaniya, traditional attire, and a shared history as nomadic pastoralists (Mormul, 2021, pp. 163-164). Moreover, the POLISARIO Front was established within Mauritania, specifically in the town of Zouérat, on 10 May 1973. Just ten days later, a unit of the POLISARIO Front launched an attack on the Spanish El Khanga post within the territory of Spanish Sahara. In the context of the stance taken by authorities in Nouakchott concerning the Western Saharan issue, it is notable that in 1966, the Mauritanian delegate to the Special Committee session of the United Nations in Addis Ababa called for full independence for Western Sahara (Kosidło, 2012, p. 34).

In contrast to Morocco and Mauritania, which made territorial claims to the Western Sahara area on historical, ethnic, and geographic grounds[8], from the beginning Algiers took the position that the Sahrawi people should be granted full rights to self-determination. However, from the moment the Popular Front for the Liberation of Saguia el Hamra and Río de Oro (the POLISARIO Front) was formally constituted in 1973 till November 1975 the Algerian support was rather minimal and in reality, only started in mid-1974. The origin of the POLISARIO Front can be traced to a Sahrawi nationalist organisation - the Movement for the Liberation of Saguia el Hamra and Wadi el Dhahab, which was formed with the intention of launching an armed struggle against the Spanish occupation (Zunes and Mundy 2010, pp. 40-42). The Algerian President at the time, Houari Boumédiène, sought to settle Algerian-Mauritanian and Algerian-Moroccan border disputes, so that the reconciled neighbours could more effectively put pressure on Spain to decolonise Western Sahara. To this end, he held numerous bilateral and trilateral meetings between 1970 and 1973. Additionally, in international forums, mainly in the UN and the OAU, Algeria repeatedly demanded the decolonisation of Western Sahara. In response to what is known as the "Green March," conducted in November 1975 on the initiative of the Moroccan authorities (a massive popular mobilisation followed by a peaceful march on the Western Sahara with the aim of occupying the area), Algeria brought about the passing of a resolution during the United Nations General Assembly

---

8   Both, Mauritanians and Sahrawis speak Hassaniya Arabic, they also experience a range of cultural similarities that enable good understanding on an interpersonal level (Interview with Prof. Dr. El Moctar Taleb Hende, University of Nouakchott, Nouakchott, Mauritania, February 2019).

in December 1975 stating the Sahrawis' inalienable right to self-determination (United Nations 1975, p. 117). When on 6 March 1976 Algeria acknowledged Western Saharan independence, Morocco severed all diplomatic relations with it, while in answer Algiers accused Rabat of intending to further its territorial conquests (Jensen 2012, p. 19; Kasznik-Christian 2006, pp. 422-423). When the Moroccan and Mauritanian armies began their occupation of Western Sahara, Algeria compared the Sahrawi struggle against the occupant to the fight led by the Algerian nation against the French, and directly accused Rabat of colonising Western Sahara. In answer, Morocco suggested that Algiers was making cynical use of the Western Sahara issue to enable its future subordination of the territory (Kukułka 2001, p. 256). The concentration of army forces at the border around Tindouf ultimately led to armed clashes near the Amgala Oasis at the beginning of 1976. As a result of the First Battle of Amgala (27– 29 January), the Algerian army was forced to retreat. However, during the Second Battle of Amgala (14–15 February), the POLISARIO Front, supported by Algerian units, pushed the Moroccan armed forces out of the area. In the diplomatic sphere, at the 30th session of the United Nations General Assembly (1975-1976) there was a heated debate between the representatives of Algeria and Morocco. On 27 February 1976, the POLISARIO declared the establishment of the Sahrawi Arab Democratic Republic. Concurrently, in April of the same year, Morocco and Mauritania signed an agreement delineating the border between the two countries, partitioning Western Sahara between them. This agreement was a manifestation of a confidential pact reached in 1975, whereby Nouakchott expressed apprehensions regarding Moroccan expansionism. On 14 November 1975, in Madrid, representatives of Spain, Morocco, and Mauritania signed what is known as the Madrid Accords – a pact regarding Western Sahara. Within this agreement, Madrid committed to decolonising the territory and withdrawing its military forces by the end of February 1976. During the transitional period, authority was to be gradually transferred to Moroccan and Mauritanian administrations (United Nations Peacemaker, 1975). Some scholars suggest that Morocco's prior claims and its reluctance to recognise Mauritania's independence over several years may have influenced the Mauritanian authorities' decision to occupy Western Sahara. This move led Mauritania to defensively respond with diplomatic manoeuvres, laying claim to Western Saharan lands based on ethnic kinship with the Sahrawi people inhabiting those areas. The Mauritanian approach can be seen as more defensive than expansionist, as the allocation of part of Western Sahara under the 1975 Madrid Accords was perceived by Nouakchott more as a bargaining chip in its negotiations with Rabat, aimed at bolstering its position rather than seeking territorial expansion (Szczepankiewicz, 2010, pp. 61-62; Kłosowicz, 2022, p. 60).

It is worth noting that in the initial years following the establishment of the PO-LISARIO Front, its leaders contemplated the possibility of forming a federation between Mauritania and Western Sahara. A comparable solution was applied by the UN in the case of Eritrea and Ethiopia. In 1950, by decision of the UN General Assembly, Eritrea was federated with Ethiopia as an autonomous province, with its own parliament and government (Kłosowicz, Mormul, 2018, p. 41; Kłosowicz, 2022, p. 60). Fearing Rabat's expansionist tendencies and seeking to avoid domination by their northern neighbour, the POLISARIO Front leaders favoured Mauritania due to its perceived cultural and ethnic proximity (Shelley, 2004, p. 43; Kłosowicz, 2022, p. 60).

Nonetheless, Mauritania's occupation of the southern part of Western Sahara immediately led to the rupture of previously amicable diplomatic relations with Algeria and prompted military actions against Mauritania by the POLISARIO Front. The repeated attacks on trains transporting iron ore to the Mauritanian coast and to the mining town of Zouérat, along with an assault on the state capital Nouakchott in April 1976, underscored the Mauritanian army's vulnerability and its lack of adequate preparation for military engagements. While the dispatch of Moroccan troops to Mauritanian territory temporarily allayed fears of further POLISARIO Front incursions into the capital, it also aroused concerns among those who remembered Morocco's past ambitions toward Mauritanian territories. Additionally, the occupation of Western Sahara was met with disapproval from a segment of Mauritanian society (Kowalska-Lewicka, 1976: 94; Kłosowicz, 2022, p. 61). Consequently, Mauritanian President Mokhtar Ould Daddah had to contend with strong domestic opposition against the annexation of neighbouring lands, which not only undermined the government's external legitimacy but also its internal credibility. This situation eventually precipitated an internal crisis and culminated in the overthrow of the incumbent president in a military coup in July 1978. The Military Committee for National Recovery, which assumed power in Mauritania, opted to withdraw from the occupation of Western Sahara. In August 1979, during a meeting in Algiers, Mauritanian representatives signed a peace agreement with the POLISARIO Front in which both parties renounced their mutual claims. Consequently, Mauritania withdrew from the occupied territory, which was promptly taken over by the Moroccan army. In 1984, the subsequent military regime under Mohamed Khoun Ould Haïdallah officially recognised the Sahrawi Arab Democratic Republic. The Mauritanian authorities contended that the legal institutions of Western Sahara and a significant portion of the Sahrawi population resided in the refugee camps in Tindouf. This decision severely strained Mauritania's relations with Morocco (Faria and Vasconcelos, 1996, p. 43; Kłosowicz, 2022, p. 61).

Algeria's involvement in the Western Saharan conflict had major consequences for its foreign policy. Indeed, Algeria at the time enjoyed some international recognition and a reputation as one of the most important among what
are known as the "non-aligned states". In the Memorandum Submitted by the
People's Democratic Republic of Algeria on the Convening of a Special Session
of the United Nations General Assembly, Boumédiène denounced not only the
division of the world into a political East and West, but also into an economically
rich North and a poor South (Organisation of African Unity 1974). At the time,
Algeria was enjoying the height of its diplomatic importance on the international
scene. The prestige it held after winning the war of independence manifested
itself in the fact that it was considered a respected negotiator in international
conflicts. Having fought for independence for years, Algeria also strongly supported the Palestinian cause. At any rate, commitment to the Palestinian and
Western Sahara causes would be flagship issues of Algerian foreign policy during
the Boumédiène government. However, tensions arising from the conflict with
Morocco, and eventually the severance of diplomatic relations with Rabat supported by the USA and other Western countries, had the effect of reducing Algiers' influence on other African and Arab states (Kasznik-Christian 2006, pp.
419-421). In order not to lag behind Morocco, which was being rearmed by the
USA and France, Algeria began to increasingly orient itself toward the USSR
and the Eastern Bloc countries, who supplied it with military equipment, as well
as providing economic and technical assistance, which led to the positioning of
the country more and more on one side of the Cold War conflict and eventually
caused Algiers to lose its role as one of the leaders of the non-aligned countries.[9] Furthermore, concerning the Western Sahara issue within the OAU, Algiers aligned itself with figures such as Ethiopia's controversial leader, Mengistu
Haile Mariam, who seized power in a coup in 1974, overthrowing Emperor
Haile Selassie, a revered figure in Africa. Supported by the USSR and Eastern
Bloc countries, Mengistu Haile Mariam implemented a brutal regime in Ethiopia and openly pursued a confrontational political stance towards the USA and
Western nations (Kłosowicz, 2015, pp. 84-85). It is noteworthy that in the case

---

9 Algeria was the first country outside the Eastern Bloc to receive the latest Soviet military equipment between 1975 and 1985 in the form of T-72 tanks and MiG-23 and
MiG-25 aircraft. In addition, military personnel in the amount of 3,500 men were sent
to Algeria for training purposes. Morocco, on the other hand, received $380 million
in military aid from the US between 1976 and 1980, the largest amount at the time for
any African country (Duigan and Gann 1984, p. 295).

of Western Sahara, Moscow did not actively support the Sahrawi cause. Instead, it appeared to prioritise demonstrating neutrality and averting direct confrontation between its ally Algeria and Morocco. Despite maintaining a pro-Western stance, Moscow sought to preserve favourable business relations with Morocco. By 1978, Morocco had become the Soviet Union's largest economic partner in Africa, primarily due to a bilateral phosphate deal. Under this agreement, the Soviets were tasked with developing a new phosphate mine in Meskala. The Soviets refrained from directly supplying arms to the POLISARIO Front and only reluctantly acquiesced to Algeria's provision of military support. Furthermore, following the proclamation of the Sahrawi Arab Democratic Republic, the USSR did not extend official recognition to the new entity (Zoubir, 1987, pp. 17-32). Soon, the Western Sahara issue pushed by Algeria divided the OAU so deeply that the matter even threatened to split it into two blocs (Cowell 1983). Meanwhile, Morocco, which had been falling into increasing political isolation in Africa, decided to outflank Algiers in August 1984 with forming the Arabic-African Federation (the Oujda Treaty), which stunned the world. The treaty was to create a union of states between Morocco and Libya as part of a first step toward a "Great Arab Maghreb," but it did not even last two years (Gwertzman 1984). It seems that Morocco's main goals with this move were to end Libya's provision of military aid to the POLISARIO Front, eliminate Tripoli as an ally of Algeria, and isolate Algiers in the Maghreb region by intensifying cooperation between Rabat, Tripoli, Tunis, and Nouakchott. Despite the collapse of the initiative, deemed unrealistic from the start and merely a tactical ploy employed by Hassan II, it succeeded in ending Libya's provision of military aid to the SADR and in cooling Algerian-Libyan relations (International Legal Materials 1984, p. 1022; Kosidło 2012, pp. 80-81; Daguzan 1999, p. 31). This move of the Kingdom of Morocco seems to have radicalised the mood in the inner circles of Algerian power. At the beginning of the presidency of Chadli Bendjedid (1979-1992), although the attitude towards the problem of Western Sahara was quite unambiguous – the rights of the Sahrawi people to self-determination and the need to decolonise the territory were emphasised, however, the Algerian authorities did not want to completely destroy relations with Morocco. It was even believed that they could be built on the basis of good neighbourliness. In this spirit, in September 1980, President Bendjedid participated in the ad hoc committee of the OAU on Western Sahara, convened in Freetown, in the company of Prime Minister of Morocco (Cubertafond 1981, p. 161).

For several years after this, political relations between Algeria and Morocco remained strained since the former demanded Rabat's recognition of the POLISARIO Front as a representative of the Sahrawi people and the resolution of the

Western Sahara issue as a precondition for the restoration of relations between the two countries. The POLISARIO Front maintained military bases in Algeria, while refugee camps and entire structures of the SADR state found refuge there, which showed that Algiers treated them as the government-in-exile.[10] Throughout this period, Algeria supported the Sahrawi fighters financially and militarily by supplying arms and ammunition. When Morocco finally recognized the POLISARIO Front and agreed to negotiations, a few months later, in 1988, Algeria resumed diplomatic relations with Rabat with the mediation of Saudi Arabia, and a ceasefire between the POLISARIO Front and Morocco followed in 1991. However, mutual relations remained far from good. During the Algerian civil war (1991–2002), Algiers accused Rabat of sheltering and supporting the Armed Islamic Group (*Groupe islamique armé*, GIA), which the Moroccan authorities denied, but the situation led to the closure of the border between the countries in 1994, after Morocco accused Algeria's Intelligence and Security Department of jointly (along with the GIA) planning and carrying out a terrorist attack in the Hotel Atlas Asni in Marrakech in 1994 that killed two Spaniards[11]. As Algerian extremists were implicated in the incident, Morocco implemented a visa requirement for all Algerian citizens, subsequently resulting in the closure of the border. In response, the Algerian government imposed visa requirements for Moroccan citizens and closed its borders with Morocco. This action significantly disrupted economic trade along the borders and impacted the livelihoods of communities residing in border areas. Consequently, this crisis brought an end to the reconciliation efforts between the two countries and led to the suspension of the Arab Maghreb Union (Lounnas and Messari, 2020, p. 10). Morocco rejected any initiatives put forth by representatives of African states to address the Western Sahara conflict, maintaining that only the United Nations Security Council held authority over the matter. Consequently, in 1995, Rabat declined to permit a visit to the Western Sahara region, which was under Moroccan occupation, by South African President Nelson Mandela, who was widely regarded as Africa's foremost political and moral authority at the time. It is important to note that, in turn, Mandela was extended an invitation by Algeria and visited Sahrawi

---

10 On the Sahrawi refugee camps in Algeria and its inhabitants, see: Mormul 2021, pp. 169-182.

11 It is worth mentioning that this was the third time since Algeria gained independence in 1962 that the Moroccan-Algerian border was closed. The first took place because of the Sands War (1963), the second in the aftermath of the Green March (1975) and Moroccan seizure of Western Saharan territory (Daoudi 2015, pp. 19-48).

refugee camps located within the country's territory (Kosidło 2018, p. 40). In the 1990s, as a consequence of the ceasefire, there was a gradual lowering of Algeria's involvement in the Western Sahara issue, highlighted by a reduction in economic and military aid to the POLISARIO Front. This was certainly influenced on the one hand by the end of the Cold War, and the very bloody civil war with Islamists on the other. In this situation, Algiers was not interested in stirring up a new open conflict with Morocco. The efforts of the weakened state's government were focused on strengthening its international position through the establishment of an anti-terrorist alliance with the USA and Western countries, and cooperation within regional international institutions, including broader integration with Europe, such as through the Euro-Mediterranean Partnership (EUROMED) (Szczepankiewicz 2010, p. 61). It was precisely within the framework of the latter that the Maghreb–Europe Gas Pipeline was constructed and launched in December 1996. The 1370-km long pipeline from Hassi R'Mel in Algeria runs through the territory of Morocco over a distance of 525 km and provides gas to Córdoba in Spain (Pierros, Meunier, and Abrams 2019, pp. 176-2018).

Attempts at Finding a Peaceful Solution

It seemed that economic cooperation would pave the way for a political settlement of the region's most pressing issue, i.e. the matter of Western Sahara. In addition, Hassan II, who had held an intransigent position on the status of Western Sahara, died in July 1999. His replacement by his eldest son and successor Mohammed VI, who was more open-minded and willing to enact reform, offered a chance to resolve the Sahrawi issue. It is worth noting that in 1999 the newly elected Algerian President, Abdelaziz Bouteflika, who attended the funeral of the Moroccan king Hassan II and held talks with his successor, was also the first Algerian head of state to visit Morocco since 1989 (Drozdiak 1999). In 2001, the first plan was presented by the Personal Envoy of the UN Secretary-General for Western Sahara, James Baker, which stipulated that a referendum be held on Western Sahara territory, in which all residents of the disputed territory would participate regardless of where they had been born. Meanwhile, the Algerian-backed POLISARIO Front demanded the application of what is referred to as the Spanish census, allowing only people who had lived in the Western Sahara territory while it was still a Spanish colony to vote. Baker's proposals were therefore heavily criticised by Algiers. The Algerian authorities sent a memorandum, highly critical of the draft Framework Agreement, complaining that the document prepared the ground for the future integration of the territory with Morocco and that it went against the principle of self-determination (Theofilopoulou

2006, pp. 9-10). Furthermore, Algiers and the POLISARIO Front indicated the vaguely defined powers of the legislative body in the future autonomous region, and the still-unresolved problem of voter identification among a largely predominantly immigrant Moroccan electorate. Objections to the plan were also raised by the Moroccan side, as granting Western Sahara the status of an autonomous region would imply a constitutional amendment and undermine the Kingdom's unity (Szczepankiewicz 2009, p. 186).

In May 2003, Baker's second plan, the "Peace Plan for Self-Determination for the People of Western Sahara" was presented, i.e., a developed version of the first plan including details of the electorate allowed to vote in the referendum and the legislative and executive powers of the Western Sahara autonomous region. This version was hailed by Algiers as a "historic compromise for peace." It seems that this change in Algiers' position was influenced not only by the modifications brought to the plan itself, but also to some extent by the American show of force during the US military campaign in Iraq (20 March – 1 May 2003) (Shelley 2003). The Algerian government did not want to take the risk that rejecting Baker's plan would signify embarking on a course of open conflict with Washington. This was even more important as following the end of the Cold War, Algeria, once considered socialist and an advocate of Third World interests, embarked on a path leading to a liberalised economy. The successes achieved in the civil war against Islamist terrorist groups won Algeria some favour with the USA, and the Algerian government began increasing its economic cooperation with Washington. As a result, the Algerian government was on the one hand keen not to alienate the Americans, pursuing a policy that would strengthen Algeria's position internationally *vis-à-vis* Morocco, which had so far been strongly supported by the USA, and – on the other – it was not willing to sacrifice the Western Sahara issue (Shelley 2003). Earlier, in 2003, one of the most influential Algerian generals and a former member of the High Council of State of Algeria, Khaled Nezzar, expressed the opinion that the Western Sahara issue should not divide "the two brother countries", while in the era of great regional blocs, it was necessary to construct "our own Maghreb space". Nezzar considered the best option "would be to go towards the thesis of no winner, no loser" (Shelley 2003). There can be no doubt that such statements were a signal from some representatives of the Algerian power elite directed at Washington to strengthen US-Algerian cooperation. It is also significant that the Algerian President at the time, Abdelaziz Bouteflika, had in 1975, while still Foreign Minister (1963–1979), recommended that his government move away from supporting Western Sahara in exchange for a final border agreement between Algiers and Rabat (Shelley 2003). However, Baker's second plan was abandoned due to the resistance demonstrated by Morocco, supported by France. Rabat's approach was also facilitated by new international circumstances linked to renewed concern within the US government about international terrorism, with Morocco's help in the matter deemed essential (Theofilopoulou 2006). The threat of terrorism also played a role in shaping Mauritania's evolving policy towards Western Sahara. Following his ascent to power through another coup in December 1984, Colonel Maaouya Ould Sid'Ahmed Taya officially adopted a stance of neutrality in the Western Sahara conflict and restored diplomatic ties with Morocco. Throughout the 1990s, although Mauritania maintained an official stance of neutrality in the dispute between the POLISARIO Front and Algeria on one side, and Morocco on the other, while it provided unofficial support to the Sahrawis. However, navigating this diplomatic balancing act between the conflicting parties proved challenging for Mauritanian authorities. Of particular significance is Morocco's close relationship with the United States and France, the most influential external actors in the Maghreb region. This relationship gained prominence after the September 11 attacks on the World Trade Centre, when the US government elevated the fight against Islamic terrorism to a top foreign policy priority. A series of attacks and kidnappings in the Sahel region, and notably the 11 March 2004 terrorist attacks in Madrid, which revealed the perpetrators' ties to al-Qaeda, prompted American politicians and military officials to focus on the threat of Islamic terrorism in the Sahara. Rabat adeptly capitalised on this situation in its interactions with the United States. Morocco portrayed Algeria, Mauritania, and Mali as weak states incapable of effectively controlling the region, suggesting it could become the "Afghanistan of Africa". Exploiting the terrorism threat, Moroccan politicians successfully distanced the involved states from the Western Sahara issue and convinced American counterparts that Moroccan armed forces maintaining control over Western Sahara was crucial to preventing terrorist infiltration in the area (Kłosowicz, 2022, pp. 61-62).

In July 2004, Rabat lifted visa requirements for Algerians travelling to Morocco, and two years later, in April 2006, the Algerian president reciprocated the gesture. It seemed as if the border issues were close to being resolved, which would have been a manifestation of a new chapter in the relations between the two countries. Talks about opening the borders were undertaken during a visit by the Moroccan communications minister to Algiers in March 2012. At the time, it seemed that the two countries would be united by a new common enemy – al Qaeda in the Islamic Maghreb (AQIM), an alliance of Algerian and Mauritanian Islamists attacking military targets and kidnapping tourists throughout the region. To combat it effectively, regular meetings between Moroccan and Algerian intelligence chiefs began in 2007. In January 2012, for the first time in years,

there was a ministerial meeting on the issue. Moreover, Algeria needed its soldiers elsewhere than at the Moroccan border. Things had become dangerous on
the border with Libya, from where armed militants had begun to infiltrate the
country after the fall of Muammar Gaddafi, such as Tuareg groups, previously
fighting under the dictator, which were now travelling through Algeria to Mali,
where they fomented a new uprising. There, the Islamists began establishing
their bases, and thousands of unregistered weapons stemming from the Libyan
conflict were estimated to be circulating in the region. The military was therefore
needed more in the east and south of the country (Tziarras and Fredriksen 2020,
pp. 20-21). Meanwhile, another attempt was made to resolve the Sahara issue. In
2009, a new UN envoy to Western Sahara was appointed, a former US diplomat
who had served as United States Ambassador to Algeria and Syria, Christopher
W. S. Ross, who led three-day negotiations in Long Island in November 2010
between Morocco's envoys and representatives of the POLISARIO Front, accompanied by delegations from Algeria and Mauritania. Indeed, Ross was aware
that any talks and resolutions involving POLISARIO representatives alone were
pointless, as they would not be binding without the explicit approval of the Algerian side, although officially the Algerian delegation, like the Mauritanian one,
are not parties of the Morocco-POLISARIO dispute. The talks yielded no results.
Morocco offered the Sahrawis autonomy, while the POLISARIO demanded a
referendum on the region's independence (The Economist 2010, p. 48). A year
later, the Moroccan authorities, reproaching Ross for previously serving as ambassador to Algeria, accused him of lacking impartiality and supporting only
one side of the dispute – the POLISARIO Front and Algeria, and declared him
persona non grata (Allilou 2015).

This situation led to yet another cooling of relations between Algiers and
Rabat. Two years later, in 2014, there was an incident at the border. According
to accounts released to the world by the Moroccan government, an Algerian
border guard allegedly opened fire on more than a dozen unarmed civilians,
one of whom sustained three serious gunshot wounds. The incident occurred
near the north-eastern city of Oujda in northern Morocco. Morocco's foreign ministry summoned the Algerian ambassador to explain the situation,
while the Minister of the Interior Mohammed Hassad demanded that Algiers
take disciplinary action against the soldier. The official statement issued by
the government in Rabat referred to the "grave incident" as part of a series
of Algerian border provocations. The Algerian authorities commented on
the whole incident as targeting "Moroccan smugglers who pelted them with
stones." In addition, Algerian officers were said to have fired only into the air
(Dyduk 2014). In fact, the problem of drug smugglers from Morocco is often

mentioned in the Algerian narrative regarding the closed Morocco-Algeria border. According to Algiers, open borders would obviously be better for the development of mutual relations and could stimulate regional cooperation, but on the other hand, there is still need, in the face of Moroccan reluctance to engage in dialogue on borders, to fight drug smuggling from Morocco and protect Algerian market of basic food products and gasoline, which in Algeria are heavily subsidized by the state[12]. The Algerian government has also consistently opposed Moroccan efforts to exclude the Western Sahara from the African Union. Algeria, as a supporter of the SADR and the POLISARIO Front, announced that it would boycott AU meetings if the SADR was excluded from the AU (in 2015, Algeria became the seat of the centre of the regional African security and counterterrorism effort, The African Union Mechanism for Police Cooperation – AFRIPOL) (AFRIPOL 2022).

Meanwhile, in April 2018 the USA blocked a resolution to extend the mandate of the United Nations Mission for the Referendum in Western Sahara (MINURSO) for another year, agreeing to extend the mission for only another six months (United Nations Security Council 2018). This was in line with Washington's policy of reducing American involvement in world politics and withdrawing US funding of some UN initiatives, including peacekeeping missions. According to President Donald Trump's National Security Advisor John Bolton, it was time to end the funding of unproductive missions, the costs of which were burdening the US budget, as the country practically financed 30% of the cost of their activities (Reuters 2018). The USA's loss of patience with the lack of progress in the peace process was even more pronounced as MINURSO has been one of the longest running UN peacekeeping missions; it was launched in 1991 with a year-long mandate renewed every year, without any tangible effects (United Nations Security Council 1991). It seems that the US authorities may also have wanted to put pressure on Morocco and Algeria to finally enter constructive talks. There was no need to await the results of these actions too long, as shortly thereafter the UN Secretary General's personal envoy for Western Sahara Horst

---

12 Interview with Dr. Saïd Ayachi, Chairman of the Algerian National Committee of Solidarity with the Sahrawi People, Algiers, Algeria, May 2023. The threat of drug smuggling from Morocco also appears frequently in the Algerian press. During the authors' last visit to Algeria, it was very common to read about the Algerian border guards' or military successes in thwarting of another smuggling operation (i.e. Le Patriote 2023: 24).

Köhler organised a roundtable for all parties interested in the Western Sahara issue, which took place in two rounds, the first on 5-6 December 2018 in Geneva, and the second on 21-22 March 2019. In addition to Köhler and envoys from Morocco and the POLISARIO Front, the meeting was also attended by delegations from Algeria and Mauritania. The goal of the meeting was "to achieve a just, lasting, and mutually acceptable political solution, based on compromise, which will provide for the self-determination of the people of Western Sahara in the context of arrangements consistent with the principles and purposes of the Charter of the United Nations" (United Nations Security Council 2019). These were the first talks in six years, resuming the peace process interrupted in 2012. Unfortunately, the talks did not lead to a breakthrough, as both sides remained intransigent in their positions. The POLISARIO Front and Algeria wanted a referendum, Morocco agreed only to talks on the region's broad autonomy. The matter was complicated by Algeria's approach, as it did not want to be an official party to the talks but act only as an observer, while Rabat believed that Algiers' support for the POLISARIO was the real sticking point to the dispute.[13]

After decades of political instability, Mauritania entered a peaceful era under the leadership of former army general Mohamed Ould Abdel Aziz, who both curtailed the activities of the POLISARIO Front within Mauritania and maintained official relations with the SADR. This was evidenced by official visits from Sahrawi representatives to Nouakchott (Sahara Press Service, 2016). Following the presidential election in August 2019, former Defence Minister Mohammed Ould el-Ghazouani assumed power, marking the first peaceful change of government in the country's history. Shortly after taking office, the new president expressed his stance on the Western Sahara issue, advocating for a just and lasting solution to the conflict that would be accepted by all parties and alleviate civilian suffering. Mauritanian observers and political analysts believe that the appointment of Ismail Ould Cheikh Ahmed as the new foreign minister by the president was not coincidental. He has consistently advocated for Mauritania to disengage from the Sahrawi foreign policy issue and transition from a policy of balancing between Algeria and Morocco to one that takes proactive initiatives regarding the Western Sahara problem. Nouakchott can indeed play an active and significant role in negotiations due to its open channels of communication with the

---

13 Following the fiasco of the March talks, Horst Köhler resigned from the function of Special UN Envoy, officially for health reasons (United Nations Secretary-General 2019).

POLISARIO Front, good relations with Sahrawi tribal leaders, and important contacts with both Rabat and Algiers. However, politicians in Nouakchott are mindful that Mauritania is also considered an integral part of the "Greater Morocco", a notion occasionally emphasised by nationalist Moroccan politicians. In December 2016, the Secretary General of the Istiqlal (Independence) Party officially stated that Mauritania lies on Moroccan soil, leading to tensions at the time. Yet, three months later in March 2017, King Mohammed VI visited Mauritania on an official visit to ease relations and discuss security concerns on the southern border related to the activities of the POLISARIO Front (Igrouane, 2017; Kłosowicz, 2022, p. 63). In recent years, Mauritania has made it clear that it seeks to resolve the Western Sahara issue, which has divided Morocco and Algeria since the mid-1970s. Authorities in Nouakchott find themselves caught between conflicting interests, striving to avoid conflict with either neighbouring country. In a press conference in November 2019, Mauritanian Foreign Minister emphasised that Mauritania is actively engaged and seeks a solution to the conflict that will be acceptable to all parties involved, thereby addressing the regional dispute that has hindered the Arab Maghreb Union (The Arab Weekly, 2019; Kłosowicz, 2022, p. 64). According to Moroccan news sources, "Although Morocco and Mauritania have taken opposing stances on the Western Sahara issue in the past, Mauritania's official 'neutrality' on the matter has facilitated cordial relations with Morocco. Mauritania is a key participant in the ongoing UN-led negotiations on Western Sahara, and Morocco is eager to secure Mauritanian support for its Autonomy Plan" (Hekking, 2020).

During fieldwork conducted in Mauritania in February 2019 and in meetings with representatives of the country's political elite in Nouakchott, a sense of fatigue was palpable among Mauritanian politicians. They expressed frustration with the unresolved Western Sahara issue, which they felt was holding Mauritania hostage. Additionally, conversations with residents of Nouakchott or Nouadhibou about the Western Sahara issue revealed sympathy and compassion for the Sahrawi people and their plight. However, few believed that a resolution to the problem was feasible. Furthermore, Mauritania's economic stagnation is also attributed to the unresolved Western Sahara conflict. According to the interviewees, this hinders greater economic cooperation among Maghreb countries, to which Mauritania aspires to belong. Additionally, the political instability resulting from the Western Sahara issue deters foreign investors (Interviews and observations during field research in Mauritania, February 2020; Kłosowicz, 2022, pp. 66-67).

Changes on the Chessboard

In 2019 a planned POLISARIO convention was held, taking place a week after Algeria's 12 December 2019 presidential election. The POLISARIO authorities were thus able to get some idea of what the future president's political approach would be, and – therefore – about the course Algeria would take in its foreign policy. Would it continue to consistently support the Sahrawi cause or open up to dialogue with Rabat? The election was won by former Prime Minister Abdelmadjid Tebboune, a 74-year-old politician who hails from the elite that had previously held power in Algeria (Al Jazeera 2019). The new president did not change Algeria's position on the Western Sahara issue. Speaking after the inauguration ceremony in Algiers, he stated that "the Western Sahara question is about decolonisation." Tebboune added that the territorial dispute was being settled under the auspices of the United Nations and the African Union. However, he expressed hope that his country's position would not affect relations with Morocco. This was not a major surprise, as Tebboune had already expressed a similar opinion on Western Sahara during the election campaign, on 11 November 2019, emphasising that the dispute was a "decolonisation question that must be settled by granting the right of self-determination to Sahrawis and allowing them to have a say on whether they want to be Moroccans (…) or free" (Babas 2019).

Meanwhile, Morocco's Ambassador to the UN Omar Hilale expressed his government's position, stating that Morocco would offer the POLISARIO and the Sahrawi people broad autonomy, including control of the executive, legislative and judicial branches within Western Sahara, as well as 100% economic control over the extraction of natural resources with the profits benefitting the local population. He claimed that the POLISARIO, instead of being mentally stuck in the 1970s, should change its hard-line stance and vision for resolving the conflict, otherwise future generations would waste time seeking independence that would never come (Lederer 2019). He took the opportunity to condemn Algeria's hostile moves against Morocco's territorial integrity at the UN Committee meeting on 17 June 2019 in New York, thus referring to the Algerian support for the Western Sahara self-determination, without mentioning that the territory in question is not legally part of Morocco and is considered by the United Nations as a non-self-governing territory (United Nations 2022). The Moroccan ambassador expressed his government's position that Algeria was unquestionably responsible for the conflict, stating that "if Algeria is only an observer, why does it arm, finance, shelter and diplomatically mobilize for the POLISARIO, an armed non-state separatist movement?" and that "if Algeria is not a main party, why does it foster the culture of hatred of Morocco and separatism among children in primary education by introducing it into the school curriculum and end-of-year examinations." He finished his speech with the following telling sentence: "The Sahara will never be independent and will always be an integral part of Morocco" (Kasraoui 2019).

In early December 2020, authorities in Algiers were shocked to hear the official news from the White House that President Donald Trump, during a phone call with King Mohammed VI of Morocco, had reached an agreement according to which the United States would change its position on the occupation of Western Sahara and recognise Moroccan sovereignty over the territory in exchange for Rabat establishing full diplomatic relations with Israel. In addition, the USA was to open its consulate in the occupied territories in the city of Dakhla (White House 2020). A White House proclamation stated the United States believed an independent Sahrawi State was "not a realistic option for resolving the conflict and that genuine autonomy under Moroccan sovereignty is the only feasible solution" (France24 2020a, Web). In Algeria's first reaction to the US decision, Prime Minister Abdelaziz Djerad said that "there are foreign manoeuvres which aim to destabilise Algeria" (France24 2020b, Web). In Algiers, the Foreign Ministry stated that the US decision "has no legal effect because it contradicts UN resolutions, especially UN Security Council resolutions on Western Sahara". Further, "the proclamation would undermine the de-escalation efforts made at all levels in order to pave the way for launching a real political process," as the ministry issued in a statement on the matter (Reuters 2020b, Web). Algerian authorities took the news doubly badly, as it not only struck at its policy of supporting Western Sahara independence, but also paved the way for already official and extensive political-economic-military cooperation between Israel and their biggest rival in the region, the Kingdom of Morocco. "The Israeli army is at our borders," Algerian journalist and analyst Abed Charef wrote, continuing that "The rapprochement between Morocco and Israel opens the way, if it has not already happened, for Israeli aid to support Morocco's army" (Reuters 2020b, Web).

The situation was even more perilous than commonly acknowledged, as for years, the two countries had been engaged in an unofficial arms race, placing significant strain on their national budgets. However, the arms race between the countries has notably intensified in recent years. In 2020, Rabat announced a plan to construct a military base on a 23-hectare area in Jerada province, a mere 38 kilometres from Algerian territory. Algerian authorities assert that the base will be equipped with advanced electronic systems supplied by Israel (Hernández, 2020). In August 2021, Algiers broke off diplomatic relations with Morocco due to "hostile actions against Algeria and using Pegasus spyware against its officials, supporting a separatist group and failing in bilateral commitments, including on the Western Sahara issue" (Reuters 2021). Algeria also stopped supplying natural gas to Morocco through the Maghreb-Europe pipeline as of 1 November 2021 (Rashad, Ould Ahmed, and Chikhi 2021).

Conclusions

With Morocco's efforts to expand military installations and purchase modern weapons, there has been growing concern in Algiers that this could be a preparation for Rabat to continue a search for a final military solution to the Western Sahara conflict. A similar situation occurred in the Caucasus, when in the autumn of 2020 Azerbaijan decided to initiate a war with Armenia to regain the Nagorno-Karabakh area, which for the previous 30 years had functioned as an unrecognised state supported by Armenia. It seemed that the world, exhausted by the two-year COVID-19 pandemic, would not pay much attention to peripheral conflicts, while both the Nagorno-Karabakh issue and Western Sahara were regarded as such. Meanwhile, Russia's aggression against Ukraine on 24 February 2022 seems to have caused an absolute re-evaluation of the approach to aggressor states, at least in the West. A series of sanctions were introduced against Russia, both political and, which is historically unprecedented, economic, including on some of its main sources of income – oil and gas. In this situation, interest in alternative suppliers of the raw materials has grown exponentially. One of the main countries with rich deposits of these resources is Algeria. It should therefore come as no surprise that a senior US administrative official with the rank of Secretary of State, Antony J. Blinken, visited Algiers as early as on 30 March 2022. This was the first visit by a US representative since the Donald Trump administration had recognised Moroccan sovereignty over the Western Sahara territory and approved the plan for Western Sahara autonomy within the Moroccan state. Since that event, relations between Washington and Algiers had severely deteriorated. In Algeria, Blinken met with President Abdelmadjid Tebboune, seeking to persuade Algeria to reopen the pipeline that transported Algerian natural gas through Moroccan territory to Spain. This was aimed at assisting European countries in reducing their energy dependence on Russia. The GME pipeline was closed in 2021 after Algiers declined to renew a 25-year export contract following heightened bilateral tensions. In Algiers, Blinken was also scheduled to discuss regional security and stability issues, as well as trade cooperation. On the Western Sahara issue, the US Secretary of State reiterated the previous American administration's expressed support for the Moroccan autonomy plan for Western Sahara, which he described as "serious, credible and realistic" (France24 2022, Web). However, at a press conference in Algiers, Blinken, when asked by reporters about this, was less categorical and gave the evasive answer that the United States fully supported UN efforts to resolve the situation: "We're very focused on diplomacy". There are many indications that Algeria now has an opportunity, in the current political and economic realities related to the war in Ukraine, to take advantage of its position in the region and strengthen it, not only in the interests of Algiers, but also those of the SADR. As T. M. Hill put it "If increasing energy exports to Europe from Algeria was the primary U.S. request, what did the United States offer Algeria — and what might Algeria have asked for? It's conceivable that Algeria would have asked the Biden administration to walk back the U.S. recognition of Moroccan sovereignty over the Western Sahara — a step that would create significant U.S.-Moroccan tensions" (Hill 2022). Whether this will have any real impact on resolving the Western Sahara issue, only time will tell. The Western Saharan conflict is once again on the radar of geopolitics, but this time Moscow also takes an active stance, not only because of its traditionally good relations with Algiers, but also because of its growing interest in the presence on the African continent, which had started years before February 2022 (Roussellier 2018). In November 2022 Algeria announced that it had formally applied to join the BRICS and it has the support of Russian and Chinese authorities. On the UN forum Algerian representatives since March 2022 have abstained from voting against Russia. As Akram Belkaïd put it "Algerian diplomats [...] insisted that abstention does not amount to unquestioning support for Russia – unlike countries such as North Korea, Syria, Belarus and Eritrea, which automatically vote against UN resolutions critical of Russia" (Belkaïd 2023). This explanation was also provided to the authors during their last stay in Algiers in May 2023. Furthermore, in Algeria the Russian invasion of Ukraine is rather seen as yet another conflict between the great powers. Even if the Ukrainians' suffering evokes sympathy (and it does), there is a conviction that the conflict will be decided in Moscow and Washington, which is reminiscent of the times of the Cold War[14]. Similarly, the question of the already mentioned re-evaluation of the approach to aggressor states remains open and raises an issue of its scope. Will it be also applied to the protracted unsolved conflicts, such as Western Saharan one or is it just another example of double standards, as the Sahrawis and

---

14 Interview with Prof. Smail Debeche, University of Algiers 3, Algiers, Algeria, May 2023; Interview with Dr. Saïd Ayachi, Chairman of the Algerian National Committee of Solidarity with the Sahrawi People, Algiers, Algeria, May 2023.

their allies put it?[15]. Currently, there is no sign that the United States, France, or Spain will be re-evaluating their support for the Moroccan policy towards Western Saharan issue. On the other side, any kind of support or attempt of rapprochement with Moscow may be a dangerous path for the Sahrawi cause and the Algerian international position, short-term gains may turn out to be long-term losses, especially in the face of the uncertain future of the Russian state in the coming years.

References

"Libya-Morocco: treaty instituting the Arab-African Union of States." 1984. *International Legal Materials* 23 (5) September, pp. 1022-1026.

AFRIPOL: Retrieved 20.10.2022, from https://afripol.africa-union.org/

Al Jazeera: "Abdelmadjid Tebboune: Who is Algeria's new president?" 13 December 2019. Retrieved 27.2.2020, from https://www.aljazeera.com/news/2019/12/abdelmadjid-tebboune-algeria-president-191213161923647.html

Allilou, Aziz: "Morocco declares Christopher Ross persona non grata in Western Sahara." *Morocco World News,* 8 November 2015. Retrieved 20.7.2020, from https://www.moroccoworldnews.com/2015/11/172144/morocco-declares-christopher-ross-persona-non-grata-in-western-sahara/

Amirah Fernández, Haizam: "Morocco returns to the African Union amidst unresolved issues." Real Instituto El Cano. 16 February 2017. Retrieved 28.3.2022, from https://www.realinstitutoelcano.org/en/blog/marruecos-vuelve-a-la-union-africana-entre-interrogantes/

Babas, Latifa: "The Western Sahara issue is about decolonization, Algeria's new president says." *Yabiladi.* 19 December 2019. Retrieved 27.2.2020, from https://en.yabiladi.com/articles/details/86904/western-sahara-issue-about-decolonization.html

Bardonnet, Daniel: "La question des frontières marocaines." In Daniel Bardonnet and Driss Basri (eds.) *La Marche Verte.* Paris: Plon, 1990, pp. 93-116.

Cowell, Alan: "African Unity Organization ends its summit gathering in disunity." *The New York Times,* 13 June 1983. Retrieved 17.1.2022, from https://www.nytimes.com/1983/06/13/world/african-unity-organization-ends-its-summit-gathering-in-disunity.html

---

15 Interview with Mr. Abdelkader Taleb Omar, Ambassador of the SADR in Algeria and the Member of the National Secretariat of the POLISARIO Front, Algiers, Algeria, May 2023.

Belkaïd, Akram: "Algeria and Morocco vie to keep Russia onside". *Le Monde Diplomatique*, February 2023. Retrieved 19.4.2023, from https://mondediplo.com/2023/02/06maghreb-ukraine

Cubertafond, Bernard: "L'Algérie du président Chadli." *Politique étrangère*, 46 (1) 1981, pp. 151-162.

Daguzan, Jean-François: "MAGHREB. Les armées en politique: des trajectoires divergentes." *Confluences Méditeranée*, Printemps 29, 1999, pp. 21-28.

Daoudi, Fatiha: *Analyse de situation aux frontières terrestres algéro marocaines: vie quotidienne d'une population partagée* (PhD thesis). Grenoble: Université Grenoble Alpes, 2015.

Drozdiak, William: "Funeral Becomes Forum for Peace Talk." *The Washington Post*, 26 July 1999. Retrieved 20.12.2021, from https://www.washingtonpost.com/archive/politics/1999/07/26/funeral-becomes-forum-for-peace-talk/4bb027b1-69ab-4905-a3a2-10d65cd5e052/

Duignan, Peter / Gann, L. H: *The United States and Africa. A History*. Cambridge: Cambridge University Press, 1984.

Dworkin, Anthony: *North African standoff: How the Western Sahara conflict is fuelling new tensions between Morocco and Algeria*. European Council on Foreign Relations, 8 April 2022. Retrieved 13.6.2022, from https://ecfr.eu/publication/north-african-standoff-how-the-western-sahara-conflict-is-fuelling-new-tensions-between-morocco-and-algeria/

Dyduk, Daniel: *Maroko-Algieria: niespokojnie na granicy*. Polskie Centrum Studiów Afrykanistycznych, 4 November 2014. Retrieved 12.5.2022, from https://pcsa.org.pl/maroko-algieria-niespokojnie-na-granicy/

Faria, Fernanda / Vasconcelos, Alvaro: *Security in Northern Africa: Ambiguity and Reality*, Institute for Security Studies. Challiot Papers, 25 (September 1996), pp. 1-44.

Farsoun, Karen / Paul, Jim: "War in the Sahara: 1963". *MERIP Reports* 45 (1976), pp. 13-16. https://doi.org/10.2307/3011767.

Ferrer Lloret, Jaume: "Morocco, occupying power of Western Sahara: some notes about Spain's foreign legal policy, the role of the Spanish doctrine and the rule of law in international relations". *Spanish Yearbook of International Law*, 26 (2022), pp. 197-246.

France 24. 2020a. "Israel and Morocco agree to normalise ties in latest US-brokered deal." 12 December. Retrieved 31.12.2020, from https://www.france24.com/en/middle-east/20201210-israel-and-morocco-agree-to-normalise-ties-in-latest-us-brokered-deal

France 24. 2020b. "Algeria slams 'foreign manoeuvres' over US-brokered deal on Western Sahara." 12 December. Retrieved 24.12.2020, from https://www.

france24.com/en/africa/20201212-algeria-slams-foreign-manoeuvres-over-us-brokered-deal-on-w-sahara

France 24. 2022. "Blinken visits Algeria in shadow of Ukraine war." 30 March. Retrieved 5.2.2022, from https://www.france24.com/en/live-news/20220330-blinken-visits-algeria-in-shadow-of-ukraine-war

Gwertzman, Bernard: "A Moroccan-Libyan 'Union' Jolts U.S." *The New York Times*, 26 August 1984. Retrieved 16.1.2022, from https://www.nytimes.com/1984/08/26/weekinreview/a-moroccan-libyan-union-jolts-us.html

Hekking, Morgan: "Morocco, Mauritania Move Towards Concrete Bilateral Cooperation", *Morocco World News,* 15.1.2020, retrieved 22.2.2021, from https://www.moroccoworldnews.com/2020/01/291196/morocco-mauritania-move-bilateral-cooperation/

Hernández, Henar: "Algeria to build a military base near the border with Morocco." *Atalayar*. 26 June 2020. Retrieved 30.12.2020, from https://atalayar.com/en/content/algeria-build-military-base-near-border-morocco

Hill, Thomas M.: *Ukraine War Puts New Focus on Conflict in Western Sahara. Amid new tensions, can diplomacy unstick a long-stalled peace process with Morocco and Algeria?* United States Institute of Peace. 14 April 2022. Retrieved 15.5.2022, from https://www.usip.org/publications/2022/04/ukraine-war-puts-new-focus-conflict-western-sahara

Igrouane, Youssef: "King Mohammed VI to visit Mauritania during his next round tour in Africa". *Morocco World News*, 2.3.2017. Retrieved 15.4.2022, from https://www.moroccoworldnews.com/2017/03/209874/king-mohammed-vi-visit-mauritania-next-round-tour-africa/ [15.04.2022].

Informal talks with the participants of the 44th European Conference of Support and Solidarity with the Sahrawi People (EUCOCO), Vitoria-Gasteiz, Spain, 22-23 November 2019.

Interviews and observations during field research in Mauritania, February 2020.

Interview with Dr. Saïd Ayachi, Chairman of the Algerian National Committee of Solidarity with the Sahrawi People, Algiers, Algeria, May 2023.

Interview with Mr. Abdelkader Taleb Omar, Ambassador of the SADR in Algeria and the Member of the National Secretariat of the POLISARIO Front, Algiers, Algeria, May 2023.

Interview with Mr. Hamdi Bueha, Secretary-General of the Ministry of Foreign Affairs of the Sahrawi Arab Democratic Republic, and Mr. Mohamed Hammadi from the Department of Europe and the Arab World of the MFA of the SADR, Rabouni refugee camp, Algeria, May 2016.

Interview with Mrs. Fatma Mehdi Hassam, Secretary-General of the National Union of the Sahrawi Women, Boujdour refugee camp, Algeria, April 2016.

Interview with Prof. Dr. El Moctar Taleb Hende, University of Nouakchott, Nouakchott, Mauritania, February 2019.

Interview with Prof. Smail Debeche, University of Algiers 3, Algiers, Algeria, May 2017.

Interview with Prof. Smail Debeche, University of Algiers 3, Algiers, Algeria, May 2023.

Isidoros, Konstantina. 2018. *Nomads and nation-building in the Western Sahara. Gender, Politics and the Sahrawi.* London: I.B. Tauris.

Jajili, Youssef: *Éclairages sur le Sahara (Interview avec Mohamed Elyazghi).* Casablanca: Les Editions Maghrébines, 2018.

Jensen, Erik: *Western Sahara. Anatomy of a stalemate?* Boulder/London: Lynne Riener Publishers, 2012.

Jensen, Geoffrey: *War and Insurgency in the Western Sahara.* Carlise Barracks: Strategic Studies Institute and U.S. Army War College Press, 2013.

Kasraoui, Safaa: "Morocco's Omar Hilale: Western Sahara will never be independent." *Morocco World News.* 18 June 2019. Retrieved 23.7.2020, from https://www.moroccoworldnews.com/2019/06/276139/morocco-western-sahara-algeria/

Kasznik-Christian, Aleksandra: *Algieria.* Warszawa: Wydawnictwo TRIO, 2006.

Kłosowicz, Robert: "The role of Ethiopia in the regional security complex of the Horn of Africa." *Ethiopian Journal of Social Sciences and Language Studies* 2(2) 2015, pp. 83-97.

Kłosowicz, Robert: *Problemy dysfunkcyjności państw Afryki Subsaharyjskiej.* Kraków: Wydawnictwo Uniwersytetu Jagiellońskiego, 2017.

Kłosowicz, Robert: „Między Marokiem a Algierią. Mauretania wobec kwestii Sahary Zachodniej." *Politeja* 18, 6 (75) 2021, pp. 143-157, https://doi.org/10.12797/Politeja.18.2021.75.07

Kłosowicz, Robert: "Policies of the Maghreb Countries Toward Western Sahara: Mauritania's Perspective". *Hungarian Journal of African Studies* 16 (1) 2022, pp. 57-70.

Kłosowicz, Robert / Mormul, Joanna: *Erytrea i jej wpływ na sytuację polityczną w Rogu Afryki.* Kraków: Wydawnictwo Uniwersytetu Jagiellońskiego, 2018.

Kosidło, Adam. 2012. *Sahara Zachodnia. Fiasko dekolonizacji czy sukces podboju 1975 – 2011.* Gdańsk: Wydawnictwo Uniwersytetu Gdańskiego.

Kosidło, Adam: „Maroko - trudny powrót do Unii Afrykańskiej, cz.1: Poszukiwanie drogi". *Colloquium* 10 (3) 2018, pp. 25-56.

Kowalska-Lewicka, Anna: *Mauretania.* Wiedza Powszechna, Warszawa, 1976.

Kukułka, Józef: *Historia współczesnych stosunków międzynarodowych 1945-2000*. Warszawa: Wydawnictwo Naukowe SCHOLAR, 2001.

Lederer, Edith M.: "UN welcomes momentum on Western Sahara, but parties at odds." *Associated Press*. 30 April 2019. Retrieved 21.7.2020, from https://apnews.com/1a29f01a230243e2b9d5c5294a681839

Lounnas, Djallil / Messari, Nizar: Algeria – Morocco relations and their impact on the Maghrebi regional system. Working Papers 20, October 2020, Middle East and North Africa Regional Architecture: Mapping Geopolitical Shifts, Regional Order and Domestic Transformations (MENARA), Istituto Affari Internazionali. Retrieved 21.8.2021, from https://www.iai.it/sites/default/files/menara_wp_20.pdf

Le Patriote: "Plus de 5 quintaux de kif saisis, 41 narcotrafiquants arrêtés", 11 May 2023. No. 42177: 24.

"Mauritania says 'time has come' for a solution to Western Sahara conflict. The remarks seemed to indicate a foreign policy shift in favour of Morocco". *The Arab Weekly*, 15.11.2019. Retrieved 15.4.2022, from https://thearabweekly.com/mauritania-says-time-has-come-solution-western-sahara-conflict

Mormul, Joanna: „Hijos de las nubes i 45 lat marzeń: uchodźcy Saharawi na terytorium Algierii." *Politeja* 18, 6 (75) 2021, pp. 169-182. https://doi.org/10.12797/Politeja.18.2021.75.08

Organisation of African Unity: Memorandum Submitted by the Democratic and People's Republic of Algeria on the Convening of a Special Session of the United Nations General Assembly, Council of Ministers Twenty Second Ordinary Session, Kampala, 1-4 April 1974. Retrieved 2.3.2022, from https://archives.au.int/bitstream/handle/123456789/9161/CM%20567%28XXII%29_E.pdf?sequence=1&isAllowed=y

Ożarowski, Rafał: „Sahara Zachodnia jako przykład afrykańskiego quazi-państwa." *Cywilizacja i polityka* 10, 2012, pp. 204-226.

Pierros, Filippos / Meunier, Jacob / Abrams, Stan: "The Euro-Mediterranean Partnership, 1994–1998." In Filippos Pierros, Jacob Meunier, and Stan Abrams. *Bridges and Barriers. The European Union's Mediterranean Policy, 1961–1998*. London: Routledge, 2019, pp. 176-218. https://doi.org/10.4324/9780429027024

Rashad, Marwa / Ould Ahmed, Hamid / Chikhi, Lamine: "Algeria to end gas supplies to Morocco; supply Spain directly – sources." *Reuters*. 25 October 2021. Retrieved 5.2.2022, from https://www.reuters.com/world/africa/algeria-end-gas-supplies-morocco-supply-spain-directly-sources-2021-10-25/

Reuters. 2018. "Bolton frustrated Western Sahara conflict has not been resolved." 13 December. Retrieved 20.7.2020, from https://www.reuters.com/article/

us-westernsahara-usa/bolton-frustrated-western-sahara-conflict-has-not-been-resolved-idUSKBN1OC26U

Reuters. 2020a. "Fears grow of new Western Sahara war between Morocco and Polisario Front." 13 November. Retrieved 5.12.2020, from https://www.reut ers.com/article/us-morocco-westernsahara-idUSKBN27T15S

Reuters. 2020b. "Algeria rejects Trump's stance on Western Sahara." 12 December. Retrieved 31.12.2020, from https://www.reuters.com/article/algeria-westernsahara-usa-idUSKBN28M0MZ

Reuters. 2021. "Algeria cuts diplomatic relations with Morocco." 25 August. Retrieved 5.2.2022, from https://www.reuters.com/world/algeria-says-cutt ing-diplomatic-ties-with-morocco-2021-08-24/

Riedel, Bruce: "Kennedy, Cuba, and the "War of the Sands"". *Brookings.* 19 July 2021. Retrieved 14.5.2022, from https://www.brookings.edu/blog/order-from-chaos/2021/07/19/kennedy-cuba-and-the-war-of-the-sands/

Roussellier, Jacques: "A Role for Russia in the Western Sahara?". *Carnegie Endowment for International Peace.* 5 June 2018. Retrieved 2.5.2022, from https://carnegieendowment.org/sada/76532

Sahara Press Service. "President of Republic Special Envoy received by President Mohamed Ould Abdel Aziz", 13.8.2016. Retrieved 20.3.2002, from https://www.spsrasd.info/news/en/articles/2016/08/13/3584.html

Secretary Blinken News Conference in Algiers, 30.3.2022, retrieved 6.5.2022, from https://www.c-span.org/video/?519082-1/secretary-blinken-russia-speak-truth-power-ukraine

Shelley, Toby: *Endgame in the Western Sahara. What Future for the Last Africa's Colony?* London-New York: Zed Books, 2004.

Shelley, Toby: "Behind the Baker Plan for Western Sahara." *Middle East Report Online,* 1 August 2003. Retrieved 19.7.2020, from https://merip.org/2003/08/behind-the-baker-plan-for-western-sahara/

Szczepankiewicz, Ewa: „Niedokończona dekolonizacja Sahary Zachodniej – historia i perspektywy rozstrzygnięcia konfliktu." *Politeja* 1(11) 2009, pp. 177-194.

Szczepankiewicz, Ewa: *Region Maghrebu w polityce Unii Europejskiej: założenia, uwarunkowania, efekty współpracy.* Kraków: Oficyna Wydawnicza ABRYS, 2010.

Szeptycki, Andrzej: "Algieria: wrota do Afryki". In Marcin F. Gawrycki and Wiesław Lizak (eds.) *Kuba i Afryka. Sojusz dla rewolucji.* Warszawa: Oficyna Wydawnicza ASPRA-JR, 2008, pp. 209-232.

The Economist. 2010. "Diplomacy over Western Sahara. Morocco v Algeria", 6-12 November. 2010.

Theofilopoulou, Anna: "The United Nations and Western Sahara: A Never-ending Affair." *United States Institute of Peace. Special Report* 166, 2006, pp. 1-20. Retrieved 5.4.2022, from https://www.usip.org/sites/default/files/sr166.pdf

Tziarras, Zenonas / Fredriksen, Sigvart Nordhov: "The Libya Conflict and its Implications for the Broader Region." *Re-imagining the Eastern Mediterranean Series: PCC Report* 4. Nicosia: PRIO Cyprus Centre, 2020. Retrieved 20.3.2022, from https://www.prio.org/publications/12195

United Nations: *The United Nations and Decolonization. Non-Self-Governing Territories.* 10 May 2022. Retrieved 20.4.2023, from https://www.un.org/dppa/decolonization/en/nsgt

United Nations Peacemaker: *Declaration of Principles on Western Sahara by Spain, Morocco and Mauritania* (Madrid Accords), 14 November 1975. Retrieved 5.4.2021, from https://peacemaker.un.org/sites/peacemaker.un.org/files/MA-MR-ES_751114_DeclarationPrinciplesOnWesternSahara_0.pdf

United Nations Secretary-General: "Note to correspondents: Resignation of the Personal Envoy of the Secretary-General for Western Sahara, former President of Germany, Horst Köhler." 22 May 2019. Retrieved 11.5.2022, from https://www.un.org/sg/en/content/sg/note-correspondents/2019-05-22/note-correspondents-resignation-of-the-personal-envoy-of-the-secretary-general-for-western-sahara-former-president-of-germany-horst-k%C3%B6hler

United Nations Security Council: *The United Nations Mission for the Referendum in Western Sahara (MINURSO), Resolution 690* of 29 April 1991. Retrieved 10.3.2020, from https://www.securitycouncilreport.org/atf/cf/%7B65BFCF9B-6D27-4E9C-8CD3-CF6E4FF96FF9%7D/MINURSO%20SRES690.pdf

United Nations Security Council: *Resolution 2414,* adopted by the Security Council at its 8246th meeting on 27 April 2018. Retrieved 15.7.2020, from http://www.securitycouncilreport.org/atf/cf/%7B65BFCF9B-6D27-4E9C-8CD3-CF6E4FF96FF9%7D/s_res_2414.pdf

United Nations Security Council: *Resolution 2494,* adopted by the Security Council at its 8651st meeting on 30 October 2019. Retrieved 22.7.2020, from https://www.securitycouncilreport.org/atf/cf/%7B65BFCF9B-6D27-4E9C-8CD3-CF6E4FF96FF9%7D/S_RES_2494.pdf

United Nations, General Assembly-Thirtieth Session, 3458 (XXX), Question of Spanish Sahara/A/2435th plenary meeting, 10 December 1975, retrieved 17.1.2022, from https://www.usc.es/export9/sites/webinstitucional/gl/institutos/ceso/descargas/A_RES_3458_1975.pdf

White House: *Proclamation on Recognizing the Sovereignty of The Kingdom of Morocco over The Western Sahara.* 10 December 2020. Retrieved 20.2.2022,

from https://trumpwhitehouse.archives.gov/presidential-actions/proclamat
ion-recognizing-sovereignty-kingdom-morocco-western-sahara/

Zoubir, Yahia: "Soviet Policy toward the Western Sahara conflict". *Africa Today,*
3rd Qtr., 34 (3) 1987, pp. 17-32.

Zunes, Stephen / Mundy, Jacob: *Western Sahara: war, nationalism, and conflict
irresolution.* Syracuse, New York: Syracuse University Press, 2010.

Robert Kłosowicz, Ewa Szczepankiewicz-Rudzka

Chapter 7. North African States Not Bordering Western Sahara in the Face of the Problem of Its Independence[1]

The issue of Western Sahara has been a major source of division in the North African region for over fifty years. This problem not only impacts political relations but also hinders economic cooperation. The division between states supporting Western Sahara's independence and those backing Morocco's stance has created strong polarisation, not only within the region but also across the African continent and the Middle East. The aim of this chapter is to analyse the attitudes of North African countries not bordering the territory of Western Sahara, namely Libya, Tunisia, and Egypt, toward the Sahrawi Arab Democratic Republic (SADR) and the question of its independence, both before and after the Arab Spring. The analysis considers the region's history, with a focus on the Arab Spring as a significant turning point. The outbreak of the Arab Spring caused a political reshuffle in the North African states, and among many changes, there was also a shift in the approach of Libya and Egypt towards the Western Saharan issue, while Tunisia consistently attempted to implement a policy of positive neutrality.

Keywords: Western Sahara, Tunisia, Libya, Egypt, foreign policy, *de facto state,* North Africa

Introduction

The issue of delimiting borders within the Sahara was on the agenda of countries located in the North African region, practically at the dawn of independence. This problem concerned not only the issue of Western Sahara, Morocco, Algeria, and Mauritania, but also all the Maghreb states, including Tunisia and Libya, and extending also to the neighbouring countries of Sub-Saharan Africa (specifically the Sahel region) such as Mali, Niger, and Chad, whose territories lie within the Sahara. The long border between the Egypt and Sudan is also not free of disputes[2]. All these reciprocal claims were the aftermath of the artificial borders drawn by the European colonisers as a result of their agreements and rivalries. For the newly established North African states, territorial issues took on special

---

1   This chapter is the result of a research project financed by the National Science Centre (Narodowe Centrum Nauki), Poland, grant ID: 2017/25/B/HS5/00958.

2   The two disputed areas along their borders are Halaib Triangle and Bir Tawil.

importance, as they served to consolidate their subjectivity and identity. Therefore, disputes over the demarcation of borders in the Sahara were fraught with serious frictions between the states, sometimes escalating into armed conflicts (see Table 4). The dispute over the status of Western Sahara exemplifies a post-colonial conflict stemming from the disparity between Spain's hurried departure from Africa and the physical demarcation of borders on the map. Historical and ethnic claims asserted by the successors of Spanish Sahara, namely Mauritania and Morocco, alongside the disregard for the indigenous Sahrawi population's aspirations for their own state, have led to a protracted conflict involving both neighbouring countries and those further afield (Roggero 2022, pp. 13-16).

Table 4. Border conflicts between states in North Africa and the Sahel region

conflict parties	conflict period	status
Algeria - Tunisia	1961-1970	Agreement in 1970
Algeria - Morocco	1962-1970	Agreement in 1970
Mali-Mauritania	1960-1963	Agreement in 1963
Chad - Libya	1935 - 1964	International Court of Justice, decision in 1994
Egypt-Sudan	1956-open	No Agreement
Tunisia - Libya	1990-1994	International Court of Justice, decision in 1994
Mali – Burkina Faso	1963, 1974-1975, 1985-1986	No Agreement
Western Sahara[3] - Morocco	1975 - open	No Agreement

Source: own study based on *Africa's international borders as potential sources…2012*

Although Tunisia, Libya and Egypt are countries without a direct border with Western Sahara, they have been – to a greater or lesser extent – involved in the

---

3   By Western Sahara we understand the Sahrawi Arab Democratic Republic (SADR) – partially recognised state proclaimed on 27 February 1976 by the POLISARIO Front and currently in control of the 20% of the territory it claims rights for.

Western Saharan conflict since the beginning, through the fact that they belong to the same region of North Africa. Libya, following the example of Algeria, for a certain period, especially at the beginning of the conflict, strongly supported the POLISARIO Front, the pro-independence movement of the Sahrawi people, providing it with financial and military assistance. On the other hand, successive Tunisian governments consistently tried to pursue a policy of so-called "positive neutrality" on the Western Saharan issue, attempting to maintain a neutral position as much as possible. Egypt, which is particularly evident under the presidencies of Anwar Sadat, Hosni Mubarak and now, has been more focused on the area of the Middle East and East Africa and not greatly concerned with the issues of the independence of Western Sahara. To sum up, while in the case of Libya there was a certain favourable attitude, and in the first period of Gaddafi's rule even support for the Western Sahara independence option, both Tunisia and Egypt adopted a policy of not taking sides in the conflict (Damis 1983, pp.169-179).

Tunisia's policy towards Western Sahara until the outbreak of the Arab Spring in 2011

Against the backdrop of the aroused territorial ambitions of its neighbours, from the beginning of Tunisia's independence, i.e., 1956, President Habib Bourguiba sought to pursue what is referred to as a "policy of positive neutrality." The peculiar *idée fixe* of Tunisia's first president can be boiled down to a formula from his 1959 statement that *"the Sahara does not represent land to be conquered, but capital to be exploited."* (Lacouture 1961). Indeed, Bourguiba placed less importance on extending political sovereign authority over new territories, opting instead to seek solutions based on collective cooperation in the region. This was the principle behind Bourguiba's abandonment of territorial claims in the Sahara during the Libyan-Tunisian-Algerian border settlement. The disputed case concerned border marker 233 (*l'affaire du borne* 233) and was based on a Tunisian claim originally made to the territories in the south-west of the country, between Bir-Romane, Fort-Saint and Garet-el-Hammel, about 300 kilometres long and about 100 kilometres wide (Ben Salem 2022).

In his policy towards neighbouring countries, Bourguiba was ahead of the spirit of the times and envisioned the exploitation of the Sahara within the framework of a regional community of states, encompassing its territory under common administration. In the name of good neighbourly relations, after Algerian independence in 1962, he agreed to sign a border protocol six years later (April 16, 1968) marking the tripartite border at Fort Saint, thereby abandoning his claim to the border strip between markers 223-233 (Fort Saint and Garet-el-Hamel) (Lacouture 1961).

Tunisia's conciliatory approach to the division of the Sahara was the opposite of the Moroccan take on the border issue. In turn, Morocco made demands to extend its authority to an area five times larger than the one it covered after independence. The idea of a "Greater Morocco", intensively and consistently promoted by successive Moroccan rulers, beginning with Mohammed V, was woven into the country's identity politics in the following decades. In its understanding, the historical borders of the monarchy extended to Niger and Senegal, encompassing the western Algerian regions of Colomb-Béchar and Tindouf, the northwestern part of Mali, Mauritania, and the entirety of the Spanish Sahara (de la Serre 1966, p. 321).

Not surprisingly, prior to Mauritania's declaration of independence in November, Rabat published a White Paper that also contained a list of areas targeted for Moroccan revindication, including Mauritanian lands. The Mauritanian government responded by issuing what is referred to as the Green Book, which refuted Morocco's claims to its territories and accused Mohammed V of imperialist inclinations (Misra 1964). The Alawite monarchy also took steps in the wider international forum and a month before the official declaration of the Islamic Republic of Mauritania's independence, i.e. in October 1960, the King of Morocco submitted a request to the United Nations General Assembly to investigate the issue of Moroccan rights to Mauritania. Mohammed V had the support of all Arab states in this regard except Tunisia. Tunisia was also one of the first countries to recognise Mauritania's independence and later, along with France and Liberia, gave it diplomatic support in its application to join the United Nations (Constantin / Coulon 1979, p. 343).[4]

The Tunisian position towards the regarding Mauritania's post-colonial status was indirectly expressed in the White Paper, which stated that "[...] the Moroccan claim does not take into account Mauritania's current social and political situation" (Livre blanc... 1961, p. 327). However, the authorities in Rabat were not about to give up and did not recognise Mauritania's independence, official national mourning was declared in Morocco in protest the day after the event. As a result, Morocco did not establish diplomatic relations with Mauritania,

---

4   On 27 October 1961, the Islamic Republic of Mauritania was officially recognised as a member of the organisation with the USSR abstaining in the UN Security Council and with 68 supporting votes, 13 against (Arab states except for Tunisia) and 20 abstaining in the General Assembly (Constantin / Coulon 1979, p. 343).

ostentatiously boycotting the country internationally and undermining its membership in the UN (Kłosowicz 2022a, p. 59).

Nouakchott needed to consolidate its position in the region and, above all, settle relations with its closest neighbours, and the establishment of diplomatic cooperation with Tunisia served Mauritania in emphasising the country's Arab and Islamic identity. Friendly relations between the two states continued in the following years. In 1961, President Moktar Ould Daddah gave his full support to Tunisia to evacuate the French military base located in Tunisia's Mediterranean port of Bizerte. In 1963, a Mauritanian political delegation travelled to Tunisia, and in July 1964, in turn, President Daddah visited Tunis in July 1964. As a result of these visits, several cultural, technical, commercial, and consular cooperation agreements were signed in Nouakchott (Santucci 1979, pp. 372-376).

As already mentioned, Bourguiba's acceptance of the role of Mauritania's promoter in its efforts to become a member of the UN resulted in a deterioration of relations with Rabat, the outward manifestation of which was Morocco's recalling of its ambassador to Tunis in late November 1961. Mutual diplomatic relations were not restored until three years later at the 1964 Pan-African Conference in Cairo. During the Cairo Conference, Bourguiba also made efforts for political rapprochement between King Hassan II of Morocco and Mauritanian President Moktar Ould Daddah. These initial talks set in motion the process as a result of which Hassan II decided in 1969 to recognise Mauritanian independence (Santucci 1979, p. 379).

The position that Morocco took towards Mauritania foreshadowed Rabat's later determination regarding the Spanish colony, which was then Spanish Sahara (now Western Sahara). It should therefore come as no surprise that after Spain withdrew from this territory, the issue of its legal status became a hot topic in the region due to Moroccan claims to these areas. Following the signing of the Tripartite Agreement in Madrid on 14 November 1975 between Spain, Mauritania, and Morocco, which established Morocco and Mauritania as the successors to the Spanish Sahara, concerns arose in Tunis about the resumption of mutual territorial claims and the deterioration of relations in the Maghreb region. Bourguiba rightly predicted that Spain's unilateral decision to withdraw from the Western Saharan territories would reignite a conflict over their status. Therefore, at the height of the conflict between the POLISARIO Front, backed by Algeria and Libya, and Morocco in 1976, when the Sahrawi issue took an armed turn, Tunisia officially declared neutrality and offered its services to facilitate a peaceful path to settling the dispute (Brésillon 2022, p.12). At that time, Tunis opted for international engagement and seeking a solution at the UN or the Organisation of African Unity. A parallel diplomatic offensive was conducted by Tunisian diplomacy in Rabat and Algiers with the aim of reaffirming the position of non-alignment. For Tunisia, the Algiers-Rabat dispute was a serious problem, and balancing between the feuding parties was increasingly difficult. As a result, Tunis did not recognise the Algiers-backed POLISARIO Front, considered the political representation of the Sahrawi people, while at the same time not denying the Sahrawis the right to self-determination (Moshen-Finan 1997).

The policy of positive neutrality was also pursued by the subsequent president of the Republic of Tunisia, Zine El Abidine Ben Ali. Serving as prime minister during the waning years of Bourguiba's presidency and being his close associate, Ben Ali naturally continued Tunisia's approach to the Western Sahara issue (Brésillon, p. 17). The period of his rule saw some easing of tension in relations between the region's states. In 1989, the Arab Maghreb Union (AMU) was established, an integrative grouping that held hopes of reviving economic cooperation and stability in the region. With the AMU, there were plans to ease visa restrictions to aid tourism and family movement, as well as lowering tariffs. Regional cooperation was seen as something that could bring huge benefits to all countries in the region, creating opportunities for the development of new industries, for example, the mutual exploitation of resources could open opportunities for global-level fertiliser production through cross-border cooperation, based on combining Algerian and Libyan energy sources with phosphates from Morocco (Jensen 2012, pp. 116-117). Moreover, the rationale for ending the impasse over Western Sahara was fuelled by the transfer of the dispute to the international level. In 1991, a ceasefire was made official and the United Nations Mission for the Referendum in Western Sahara (MINURSO) was established. The mission's mandate, which began in 1991, was to monitor compliance with the ceasefire and hold a referendum on the future of Western Sahara (Theofilopoulou 2017; Szczepankiewicz 2009, pp. 186-187).

Diplomatic leaks published on the *Wikileaks* in 2010 suggest that, in essence, the Tunisian position took a more pragmatic turn. During a meeting between Zine El Abidine Ben Ali and US Assistant Secretary of State for Near Eastern Affairs David Welch in February 2008, the Tunisian president was said to have used a phrase that made it clear that the impasse in resolving the dispute lies with Algeria and its insistence on creating an independent state at all costs, i.e., the Sahrawi Arab Democratic Republic (Belkaid 2017).

This fact allows for the conclusion that while, as in the case of the Bourguiba government, it was in Tunisia's interest to quickly resolve the dispute over Mauritanian independence and revive regional cooperation, Ben Ali's government was ready to recognise Rabat's claims in regard to the Western Sahara issue. This position did not find expression in official documents, although it can be assumed with a high degree of probability that the Tunisian authorities would have been able to sacrifice the issue of Western Saharan independence, which they believed was holding the issue of cooperation within the Arab Maghreb Union hostage.

Libya's policy towards Western Sahara until the outbreak of the Arab Spring in 2011

Compared to Tunis flexible stance, balancing between idealism and political realism, Libya's approach to the Sahrawi dispute was more explicit. When Muammar Gaddafi took power in Tripoli, he tried to emulate the Pan-Africanism and Pan-Arabism of Egyptian President Gamal Abdel Nasser, and when in September 1970, Nasser died, he tried to portray himself as his successor for the leader of African states. By dabbling in anti-imperialist and anti-Zionist slogans, he became an advocate of the rekindled Arab pride, a role model for those committed to Arab unity, and a dedicated supporter of the Palestinian cause and, later, also the Sahrawi cause. Since Gaddafi overthrew King Idris I, who had a good relationship with Hassan II, in a coup, and due to his undisguised hostility towards monarchs whom he regarded as impediments to progress, relations between Gaddafi and the Moroccan king were not good from the start, especially since Hassan II openly opposed Gaddafi's radical views (Harris 1986, p. 86). After the 1971 coup in Morocco, aimed at overthrowing the Alawite monarchy and proclaiming a republic, Hassan II accused Gaddafi of supporting those behind the coup, while the Libyan leader publicly gave moral support to the organisers of the coup. The result was a break in diplomatic relations between Rabat and Tripoli (Miller 2013, pp. 174-178). The mutual relations only improved during the war between Israel and the Egyptian-Syrian coalition (the Yom Kippur War) in 1973[5].

In addition, the two countries also differed in terms of their foreign policy. Gaddafi advocated for the independence of Moroccan-occupied Western Sahara and supported the POLISARIO Front, while Hassan II considered the Western Saharan lands part of Morocco. Hassan II was also regarded as an ally of the USA and France, maintaining clandestine relations with Israel (Lobban Jr 2014, p. 70). An interesting event is Gaddafi's organization of a "green march" in 1973, which consisted of a cavalcade of twenty thousand vehicles that travelled more than a thousand kilometres along the coast from Tripoli to the Egyptian border (Hilsum 2013). This action was intended as a manifestation of the will of the

---

5   Diplomatic relations were resumed in January 1975.

Libyan people expressing their readiness to unite with Egypt. Two years later in November 1975, Hassan II would also organise a "green march" to the Western Sahara areas, attended by thousands of Moroccans in order to "annex Western Sahara to Morocco as an expression of the will of the popular masses." The similarity between the two initiatives is very interesting, and consequently raises the question of whether Gaddafi inspired Hassan II in this regard.

As already mentioned, from the beginning of the conflict in Western Sahara, Gaddafi supported the POLISARIO Front, which he expressed, for example, in January 1976, when he announced that he condemned the division of Western Sahara between Mauritania and Morocco, and then provided assistance to the POLISARIO Front in building up its armed forces. During their warfare with Mauritania and Morocco, he also established military training camps on Libyan territory, providing weapons and radio broadcasting equipment. It is worth noting that before Algeria became the main supporter of the Sahrawi cause, it was previously Libya which supported the POLISARIO Front since its inception in 1973 (Shelley 2004, p. 194).

Gaddafi also acted as one of the mediators of the agreements concluded between Mauritania and the POLISARIO Front when, after the overthrow of President Moktar Ould Daddah in 1978, his successor Mustafa Ould Salek leaned towards an agreement with the Sahrawis. This resulted in signing a peace treaty in Algiers on 5 August 1979, under which Mauritania withdrew from the occupied area of Western Sahara and recognised the POLISARIO Front as the only representative of the Sahrawi people. In August 1979, Libya reciprocated by concluding several agreements on economic and cultural cooperation with Mauritania. (Kłosowicz 2022a, p. 61).

Libya was among the countries that sent a letter to the Secretary-General of the Organisation of African Unity in July 1980, expressing support for the admission of the Sahrawi Arab Democratic Republic (SADR) to the organisation. In later years, Gaddafi vehemently rejected the Moroccan autonomy plan for Western Sahara, asserting that the Sahrawis should be allowed to choose between two options in a referendum: integration with Morocco or independence (Theofilopoulos 2007, pp. 22-23). These actions by Gaddafi heightened diplomatic tensions between Rabat and Tripoli, leading Morocco to sever diplomatic relations with Libya in April 1980. Relations were only re-established fourteen months later, in July 1981 (Mark 2004).

In April 1981, Gaddafi organised a meeting in Tripoli attended by the Mauritanian Prime Minister Maaouya Ould Sid'Ahmed Taya, Secretary-General of the POLISARIO Front Mohamed Abdelaziz, leader of the Lebanese National Resistance Front Walid Kamal Jumblatt and Secretary-General of the Popular Front for the Liberation of Palestine Ahmed Jibril. At the meeting, Gaddafi came up with a proposal to proclaim a union between the SADR and Mauritania, as well as to create a pact grouping the SADR, Libya, Algeria, and Mauritania. However, once again, Gaddafi's unification proposals did not come to pass.

In June 1981, Libya went international with a new peace initiative to resolve conflicts in the Arab world, including the Western Sahara (Gupte 1981). Soon, the Western Sahara issue, pushed by Algeria and Libya, divided the Organisation of African Unity so sharply that it was even at risk of splitting into two blocs. In addition, the prolongation of the conflict over Western Sahara caused regional alliances in Cold War realities to become part of the US-Soviet rivalry. On the one hand, Morocco was supported by the USA and France, while – on the other – Algeria and Libya enjoyed the support of the Soviet Union. The tightening political course of the new US administration under President Ronald Reagan toward the USSR led to demonstrations of American strength in North Africa, such as the shooting down of two Libyan military aircraft by US fighter jets from the Sixth Fleet over the Gulf of Sirte near Libyan territory in August 1981(Jackson 1984, p. 221).

Despite the support of the USA and France, the Moroccan authorities, who were slipping into increasing political isolation in the region, decided on a surprising move to outflank Algiers through an alliance that in August 1984 stunned the world, primarily its allies, such as the US and France. Hassan II and Gaddafi signed the Oujda Treaty (also known as the Arabic–African Federation Treaty). The aim of which was to establish a "union of states" between the two, and eventually to create a "Great Arab Maghreb". An important element of the union was the provision that an attack on one of the states would be considered an act of aggression against the other signatory, which automatically deprived the POLISARIO Front of support from Tripoli. As history has shown, however, the union did not even last two years. The main goal of the Moroccan ruler, it seems, was to end Libya's military aid to the POLISARIO Front, isolate Algiers in the Maghreb region, and intensify cooperation between Rabat and Tripoli, as well as Tunis and Nouakchott. In turn, Gaddafi aimed to implement Nasser's idea of building pan- Arab unity and to draw Morocco away from allied relations with the United States and the Western world in general. Despite the collapse of this initiative, which seemed unrealistic from the beginning. Hassan II succeeded in blocking Libya's military aid to the SADR for a time and in cooling Algerian-Libyan relations (Schumacher 1984; Kosidło 2012, p. 91; Jensen pp. 45-46).

In 2009, Gaddafi returned to the idea of supporting the POLISARIO Front and the Sahrawi issue, which was manifested, for example, in the gesture of inviting the president of the Sahrawi Arab Democratic Republic, Mohamed

Abdelaziz, to participate in the ceremonies commemorating the September Revolution of 1969. This fact obviously angered King Mohammed VI, who ordered the Moroccan delegation to withdraw from the festivities and leave Libya. In an interview with the France24 television channel in July 2010, Gaddafi stated that "there is no alternative to the referendum in Western Sahara and those who oppose will pay a heavy price." In addition, also on the occasion of the Arab League Summit held in Sirte, Libya in March 2010, Gaddafi re-welcomed the SADR leader Mohamed Abdelaziz with all honours. These diplomatic moves angered the Moroccan authorities and raised questions about the Libyan leader's true intentions (Dahmani 2019).

The problem with Gaddafi's inconsistent attitude to the Western Saharan issue, which he once strongly supported, and in other moments of his rule he distanced himself from it, is related to a certain *idée fixe* of the Libyan dictator, who wanted to unite initially the countries of North Africa, and later all the tribes inhabiting the Sahara. Thus, Gaddafi wanted to make political efforts to build the institutional unity of North African states, in light of which the creation of Western Sahara would be, in his mind, a form of Balkanisation of the Maghreb, in which the cooperation of quarrelling and mutually not recognised states would be very difficult, if at all possible. Moreover, for the Libyan leader, the fighting in the Western Sahara area was in a sense a testing ground that would later bear fruit during the Libyan-Chadian war. In 2005, Gaddafi launched his concept of uniting all the nomadic tribes living in the Sahara under the banner of a borderless Islamic Republic of the Sahara, hoping to become the leader of all the peoples living in the area (Kłosowicz 2016; Lewis 1981, pp. 412-413; Malinowski 2001, p. 211)[6]. In 2006, the Libyan dictator, as was his style, announced the formation of the Popular and Social League of the Great Sahara Tribes in Timbuktu. Gaddafi considered all the borders dividing the Sahara completely artificial. At the same time, by his actions, he encouraged the Tuaregs of Algeria, Mali, and Niger to unite and supported their rebellion (UN Security Council, Web)[7]. In some of his speeches, he extended the concept of a Greater Sahara to encompass an area from Mauritania to Iraq, and even Saudi Arabia (Lacoste 2011, pp. 14-16).

---

6   Earlier, Gaddafi took military steps to weaken the government in Chad by getting involved in the power struggle in the Central African Republic, where he sent reinforcements of troops.

7   Currently, since 2015, the terrorist group Islamic State in the Greater Sahara has been operating in this area.

In a sense, Gaddafi's ideas were fulfilled in the subsequent Tuareg revolt in Mali and the establishment in January 2012 of the National Movement for the Liberation of Azawad (*Mouvement national pour la libération de l'Azawad*, MNLA) who, together with Islamic armed groups including Ansar Dine, Al-Qaida in the Islamic Maghreb (AQIM) and Movement for Unity and Jihad in Western Africa (*Mouvement pour l'unicité et le jihad en Afrique de l'Ouest*, MUJAO) initiated a series of attacks against Government forces in the north of the country[8]. These incidents were a direct consequence of the fall of the Gaddafi regime in Libya in October 2011, when the Tuareg mercenary fighters fighting in his service returned to Mali with stolen weapons from Libyan warehouses, which enabled them to start fighting for the independence of Azawad in January 2012. As a result of the Tuareg revolt from January to March 2012, the central authorities lost control of several cities, and the rebels gained control of most of Azawad with the most important cities in the north: Kidal, Gao, and Timbuktu. As a result of fighting in the north of the country, Mali became destabilised, there was a military mutiny in Bamako followed by a coup d'état that overthrew President Amadou Toumani Touré. The Tuaregs took advantage of this situation and on 6 April 2012, they announced the end of military operations against the Malian authorities and declared the independence of Azawad, comprised the northern part of Mali. The Tuaregs declared the city of Gao as the capital of their new country (Al Jazeera 2012). In this way, a short-lived unrecognised state was created (Azawad survived only a few months from the beginning of April 2012 to January 2013), which was put to an end by a military operation carried out by West African states associated in the Economic Community of West African States (ECOWAS) with military support of France (Operation Serval) (Boeke/Schuurman 2015). Thus, paradoxically, the fall of Gaddafi began, at least in part, the implementation of his concept of a Saharan state, whose short episode as an unrecognised state is now part of the history of separatist movements in Africa.

It is also worth mentioning that for years, until the fall of Gaddafi's rule, Libya, along with Algeria, Cuba, and Syria, was the main place Sahrawi youth living in refugee camps on Algerian territory to continue their higher education (Mormul 2021, p. 174).

---

8   The United Nations Multidimensional Integrated Stabilisation Mission in Mali (MINUSMA) was established by the UN Security Council resolution 2100 of 25 April 2013.

Egypt's policy towards Western Sahara until the outbreak of the Arab Spring in 2011

Compared to the clear stance of its Maghreb neighbours, the Western Saharan issue did not dominate the foreign policy of the first decades of independent Egypt, on the contrary, it was practically absent from the political discourse in Egypt. The coming to power of Gamal Abdel Nasser as a result of the Egyptian Revolution[9] on 23 July 1952 not only led to political and social changes in Egypt itself, but also guaranteed him the role of a leader in the Arab world and a promoter of anti-colonial movements on the African continent. Egypt's diplomatic victory in the Suez Crisis of 1956 cemented this position, and consequently the Nasser ideology of Pan-Arabism and the policy of supporting fellow Arabs fighting external oppression inspired liberation movements throughout North Africa, the African Sahel, the Middle East, and the Arabian Peninsula. It also had a particularly strong resonance in Algeria, which was under the rule of France, in Western Sahara, which was a Spanish colony, and Libya, which was then a monarchy.

Fathi el Dib, President Nasser's delegate for contacts with the Algerian National Liberation Front (*Front de libération nationale*, FLN), recalls that "[…] Nasser has repeatedly said that Egypt will not be able to feel fully free as long as any Arab country is occupied." The liberation of North Africa-Arab Maghreb, "[…] the most dominated and most deeply colonized Arab lands, should be a priority" (Gilbert 1990, p. 96). Political declarations are accompanied by deeds. In 1954, the Committee for the Liberation of the Arab Maghreb is founded in Cairo, and Egypt's diplomatic activities in the 1950s focused on supporting the Algerian War of Independence[10]. It is no coincidence that political meetings of the Algeria's National Liberation Front were held in Cairo. Importantly, it was also where the leader of the FLN, Ferhat Abbas, on 19 September 1958, announced the creation of the Provisional Government of the Algerian Republic (*Gouvernement provisoire de la République algérienne*, GPRA) and thus Cairo became the seat of the Algerian government fighting for the country's independence (Gilbert, p. 98).

---

9   Also known as the Egyptian Revolution of 1952, the 1952 Coup d'état, the 23 July Revolution.
10 Libya gained independence in 1951, Tunisia in 1956, Morocco in 1956, and Sudan in 1956.

Besides diplomatic support, Egypt provided the Algerian revolutionaries with military and technical assistance. In historical narratives concerning the era of Nasserism, the common elements between the Egyptian Revolution of 1952 and the Algerian Revolution of 1954-1962, as well as the real support for the anti-colonial struggle that followed are prominent in Nasser's activities. What may be surprising, however, is the lack of emphasis on the Western Sahara issue in Egypt's policy at that time. The postulate of decolonisation of the Spanish Sahara is only mentioned by Nasser, but it was not prioritised in the agenda of his foreign policy, although it fully aligned with the interests of the Maghreb Liberation Committee. This was likely due to the choice of priorities, with the primary focus being on achieving independence for the North African states - Morocco, Tunisia, and Algeria. In the case of the latter, urgent support was provided for the Algerian liberation struggle against French colonialism. It is significant to note that the "annexation of the Sahara" as a result of the Green March occurred after the death of Gamal Abdel Nasser in 1970. This circumstance facilitated King Hassan II of Morocco in making political manoeuvres towards Western Sahara, as there was no other politician of comparable significance and authority in the region as Nasser (Yasmine 2010, pp. 189-193).

The signing of the tripartite agreement in Madrid in 1975, which sealed the withdrawal of Spain from Western Sahara and its division between Morocco and Mauritania, omitting its indigenous people - Sahrawis, as mentioned above, took place during the presidency of Muhammad Anwar el-Sadat. This agreement moved the territorial "dispute" from the level of Spain-Maghreb countries to the wider regional level. Egypt decided not to participate in it, bearing in mind historically good, even brotherly relations with Algeria. Sadat did not take a clear stance on the Sahrawi aspirations to create an independent state, nor did he officially recognise the POLISARIO Front and the Sahrawi Arab Democratic Republic. This decision can be interpreted through the perspective of his strategy of not opening new conflict fronts in relations with the Arab world. Supporting the POLISARIO Front would mean entering conflict with the Kingdom of Morocco, while recognising the Alawites' claims to the Western Saharan territory would inflame relations between Cairo and Algiers, which had already been severely damaged by the signing of the peace agreement with Israel in Camp David in 1978 (Yasmine 2010, pp. 194-196).

The normalisation of relations with the Jewish state, on the one hand, condemned Egypt to criticism, even banishment, from its Arab partners, staunch enemies of Israel, on the other hand, it set a new direction for Egyptian foreign policy. From then on, it would be based on a strategic partnership with the United States and a turn towards the Persian Gulf states, especially Kuwait and the UAE, which Cairo had shared political and economic interests with (Yasmine 2010, p. 197). This was due to the fact that Sadat at that time was very interested in resolving the economic crisis faced by Egypt, fighting the Islamists of the Muslim Brotherhood, and strengthening the social legitimacy of his power by regaining the Sinai Peninsula, lost to Israel in 1967. The strategic alliance with the US and the partnership with the rich countries of the Arabian Peninsula guaranteed their implementation. Ideological issues, political goals of secondary importance, including the problem of the status of Western Sahara, which is geographically distant, were marginalised in Egypt's political activity. Despite the ambitions of being a regional power to which Nasser's Egypt aspired, Sadat pursued a reactive policy, skilfully adapting to changes in his regional environment.

The strategy of subordinating foreign policy to the needs of domestic policy was continued by Hosni Mubarak. Remaining in the sphere of US influence, Egypt was content to play an auxiliary role to Washington policy in the Middle East and North Africa. Egypt's involvement in the Gulf War on the US side, in exchange for the cancellation of half of the country's national debt, was a clear proof of this (Abdelrahim 2022, pp. 10-11).

Evolution of the position of Tunisia, Libya, and Egypt towards the Western Saharan dispute after the events of the Arab Spring

The revolutions that swept through North Africa and the Middle East in late 2010 and early 2011 changed the political landscape in the region. According to Noam Chomsky, the Arab Spring began in October 2010, when the people of Western Sahara revolted against their Moroccan occupiers (Tangerino 2015). In October 2010, in Gdeim Izik, 12 km southeast of Laayoune, the capital of occupied Western Sahara, thousands of Sahrawis set up a camp in an act of mass protest against their marginalization under the decades-long Moroccan occupation of their land (Hicham 2013; Mormul 2014, pp. 18-019). However, the events of late 2010 and early 2011 are taken to be the actual beginning of the Arab Spring, which began in Tunisia and in a short period of time covered most of North Africa and the Middle East, leading to the overthrow of the long-standing regimes of Ben Ali in Tunisia, Muammar Gaddafi in Libya, and Hosni Mubarak in Egypt. Participants in the protests blamed the political class for corruption, economic stagnation, and authoritarian rule. The revolution was a historical moment of great significance and brought hope for political transformation in the Arab states of North Africa.

From the very beginning of what is referred to as the Arab Spring in North Africa, Sahrawi activists intensified their diplomatic struggle with Morocco in an effort to sway public opinion in Tunisia, Libya and Egypt to their side in the fight for recognition of their right to self-determination. This found expression, for example, at the 13th annual POLISARIO Front Congress, which took place on 15-21 December 2011 in Tifariti. One of the leading themes of the congress was the Arab Spring and its potential impact on the possibility of gaining independence by Western Sahara. The SADR's representative to the African Union, Sidi Mohamad Omar, stated that he hoped that "the winds of change that are blowing over North African countries will benefit the Sahrawi" (Western Sahara Since the Arab Spring, Web, 2015).

Tunisia on the Sahara issue after the outbreak of the Arab Spring

The events of the Arab Spring in Tunisia led to the overthrow of the Ben Ali dictatorship in January 2011 and began the process of democratic transition. The restoration of freedom of speech and right of association brought previously uncomfortable topics into the sphere of public debate, one of which was the Western Sahara issue. An example of this was the World Social Forum, an alter-globalist movement, which brought together a sizable number of NGOs from around the world during a session in Tunis in 2015. Moroccan, Algerian, and Sahrawi organizations also participated in the forum. The panel deliberations were disrupted by verbal clashes between representatives of delegations representing conflicting points of view in the dispute. Interestingly, activists from Tunisia sided with the Sahrawi case, a stance they could not previously afford under the censorship of the authoritarian state (Sellami 2015).

This was a significant development because while the Sahrawi topic functioned in the social sphere after 2011, it was mostly absent from political debate. Questions related to Western Sahara's freedom or support for either side were ignored by parties of virtually all political options, including left-wing parties, traditionally negative towards all forms of imperialism and committed to side with national liberation movements (Belkaid 2017). The presidents and government teams of what is referred to as the transition period adopted a strategy of not aggravating relations along the Tunis-Algiers-Rabat line, which, if analysing the position of the smallest Maghreb state, translated into maintaining a political *status quo* in the Western Saharan impasse.

The presidency of Moncef Marzouki, who was elected for the 2011-2014 term by the Constituency, was a test of strength in this regard. The human rights activist and long-time opposition activist during the Ben Ali regime did not have good press in Algerian political circles, who believed that he pursued a pro-Moroccan policy on the Western Sahara issue. Marzouki took the position that Algeria's support for POLISARIO ambition to proclaim a new state in the Maghreb was undermining the common regional interest of creating a functional Maghreb union. In his opinion, the solution to the Western Sahara issue should not be the pursuit of creating a state, but efforts to find a solution in the form of broad autonomy within Morocco. Controversy arose over his human rights work in international organisations, which also focused on violations of civil liberties in Algeria (Mandraud 2012).

More caution in this regard was represented by the next president, Beji Caid Essebsi, who refused the Moroccan monarch's invitation to visit the Sahrawi city of Dakhla, located in the occupied territories. On the other hand, the phrase 'Western Sahara' was not mentioned in government speeches, so as not to undermine Moroccan sovereignty over the territory (Belkaid 2017).

Tunisia's current president, Kais Saied, continues the policy line of "positive neutrality" chosen some years ago. In his program during the 2019 presidential elections, he announced an initiative to create a Maghreb Committee for the resolution of the Western Sahara issue, clearly expressing the political will to be a mediator in the conflict. Such an option seems to be the only appropriate one in a situation in which Morocco is sparing no diplomatic efforts to ensure Tunis takes sides. Algerian diplomacy has been less active to pull Tunis to its side. While in the first period of the dispute, President Houari Boumédiène resented Habib Bourguiba's failure to recognise the POLISARIO Front and the SADR government-in-exile in Algeria, the position of subsequent Algerian presidents has been less radical and more pragmatic. This position is best expressed by a statement by one of the ministers in the current government, Najla Bouden, who noted in an anonymous interview that "for Algeria, the situation will be acceptable as long as Tunis maintains "positive neutrality"" (Belkaid 2017).

Not exacerbating relations with a more powerful neighbour and an ally in the fight against terrorism is a political and geostrategic imperative, especially with the weak structures of the post-authoritarian state and the unstable situation in neighbouring Libya. Tunisia and Algeria undoubtedly have similar security issues related to securing their borders. The two countries share a 965-kilometer-long border, and the usefulness of Algeria's extensive security apparatus in the form of border guards and anti-terrorism units guarding borders prone to infiltration by terrorist organisations and contraband is a no-brainer for its smaller neighbour ("L'Algérie et la Tunisie veulent renforcer leur cooperation" 2013, Web).

Just how thin the line is between a non-aligned status and a henchman status in the dispute was demonstrated by the vote on Security Council Resolution 2602 on 29th October 2021 on the extension of the mandate of the UN Mission for the Referendum in Western Sahara (MINURSO) until 31st October 2022. Tunisia, as a non-permanent member of the United Nations Security Council for the 2020-2021 term, abstained as one of two Security Council members (along with the Russian Federation). This seemingly neutral move was interpreted by the Moroccan side as a break with the principle of previous neutrality in the dispute over Western Sahara and even "playing to the dictates" of Algiers (Ange Touré 2021). Indeed, Algeria repeatedly opposed the text of the resolution, which it described as biased and unfair. It criticised the phrases in the text, i.e., "a political process," "a round table," or "a just, lasting and mutually acceptable political solution based on compromise," which was read in Algiers as support for the Moroccan proposal for autonomy for Western Sahara within the Kingdom of Morocco. On the day of the United Nations Security Council session at which the resolution was adopted, in a televised address, Walid Hajjem, an adviser to President Kais Saied and his unofficial spokesman, gave a statement to the Tunisian news agency TAP that "Tunisia welcomes the news that the resolution has been adopted." (Ange Touré 2021).

Putting the matter this way and, as it were, giving support to the resolution *post facto*, has been portrayed in the Moroccan media as an attempt to maintain the illusion of neutrality, which is essentially a sham. Some sources also claim that President Kais Saied was unaware of the abstention decision taken by the Foreign Ministry, which he was informed of only after the fact (Ange Touré 2021). It seems that the version, presented by the president's close circle, was only intended to soften criticism from Morocco.

The situation was similar when Tunisian President Kais Saied invited Brahim Ghali - the leader of the POLISARIO Front to the Eighth Tokyo International Conference on African Development (TICAD8), held on 27-28 August 2022. In response, Moroccan authorities called it a "hostile" and "unnecessarily provocative" act, Morocco immediately withdrew its ambassador in Tunis for consultations and cancelled its own participation in the conference. Furthermore, a diplomatic crisis spilled over into the sporting world when the Royal Moroccan Handball Federation announced on August 29 that its clubs would not participate in the 37th Arab Club Handball Championship to be held in Tunisia (Ltifi 2022; France24 27 August 2022, Web).

According to historian Sophie Bessis, Ghali's reception, which was worthy of a head of state, drew Rabat's ire as the Tunisian president greeted him personally at the airport. Had Tunisia only sent a foreign ministry representative to greet the

Secretary-General of the POLISARIO Front (and at the same time the President of the SADR), Morocco's reaction might have been less violent. Such an official reception is even more surprising given that Tunisia has never recognised the SADR. The Tunisian Ministry of Foreign Affairs expressed "surprise" at Morocco's reaction and issued a statement asserting that Tunis "maintained its total neutrality on the issue of Western Sahara in accordance with international laws" advocating a "peaceful solution acceptable to all parties" (Blaise 2022). However, for many observers, the Tunisian president's gesture marks a break with the policies of his predecessors, seen as a result of increasingly clear Algerian influence as Kais Saied has moved closer than ever to Algiers since his election in 2019 (Blaise 2022).

The official position of "positive neutrality" on the Western Sahara issue upheld by successive Tunisian governments is a result of its interests, both political and economic. On the one hand, it is vitally important to revive cooperation within the Arab Maghreb Union so that, following the example of other regional free trade zones, it brings real economic benefits. On the other, it is imperative for Tunis to maintain good neighbourly relations with Algeria, a very important ally in the fight against terrorism.

In the context of the position of a neutral state, to which Tunisia seems to aspire, at least in the declaratory sphere, one may wonder to what extent a small state in Africa, with a weak economy and an unconsolidated political system, is able to follow an independent foreign policy in the very difficult conditions of the strong polarisation of the positions of the two main countries in the region, Algeria and Morocco, towards the Sahrawi issue. Security interests, the economy and the immediate neighbourhood argue for the need to take a pro-Algerian course. Considering the above, the declarations of Rached Ghannouchi, leader of the Islamist *Ennahda* party and speaker of Tunisia's parliament in 2019-2022, need to be mentioned, regarding the formation of an alliance among Tunisia, Algeria and Libya as the hard core of the AMU. The proposal simultaneously overshadowed Morocco and Mauritania (Lafrance 2021). On the other hand, openly antagonising Morocco is not in Tunisia's interest. The position of the Alawite monarchy is gradually growing both regionally and internationally. It is impossible not to note Morocco's return to the ranks of African Union states, its close cooperation with Europe in managing the migration crisis, or military cooperation with the US.

Regardless of whether the period of Kais Saied's presidency actually set a pro-Algerian course in the regional dispute or is rather the result of chaotic and uncoordinated state actions during the transformation period, one thing should be noted. Modern Tunisia is very different from Bourguiba's Tunisia. Predictability and the attempt at maintaining the political *status quo* are what was placed by the wayside with the events of the Arab Spring revolutions and the autocratic moves of the current president Saied, while the ideals of peaceful coexistence and shared governance of disputed territories promoted by the father of independent Tunisia have given way to the interests of the state perceived in the spirit of political realism.

Libya and the Sahara question after the outbreak of the Arab Spring

Shortly after the outbreak of the revolution in Libya, the Moroccan government allied itself with Libya's National Transitional Council (NTC), disassociating from the Gaddafi regime, in the hope that the new Libyan establishment would remember Morocco's early recognition of the Libyan revolutionaries, and would return the favour in due course by lending support to Moroccan claims to Western Sahara. When Libyan rebels announced their victory, Morocco was one of the first countries to send its foreign minister, Taieb Fassi Fihri, to Benghazi to express support for the new Libyan regime – National Transitional Council (NTC) (Morocco World News, 20 October 2011, Web). Moroccan authorities have also sought to discredit the POLISARIO Front in the eyes of Libyan revolutionaries by accusing it of sending hundreds of Sahrawi fighters to Libya, with the Libyan regime paying these mercenaries $500 a day to support Gaddafi (Bennis 2011). The accusations were immediately dismissed by the SADR representatives.

Morocco's support for the insurgent government was invaluable, which is why members of the new Libyan authorities decided to make some political gestures aimed at satisfying Rabat. One such gesture was a NTC position on Western Sahara presented through the mouth of London-based government spokesman Guma El-Gamaty[11], who made it clear on regional television in Laayoune that Western Sahara's future is within Moroccan statehood: "*The future of the Sahara can only be conceived under the sovereignty of Morocco*" (Al-Arabiya News, 10 September 2011, Web). The civil war in Libya as well as the confusion caused by the "Arab Spring" in other North African countries, Tunisia and Egypt, were used by the Moroccan authorities to strengthen Rabat's position in the international

---

11 Guma El-Gamaty was UK coordinator for the Libyan National Transitional Council (NTC), working closely to liaise between the NTC and the British government throughout the period of the Libyan revolution in 2011.

arena, and Moroccan decision-makers focused on positioning the kingdom as a regional supplier of stability and mediator, especially in Libya.

On 17 September 2015, under the auspices of the United Nations, Morocco brought together all Libyan parties to sign an agreement in Skhirat, which resulted in the international recognition of the Government of National Accord (GNA) as Libya's sole legitimate authority. It was a key peace deal in Libya after the fall of Muammar Gaddafi's regime in 2011. The Skhirat Agreement was an important Moroccan initiative aimed at bringing the various Libyan parties involved in the civil war to achieve a peaceful resolution. Morocco has tried to maintain a neutral position towards all parties in Libya, playing the role of an "honest broker", which allows it to gain the trust of all parties to the conflict and consolidates Rabat's influence in Libya (Hassan 2020). Moreover, this role is intended to make it easier for Rabat to limit Algeria's influence in North Africa. (Abouzzohour 2021).

The political activity of the Alawite dynasty in the Libyan issue in the following years is a consequence of the above objectives, it seeks to consolidate Moroccan position in the region and push Algiers out of regional initiatives. There is a reason why the next meeting of representatives of the "warring political factions", on the one hand, the GNA and the House of Representatives, on the other, took place, as in 2015, in Morocco in the town of Bouznika, a few kilometres south of Rabat. The date of the reconciliation meeting, 6-7 September 2020, coincided with the period of intensified Algerian diplomacy within the AU regarding the convening of an informal peace conference in Algiers (Hamamdijan 2020). Moreover, Rabat successfully lobbied to reject the candidacy of former Algerian Foreign Minister Ramtane Lamamra for the post of the UN special envoy for Libya (Special Representative of the Secretary-General for Libya and Head of the United Nations Support Mission in Libya). Despite the approval of the African Union, the Rabat offensive turned out to be a hit and resulted in the rejection of the Algerian candidacy by two non-permanent members of the Security Council: Egypt and the UAE, and finally also the US. As a result, an American, Stephanie Williams, deputy head of UNSMIL, was appointed temporary envoy for Libya ("Crise en Libye: les Américains derrière le blocage de la candidature de l'Algérien Lamamra à l'ONU", 9 April 2020, Web).

The above facts may indicate that in Morocco's strategy, the search for effective ways to end the Libyan conflict "based on compromise and transparency of the political process" is a priority (Abouzzohour 2021). On the other hand, Rabat effectively blocks the influence of other countries in the region, especially Algeria, in order to maintain an undisputed monopoly in this matter.

In the face of the civil war lasting over a decade and the fragility of the Government of National Unity, established in March 2021, an interim government resulting from a compromise between the rival centres of power, it is difficult to expect that the issues of the national aspirations of the POLISARIO Front and the independence of Western Sahara will be included in Libya's political agenda. The situation in the country remains unstable and much help will be needed to rebuild the Libyan state institutions and economy after a long internal conflict. In this regard, the authorities in Tripoli also count on the countries of the region, including Morocco and Algeria. Therefore, it seems that in the current situation and in view of "diplomatic rivalry" on the Libyan issue between two strong Maghreb players, it is not a priority for the Libyan government to adopt a specific position on the Western Sahara issue, which would certainly antagonise Libya with Algiers or Rabat.

Egypt on the Sahara issue after the outbreak of the Arab Spring

In January 2011, mass social protests erupted against the rule of President Hosni Mubarak and in response to the general political and economic situation in the country, leading to riots and the deaths of over 300 people. Consequently, these events marked the end of Mubarak's nearly 40-year rule. In free and democratic elections, the Islamists from the Muslim Brotherhood gained control of the parliament, and the movement's leader, Mohamed Morsi, was elected president of the country. However, in July 2013, he was overthrown in a military coup, and Abdel Fattah el-Sisi assumed the presidency (Democracy Index 2014).

In terms of shaping foreign policy, Sisi has limited options, and his activities are focused primarily on gaining international legitimacy of his power. From the beginning, he could enjoy unofficial support from Washington. While expressing concern over the violent political events in Egypt, the US administration did not call El-Sisi's extra-constitutional takeover of power a coup. The US is also continuing to provide military aid to Egypt, in the amount of USD 1.3 billion a year, which is another sign of support for the El-Sisi's government (Sallone 2021). Solid support also comes from the Arab states of the Persian Gulf (Farouk 2014).

In the first years of El-Sisi's rule, there was a certain opening in bilateral relations with Algeria. Both countries share similar political systems, leaning towards autocracy, and the threat of Islamism. Moreover, Cairo was looking for political recognition and economic partners, while Algeria was interested in increasing support for its regional policy and building a coalition of Arab states favourable to the option of an independent Western Sahara. It is significant that

El-Sisi chose Algiers as the destination of his first official trip abroad. At the end of December 2014, both countries signed an agreement under which Algeria committed to exporting 750,000 m3 of liquefied natural gas to Egypt in 2015. This fact did not go unnoticed in Rabat, and commentators in Morocco were critical of Algiers' cooperation with Cairo, seeing it as an expression of Egypt's support for Algerian policy in regard to Western Sahara in exchange for increased gas supplies. Moreover, the Moroccan authorities, according to the report of the Economist Intelligence Unit, expressed concern about the participation of the Egyptian delegation in December 2014 in a conference supporting the POLISARIO Front. This fact reinforced the fears of the Alawite monarchy about the transition of Cairo into the Algerian sphere of influence. It is therefore not surprising that the Moroccan media launched a critical campaign against Egypt, and President El-Sisi in particular, calling the overthrow of President Morsi "a coup which put a halt to a democratic process" (Jaabouk 2015).

Indeed, the SADR invited Egyptian journalists to the Sahrawi refugee camps, located near Tindouf in Algeria, in June 2014. This visit was followed by another, more official one, in October of the same year, in which an Egyptian delegation headed by the undersecretary of the Ministry of Culture visited the refugee camps and met with the SADR President Mohamed Abdelaziz. However, as early as on 16 January 2015, Egypt sought to improve bilateral relations with Morocco during the visit of the Egyptian foreign minister to Rabat, where he was received by his Moroccan counterpart as well as the king of Morocco. During this visit, Rabat was assured of Egyptian support for Morocco's proposal for Western Sahara autonomy (Jaabouk 2015). However, on 14 October 2016, the Egyptian authorities again invited the delegation of the POLISARIO Front, granting the members of the group visas to enter their territory to participate in the ceremony on the 150th anniversary of the establishment of the Egyptian parliament, which was held in the city of Sharm El-Sheikh (Hassan 2020).

In mid-November 2020, an exchange of fire occurred between Moroccan troops and POLISARIO fighters, initially in Guerguerat and subsequently in several other locations along the ceasefire line dividing Western Sahara between the part occupied by Morocco and the part controlled by the POLISARIO Front. Despite Rabat's expectations of receiving support from Cairo, Egypt refused to endorse Morocco in its actions against the POLISARIO Front (Drury 2019, p. 325). Egypt's foreign ministry stated on its Facebook page on November 15 that the country was closely following developments in the region, at the same time Cairo called on both belligerent parties to exercise restraint and refrain from any provocative actions that could be detrimental to economic interests and trade in the Guerguerat region. Egypt further called on both sides to engage in dialogue and restart political process to resolve the crisis, which was disapproved of by Rabat (Hassan 2020).

Although there were reasons for the adoption of a pro-Sahrawi position by Egypt in the first period of El-Sisi's rule, the events of the following years clearly indicate that Egypt has moved to a neutral position. Such an evolution of Egypt's policy in the dispute resounds in the official communication coming from Cairo. In January 2021, Achraf Ibrahim, Egypt's ambassador to Morocco, noted that "Egypt has never recognised the POLISARIO Front, and Egypt's position on Western Sahara has so far remained unchanged and will not change overnight" ("L'Égypte n'a jamais reconnu le Polisario", 26 February 2021, Web). In a statement, he also denied Moroccan media reports that Egypt was planning to open a consulate in Rabat-controlled Laayoune ("L'Egypte dément avoir eu l'intention d'ouvrir un consulat au Sahara occidental occupé", 3 January 2021, Web). Opening a consular post in the disputed territory would mean a *de facto recognition* of Moroccan claims. However, a few months later, Egypt's official position on the Western Sahara issue began to evolve towards the Moroccan stance, and the messages from Cairo have become increasingly less neutral. On 9 May 2022, Egypt openly reaffirmed its support for Morocco's territorial integrity and called for a solution to be sought under UN Security Council Resolution 2602 of 2001, which advocates for negotiations between the parties involved in the conflict to ultimately determine the status of Western Sahara (UN Security Council Resolution No. 2602, 2021). The government's announcement is a clear signal for Algiers that Cairo has abandoned its support for the self-determination referendum in Western Sahara in favour of consultations on the scope of autonomy within the Kingdom of Morocco. For Algeria, the advocate of an independent Sahrawi state, this decision represented a severe diplomatic setback, especially since the communication was made public less than four months after the official trip of Algerian President Abdelmadjid Tebounne to Cairo to increase regional support for the POLISARIO claims ("Visite du Président Tebboune en Egypte: renforcement de la coopération et de l'action commune", 25 January 2022, Web).

The Egyptian position on the issue of Western Sahara cannot, however, be considered through the perspective of relations between Cairo and Algiers but rather as the result of strategy and political goals. These, in the case of Cairo, consist in closer cooperation with the Gulf states and the US, whose financial support the El-Sisi regime depends on. The Washington administration supported Moroccan claims under the Abrahamic Accords of August 2020. Most of Arab League member states, including the UAE, Kuwait, and Saudi Arabia, stand by the position of upholding Morocco's territorial integrity (Kasraoui 2022). The failed offensive by Algiers to establish an official map used by the Arab League with the separated territory of Western Sahara is symbolic in this regard, as well as the failed attempts to include in the agenda of the Arab League summit (in 2022 taking place in Algiers) the postulate of inter-Arab solidarity and support for the Sahrawi people.

In the absence of unequivocal support from the majority of Arab states, as well as a direct interest for Egypt, the likelihood of a change in the policy towards Western Saharan issue by El-Sisi and greater involvement in this ongoing conflict on the other side of the African continent is rather slim.

Conclusions

The unresolved Western Sahara issue continues to cast a shadow over the entire North African region, affecting the Maghreb countries to the greatest extent. During the Cold War, the division between states supporting the cause of Western Sahara's independence and those supporting Morocco's position greatly polarised the region, not only of the Maghreb, but also of the African continent, a fact that was repeatedly reflected in the Organisation of African Unity and, later, the African Union. Moreover, during the Cold War, the dispute was part of the division between states aligned with the Western camp (supporting Morocco) and those that identified with the Eastern Bloc and socialism, such as Algeria and Libya, which in turn translated into the forum of the UN. Tunisia was the only country in the region that consistently tried to pursue a policy of "positive neutrality" and was doomed to attempts at doing a balancing act not only in the region's alignment, between Algeria and Morocco, but also in the bipolar world between the West and the Eastern bloc. Egypt, on the other hand, did not express much interest in the issue of Western Sahara, as its foreign policy was more focused on the area of East Africa and the Middle East. In recent years, Egypt has been very much involved in its foreign policy in stopping Ethiopian investments related to the construction of hydroelectric power plants and dams on the Blue Nile. In addition, Cairo has expressed great interest in Somaliland, another unrecognised state in Africa, apart from Western Sahara.

However, as mentioned earlier, the problem of Western Sahara concerns primarily the Maghreb countries. The much-promised AMU cooperation has been paralysed by the Western Sahara issue, and not even the events of the Arab Spring have changed that. According to a World Bank report published in 2010, the economic integration of Maghreb countries could have increased GDP per capita by 34% for Algeria, 27% for Morocco and 24% for Tunisia between 2005 and 2020. In contrast, an analysis by the United Nations Economic Commission for Africa shows that with AMU, five countries in the region[12] would have gained the equivalent of 5% of its total gross domestic product per year (Kadri 2021). Meanwhile, there is no immediate prospect of this situation changing, and in addition, the war in Ukraine has caused complications because of the fuel and food crisis. These events strengthen the position of raw material countries, such as Algeria and Libya, and threaten countries that depend on raw materials like Tunisia, which additionally faces a serious food crisis.

Regardless of how the Libyan, Tunisian and Egyptian positions on the Western Sahara dispute evolve, the key to resolving the conflict lies with the strongest states in the region – Morocco and Algeria – and is a direct result of their geo-strategic position. Maintaining good relations with the Kingdom of Morocco is in the interest of the European Union. Given that the security of the Schengen external borders, the Spanish exclaves of Ceuta and Melilla, is dependent on Morocco, which gives Rabat the possibility of what is referred to as *weaponization* through migration processes, which could hit Europe hard. Mohammed VI, for the rest, did not hesitate to "play this card" in 2021 to force Madrid to change its position on Western Sahara[13]. The Alawite monarchy also has the favour of the US, which in 2020 recognised the legitimacy of Moroccan claims to Western Sahara in exchange for recognition of the state of Israel ("Donald Trump annonce que le Maroc reconnaît à son tour Israël", 11 Decemeber 2020, Web). The Rabat-Washington political alliance is also strengthened by military cooperation, especially in the field of counterterrorism. Military cooperation is also central to US relations with Algeria. This North African country ranks among the top ten countries as the largest importers of arms, including American ones ("International arms transfers level off after years of sharp growth", 15 March 2022, Web). Its role is also key, by virtue of its geographic location and developed intelligence services, in carrying out joint counterterrorism operations in the Sahel region. Algeria's geostrategic position has also increased in its relations with Europe in the context of the recent months of the war in Ukraine and the accompanying energy crisis. It is also significant that Algeria, the world's tenth largest

---

12 Morocco, Algeria, Tunisia, Libya, and Mauritania.
13 In May 2021, Moroccan border guards loosened the border crossing around the Spanish exclave of Ceuta for several days, resulting in an illegal influx of some 10,000 people into Spain. Morocco refused to accept the refugees again, pending recognition by the Madrid government of Rabat's rights to Western Sahara and the surrender of Brahim Ghali, leader of the POLISARIO Front, undergoing treatment in Spain, considered a terrorist by the Moroccan monarchy (Stasiński 2021).

gas producer, would be a natural partner for the EU in achieving its goal of be-coming independent from Russian gas supplies (Meddi 2022).

Faced with the geostrategic advantages of the region's two strongest states, minor states like Tunisia and Libya, weakened by a long-running war, have far fewer assets and opportunities to play a significant role in the Western Sahara crisis. They remain observers or, indirectly, as in the case of Tunisia, victims of this dispute, which has adversely affected regional relations for almost half a century, with no indication of change in the near future.

References

Abdelrahim, Amr : *Le retour de l'Égypte comme puissance régionale?,. Études de l'Ifri.* décembre 2022, pp.10-11.

Abouzzohour, Yasmina. "Order from Chaos. Israel, Africa, and Libya: Morocco's foreign policy trump cards". Brookings Institute. 27.07.2021. https://www.brookings.edu/blog/order-from-chaos/2021/07/27/israel-africa-and-libya-moroccos-foreign-policy-trump-cards/.

"Africa's international borders as potential sources of conflict and future threats to peace and security". Institute for Security Studies. May 2012. No 233, Retrieved 20.5.2023, from https://www.files.ethz.ch/isn/145411/Paper_233.pdf (15.04.2023)

Ange Touré, Frédéric: „Sahara occidental: la Tunisie entre le marteau et l'en-clume".*Le Journal 2L'Afrique.* 21.11.2021. Retrieved 20.5.2023, from https://lejournaldelafrique.com/lafrique-daujourdhui/sahara-occidental-la-tunisie-entre-le-marteau-et-lenclume/.

Belkaid, Akram: „Sahara: Tunisia faced with the Algerian-Moroccan rivalry". *OrientXXI*, 9.03.2017. Retrieved 20.5.2023, from https://orientxxi.info/magaz ine/sahara-tunisia-faced-with-the-algerian-moroccan-rivalry,1753.

Ben Salem, Mohamed: *L'affaire de la borne 233*, (Mémoire DES, Faculty of Law, University of Tunis). ([master's thesis) 1972. Retrieved 20.5.2023, from http://www.habib-bourguiba.net/ben-salem-memoire-des-laffaire-de-la-borne-233/.

Bennis, Samir: "Libya: Over 556 of the Polisario mercenaries in the hands of NTC". *Morocco World News.* 25.08.2011. Retrieved 20.5.2023, from https://www.moroccoworldnews.com/2011/08/7772/libya-polisario-mercenar ies-in-the-hands-of-ntc

Blaise, Lilia: "Morocco and Tunisia feud after self-proclaimed Western Sahara leader visits Tunis". *Le Monde*, 1.09.2022. Retrieved 20.5.2023, from https://www.lemonde.fr/en/le-monde-africa/article/2022/09/01/the-diplomatic-cri

sis-between-tunis-and-rabat-over-western-sahara-is-showing-no-signs-of-abating_5995479_124.html.

Boeke, Sergei/Schuurman, Bart: *Operation Serval: the French Intervention in Mali*. Leiden Universiteit. Leiden security and global affairs blog. 9.4.2020. Retrieved 20.5.2023, from https://www.leidensecurityandglobalaffairs.nl/articles/operation-serval-the-french-intervention-in-mali.

Brésillon, Thierry: „Mise à mal de la neutralité tunisienne". *Le Monde Diplomatique*. février-mars. 2022, p. 12.

Constantin, François/Coulon, Christian: „Les relations internationales de la Mauritanie". In : *Introduction à la Mauritanie*. Centre de recherches et d'études sur les sociétés méditerranéennes. Centre d'étude d'Afrique noire. Aix-en-Provence.1979.

"Crise en Libye: les Américains derrière le blocage de la candidature de l'Algérien Lamamra à l'ONU". *Jeune Afrique*. 9.4.2020. Retrieved 20.5.2023, from https://www.jeuneafrique.com/924803/politique/crise-en-libye-les-americains-derriere-le-blocage-de-la-candidature-de-lalgerien-lamamra-a-lonu/.

Dahmani, Youssef: „When Muammar Gaddafi angered king Mohammed VI by calling him «my son»". *Yabiladi News*. 22.1.2019. Retrieved 20.5.2023, from https://en.yabiladi.com/articles/details/73640/history-when-muammar-gaddafi-angered.html.

Damis, John: "The Western Sahara Conflict: Myths and Realities", *Middle East Journal*, vol. 37, no. 2, 1983, pp. 169–179. Retrieved 20.5.2023, from http://www.jstor.org/stable/4326560.

"Death of Gaddafi: A new era is dawning in Moroccan-Libyan relations", *Morocco World News*. 10.10.2011. Retrieved 20.5.2023, from https://www.moroccoworldnews.com/2011/10/12408/death-of-gaddafi-a-new-era-is-dawning-in-moroccan-libyan-relations.

Democracy Index 2014, A Report from The Economist Intelligence Unit. Retrieved 20.5.2023, from https://www.sudestada.com.uy/Content/Articles/421a313a-d58f-462e-9b24-2504a37f6b56/Democracy-index-2014.pdf.

„Donald Trump annonce que le Maroc reconnaît à son tour Israël", *Le Monde*, 11.12.2020. Retrieved 20.5.2023, from https://www.lemonde.fr/international/article/2020/12/10/donald-trump-annonce-que-le-maroc-reconnait-a-son-tour-israel_6062948_3210.html.

Drury, Mark. „On the Border in Northern Mauritania", *L'Année du Maghreb*. 21.2019, p. 325. Retrieved 20.5.2023, from https://journals.openedition.org/anneemaghreb/5910.

Farouk, Yasmine: „More than Money: Post-Mubarak Egypt, Saudi Arabi, and the Gulf", Gulf Research Center, GRC GULF PAPER. April 2014. P.11. Retrieved

20.5.2023, from https://www.files.ethz.ch/isn/179860/Egypt_Money_new_ 29-4-14_2576.pdf.

Farouk, Yasmine : „L'Egypte est-elle encore une puissance régionale? ". *Confluences Méditerranée*. vol. 75. no. 4. 2010, p. 217.

Farsoun, Karen/ Jim Paul: „War in the Sahara: 1963". *MERIP Reports*, no. 45, 1976, s. 13–16. Retrieved 20.5.2023, from https://doi.org/10.2307/3011767.

Gdeim, Izik: *The First, Forgotten Spark of the Arab Uprisings*. OpenDemocracy. 24.2.2013. Retrieved 20.5.2023, from http://www.opendemocracy.net/hic ham-yezza/gdeim-izik-first-forgotten-spark-of-arab-uprisings.

Gupte, Pranay, B.: "Libya announces peace efforts in Sahara, Lebanon and Persian Gulf". *New York Times*. 20.6.1981. Retrieved 20.5.2023, from https:// www.nytimes.com/1981/06/20/world/libya-announces-peace-efforts-in-sah ara-lebanon-and-persian-gulf.html.

Hamamdijan, Thomas: „Crise en Libye: pourquoi le Maroc joue les facilitateurs". *Jeune Afrique*. 7.9.2020. Retrieved 20.5.2023, from https://www.jeuneafrique. com/1041087/politique/crise-en-libye-pourquoi-le-maroc-joue-les-facili tateurs/.

Harris, lilian, C: *Libya: Qadhafi's Revolution and the Modern State*. Boulder: Westview Press. 1986.

Hassan, Khalid: "Egypt backs Polisario Front, risks relations with Morocco". *Al.-Monitor*. 23.11.2020. Retrieved 20.5.2023, from https://www.al-monitor.com/ originals/2020/11/egypt-support-polisario-front-western-sahara-morocco. html#ixzz7ynKLq6Pc.

Hilsum, Lindsay: *Burza piaskowa. Libia w czasach rewolucji*. Wydawnictwo: Sonia Draga. Katowice, 2013.

International arms transfers level off after years of sharp growth, Stockholm International Peace Research Institute (SIPRI). 23.11.2020. Retrieved 20.5.2023, from https://www.sipri.org/media/press-release/2021/international-arms-transfers-level-after-years-sharp-growth-middle-eastern-arms-impo rts-grow-most.

Islamic State in the Greater Sahara (ISGS), United Nations Security Council. Retrieved 20.5.2023, from https://www.un.org/securitycouncil/content/isla mic-state-greater-sahara-isgs.

Jaabouk, Mohammed: *Sahara: L'Egypte d'Al Sissi Soutient la Proposition Marocaine d'Autonomie.* Yabiladi. 16.1.2015. Retrieved 20.5.2023, from http://www. yabiladi.com/articles/details/32681/sahara-l-egypte-d-al-sissi-soutient.html.

Jaabouk, Mohammed: *Maroc: L'Egypte S'Approche du Polisario et ses Médias Attaquent le Roi….* AfriqueAsie.fr. 4.1.2015. Retrieved 20.5.2023, from http://

www.afrique-asie.fr/menu/maghreb/8709-maroc-l-egypte-s-approche-du-polisario-et-ses-medias-attaquent-le-roi.html.

Jackson, Henry, F.: *From the Congo to Soweto. U.S. Foreign Policy Toward Africa Since 1960*. W. Morrow: New York. 1984.

Jensen, Erik: *Western Sahara. Anatomy of a Stalemate?* Lynne Rienner: London. 2012.

Kadri, Ghalia: „Les tensions entre le Maroc et l'Algérie paralysent les échanges économiques". *Le Monde Afrique*. 7.10.2021. Retrieved 20.5.2023, from https://www.lemonde.fr/afrique/article/2021/10/07/les-tensions-entre-le-maroc-et-l-algerie-paralysent-les-echanges-economiques_6097518_3212.html.

Kasraoui, Safaa: *Arab League Slams Algerian Media for Challenging Morocco's Territorial Integrity*. Morocco World News. 30.10.2022. Retrieved 20.5.2023, from https://www.moroccoworldnews.com/2022/10/352119/arab-league-slams-algerian-media-for-challenging-moroccos-territorial-integrity.

Kłosowicz, Robert: "Central African Republic: Portrait of a Collapsed State After the Last Rebellion". *Politeja* 13 (3 (42). Wydawnictwo Akademicka: Kraków, 2016.

Kłosowicz, Robert: "Policies of the Maghreb Countries Toward Western Sahara: Mauritania's Perspective". *Hungarian Journal of African Studies,* Vol 16. No 1. 2022a.

Kosidło, Adam: *Sahara Zachodnia. Fiasko dekolonizacji czy sukces podboju? 1975-2011*. Wydawnictwo Uniwersytetu Gdańskiego: Gdańsk. 2012.

L'Égypte n'a jamais reconnu le Polisario. Bladi.net, 26.2.2021. Retrieved 20.5.2023, from https://www.bladi.net/egypte-reconnaissance-polisario,80226.

Lacoste, Yves : „*Sahara, perspectives et illusions géopolitiques*". Hérodote. vol. 142, no. 3. 2011, pp. 12-41. Retrieved 20.5.2023, from https://www.cairn.info/revue-herodote-2011-3-page-12.html.

Lacouture, Jean : „Maroc et Tunisie : revendications à Rabat et pragmatisme à Tunis une surface à conquérir ou un capital à exploiter", „Le Monde Diplomatique", March 1961. Retrieved 20.5.2023, from https://www.monde-diplomatique.fr/1961/03/LACOUTURE/24155.

Lafrance, Camille: „*Tunisie – Rached Ghannouchi et l'UMA*", Jeune Afrique, 10.3.2021. Retrieved 20.5.2023, from https://www.jeuneafrique.com/1133995/politique/tunisie-rached-ghannouchi-et-luma-tous-les-peuples-du-maghreb-soutiennent-les-droits-legitimes-des-palestiniens/.

L'Algérie et la Tunisie veulent renforcer leur coopération contre le terrorisme. RFI. 7.8.2013. Retrieved 20.5.2023, from https://www.rfi.fr/fr/afrique/20130807-algerie-tunisie-terrorisme-jihadistes-chaamb.

L'Egypte dément avoir eu l'intention d'ouvrir un consulat au Sahara occidental occupé. Algérie Presse Service. 3.1.2021. Retrieved 20.5.2023, from https://www.aps.dz/monde/115340-l-egypte-dement-avoir-eu-l-intention-d-ouvrir-un-consulat-au-sahara-occidental-occupe.

Lewis, William, H.: *"Western Sahara: Compromise or Conflict".* Current History, vol. 80, no. 470. 1981. University of California Press.

Livre blanc sur les différends entre le gouvernement de la République Tunisienne et le gouvernement chérifien du Maroc, Tunis, 1961.

Lobban, Richard, A. Jr./Dalton, Christopher, H.: *Libya: History and Revolution,* Praeger: Santa Barbara. 2014.

Ltifi, Mohamed Ali: *Western Sahara dispute spills into Tunisia.* Al Monitor. 5.9.2022. Retrieved 20.5.2023, from https://www.al-monitor.com/originals/2022/09/western-sahara-dispute-spills-tunisia.

Malinowski, Mariusz: *Sahara Zachodnia. Konflikt terytorialny między Marokiem a Hiszpanią w latach 1956–1976.* Wydawnictwo Adam Marszałek: Toruń, 2001.

Mandraud, Isabele. „*Tunisie: les cent jours de Moncef Marzouki".* Le Monde. 22.3.2012. Retrieved 20.5.2023, from https://www.lemonde.fr/tunisie/article/2012/03/22/tunisie-les-cent-jours-de-moncef-marzouki_1674198_1466522.html.

Mark, Clyde, R: *Libya.* Foreign Affairs, Defense, and Trade Division, CRS Issue Brief for Congress. 29.11.2004. Retrieved 20.5.2023, from https://www.everycrsreport.com/files/20041129_IB93109_6e5e2b78a06460d06f2bde8605b0f3fac00e4767.pdf

Meddi, Adléne: „Guerre en Ukraine: le gaz algérien, une manne pour l'Europe?" *Le Point.* 10.3.2022. Retrieved 20.5.2023, from https://www.lepoint.fr/afrique/gaz-algerien-vers-l-europe-plus-complique-qu-il-n-y-parait-09-03-2022-2467482_3826.php.

Meynier, Gilbert : „Les Algériens vus par le pouvoir égyptien pendant la guerre d'Algérie d'après les mémoires de Fathi al Dib". In *Cahiers de la Méditerranée. États et pouvoirs en Méditerranée (XVIe-XXe siècles). Mélanges offerts à André Nouschi.* n°41. 1. 1990.

Miller, Susan, G.: *A History of Modern Morocco,* Cambridge University Press. New York, 2013.

Misra, K. P: "Recognition of Mauritania - A Case Study with Particular Reference to India's State Practice" „India Quarterly", Vol. 20, No. 3, July-September 1964, pp. 239-257.

Mormul, Joanna: „Hijos de las nubes i 45 lat marzeń: uchodźcy Saharawi na terytorium Algierii". *Politeja,* 75(6). Wydawnictwo Akademicka: Kraków, 2021.

Mormul, Joanna: *Jaśminowa rewolucja w Tunezji: zwycięstwo społeczeństwa obywatelskiego czy przebudzenie islamistów?* In Szczepankiewicz-Rudzka, Ewa (eds.) *Arabska wiosna w Afryce Północnej*. Wydawnictwo Akademicka. Kraków, 2014.

Moshen-Finan, Khaduja: *Sahara occidental, Les enjeux d'un conflit régional*, CNRS Edition : Paris. 1997, pp. 182-190

"Qaddafi's fall strengthens Morocco over Western Sahara". Al-Arabiya News. 10.9.2021. Retrieved 20.5.2023, from https://english.alarabiya.net/.

Rahhlou, Jihane: "Libyan Crisis: Egypt Confirms Support for Solution Under Skhirat Agreement". *Morocco World News*. 8.3.2023. Retrieved 20.5.2023, from https://www.moroccoworldnews.com/2023/03/354369/libyan-crisis-egypt-confirms-support-for-solution-under-skhirat-agreement.

Roggero, Caterina: *L'Algérie au Maghreb. La guerre de libération et l'unité régionale*. Mimesis: Paris, 2013.

*Sahara: l'Égypte réaffirme son soutien à l'intégrité territoriale du Maroc et aux résolutions du conseil de sécurité (Communiqué conjoint).*Agence Maroccaine de Presse. 9.5.2022. Retrieved 20.5.2023, from http://www.mapnews.ma/fr/actualites/politique/sahara-l%C3%A9gypte-r%C3%A9affirme-son-soutien-%C3%A0-lint%C3%A9grit%C3%A9-territoriale-du-maroc-et-aux.

„Sahara: pourquoi la Tunisie s'est abstenue à l'ONU". *Jeune Afrique*. 8.11.2021. Retrieved 20.5.2023, from https://www.jeuneafrique.com/1262867/politique/sahara-pourquoi-la-tunisie-sest-abstenue-a-lonu/.

Sallon, Hélène: „Washington renonce à utiliser son aide militaire comme un levier de pression sur Le Caire", *Le Monde*, 16.10.2021. Retrieved 20.5.2023, from https://www.lemonde.fr/afrique/article/2021/09/16/washington-renonce-a-utiliser-son-aide-militaire-comme-un-levier-de-pression-sur-le-caire_6094888_3212.html.

Santucci, Jean-Claude : „La Mauritanie dans les relations intermaghrébines". In: *Introduction à la Mauritanie*. Centre de recherches et d'études sur les sociétés méditerranéennes. Centre d'étude d'Afrique noire. Aix-en-Provence.1979.

Schumacher, Edward: "Morocco-Libya Pact: The Aftershock". *The New York Times*. 9.9.1984. Retrieved 20.5.2023, from https://www.nytimes.com/1984/09/09/world/morocco-libya-pact-the-aftershock.html.

Security Council Resolution no. 2062 (2021) S/RES/2602 (2021). Retrieved 20.5.2023, from https://digitallibrary.un.org/record/3946431?ln=en&v=pdf

Segura I Mas, Antoni : „La question du Sahara dans la dynamique géopolitique du Maghreb". *Confluences Méditerranée*". 31 Automne. 1999, p. 24.

Sellami, Mohammad. „Forum social mondial: Incidents à Tunis ". *El Watan*. 25.3.2015. Retrieved 20.5.2023, from https://www.elwatan.com/edition/actualite/forum-social-mondial-incidents-a-tunis-28-03-2015.

Serre, de la, Françoise : „Les revendications marocaines sur la Mauritanie", *Revue française de science politique*, 1966, 16-2.

Shelley, Toby: *Endgame in Western Sahara. What future for Africa's last colony?*. Zed Books Ltd London. 2004.

Stasiński, Maciej: „Maroko nie chce przyjąć z powrotem uchodźców z Ceuty. Przypomina o sprawie Sahary Zachodniej". Wyborcza.pl. 6.6.2021. Retrieved 20.5.2023, from https://wyborcza.pl/7,75399,27154049,maroko-nie-chce-przyjac-z-powrotem-uchodzcow-z-ceuty-przypomina.html.

Szczepankiewicz, Ewa: „Niedokończona dekolonizacja Sahary Zachodniej: historia i perspektywy rozstrzygnięcia konfliktu". *Politeja*, nr 1 (11). Wydawnictwo Akademicka: Kraków. 2010..

Tangerino, Beduino. *Noam Chomsky and Western Sahara*, YouTube, 21.3.2011. Retrieved 20.5.2023, from http://www.youtube.com/watch?v=JTjOt0Pz0BQ.

The United Nations Multidimensional Integrated Stabilization Mission in Mali (MINUSMA). The UN official website. Retrieved 20.5.2023, from https:// minusma.unmissions.org/en/history.

Theofilopoulou, Anna: *Western Sahara – How not to Try to Resolve a Conflict*, Center for Strategic and International Studies. 2007. Retrieved 20.5.2023, from https://www.csis.org/analysis/western-sahara-%E2%80%93-how-not-try-resolve-conflict.

Theofilopoulous, Anna: "United Nations Mission for the Referendum in Western Sahara (MINURSO)". In: Koops, Joachim, A./ Tardy, Thierry/MacQueen, Norrie/ Williams, Paul: *The Oxford Handbook of United Nations Peacekeeping Operations*. Oxford Handbook. 2017. Retrieved 20.5.2023, from https://www. oxfordhandbooks.com/view/10.1093/oxfordhb/9780199686049.001.0001/ oxfordhb-9780199686049-e-33.

Tuaregs claim 'independence' from Mali. Rebel group proclaims "independence of Azawad" following gains in northern Mali, as Algerian consulate staff abducted, Al Jazeera 6.4.2012. Retrieved 20.5.2023, from https://www.aljazeera.com/ news/2012/4/6/tuaregs-claim-independence-from-mali.

Tunis recalls ambassador to Morocco over Western Sahara dispute. France24. 27.8.2022. Retrieved 20.5.2023, from https://www.france24.com/en/afr ica/20220827-tunis-recalls-ambassador-to-morocco-over-western-sahara-dispute.

Visite du Président Tebboune en Egypte: renforcement de la coopération et de l'action commune, Algérie Presse Service, 25.1.2022. Retrieved 20.5.2023, from

https://www.aps.dz/algerie/134682-visite-du-president-tebboune-en-egypte-
renforcement-de-la-cooperation-bilaterale-et-de-l-action-commune.

Western Sahara Since the Arab Spring. African Centre for the Constructive Resolution of Disputes. ACCORD. 11.4.2015. Retrieved 20.5.2023, from https://
www.accord.org.za/conflict-trends/western-sahara-since-arab-spring/.

Robert Kłosowicz

Chapter 8. The Problem of *De Facto States* in Africa from the Historical Perspective. The Case of Katanga[1]

Within the recent history of Sub-Saharan Africa, there have been several secession attempts, most of which have ended in failure. Some came close to achieving their goal, such as Katanga in the Belgian Congo or Biafra in Nigeria, while others never had any practical chance of coming into existence, such as Cabinda's desire to separate from Angola. The first instance of a civil war erupting and separatism emerging in an independent state from this region was in the Republic of Congo (now the Democratic Republic of Congo). This former Belgian colony, which gained independence on June 30, 1960, found itself embroiled in internal conflict just two weeks later. Politicians from the mineral-rich province of Katanga seized the opportunity presented by the army revolt and the ensuing chaos following the declaration of independence. The conflict became a component of a broader international political game involving the Western world, the Eastern bloc, and non-aligned states. To date, Katanga stands as the sole example where the international community made efforts to end a secession and restore the country's unity by deploying UN military forces. The objective of this chapter is to conduct a historical analysis of the political situation during that period and evaluate the likelihood of Katanga's actual existence from today's perspective, while considering current state of research regarding *de facto states* in Africa.

Keywords: *de facto states*, Katanga, Congo, the DRC, decolonisation

Katanga's secession took place during an exceptionally tense moment in international relations as it occurred during the peak of the Cold War. The majority of authors analyse the secession that occurred in Congo at the threshold of gaining independence within the framework of the Cold War and neo-colonialism (Kent 2017; MacFarlane 2002, p. 41). The latter as the reason behind the secession in Congo was especially strongly emphasised by African authors. The most well-known among them, the first president of the independent Ghana, Kwame Nkrumah, wrote two important texts in which he tackles the issues of

1   The publication was funded by the Priority Research Area Society of the Future under the program "Excellence Initiative – Research University" at the Jagiellonian University in Krakow".

neo-colonialism and secession: *Neo-colonialism: The Last Stage of Imperialism* and *Africa Must Unite*. In these texts, he argued that a state subjected to neo-co-lonialism, though theoretically politically independent, was *de facto* politically subordinate due to its economic dependency. In turn, he referred to African po-litical leaders attempting to secede as puppets acting in the interests of former colonisers (Nkrumah 1963). However, in recent times, texts have been published that attempt to analyse the secession attempt in Congo from the perspective of the aspirations of the Katanga region's populace towards emancipating them-selves from the central government, who could not curb the chaos in the country following independence. There is also a more objective assessment of the po-litical leaders aspiring towards secession as people who cared not only about their own political interests linked to staying in power, but as ones who should also not be denied having a vision and legitimacy in their struggle for indepen-dence (Larmer / Kennes 2014). This is confirmed by the words stated by Francis Terry McNamara, an officer in the American consulate in Elisabethville between 1961 and 1963 and an eyewitness to the events in Congo (Association for Dip-lomatic Studies and Training: *Congo in Crisis*, Web). Of course, both approaches do not have to exclude each other. Former colonial civil servants in Katanga and the mining lobby benefitted from the actions of the secessionist politicians and financed them. The politicians mobilised the population inhabiting the southern part of Katanga according to an ethnic key by arguing that the profits from the natural resources in these provinces should fall to the "authentic" inhabitants of Katanga. All the above-mentioned issues should not veil the role and scope of external involvement, which – as it turned out – had a decisive impact on how the situation evolved.

Congo became a symbol of colonial exploitation and appalling governance. This Belgian colony was one of the least developed and most underinvested in Africa. As a result of this situation, this country with an enormous territory did not have educated elites that could carry its independence, which later led to ter-rible consequences. Towards the end of the 1950s, Congo was still an enterprise that brought in enormous profits. At the time, the colony provided almost 10% of global copper production, 50% of the cobalt and 70% of the industrial diamonds, with one of its richest provinces being Katanga.

The riots that rippled through Congo and the aspirations towards indepen-dence among the colony's inhabitants led the Belgians, afraid of the eruption of an open conflict like what had occurred in French Algeria, to establishing a schedule and the principles of transferring power with the Congolese elites. To this aim, in January 1960, a Belgian-Congolese roundtable took place in Brussels, during which an agreement was reached concerning granting Congo independence and transferring power to the people of the country. The Belgians proposed the gradual transfer of power drawn out over time (about four years); however, the Congolese leaders demanded immediate independence. On 30 June 1960, the inhabitants of the former Belgian colony formally took power over the country. As a result of the first elections, conducted in June of that year, Patrice Lumumba from the Congolese National Movement (*Mouvement national congolais, MNC)* became the prime minister and Joseph Kasavubu from the Alliance of Bakongo Association (*Alliance des Bakongo /Association des Bakongo pour l'unification, la conservation et l'expansion de la langue Kikongo,* ABAKO) became president.[2]

Nonetheless, the situation in the country remained tense and unstable. Two days after independence was declared, revolts of the *Force Publique* soldiers erupted, as they were dissatisfied with their low wages and lack of possibilities for promotion, which they had been counting on following independence[3]. The army rebellion not only plunged the country into chaos, but also led to the collapse of the standing of Patrice Lumumba's government and caused panic among the Europeans residing in Congo, leading to a mass evacuation of Belgian civil servants and the complete crash of the administrative apparatus. The Belgian government declared that it would send an army to Congo in order to ensure safety for their citizens.[4] Despite the lack of consent from Lumumba for the Belgian army's intervention, Brussels transferred airborne units to both its bases in the country. Soon military forces amounting to 10,000 soldiers proceeded to disarm the Congolese army (Leśniewski 2000, p. 382).

The Katanga State (*État du Katanga*) 1960 -1963

In these circumstances, seeing the opportunity for gaining independence, on 11th July 1960, the province of Katanga declared its secession from the newly

---

2 The colours of the Ethiopian flag were adopted as the national colours on the Congolese flag, which had a symbolic dimension, because Ethiopia was an African country that had never been colonised. This in fact was nothing special for that time as the same principle was adopted in many other African states during the decolonisation period (Kłosowicz / Mormul 2018, p. 154).

3 The *Force Publique* (Public force), Belgian paramilitary police force established by King Léopold II to secure the Congo Free State, which consisted of soldiers from many African tribes and Congolese conscripts, commanded by white officers. It was responsible for many of the atrocities committed in the Congo Free State.

4 At the time, the Belgians had two military bases in Congo.

formed Congolese state. Moïse Tshombe, who was in favour of cooperating with the Belgian colonial administration, became the president of Katanga. Tshombe was also the leader of the Confederation of Tribal Associations of Katanga (*Confédération des Associations Tribales du Katanga*, CONAKAT), which was regional in character and cooperated with white settler organisations and the largest company in Katanga, i.e., the *Union Minière du Haut-Katanga* (UNHK). At the moment of declaring Katanga's secession, Tshombe accused Prime Minister Lumumba of connections with communists and bad governance, which led to chaos in the state, while simultaneously approaching the Belgians to ask for their help and international recognition. The prime minister of Belgium, Gaston Eyskens, initially decided to acknowledge Katanga's independence and planned to do it on 16th July; however, some of his associates dissuaded him from taking such steps, including Albert Schöller, who knew the realities of the area very well as the former governor-general in Congo in 1958-1960 (Boehme 2005, p. 3). It is worth emphasising that a Belgian contingent amounting to 6,000 soldiers was stationed in Katanga, whose commander, Colonel Guy Weber, became a trusted advisor to Tshombe and immediately set about organizing military forces in the rebelling province, known as the Katangese gendarme (Langellier 2019, p. 65). Lumumba was convinced that the secession had taken place as a result of a Katangese-Belgian conspiracy, which aimed to undermine the independence of the new state and extract a province rich in natural resources from Congo. His suspicions corresponded with the facts as Belgian airborne units landed in Léopoldville on the same day that Katanga declared independence. In response, on 14th July, Congo severed diplomatic relations with Belgium (Calvocoressi 2002). Right after Katanga declared independence, the *Union Minière du Haut-Katanga* transferred 1,250 million Belgian Francs to Tshombe's separatist government as a form of support. The fact that the Belgians maintained mining operations was also hugely significant, as the mining royalties financed the Katangese armed forces (Boehme 2005, p. 4).

Katanga's separatist aspirations were nothing new as the province – for historical (the kingdoms of Kazembe, Luba and Lunda), geographic (the province is surrounded in 2/3 by the territory of present-day Zambia, which was then the British colony of Northern Rhodesia) and economic reasons (located in what is referred to as the *Copperbelt* with copper, silver, gold, coal, zinc, lead and cobalt deposits) – was more linked to their neighbour from the south, the aforementioned Northern Rhodesia. The Katangese leaders also had a more conciliatory approach to the former colonisers and did not want to follow in Lumumba's footsteps by breaking mutual relations and ties with Belgium and its industrial companies. In fact, Katanga had already for a long time maintained a quasi-independent existence separated from the rest of Congo. The white settlers had demanded more autonomy since as early as 1920, and separatist sentiments became even stronger after the Second World War (Kisangani 2012, pp. 38-39).

As already mentioned, Katanga was the most important industrial area of Congo. In 1906, the *Union Minière du Haut-Katanga* company was formed, receiving exclusive rights for the extraction of copper in Katanga and becoming one of the largest producers of cobalt and copper in the world and the most important employer in the province (Gobbers 2016). The main shareholder was Belgium and some private Belgian and British companies (Boehme 2005, p. 5). Since 33.7% of Congo's profits came from the sale of copper extracted in Katanga, this province was exceptionally important for the newly formed state, as well as for European companies that could lose their profits. Thus, it should come as no surprise that practically from the very beginning of the secession the Katangese politicians received support from the Belgian authorities and unofficially from the Union of South Africa (since 1961 Republic of South Africa) and Portugal, as well as from international mining companies. It is also significant that there was no collapse of the administration in Katanga, as the majority of the Belgian civil servants remained at their posts, feeling relatively safe in the province as compared to the rest of Congo. Belgium also expanded its efforts to support the secessionists' armed forces and between 11 July and 8 September 1960 provided Katanga with over 100 tonnes of arms and ammunition. In addition, the Belgians also delivered 25 Belgian air force planes to Katanga. Eighty-nine Belgian officers served in Tshombe's advance guard, while 326 Belgian non-commissioned officers and technicians acted as "volunteers" helping to expand and train Katanga's military forces (Haskin 2005, p. 28).

Tshombe also attempted to construct an independent monetary system for Katanga as quickly as possible, wanting in this way to emphasise the distinctiveness of the secessionist province. The only road to achieve this led through creating a central bank, independent of Congo, and the introduction of its own currency – the Katangese Franc, with an exchange rate that was to be equal to that of the Belgian Franc. On this matter, Tshombe approached the Belgian authorities, who promised him technical and financial support. On 8 August 1960, the National Bank of Katanga (*Banque Nationale du Katanga*) was created, while the first banknotes with the image of Tshombe on the obverse side were issued at the beginning of 1961 (Boehme 2005, pp. 4-19).

From the very moment it proclaimed independence, Katanga could count on the support of some African and European countries which had a vested interest in Africa. The Union of South Africa, implementing the politics of the apartheid government, supported the secession of Katanga. Tshombe and some of his ministers met with South African politicians, including Prime Minister Hendrik Verwoerd, as early as in September 1960. Pretoria actively provided support to Katanga and a few weeks after it proclaimed its independence, the Department of Foreign Affairs of the Union of South Africa considered recognising it internationally. However, the parties reached the conclusion that declaring official support to Katanga by the Union would not be perceived well by other African nations due to the apartheid system and the Sharpeville massacre, which occurred in March 1960 and caused quite a stir both throughout Africa and around the world. Thus, Pretoria's support for Katanga was to be unofficial in nature (Passemiers 2016). In fact, the crisis in Congo was very skilfully taken advantage of by the government formed by the National Party for the defence and justification of the apartheid ideology and in order to mobilise white inhabitants to support the government. Many white inhabitants of the RSA saw what occurred in Congo as a lesson from which conclusions should be drawn, so that in future the decolonisation process would not move further south, which would have threatened the position of the white inhabitants and their maintenance of their political and economic position in the country (Saunders 2020).

The white leaders of the Federation of Rhodesia and Nyasaland openly sympathised with secessionist Katanga. As early as in 1958, before Congo gained independence, the Europeans residing in Katanga called for a union with the Federation of Rhodesia and Nyasaland. The prime minister of the federation, Roy Welensky, became engaged in these actions. Welensky later also played an important role in talks between the politicians of Katanga and the Federation of Rhodesia and Nyasaland. However, the relations between independent Katanga and the federation were based primarily on economic ties. This resulted from the fact that the *Copperbelt* region encompassed the borderland area between Northern Rhodesia and Katanga, while the European staff of UMHK hoped to maintain good contacts with the white settlers from Northern Rhodesia (Hendricx 2021).

Finally, Katanga enjoyed the "veiled support" of the Brazzaville Group, made up of former French colonies that had recently become independent and wanted to maintain close ties with the former coloniser. In particular, the Congo-Brazzaville president, Abbé Fulbert Youlou, would have welcomed the break-up of the powerful neighbouring state into smaller units. Although Congo-Brazzaville never recognised Katanga, Youlou was a consistent ally of Tshombe, whom he called "a courageous, intelligent and responsible leader of his people", and intervened personally on more than one occasion in support of Tshombe's regime (Hendricx 2021).

António de Oliveira Salazar's Portugal, governing over the colony of Angola, right by the north-western border of Katanga, was of extreme importance to the secessionist state. The Katangese minister of foreign affairs, Évariste Kimba, travelled to Lisbon as early as in August 1960 and, more importantly, the arms delivered by Angola were a significant help in ensuring Katanga's survival at the very beginning of its secession (Gonze 1962).

A day after Katanga proclaimed its secession, Lumumba and President Kasavubu approached the UN Secretary General Dag Hammarskjöld with a request for the provision of military support to the Congolese government in a mission to maintain the country's unity. Two weeks later, on 14 July, a UN Security Council resolution established the United Nations Operation in the Congo (*Opération des Nations Unies au Congo*, ONUC). The mission mandate encompassed: ensuring the withdrawal of Belgian forces from the Republic of Congo, assisting the local government in maintaining order and security, providing technical assistance (S/RES/143 (1960)).

When on 8 August, Southern Kasai proclaimed its secession, it became obvious that other provinces could follow in the footsteps of Katanga, which could have led to the complete disintegration of the Congolese state and an increase in the chaos. To counter further attempts at separatism, on 9 August, the UN Security Council issued a new resolution ordering Belgium to withdraw its troops from Katanga to be replaced by "blue helmet" troops. As a result, despite Tshombe's objections, Belgian troops left Katanga by September, with only more than two hundred Belgian officers and soldiers remaining there to serve as advisers to the Katanga gendarmerie (Leśniewski 2000, p. 384). Significantly, the resolution caused the Belgian government to stop believing in Katanga's chances of gaining independence (Boehme 2005, p. 3).

Hammarskjöld visited the capital of the province Elisabethville in August 1960, partially in order to supervise the peaceful introduction of UN troops into Katanga, but also to personally assess the situation and attempt negotiations with Tshombe. He deliberately avoided consulting Lumumba on the way through Leopoldville for fear that the Congolese prime minister would disrupt the plans carefully negotiated in Brussels to replace Belgian troops in Katanga with UN forces. However, the introduction of ONUC mission troops mission and the opening of dialogue with Tshombe infuriated Lumumba, who accused the secretary-general of ignoring his government. Lumumba saw the UN force as a means by which he could militarily end secession (O'Malley 2016).

Not long afterwards, dissatisfied with the UN's military activities, the desperate Lumumba approached the USA to request help in the transport of army forces, tasked with suppressing the secession. Upon meeting with refusal, he

made a similar request to the USSR, which responded positively and sent transport planes, weapons, food, medical supplies, and trucks to carry Congolese soldiers to Katanga. Lumumba's moves reinforced Washington's belief that he was a
pro-Soviet politician and they came to the decision to become involved in stopping the spread of Moscow's influence in the Congo and, in cooperation with
the Belgians, remove him from power. For the US, a repeat of Cuba, where the
1959 revolution brought pro-Communist guerrillas led by Fidel Castro to power,
was unacceptable. With the approval of President Dwight Eisenhower, the director of the CIA Allen Dulles cabled the CIA station in Léopoldville in August
1960: "We conclude that his removal must be an urgent and prime objective and
that under existing conditions this should be a highly priority of our covert action" (Duignam / Gann 1984, p. 290; Weissman 2014, p. 14-15).

At the same time, internal rivalries within the Congolese government con-
tinued, with the main conflict running between President Joseph Kasavubu and
Prime Minister Patrice Lumumba. In September 1960, the chief of staff of the
Congolese government army, Colonel Joseph Mobutu, deposed Prime Minister
Lumumba and in January 1961 ordered him to be transported as a prisoner to
Katanga, where he was assassinated. Lumumba's death caused an international
upheaval, which radicalised the more neutral members of the Afro-Asian bloc,
who immediately condemned the role of Britain, the United States, and the UN.
This came as a result of growing pressure on the United States to take some decisive steps to support UN efforts in the Congo. In a telegram from the US ambassador in Brussels, William Burden stressed the importance of developing a
coherent position on the issue, urging them to act according to the following
instructions:

> I am fully aware that unilateral measures outside the framework of general Western
> policy can serve only to destroy the position of Belgium and the West in the UN and in
> Africa without any countervailing advantage, but the situation is in part a result of the
> vacuum created by failure to formulate clear and effective US policy. If we are not able to
> formulate clear US policy on Congo … to deal with the rapidly detonating situation and
> sell it to our allies rather soon, different elements in Belgium will … continue to supply
> their own paramilitary ad hoc solutions ("Telegram from the Embassy in Belgium…"
> 1961; O'Malley 2016).

On 1 February 1961, the new US president, John F. Kennedy endorsed a revised USA-Congo policy, the three main elements of which were as follows: a
new mandate for ONUC that would increase their authority to control all military elements in Congo, the restoration of a functioning government in Léopoldville and increased efforts to block external aid to separatist movements.
However, regardless of US efforts, the situation began to spiral out of control

when the Afro-Asian bloc tabled a draft resolution calling for UN troops to be granted the right to use force to prevent the outbreak of civil war (Weissman 2014, p. 142). UN Secretary-General Dag Hammarskjöld, acting under Article 99 of the UN Charter, asked the Security Council to provide technical assistance to the Congo and to consider restoring law and order in the country. The UN Security Council authorised him to send military assistance to the Congolese government with the provision that UN troops could only use force in self-defence. On 21 February 1961, the UN Security Council adopted Resolution 161 extending ONUC's mandate to include actions aimed at maintaining Congo's territorial integrity and political independence, to prevent the possibility of civil war and to ensure that all foreign military forces were withdrawn from its territory. The resolution, in fact condoning armed intervention in Katanga, resulted in the departure of most Europeans and Belgian troops from the rebellious province (S/RES/161 (1961); *United Nations Operation in the Congo*).

In March 1961, the government of Congo proposed to end the crisis by introducing autonomy for the province, but this proposal was rejected by Katanga, resulting in the start of hostilities in late July and early August. During this time, the Katanga government increased the number of gendarmerie troops and began recruiting mercenaries.

Initially, UN troops suffered defeats in clashes with Katanga forces. This was influenced by the inferior armament and training of the UN troops. The lack of air support was particularly acute. To add to this, on the night of 18 September 1961, the UN Secretary-General, Dag Hammarskjöld, was killed along with other members of the UN delegation in a plane crash in the British protectorate of Northern Rhodesia. Hammarskjöld was travelling to meet with Tshombe to negotiate a truce in the ongoing conflict. After Hammarskjöld's death, his successor, Sithu U Thant, took more decisive action to end Katanga's secession as quickly as possible.

Meanwhile, the UN was expanding its military forces in Katanga, and contingents from Ethiopia, India and Sweden were eventually reinforced with an air component. However, US support was crucial, as its aviation helped to transport UN troops to Katanga, allowing the troops to go on the counterattack in mid-December 1961, forcing Tshombe back to the bargaining table. Under the agreement signed in Kitona on 20 December, Tshombe recognised Congo's unity and the authority of the central government. However, complications soon arose as Tshombe played for time by refusing to ratify the signed agreement. The situation is well reflected in correspondence between the US State Department and the US embassy in Belgium. The telegram shows that Washington was concerned that Tshombe appeared to remain unconvinced of the absolute necessity of implementing the Kitona Agreement and that on his return to Elisabethville he might succumb to pressure from his advisers to withdraw from it. He was playing a game to delay the implementation of the agreement by arguing that the document required ratification by the Katanga government. It was feared that the fragile truce between UN forces and Katanga could soon collapse and easily lead to a resumption of armed fighting:

> ...we believe it imperative Tshombe be made understand that present UN stance Katanga, backed by majority world opinion, leaves him no alternative but to see negotiations through to successful conclusion. Specifically, Tshombe must realize UN now in position effectively isolate Katanga economically from rest of world, and that if he stalls on negotiations with Adoula, his economic and financial position will only deteriorate ("Telegram from the Department of State..." 1961).

The United States undertook diplomatic activities towards Belgium, putting pressure on the government of the country to force Tshombe to implement the agreement from Kitona ("Telegram from the Department of State..."). In the end, the Kitona agreement proved futile, as Tshombe anticipated that the United Nations (UN) would withdraw from the Congo due to financial constraints, thereby allowing Katanga to sustain itself. Throughout 1962, numerous diplomatic efforts were made to resolve the conflict, yet yielded minimal progress. The closest the UN appeared to approach a resolution was in mid-August 1962, when it endorsed a proposal for a "national agreement". This agreement proposed the implementation of a federal constitution in the Congo, with proceeds from Katanga's mines evenly distributed between the central government and the province. Additionally, the agreement outlined plans for a monetary union and the integration of Katanga's troops with those of the Congolese. However, Tshombe's obstructive actions prevented the implementation of this plan as well (Leśniewski, 2000, pp. 387-388).

In December 1962, it was already clear that further negotiations would not work and that a settlement had to be reached through military confrontation. On 28 December 1962, UN forces launched Operation Grandslam, deciding to launch a final offensive. On 15 January 1963, UN forces occupied Elisabethville, which *de facto* marked the end of Katanga's secession. The withdrawal of UN troops from Congolese territory took place in the summer of 1964, when the last ONUC troops left the country. Despite the fact that the UN managed to put an end to Katanga's secession and maintain Congolese territorial integrity, political instability in the region still persisted when another series of bloodshed-filled conflicts occurred in the newly named Democratic Republic of the Congo. In consequence, in late 1999, the UN launched the United Nations Mission in the

Democratic Republic of Congo (*Mission de l'Organisation des Nations Unies en République démocratique du Congo*, MONUC), later renamed the United Nations Organization Stabilization Mission in the Democratic Republic of the Congo (*Mission de l'Organisation des Nations Unies pour la stabilisation en République démocratique du Congo*, MONUSCO), which remains in operation to this day. ONUC continues to be considered the UN's greatest failure during the Cold War (Duică 2016).

Tshombe and all his ministers remained in Katanga after the hostilities ended; moreover, on behalf of CONAKAT, he pledged support for the reunification of Congo. In mid-1963, by a decision of the central government, the six large colonial-era provinces were divided into 21 *provincettes*, which were intended to better reflect the ethnic division. Katanga was divided into three smaller provinces: Katanga East (*Katanga Oriental*), Lualaba and Katanga North (*Katanga Nord*). Although Tshombe protested the 'Balkanisation' of the province, he cooperated with the central authorities and by April had established his own provincial government in South Katanga (Van Reybrouck 2016, pp. 411-412).

However, Tshombe once again came into conflict, this time with the General Association of the Baluba of the Katanga (*Association Générale des Baluba du Katanga*, BALUBAKAT) leader Jason Sendwe, a northern Katanga politician, which led to ethnic fighting in Jadotville. The following month, Congolese army soldiers seized Tshombe's residence on suspicion that he was maintaining a private militia. Documents revealing his contacts with foreign mercenaries fell into the hands of the central government. Fearing arrest, Tshombe fled to Paris in June 1963. He then settled in Madrid, Spain, from where he and other Katanga commanders drew up plans to return to power.

Conclusions

The Congo crisis and the secession of Katanga had serious repercussions internationally. It was obvious that the conflict was part of the Cold War logic dividing the world along the East-West line, but the divisions went further and also affected Western countries. Cracks appeared in relations between the US and Belgium, as well as the United States and the UK, revealing their fundamentally different approaches to decolonisation in Africa. This crisis challenged British economic and political interests in Africa. The UK's refusal to consider the use of force to end Katanga's secession was a consequence of the desire to protect British economic interests in the province, which in turn was linked to the influence of the *Tanganyika Concessions* company, which had a 14.5 per cent stake in the Belgian company *Union Minière du Haut Katanga* in control of most of Congo's resources. In addition to the business interests of companies such as Shell and Unilever, Katanga was critically important to the Central African copper belt, which extended to the border of Northern Rhodesia (O'Malley 2016).

For the United States, Congo was of particular interest not only due to the growing hostility in relations with the USSR, but also because Katanga was a source of uranium used in the US nuclear energy programme. Thus, the debate that unravelled over ONUC's actions caused a serious difference of opinion in the Western world. When Hammarskjöld first presented the issue of the intervention in Congo to the UN Security Council on 13 July 1960, both Great Britain and France abstained from voting in favour of the resolution ordering intervention. In addition, the tendency to avoid any official statement on UN intervention indicated that the UK was resisting UN efforts in Congo. This was in stark contrast to the clear support the US gave to ONUC. There is no doubt, therefore, that one of the important factors determining the direction of UN action in Congo was the growing tensions between the members of the UN Security Council derived from the differing interests of the great powers (Duică 2016, p. 42).

Congo paid a very high price for the chaos that accompanied the first months of its independence. In the years that followed, the country was the scene of armed clashes between warring factions, mercenary escapades, and civilian massacres, leading to the exile of hundreds of thousands of people. In 1964, revolts broke out on a massive scale in the eastern part of the country. Practically in a matter of days, the government in Léopoldville lost control of half of the country's territory, on which the People's Republic of Congo, formed by Lumumba's supporters, was established. The revolutionaries often cruelly killed anyone they considered an enemy. About 20,000 people were killed in executions at the time, mostly teachers and officials. In order to prevent the inevitable break-up of the country, the USA and Belgium provided serious military and financial support to the DRC. It is calculated that around one million Congolese were killed in the rebellion that lasted until 1965 (Meredith 2005, pp. 114-115).

The episode involving Katanga's attempt at independence had an impact on regional governance in Africa and approaches to self-determination in the period after the second wave of decolonisation. In a sense, the example of Katanga's secession led the Organisation of African Unity (OAU) to consolidate colonial boundaries as the only legitimate basis for post-colonial states in 1963 (Hendricx 2021). It is significant that, as early as on 13 July 1964, the foreign ministers of the OAU member states, who had begun preparations for the Second OAU Conference in Cairo, with deliberations lasting from 17 to 21 July, notified Congolese President Joseph Kasavubu by telegram that they did not wish the Congolese delegation to include Prime Minister Moïse Tshombe, who, after the collapse of the Katanga secession plans, had held the post of Congolese prime minister for a month following the resignation of his predecessor, Cyril Adoula. In the end, no representative of Congo-Léopoldville attended the conference. As Józef Chałasiński rightly points out, the moral assessment, or rather disqualification, of Tshombe's actions in relation to his attempts at secession deserves attention. In this sense, representatives of almost all independent African states sided with the assassinated Prime Minister Lumumba against Tshombe. This was a clear vote against secessionism; thus, on the issue of borders, the conference passed a resolution that member states commit themselves to respecting those borders that existed at the time of gaining independence (Chałasiński 1965, pp. 38-39). The basis for *uti possidetis* was Article 3 Paragraph 3 of the 1963 Charter of the Organisation of African Unity: "respect for the sovereignty and territorial integrity of each State and for its inalienable right to independent existence" (*The Organisation of African Unity Charter* 1963), and the *Border Disputes Among African States* resolution adopted by the Assembly of Heads of States and Governments of the Organisation of African Unity at the meeting in Cairo in 1964. The resolution stated the following:

> Considering that border problems constitute a grave and permanent factor of dissention; Conscious of the existence of extra-African manoeuvres aimed at dividing African States; Considering further that the borders of African States, on the day of their independence, constitute a tangible reality; Recalling the establishment in the course of the Second Ordinary Session of the Council of the Committee of Eleven charged with studying further measures for strengthening African Unity; Recognising the imperious necessity of settling, by peaceful means and within a strictly African framework, all disputes between African States; Recalling further that all Member States have pledged, under Article IV of the Charter of African Unity, to respect scrupulously all principles laid down in paragraph 3 of Article III of the Charter of the Organization of African Unity:1. SOLEMNLY REAFFIRMS the strict respect by all Member States of the Organization for the principles laid down in paragraph 3 of Article III of the Charter of the Organization of African Unity; 2. SOLEMNLY DECLARES that all Member States pledge themselves to respect the borders existing on their achievement of national independence (*Border Disputes Among African States* 1964).

It is therefore not surprising that it is the 1964 Cairo Declaration, proclaiming the principle of territorial integrity, that is cited as the source of the acceptance of *uti possidetis* in the African region. It should be noted that even before the adoption of the declaration, various proposals were made to establish borders based on historical and ethnic criteria. The declaration was opposed from the outset by the two states of Morocco and Somalia, which made territorial claims and referred to the findings of the 1958 Accra Pan-African Conference, where the leaders of eight African states declared that the artificial borders established by imperialists and dividing African peoples were working to the detriment of Africans and should be abolished or revised (Srogosz 2011, pp. 70-71). Nonetheless, it should be mentioned that even before the OAU adopted the Cairo Border Declaration in 1964, not all colonies during the decolonisation period became independent states, British Somaliland was incorporated into Somalia in 1960, Zanzibar merged with Tanganyika to form the United Republic of Tanzania in 1964, and even before the decolonisation process in Africa, Eritrea was incorporated into Ethiopia in 1952 (Kłosowicz / Mormul, pp. 39-41).

One important question is why Katanga's secession failed even though, in retrospect, there seems to have been a moment when it had stood a chance to gain its independence. Several reasons contributed to this. The Congolese conflict took place in the period of Cold War divisions between the Western world, led by the USA, and the bloc of communist states, led by the USSR. The third actor on the Cold War stage was the non-aligned movement in which Indian Prime Minister Nehru played an important role, as well as various leaders of African states, such as Kwame Nkrumah (Ghana), Ahmed Ben Bela (Algeria) or Gamal Abdel Nasser (Egypt). One should add to this the decolonisation of Africa, whereby 29 African states gained independence over the course of only five years, 1960-1964, and in the wave of enthusiasm associated with the liberation from the shackles of colonialism, the principle of unity was strongly emphasised. Any attempt at separatism was perceived as an impure behind-the-scenes imperialist affair. This attitude, as well as the experience of the civil war in Congo and the secession of Katanga, gave rise to the idea that the decolonisation of Africa should be based on the principle of *uti possidetis iuris*, which would guarantee the inviolability of the borders of the newly created states and prevent conflicts between African states.

Another obstacle, it seems, was the separatist provincial leader Moïse Tshombe, who was regarded largely as a Belgian puppet, and Katanga under his leadership was considered a "white man's enclave" controlled mainly by the Belgian mining company *Union Minière du Haut-Katanga* and *Tanganyika Concessions*. Consequently, Katanga had no support among other African countries. UN support for the restoration of the unity of the state was also very important, as was the policy put forward by Washington, which, by betting on Mobutu, recognised that he would be a loyal US ally who would prevent the communists from taking power in Congo (Weissman, pp. 14-24). Washington therefore lost interest in a possible secession, recognising that through Mobutu the Western world would control the whole of the Congo, along with its natural resources.

In summary, Katanga is the only example to date in which the international community vis-à-vis an unrecognised state made an effort to end its secession and restore the unity of the state using UN military forces. 40 years later, part of the international community represented by NATO took military action against Serbia in defence of Kosovo, i.e., in defence of an unrecognised state (Anderson 2011, p. 191).

References

"'Telegram from the Department of State to the Embassy in Belgium', Washington, December 21, 1961". *Foreign Relations of the United States, 1961–1963* 20(178), Congo Crisis.

"'Telegram from the Embassy in Belgium to the Department of State', Brussels, January 23, 1961". *Foreign Relations of the United States, 1961–1963* 20(22).

Anderson, Liam: "Reintegrating unrecognized states: internationalizing frozen conflicts". In: N. Caspersen, Nina / Gareth Stansfield (eds.): *Unrecognized States in the International System*. Routledge: London, New York 2011, pp. 183-206.

Association for Diplomatic Studies and Training: *Congo in Crisis: The Rise and Fall of Katangan Secession*, retrieved 4.3.2023, from https://adst.org/2015/09/congo-in-crisis-the-rise-and-fall-of-katangan-secession/.

Boehme, Olivier: "The Involvement of the Belgian Central Bank in the Katanga Secession, 1960-1963." *African Economic History* 33, 2005, pp. 1-29.

Border Disputes Among African States. (The assembly of Heads of State and Government meeting in its First Ordinary Session in Cairo, UAR, from 17 to 21 July 1964), retrieved 4.6.2022, from https://archives.au.int/bitstream/handle/123456789/1092/AfricanBorderDispuites_E.pdf?sequence=1&isAllowed=y.

Calvocoressi, Peter: *Polityka międzynarodowa 1945-2000 [World Politics 1945-2000]*. Książka i Wiedza: Warszawa 2002.

Caspersen, Nina / Stansfield, Gareth (eds.): *Unrecognized States in the International System*. (Exeter Studies in Ethno Politics. Series Editor: Gareth. Stansfield). Routledge: London, New York, 2011.

Chałasiński, Józef. "Organizacja jedności Afryki i kryzys kongijski", *Przegląd Socjologiczny / Sociological Review* 19(1), 1965, pp. 7-12.

Duică, Alexandra-Francesca: *The Role of the United Nations Security Council in the Evolution of Peacekeeping; Case Studies: The Congo and Somalia*, (bachelor thesis). Bucharest 2016. Retrieved 5.6.2022, from https://www.academia.edu/31629054/The_role_of_the_United_Nations_Security_Council_in_the_evolution_of_peacekeeping_Case_Studies_The_Congo_and_Somalia.

Duignan, Peter / Gann, L.H.: *The United States and Africa. A History*. Cambridge University Press: Cambridge, London, New York, New Rochelle, Melbourne, Sydney 1984.

Encyclopedia Britannica: *Democratic Republic of the Congo – Government and Society*, retrieved 10.3.2023, from https://www.britannica.com/place/Democratic-Republic-of-the-Congo.

Gobbers, Erik: "Ethnic Associations in Katanga Province, the Democratic Republic of Congo: Multi-tier system, shifting identities and the relativity of autochthony". *The Journal of Modern African Studies* 54(2), 2016, pp. 211-236. DOI:10.1017/S0022278X16000185.

Gonze, Collin: "Katanga Secession: The New Colonialism". *Africa Today* 9(1), 1962, pp. 4-6+12+16, retrieved 15.3.2023, from http://www.jstor.org/stable/4184284.

Haskin, Jeanne M.: *The Tragic State of Congo. From Decolonization to Dictatorship*. Algora Publishing: New York 2005.

Hendricx, Colin: "Tshombe's secessionist state of Katanga: agency against the odds". *Third World Quarterly* 42(8), 2021, pp. 1809-1828, DOI: 10.1080/01436597.2021.1920832.

Kabemba, Claude: "The Democratic Republic of Congo". In: Clapham, Christopher / Jeffrey Herbst / Greg Mills (eds.): *Big African States: Angola, DRC, Ethiopia, Nigeria, South Africa, Sudan*. University of Witwatersrand, Wits University Press: Johannesburg 2001, pp. 97-122.

Kent, John: "The Neo-colonialism of Decolonisation: Katangan Secession and the Bringing of the Cold War to the Congo", *The Journal of Imperial and Commonwealth History* 45(1), 2017, pp. 93-130, DOI: 10.1080/03086534.2016.1262644

Kisangani, Emizet François: *Civil Wars in the Democratic Republic of Congo, 1960–2010*. Lynne Rienner Publishers: Boulder, CO and London 2012.

Kłosowicz, Robert / Mormul, Joanna: *Erytrea i jej wpływ na sytuację polityczną w Rogu Afryki*. Wydawnictwo Uniwersytetu Jagiellońskiego: Kraków 2018.

Kłosowicz, Robert: "The problem of bad governance as a determinant of state dysfunctionality in Sub-Saharan Africa", *Politeja* 56, 2018, pp. 9-22, DOI: 10.12797/Politeja.15.2018.56.02.

Langellier, Jean-Pierre: *Mobutu*. Państwowy Instytut Wydawniczy: Warszawa 2019.

Larmer, Miles / Kennes, Erik: "Rethinking the Katangese Secession". *The Journal of Imperial and Commonwealth History* 42(4), 2014, pp. 741-761, DOI: 10.1080/03086534.2014.894716.

Leśniewski, Michał: "Kongo-Katanga, 1960-1964". In: Bartnicki, Andrzej (ed.): *Zarys dziejów Afryki i Azji. Historia konfliktów 1869-2000*. Książka i wiedza: Warszawa 2000, pp. 378-390.

MacFarlane, S. Neil: *Intervention in Contemporary World Politics*. (The International Institute for Strategic Studies). Oxford University Press: Oxford 2002.

Marshall, Tim: *Więźniowie geografii. Czyli wszystko co chciałbyś wiedzieć o globalnej polityce*. Zysk i S-ka: Poznań 2017.

Meredith, Martin: *The state of Africa. A history of the continent since independence*. Free Press: London 2005.

Mission de l'Organisation des Nations Unies pour la Stabilisation en République démocratique du Congo, retrieved 5.3.2023, from https://monusco.unmissi ons.org/en.

Ndikumana, Léonce / Kisangani, Emizet François: "The Economics of Civil War: The Case of the Democratic Republic of Congo" In: Collier, Paul / Nicholas Sambanis (eds.): *Understanding Civil War: Evidence and Analysis. Volume 1: Africa*. World Bank: Washington, DC 2005, pp. 63-88.

Nkrumah, Kwame: *Africa Must Unite*. Panaf: New York. 1963.

O'Malley, Alanna: "'What an awful body the UN have become!!' Anglo-American–UN relations during the Congo crisis, February–December 1961". *Journal of Transatlantic Studies* 14 (1), 2016, pp. 24-46, DOI: 10.1080/ 14794012.2015.1125164.

Passemiers, Lazlo: "Safeguarding White Minority Power: The South African Government and the Secession of Katanga, 1960–1963". *South African Historical Journal* 68(1), 2016, pp. 70-91, DOI: 10.1080/02582473.2015.1118882/.

Pfister, Roger: *Apartheid South Africa and African States: From Pariah to Middle Power, 1961-1994*. Tauris Academic Studies: London 2005.

Reno, William: "Congo: From State Collapse to 'Absolutism', to State Failure." *Third World Quarterly* 27(1), 2006, pp. 43-56.

S/RES/143 (1960), *United Nations Security Council Resolution*, 143 of 14th July 1960, retrieved 6.6.2020, from https://www.un.org/depts/dhl/dag/docs/ sres143ef.pdf.

S/RES/161 (1961), *United Nations Security Council Resolution* 161 [The Congo Question] of 21st February 1961, retrieved 16.6.2022, from https://www.refwo rld.org/docid/3b00f2bc1c.html

Saunders, Chris: "[Book review of] 'Decolonisation and Regional Geopolitics: South Africa and the 'Congo Crisis', 1960–1965' by Lazlo Passemiers". *South African Historical Journal* 72(2), 2020, pp. 350-352, DOI: 10.1080/ 02582473.2020.1774639.

Srogosz, Tomasz: "Charakter prawny uti possidetis w prawie międzynaro-dowym". *Państwo i prawo* 6, 2011, pp. 64-76.

The Organization of African Unity Charter, 25 May 1963, Addis Abeba, retrieved 9.3.2023, from http://www.africa-union.org/root/au/Documents/Treaties/text/OAU_Charter_1963.pdf.

United Nations Operation in the Congo, retrieved 9.3.2023, from https://www.unic.un.org.pl/misje_pokojowe/onuc.php.

Van Reybrouck, David: *Kongo. Opowieść o zrujnowanym kraju*. W.A.B: Warszawa 2016.

Vanthemsche, Guy: *Belgium and the Congo, 1885–1980*. Cambridge University Press: Cambridge 2012.

Weissman, Stephen R.: "What really happened in Congo. The CIA, the murder of Lumumba, and rise of Mobutu". *Foreign Affairs (Council on Foreign Relations)* 93(4), 2014, pp. 14-24.

Zartman, I. William: "Introduction: Posing the Problem of State Collapse." In: Zartman, I. William (ed.): *Collapsed States: The Disintegration and Res-toration of Legitimate Authority*. Lynne Rienner Publishers: Boulder, CO and London 1995, pp. 1-12.

Robert Kłosowicz, Joanna Mormul, Kateřina Ženková
Rudincová

Chapter 9. The International Relations of Somaliland[1]

The chapter aims to analyse the international relations of Somaliland as a distinctive case study of a *de facto state*. It contends that despite lacking international recognition, Somaliland has successfully forged and sustained political and economic ties with various states and entities within the global system. The chapter explores Somaliland's efforts to garner international acknowledgment through diplomatic outreach to key stakeholders while acknowledging the challenges impeding this recognition. Special emphasis is placed on the strategic significance of the port of Berbera, which serves as a crucial trade conduit for the entire region and significantly influences Somaliland's relations with Ethiopia and the United Arab Emirates. The analysis presented in this chapter has been conducted through a critical examination of relevant literature, documents, and media sources. Additionally, insights gained from field research conducted in Somaliland in 2011 have been taken into account.

Keywords: Somaliland, international relations, *de facto state*, unrecognised state, Horn of Africa

Somaliland – introduction

Somaliland is a secessionist region of Somalia with a population of 4.171 million according to 2020 government statistics (Somaliland Central Statistics Department 2022b). Although it has in fact been independent since 1991, it still lacks international recognition. Somaliland extends sovereign control over its borders, issues its own currency, maintains a foreign service, and is governed by a democratically elected government, but the international community recognises it as an autonomous region within Somalia and the authorities in Mogadishu reject Hargeisa's aspirations to independence. The UN and the African Union (AU) have also consistently stood by the principle of *uti possidetis*, i.e., the protection of existing postcolonial state boundaries in Africa. Significantly, Somalia, from which Somaliland is trying to break away, is unable to perform state

---

1 This chapter is the result of a research project financed by the National Science Centre (Narodowe Centrum Nauki), Poland, grant ID: 2017/25/B/HS5/00958.

functions and has been considered a highly dysfunctional (failed) state for years, leading the rankings of dysfunctionality. According to the "Fragile States Index", published by the Fund for Peace, Somalia was ranked number one (worst) for six consecutive years between 2008 and 2013, ranking first again in 2016. It ranked second between 2014-2015 and 2017-2022, returning to first place again in 2023 (Fund for Peace 2023; Kłosowicz 2017b). Various transitional governments have attempted to establish their authority in an internally chaotic Somalia, but – in the long run – efforts to create an effective central government have failed (Lizak 2012). The current Federal Government of Somalia (FGS) is the internationally recognised government of Somalia, but it still does not control the entire territory of the state. Meanwhile, the Somaliland government is in control of most of its territory and can perform all the basic functions of a state. Achieving international recognition has therefore been the government's main objective for 32 years, and to this end the Hargeisa-based authorities have made a number of visits to practically all the capitals of the world's most influential countries. Although the international community recognises Somaliland as part of Somalia, the Somaliland government maintains informal representations in some countries. However, these missions do not have diplomatic status under the provisions of the Vienna Convention on Diplomatic Relations (United Nations – Office of Legal Affairs 1961). Somaliland is currently represented in six African countries: Ethiopia, Djibouti, Egypt, Kenya, South Africa and Tanzania (honorary representation); in North America: Canada and the USA; in eight European countries: France, the United Kingdom, Sweden, Belgium, the Netherlands (honorary representation), Germany (honorary representation), Norway and Denmark (honorary representation); in Asia: in the United Arab Emirates, Yemen and Turkey, as well as in Australia. In addition, Somaliland has diplomatic relations with another *de facto state* that also lacks international recognition, Taiwan. The latter opened its embassy in the Somaliland capital in August 2020, and Somaliland opened a representative office in Taipei on 9 September of the same year (The Diplomat 2022). Ethiopia, Djibouti, Turkey, the UK, and Denmark also maintain representation in Somaliland (Somaliland official website 2022).

Somaliland and *uti possidetis iuris*

At the time of the decolonisation of Africa, the Conference of Heads of State and Government of the Organisation of African Unity, which met in Cairo from 17-21 July 1964, adopted a declaration entitled "Border Disputes Among African States", according to which "the borders of African States, on the day of their independence, constitute a tangible reality" and therefore "SOLEMNLY DECLARES that all Member States pledge themselves to respect the borders existing on their achievement of national independence" (Organisation of African Unity 1964). Thus, the principle of *uti possidetis iuris* was adopted to guarantee the inviolability of the borders of the newly formed states and to prevent conflicts between African states. As the history of the last 60 years has shown, this principle has not protected the states of the region from internal conflicts and separatist movements.

In its quest for independence, Somaliland invokes historical rights which, according to the *de facto state*'s politicians, do not contradict the principle of *uti possidetis*. Indeed, Somaliland was a separate colony within the British Empire, and – after decolonisation – it was briefly an independent, internationally recognised state, until it entered a state union with Somalia of its own volition in 1960. Historically, Somaliland became a British protectorate following the conclusion of treaties between Britain and various Somaliland clans in 1887, and the international boundaries of the Protectorate were defined by treaties with France (Djibouti) to the west in 1888, Ethiopia to the south in 1887, and Italy (Somalia) to the east in 1894. Following the Italians' defeat in Second World War in 1941, discussions began about the future of the former Italian colony of Somalia and the British protectorate in Somaliland. The British proposed the unification of the two former colonial areas, which would come under London's administration as a trust territory. In the end, the Big Four Commission, made up of representatives from USA, Britain, France, and the USSR, decided to establish a trust territory in the former Italian colony under the administration of Rome for a period of 10 years to prepare the people of the area for independence, which was to be declared in 1960 (Lewis 2009). On 26 June 1960, the British protectorate of Somaliland gained independence and became a sovereign state receiving congratulatory telegrams from 35 countries, including all five permanent members of the UN Security Council, in line with the practice at the time whereby international recognition was extended to newly decolonised states. Five days after independence, on 1 July 1960, Somaliland united with Somalia (comprising the area of the former Italian colony) to form a single state that would in future seek to create a "Greater Somalia", bringing together all Somalis living in the Horn of Africa. The agreed formalities for a union treaty to be concluded by both Somaliland and Somalia were not adequately fulfilled, and the people of Somaliland had little influence in the drafting of the constitution for the new Republic of Somalia. In the initial years of the union, the former Somaliland region experienced ongoing political and economic marginalisation, with political and military roles disproportionately allocated to individuals from the southern part of the state (Lewis, 2009; Carroll & Rajagopal, 1993; Somaliland Official Website, 2022). An attempted coup in 1961 by a group of senior Somali armed forces officers was a sign of disillusionment with the state union that Somaliland had joined. In the 1980s, the Issaq clans residing in the north-western region launched an armed rebellion against the authoritarian regime of President Mohammed Siad Barre. This uprising led to a devastating civil war, resulting in the loss of nearly 50,000 lives, displacing half a million individuals, and the complete destruction of Hargeisa due to aerial bombardments by government forces[2]. The war ended in spring 1991 with the overthrow of the tyrant and a new power struggle in Mogadishu. Following a meeting in Hargeisa, the Issaq clans declared Somaliland's independence within the borders of the former British protectorate on 18 May 1991 (Harper 2012). In the years that followed, Somalia plunged ever deeper into violence, lawlessness and fanaticism and became an example of a highly dysfunctional (failed) state, while Somaliland not only managed to avoid being drawn into a fratricidal war, but the clan elders disarmed the guerrillas, formed a government, established courts, a police force, established their own currency, and adopted a new constitution. With time, it has even introduced a Western model of democracy, a three-party political system comprising the following parties: Kulmiye Peace, Unity and Development Party; the Justice and Welfare Party (UCID); and the Somaliland National Party (Waddani). Since 2005, Somaliland has held what are considered free parliamentary and presidential elections (Harper 2012; Freedom House).[3]

All these efforts, however, did not have the desired effect of providing them international recognition. The Organisation of African Unity, and later its heir – the African Union, attached to the principle of the inviolability of postcolonial borders, were unwilling to recognise Somaliland's secession.

---

2   According to the Lemkin Institute for Genocide Prevention, in 1987–1989, between 50,000 and 250,000 people – members of the Issaq clan (the major clan in Somaliland) – could have been killed. This crime is now increasingly recognised as a genocide (also according to the conclusions presented in 2018 by the UN) – the Issaq genocide (or also: the Hargeysa Holocaust). As genocidal campaigns in the North by the Somali government remain little studied, they are often referred to using the term "forgotten genocide" (Lemkin Institute for Genocide Prevention 2022; Ingiris 2016; Seth 2022, p. 154).

3   According to the *Freedom in the World 2022* report, within the scope of which Freedom House, a Washington- based non-profit organization, evaluates the level of political rights and civil freedoms, taking into account data from 2021, Somaliland was identified as a "Partly Free" area (Freedom House 2022).

Somaliland's international relations

Somaliland – objectives and strategies

Somaliland's case is unique because it seceded from a highly dysfunctional (failed) state which is not currently capable of effectively reclaiming its territory. Somaliland has been able to establish relations with several states in the international system and is aware that having foreign allies/partners/quasi-patrons is necessary for promoting its independence and ensuring human and economic development. As mentioned, Somaliland has political representation in several foreign countries, including Ethiopia, the UK, and the USA. Several countries have also opened their liaison offices in Hargeisa. Somaliland's capital is the seat of representative offices of various international organisations, such as the UN Development Programme or UNHCR (Berg / Toomla 2009).

Political factors: Somaliland's claim for independence and international recognition is challenged especially by the African Union's ongoing adherence to the preservation of colonial borders in Africa. Despite the conclusions of the AU's fact-finding mission that Somaliland's case should not be linked to the notion of "opening Pandora's box" (The Mail and Guardian 2006), the AU has insisted on the territorial integrity of Somalia.

Economic factors: Somaliland's economy is highly dependent on livestock export; therefore, it is necessary to for it to search for new partners and to diversify its economic activities. The port of Berbera is the main export hub for Somaliland; it also serves the landlocked Ethiopia.

Social factors: Somaliland needs connection with the states in the region and beyond, which is provided by Ethiopian Airlines through Addis Ababa, Daallo Airlines through Mogadishu, Air Djibouti through Djibouti, as well as Flydubai and the Emirates through Dubai, even though Somaliland is not a party to the Chicago Convention (Daallo Airlines, Web; Skyscanner, Web). Several states also recognise Somaliland passports. Visas are issued by Somaliland's diplomatic missions in London or Addis Ababa (Somaliland official website 2022). As international organisations do not recognize Somaliland as an independent state, it is not a member of entities such as the Universal Postal Union. Consequently, it lacks its own internet domain or telephone code, resulting in the use of the Somali telephone code and reliance on Ethiopia for mail delivery. The sole international organisation of which Somaliland is a member is the Unrepresented Nations and Peoples Organisation. In 2005, the then-president of Somaliland, Dahir Riyale Kahin, formally requested his country's admission to the African

Union. Consequently, the AU set up a committee to look into the application, its conclusions were quite clear:

> The fact that the union between Somaliland and Somalia was never ratified and also malfunctioned when it went into action from 1960 to 1990, makes Somaliland's search for recognition historically unique and self-justified in African political history.

The committee also recommended that the African Union "find a special method of dealing with this outstanding case." However, this did not elicit the reaction Hargeisa expected (Seth 2022, p. 164).[4]

The approach taken by different actors towards Somaliland

Although the current political situation in Somaliland is relatively stable compared to Somalia, the lack of international recognition means that the *de facto state*'s stability could be shattered at any moment, making its daily existence more difficult and further threatening its security, and therefore that of the Horn of Africa region as a whole. Another risk results from the fact that disillusionment with the West's unwillingness to recognise Somaliland's independence, combined with poverty and the neighbourhood of a destabilised Somalia could result in a radicalisation of public sentiment and, consequently, the growing influence of al-Shabab jihadists. In addition, all of Somalia's neighbours are at risk of merging the irredentist rhetoric of "Greater Somalia" with Islamist ideology, to the extent that in their time both Ethiopia and Kenya have made armed interventions in Somalia (Samatar 2013; International Crisis Group 2022).

Today, however, Somaliland itself also faces a serious security problem within its own borders, more specifically in the eastern Sool and Sanaag regions bordering Puntland, as well as partly in the Togdheer region (Buuhoodle district, which according to Puntland is part of its territory – Cayn region). These territories were part of British Somaliland but are nevertheless mostly inhabited by members of the Darod clan (Dhulbahante sub-clan) rather than the Issaq clan, unlike the rest of the country's population. As such, not only do they have a strong sense of clan separateness, but they have never been supporters

---

4   Several years ago, the issue was raised of the possible membership of Somaliland, a former British colony as it were, in the Commonwealth. This was advocated, e.g., by former Somaliland Foreign Minister (now Minister of Finance) Saad Ali Shire (Shire 2018), and even earlier by Somaliland President Dahir Riyale Kahin, who in 2007 appeared at the Commonwealth Heads of Government Meeting in Kampala for this purpose (Seth 2022, p. 162).

of Somaliland independence. They were also closer to their fellow Puntlanders, among whom the Darod clan is also in the majority. The dispute over these areas between Somaliland and Puntland flared up a few years after Puntland declared autonomy within the Somali state in 1998 (in fact, in view of the apparent weakness of the Somali government, Puntland has governed itself much like Somaliland, practically on its own, except that it has never declared independence nor does its government officially seek it). The most important town in the disputed territory is Las Anod, where, in 2002, the convoy of the President of Somaliland at the time, Dahir Riyale Kahin, was attacked by Puntland forces. A few months later, Puntland occupied the disputed territory. It was not until 2007 that Somaliland regained control of these lands, but the Somaliland-Puntland borderlands remained unsettled and armed skirmishes continued to occur there. Political support for Hargeisa's rule in the region was not high either. In 2012, local politicians announced the establishment of an autonomous administrative region – Khatumo State of Somalia (SSC Khatumo[5]). That same year, the Transitional Federal Government of Somalia accepted SSC Khatumo as one of its federation states. In 2016, however, the Khatumo authorities began negotiations with Hargeisa, and in 2018 dissolved the state they had created in exchange for the promise of changes to the Somaliland constitution and government positions. Nonetheless, mutual relations were not ideal, with the assassination of a prominent politician from the Sool region in December 2022 adding fuel to the fire. The riots that erupted after his death were suppressed by Somaliland security forces (20 fatalities), who withdrew from Las Anod in January 2023 due to massive social discontent and the hostile attitude of the town's residents. In February 2023, the local government announced that it was breaking away from the sovereignty of Hargeisa and returning to the idea of SSC Khatumo as a federal state of Somalia (Guglielmo 2013, pp. 89-94; Johnson / Smaker 2014; Ker-Lindsay 2023; Haji 2023). In April 2023, Amnesty International published the results of its investigation documenting the situation in Las Anod, pointing out, e.g., that Somaliland forces were shelling the entire city, making no exceptions for hospitals, schools, mosques, causing massive casualties and panic among the civilian population. By April 2023, this had resulted in more than 100 deaths, over 600 injuries and between 154,000 and 203,000 people forced to leave their homes (Amnesty International 2023). Concern about the situation in Las Anod has been expressed by the United States, the European Union and several countries that cooperate with Somaliland in various capacities, such as the United

---

5   SSC – Sool, Saanag, Cayn.

Kingdom, Canada, and Turkey (U.S. Department of State 2023; Delegation of the European Union to Somalia 2023). The situation in Las Anod, on the one hand, is very problematic for the Hargeisa government and does not help efforts to win international recognition, and – on the other – according to some scholars (e.g., Ker-Lindsay 2023), is indirectly a consequence of the lack of international recognition of Somaliland statehood and more than 30 years of international legal limbo.

One of Somaliland's hopes for international recognition remains its geopolitical location. Somaliland's coastline lies entirely on the Gulf of Aden and thus runs opposite the coast of Yemen. The distance between Berbera, Somaliland's main port, and Aden in Yemen is only 140 nautical miles. In addition, Berbera and Zeila are ancient trading cities in the Horn of Africa that have attracted the interest of world powers for centuries due to their strategic location near the Bab el-Mandeb Strait, which connects the Gulf of Aden to the Red Sea. This location makes Somaliland's ports the region's only alternative to Djibouti in the Red Sea and Horn of Africa basin (Makinda 1992). As early as in 1896, Richard Burton, a British explorer, noted the importance of the port of Berbera, which he described as "the true key of the Red Sea, the centre of East African traffic, and the only safe place for shipping upon the western Erythroean shore, from Suez to Guardafui"[6] (Godsall 2001, p. 136).

Today, Somaliland's ports remain a focus of international interest and competition. The region's largest country with a population of 110 million, Ethiopia, has been cut off from the sea as a result of Eritrea's secession and has consequently lost important Red Sea ports (Massawa and Assab), while the use of Djibouti's congested ports, through which 80 per cent of its exports and imports pass (including 95 per cent of its maritime trade), is becoming more expensive with every year (Demissie 2021). This is causing Addis Ababa to search for alternatives with increasing urgency and, consequently, to tighten its economic ties with Somaliland, also becoming the *de facto state*'s quasi-patron (Kosienkowski / Ženková Rudincová 2022). As early as in February 2015, the Ethiopian authorities announced that they wanted to diversify their transport corridors, with plans for 5-10% of their domestic imports to pass through the port of Berbera (Mormul 2016).

In March 2018, the international logistics company Dubai Ports World,[7] the government of Somaliland and the government of Ethiopia entered into an

---

6   Cape Guardafui – today in the autonomous Puntland region.
7   An international logistics company based in Dubai, United Arab Emirates. It specialises in cargo logistics, port terminal services, maritime services, and free trade zones.

agreement on the expansion and joint administration of the port in Berbera, with Ethiopia owning 19% of its shares. The port is undergoing extensive expansion, and a highway is under construction between the port and the Ethiopian capital (DP World 2021). The port of Berbera could become a "second window to the world" for Ethiopia and its booming economy. To date, the seaports of Djibouti have earned more than one and a half billion dollars a year from Ethiopian exports and imports. Somaliland's leaders hope that the port of Berbera could achieve at least a third of this amount (British International Investment 2022).

The authorities in Addis Ababa are also considering rebuilding their military presence in the maritime waters of the Horn of Africa region, as evidenced by the military cooperation agreement signed with France in May 2019, which includes helping Ethiopia build its naval forces (although it does not specify where the landlocked state plans to dock naval units). Ethiopia's naval efforts are driven by three main factors. Firstly, these are concerns about the future of the port of Djibouti, which the International Monetary Fund classifies as being at "high debt risk" due to Chinese financing and the threat of Beijing taking control of it after Djibouti defaults on its debt obligations. Secondly, it is to protect the state-owned merchant fleet managed by the Ethiopian Shipping & Logistics Services Enterprise (ESLSE). The third factor involves creating an alternative to Djibouti, which currently effectively has a monopoly on the maritime transhipment of Ethiopian goods (International Monetary Fund 2020).

Djibouti itself maintains good relations with Somaliland, especially in the field of security, although it does not formally recognise it as a sovereign state, and Djibouti-Somaliland relations in other areas are quite limited. However, in 2015, Djibouti became the third country to open a consulate in Hargeisa – Somaliland's capital (after Ethiopia and Turkey). The main issues of contention include Djibouti's involvement in the Somali peace process, although Prof. Amina Saïd Chiré from the University of Djibouti explains that the lack of recognition of Somaliland may be primarily determined by economic considerations arising from a fear of possible competition with Somaliland's ports. Thus, from the Djiboutian perspective, it is in their national interest to maintain a quasi-state entity beyond its south-eastern border (Kłosowicz, Mormul 2017a). This approach does not seem to interfere with the ongoing bilateral cooperation regarding internal and regional security. Under the agreement signed in April 2014, Djibouti actively cooperates with Somaliland in the fight against terrorism in the Horn of Africa. This mainly involves strengthening the security of the common frontier, especially after a major terrorist attack by suicide bombers, probably from Somaliland, which took place in May 2014 in the very centre of the Djibouti capital at the La Chaumière restaurant, popular among foreigners, including foreign soldiers stationed in Djibouti (Ghorbal 2014).

Another regional power expressing interest in Somaliland's ports is the Arab Republic of Egypt. The Somaliland authorities perceive Egypt as a potential partner capable of playing a significant role in securing international recognition. Being a prominent nation in both Africa and the Arab world, Egypt is seen as having the potential to facilitate Somaliland's pursuit of recognition within both the African Union and the League of Arab States. In March 2020, a delegation from Somaliland visited Egypt, while in July, an Egyptian delegation reciprocated the visit to Hargeisa. The deepening diplomatic engagement between Somaliland and Egypt has provoked discontent from authorities in Mogadishu and Addis Ababa, leading to protests from the Somali government and Ethiopia. The latter viewed it as an attempt to politically manipulate the conflict between Addis Ababa and Cairo over the construction of a hydropower plant on the Blue Nile (Somaliland Chronicle 2020). Meanwhile, Somalia responded by cancelling the education cooperation protocol between Mogadishu and Cairo, in fact ending Egyptian cultural presence in Somalia. In addition, at the Arab League, Somalia's representative did not accede to the organisation's position supporting Egypt's stance in the conflict with Ethiopia over the Grand Ethiopian Renaissance Dam, i.e., the above-mentioned hydropower plant on the Blue Nile (Abtadoun 2020). It should also be emphasised that the Ethiopian government was especially outraged by the possibility of establishing an Egyptian army base in the port of Berbera, as according to Addis Ababa, its construction would be counter to Ethiopia's security interests (Getachew 2020). The Somaliland authorities themselves were very pleased with the Egyptian delegation's visit to Hargeisa in 2020. Press releases have even highlighted the longstanding ties between the two countries dating back to the era of Queen Hatshepsut and the Pharaohs. Egypt is regarded as a nation possessing the expertise to assist in the development of Somaliland's mining sector. Notably, amidst Egypt's dispute with Ethiopia regarding the Grand Renaissance Dam, there was a suggestion that Somaliland authorities could serve as mediators due to their amicable relations with both parties (Samir, 2020).

Somaliland established official diplomatic relations with the Republic of China (Taiwan) in July 2020. Somaliland-Taiwanese interactions date back to 2009, but previously only covered maritime security, education, and health issues. The establishment of diplomatic relations with another *de facto state* can be read as an attempt by Somaliland to strengthen its position on the international scene in the face of its lack of success in seeking international recognition from UN member states. Both China and Somalia have condemned the establishment of diplomatic relations between Somaliland and Taiwan. In contrast, the US National Security Council expressed support for the initiative. China, which has been investing in Djibouti's ports for years in an attempt to monopolise transshipment and shipping in this strategic area, saw this step as an overt political provocation (Shaban 2020)[8].

In contrast, the USA has maintained contact with Somaliland since 2001 even on the highest levels, through several meetings with President Dahir Riyale Kahin. The USA and Somaliland have cooperated in countering terrorism and piracy in the region and the democratisation process in Somaliland (Berg / Pegg 2016). Somaliland has been successful in countering pirates in the Horn of Africa, which is perceived positively by the Americans. Somaliland is generally seen as a buffer to the instability between Ethiopia and Djibouti on the one side and Somalia on the other. Engagement with Somaliland and Puntland is thus a part of the wider US security strategy in the Horn of Africa (Berg / Pegg 2016). The USA has supported the democratisation process in Somaliland through contacts with Somaliland NGOs and the diaspora (Berg / Pegg 2016). The assistance for democratisation activities was delivered through USAID and included, e.g., support for informal education or initiatives through the UN Development Program's Rule of Law program to expand judiciary and police training in Somaliland (Berg / Pegg 2016, p. 403).

The Russian Federation is also showing interest in Somaliland and would be keen to open a military base in Berbera or another Somaliland port. For Moscow, Africa is another area of confrontation with the West after Europe and the Middle East. So far, mainly Wagner Group mercenaries and Russian military advisers operate in sub-Saharan Africa, but Moscow's plans also include setting up military bases in strategic areas, including the Horn of Africa. According to the US Department of Defence, the Russians were pushing hard in 2020 to establish their first base in East Africa. Their main target was supposed to have been the port of Berbera. According to unconfirmed information, the government in Hargeisa was said to have offered to agree to the opening of a Russian naval base in the port of Berbera in exchange for Moscow's recognition of Somaliland's independence. Rumours of Russian interest in Berbera had already surfaced a few years earlier in 2017, when the annexation of Crimea in 2014 and the growing

---

8   More about the Somaliland-Taiwanese relations can be found in Chapter 10: *Cooperation of Unrecognized States in International Relations on the Example of the Republic of Somaliland and the Republic of China (Taiwan). A Model for an Unofficial Approach to the Diplomacy.*

conflict with the West led the Djibouti government to definitively refuse to allow for a permanent Russian presence in the country. Significantly, there used to be a Soviet military base in the port of Berbera, and the runway built by Soviet specialists was 4,140 metres long, making it the longest in Africa at the time. The USSR left Somalia in 1977 as it decided to support Ethiopia in the Ethiopian-Somali conflict (Payton 1980; Kłosowicz / Mormul 2018; Kentros Klyszcz 2020).

Consent to use of the port of Berbera and establishing its military base was in turn obtained by the United Arab Emirates in 2017. In their case, this was not subject to the need to recognise Somaliland statehood, but nevertheless, as already mentioned, the Emirati company Dubai Ports World has been managing, modernising and expanding the port of Berbera since 2016. The investment alone is worth more than $450 million, making UEA the largest foreign investor in Somaliland in 2021. Somaliland has a representative (liaison) office in the United Arab Emirates, and since 2021 there has been a high diplomatic representative of the UEA at the rank of consul residing in Hargeisa, who in Somaliland media is referred to using the term "ambassador" (Somaliland Standard 2021; Somaliland Chronicle 2021).

Turkey was the only country that maintained a diplomatic outpost in Hargeisa at a time when virtually no other state seemed interested in doing so, although it would be a mistake to consider Turkish policy in the region as pro-Somaliland. Turkey has long had very good relations with Somalia, which is the main bridgehead for Turkish interests in Africa. Ankara supports the territorial integrity of the Somali state. Turkish diplomats based in Hargeisa are always accredited in Mogadishu. Even on issues, in theory apolitical, such as humanitarian aid, Turkey promotes the unity of the Somali state: in Somaliland villages Turkish humanitarian aid is distributed under the Turkish flag and the Somali flag. As far as the trade balance between the two countries is concerned, there is also an imbalance: while the presence of Turkish products on the Somaliland market is increasing (mainly clothing, electronics, food products), Somaliland's main export "commodity", namely livestock and livestock products, rarely reaches Turkey. This, of course, also has implications for the trade balance. In addition, Somaliland has no official representation in Ankara. Moreover, although Somaliland grants visas to Turkish businessmen without any problems, Somaliland passports are not recognised by Ankara and citizens of Somaliland often have difficulty obtaining a Turkish visa. Thus, there is a lack of reciprocity in Turkish-Somaliland relations. In addition, Hargeisa does not approve of Ankara's good relations with Mogadishu and the fact that Turkish weapons are sold to Somalia, which rekindles the fear that they could one day be used against Somaliland. On the other hand, based on documents made public online by the Nordic Monitor portal, it appears that Turkey, despite not recognising Somaliland officially, does recognise Somaliland as a state in its operational practice. Nevertheless, for the time being, this does not translate into concrete benefits that could result in the recognition of Somaliland statehood (Rubin 2022; Kenez 2021).

As far as the African continent is concerned, the very good relations between Somaliland and Kenya are particularly noteworthy. This is despite Kenya's position that Somalia as a state is a single entity – a federal state with autonomous governments in individual regions, and this position is not changing, while Kenyan representatives stress that Hargeisa has never made any official request for recognition. Nevertheless, in April 2022, Kenya sent a new diplomatic representative to Hargeisa, and, for the first time, it was a diplomat with the rank of consul-general. Kenyan policy towards Somaliland is closely watched by the government in Mogadishu, which broke off relations with Kenya for a period of time following Somaliland President Muse Bihi Abdi's visit to Nairobi in 2020. Kenyan-Somali relations are further strained due to Kenyan involvement, politically and militarily, in Somalia's southern region of Jubaland and the unresolved issue of the joint maritime border dispute (Dahir 2021; The East African 2022; Economist Intelligence Unit 2022).

Hargeisa is also trying to find support for its efforts to gain international recognition from other African governments. Such efforts have been directed towards another African regional power, South Africa. However, the Pretoria government has suggested to the Somaliland authorities that they should start looking for support "closer to home" and, in the first instance, seek recognition from the Intergovernmental Authority on Development (IGAD), a regional organisation that groups together the countries of the Horn of Africa. In turn, IGAD is reluctant to enter into dialogue with Somaliland on the issue of its recognition, as a number of its members fear that this will set a precedent that affects their own internal situation and relations with the disaffected minorities living in their territory (Fabricius 2021). In terms of expressions of support for Somaliland in African states outside the Horn of Africa region, it is worth noting an incident in 2019 through which Guinea's relations with Somalia were significantly spoiled. The immediate cause was the visit of the Somaliland president to Guinea, where he was received according to the protocol for reception of a head of state, and he also called for international recognition of Somaliland. Following voices of protest and indignation coming from Mogadishu, Conakry unceremoniously reproached the Somali authorities in an official communiqué indicating the kind of state we are dealing with in the case of Somalia, pointing out that Mogadishu's real power is limited to Villa Somalia, the state administration was constructed by the international community and the state itself is not even capable of organising elections. The Guinean authorities contrasted it with Somaliland, which they presented as a model of democracy (Shaban 2019).

Somaliland's economic development and the importance of the port of Berbera

Somaliland's economy is driven by the private sector. The two most important sources of income and foreign exchange are remittances from the diaspora living abroad and livestock exports. The port of Berbera is a key hub for exports of the latter to Saudi Arabia, Yemen, and Oman. In 2021, GDP per capita stood at US$775. The GDP growth rate registered a slight decline in 2020 but is expected to grow at an annual rate of 2% in following years. Almost 30% of GDP comes from livestock, 24% from trade, 22% from remittances from the Somaliland diaspora, only 8% from crops, 7% from tax revenues, 6% from real estate activities, and 3% from other sectors. Livestock is the main export commodity with 59% of receipts. However, it is worth noting that its share in the exports was as high as 91% as recently as in 2012. Food insecurity and poverty remain widespread in many regions, affecting 30% of the population living in rural areas and 25% in urban areas. In addition, both low levels of investment and a low employment-to-population ratio of 28% for men and 17% for women persist. Somaliland's economy has been hit hard in recent years due to the COVID-19 pandemic, drought and locusts that infested the region (Bashir 2021; Somaliland Central Statistics Department 2017; 2022a, p. 3).

Somaliland's location near a major sea route, through which almost a third of the world's shipping passes, has helped the government attract new trade agreements and development investments. In 2021, the UK government's Commonwealth Development Corporation (CDC) group joined DP World's aforementioned project to develop the port in Berbera (Maasho 2018; Cornwell 2021).[9] The expansion of the Berbera port is expected to multiply its capacity and uplift the surrounding logistics facilities, creating a regional commercial hub. This is prognosed to provide an economic boost for Somaliland, as well as other countries in the Horn of Africa region, most notably Ethiopia. For Somaliland, the port of Berbera is expected to be one of the most important pillars of the economy and, by 2035, trade revenues are expected to account for 27% of GDP and 75% of Somaliland's total trade, which will indirectly translate into 53,000

---

9   In 2022, the CDC was renamed British International Investment (BII) as part of a strategy to deepen economic, security and development links around the world.

jobs. Various sectors are expected to benefit from the port expansion, including exporters of livestock, agricultural commodities, textiles, and construction materials. In addition, the trade enabled by the port will increase the availability and affordability of goods for more than a quarter of Somaliland's population, with the greatest benefits experienced by people dependent on imported staple foods (British International Investment 2022). The port of Berbera also plays a key role in enabling the reception of humanitarian aid reaching the region, which includes nearly two million refugees and internally displaced persons. One example is the unloading at Berbera port of 25,000 tonnes of Ukrainian grain destined for the Somali population, which arrived there by sea on 29 December 2022. (Ukrinform 2022). The first phase of the expansion at the port of Berbera has already been completed. The 234-km road corridor project, which connects the city of Berbera in Somaliland to the Ethiopian border town of Wajaale, is now complete in 85%. The completion of the road is projected to increase the volume of trade between Ethiopia and Somaliland by 30% (Somaliland Standard 2022).

The expansion of the port of Berbera poses a serious problem for Djibouti, as well as for China, which has invested huge funds in the expansion of the Djibouti ports. So far, this small state in the Horn of Africa has practically monopolised maritime transport in the Horn of Africa region. Moreover, it is in Djibouti that the world's military powers whose interests intersect in Africa – the United States, France, and China – have their military bases (Kłosowicz 2022). This is no coincidence, as Djibouti lies on the strategically important Bab al-Mandab Strait, which connects to the Suez Canal and as much as 30% of all shipping in the world passes through this point, also as a key conduit for the global oil trade. As mentioned, 80% of the cargo at the port of Djibouti is exported from and imported to Ethiopia. However, over the past decade Ethiopia has made every effort to reduce its dependence on Djibouti, convinced that only a strategy of port diversification can lead to a reduction in the high service charges it pays to its neighbour for the use of its ports. The port in Berbera is to function as such an alternative and it will surely be very serious competition for the ports in Djibouti. Landlocked South Sudan might perhaps also be interested in making use of the port. The effects are already clearly observable as – according to the Ethiopian Federal Ministry of Transport, the volume of Ethiopia's maritime trade routed through Djibouti dropped significantly in the last six months of 2021 from 95% to 83.9%. According to recent data, the port of Berbera has already taken over 5.9% of Ethiopia's trade previously handled by Djibouti ports. Ethiopia has also acquired stakes in other ports along Africa's east coast in recent years, and the country has recently expressed interest in participating in the development of the Zeila port in Somaliland, near the border with Djibouti (Desiderio Consultants Ltd 2022).

As per an agreement with the Somaliland government, Ethiopia is investing in infrastructure to construct the Berbera Corridor, envisioned as a highway. Additionally, plans are underway to construct an additional quay at the Berbera port. The second phase of the expansion includes extending the new quay from 400 metres to 1,000 metres and enabling the port to handle up to two million TEU[10] per year. In addition, as a result of the aforementioned investment, there has been renewed interest from foreign investors in Somaliland's energy and mining sector, which could provide a boost to developing energy resources. In addition to the commercial aspects of the project, the authorities in Hargeisa hope to bring the separatist region back into the political spotlight, not only catching the attention of the countries in the Horn of Africa, but also of the world powers. Seeking international recognition, Somaliland wishes to turn the port of Berbera into a symbol of stability in a troubled region (Gerding 2022).

Somalia, the country that has Africa's longest coastline, has for the past decades been mired in instability and consequently faces numerous challenges related to lack of security, armed insurgencies, and difficulties in implementing the rule of law, both on land and at sea. A particular challenge for the international community has been the fight against maritime piracy off its coasts. Therefore, the international community and the European Union are strongly committed to supporting the strengthening of Somali institutions in order to build a stable and secure society through the renewal of the architecture and structure of the security sector. Within the scope of these efforts, the European Union Capacity Building Mission in Somalia (EUCAP) was founded in 2012, and in 2014 it opened a field office in Hargeisa, where the EU police, legal and maritime experts work with Somaliland officials on a daily basis to develop and run advisory and training programmes in the area of security, governance and civil law enforcement. In the maritime sector, Somaliland institutions need support to achieve compliance with international standards and a reputation as a reliable partner in the search and rescue (SAR) field, as well as in dealing with environmental incidents. Maritime security is very important for Somaliland, as it has a real impact on economic development, regional security, and the stability of the entire region. Therefore, EUCAP cooperates in strengthening the Somaliland Coast Guard by providing training activities and equipment. Building the capacity of the Coast Guard helps to enforce the rule of law and maritime

---

10 Twenty-foot equivalent unit: a standard measure for a container for transporting goods, used to calculate how many containers a ship can carry, or a port can deal with (Cambridge Dictionary, Web).

sovereignty, maintain order at sea and combat piracy, smuggling and illegal fishing. The training programme provides Somaliland Coast Guard officers with a wide range of knowledge and tools to effectively perform their duties, including rescue services. It also supports the operationalisation of the emergency and maritime disaster response centre in the country. In 2022, joint Somaliland Coast Guard training took place, conducted by specialists from EUCAP and Sweden[11] (EUCAP Somalia 2022a). Environmental protection is also a crucial concern, given that oil spills from passing vessels pose significant hazards and have devastating effects on the environment, human health, and the economy. In this regard, EUCAP has aided Somaliland by providing seawater absorption equipment to mitigate the impact of potential oil spills (EUCAP Somalia, 2022b; European Union External Action, 2016).

Conclusions

Somaliland exhibits all the characteristics of a state that warrant international recognition. It exercises control over the majority of its territory, borders, and governance, which is duly acknowledged by its populace. Its government is democratically elected, and it fulfils the fundamental functions of a state, notably including the protection of its population. Despite the current situation in Las Anod, Somaliland remains relatively stable compared to war-torn Somalia, which steadfastly rejects the secession of Hargeisa. The historical context, highlighting Somaliland's status as a former British protectorate in contrast to Somalia's status as an Italian colony, as well as Somaliland's earlier attainment of independence and subsequent decision to merge with Somalia, should not be overlooked by the international community.

Why then does Somaliland still not have international recognition? There are certainly several reasons, apart from the principle of *uti possidetis*, which the African Union firmly upholds so as not to cause a domino effect of further secessions on the African continent. The experiences of Eritrea and South Sudan also certainly have had an impact. Both states were created as the result of a broken or ambiguous interpretation of the *uti possidetis* principle and are not good

---

11 Sweden itself is an example of a country where the Somaliland diaspora is very active and proficient, on the one hand, lobbying intensively for Stockholm's recognition of Somaliland statehood, citing, e.g., the Swedish recognition of the Palestinian state in 2014, and – on the other – mobilising significant financial resources subsequently used for humanitarian and development aid on Somaliland territory (Bulaale 2015; Horn Diplomat 2023).

examples of how to manage their independence. Eritrea is a dictatorship, responsible for several armed conflicts in the Horn of Africa and does not contribute to the region's stability. In turn, almost as soon as it gained independence, South Sudan plunged into a bloody civil war for power between conflicting ethnic groups, becoming a huge humanitarian challenge for the international community (famine and migration) and an example of a state where human rights are violated on a daily basis, and which is often described as a state in collapse. There is, however, another reason closely linked to Somaliland's geographical location, namely its 850-kilometre-long coastal strip of strategic importance both regionally and globally. The *de facto state*'s geostrategic maritime position has in fact become a point of rivalry among global players, such as the United States, China, and Russia, as well as among regional powers, Ethiopia and Egypt. Other states in the region have also joined the race, including Kenya, the Arabian Peninsula states and Djibouti. The last of these is not vitally interested in Somaliland's independence, primarily for economic reasons. As already mentioned, the expansion of the port of Berbera and the prospect of investment in other Somaliland ports will make it a serious competitor to Djibouti, which has virtually monopolised port and transhipment services in the Horn of Africa in recent years. Djibouti's current position has been sustained by the fact that more than 110 million Ethiopians have been landlocked as a result of Eritrea's secession, and relations between Addis Ababa and Asmara were not friendly until 2018, with the Eritrean ports of Massawa and Assab standing practically empty as a result. In turn, the civil war in Somalia and the breakdown of state structures, as well as the practice of piracy off its coast, meant that there was no alternative to safe ports outside Djibouti. In addition, the interest of global powers, the USA and China, which sought bases in hot spots around the globe, further strengthened Djibouti's position. For the same reasons as in the case of Djibouti, Hargeisa's independence is not supported by China, which has invested billions in the expansion of Djibouti ports over the past years. Additionally, political rapprochement between Taiwan and Somaliland is perceived in Beijing as a slap in the face and a hostile act. Finally, Somaliland independence, for obvious reasons, is not of interest to Somalia, which does not want to lose a strategically important coastal strip as a result of Somaliland's secession.

To reduce future geopolitical uncertainty and security risks in the Horn of Africa and the Red Sea, it is in the best interest of the international community to at least consider recognising Somaliland's statehood, while helping to maintain a stable internal situation. In addition, Western states must be aware that in the current geopolitical situation, such a step would probably also make it possible to keep at bay Russia, which is still keenly interested in establishing military bases in the Horn of Africa, despite the deeply uncertain future of its own statehood. For the moment, the topic of Somaliland's international recognition is very rarely raised in internal discussions in Western countries, the exception being the UK, where a parliamentary debate on London's recognition of Somaliland took place in January 2022, initiated by the Conservative MP for South Staffordshire, Gavin Williamson (Hansard. UK Parliament 2022). Is this the beginning of a new opening with the authorities in Hargeisa? For now, there is little indication of this, especially given Somaliland's current internal problems and the difficult situation on the Somaliland-Puntland border.

References

Abtadoun, Al-Shafi'l: "Egypt and Somalia had warm relations in the past, but now it is lukewarm at best". *MEMO. Middle East Monitor* 14.6.2020, retrieved 29.6.2023, from https://www.middleeastmonitor.com/20200714-egypt-and-somalia-had-warm-relations-in-the-past-but-now-it-is-lukewarm-at-best/.

Amnesty International: "Somaliland: Urgent investigation needed as fighting takes heavy toll on civilians in Las Anod". *Amnesty International* 20.4.2023, retrieved 30.6.2023, from https://www.amnesty.org/en/latest/news/2023/04/somaliland-conflict/.

Bashir, Mohamed: "Somaliland Budget Analysis". *Horn Diplomat* 14.1.2021, retrieved 5.12.2022, from https://www.horndiplomat.com/2021/01/14/somaliland-budget-analysis-2021/.

Berg, Eiki / Pegg, Scott: "Scrutinizing a Policy of 'Engagement Without Recognition': US Requests for Diplomatic Actions With *De Facto* States". *Foreign Policy Analysis* 5.2016, DOI: 10.1093/fpa/orw044.

Berg, Eiki / Toomla, Raul: "Forms of Normalisation in the Quest for De Facto Statehood". *The International Spectator* 44(4)2009, pp. 27–45, DOI: 10.1080/03932720903351104.

British International Investment: "Port of Berbera. Charting a stronger course for African trade with the rest of the world". *British International Investment* 2022, retrieved 18.11.2022, from https://www.bii.co.uk/en/story/port-of-berbera/.

Bulaale, Mukhtar: "Sweden should recognize Somaliland". *The Swedish Development Forum* 18.5.2015, retrieved 2.6.2023, from https://fuf.se/en/magasin/sverige-borde-erkanna-somaliland/.

Cambridge Dictionary, retrieved 13.10.2023, from https://dictionary.cambridge.org/dictionary/.

Carroll, Anthony J. / Rajagopal, B.: "The Case for the Independent Statehood of Somaliland". *American University International Law Review* 8 (2/3) 1993, pp. 653-681.

Cornwell, Alexander: "Dubai's DP World, UK's CDC to invest up to $1.7 bln in Africa". *Reuters* 14.10.2021, retrieved 22.11.2022, from https://www.reuters.com/world/africa/dubais-dp-world-britains-cdc-jointly-invest-africa-2021-10-12/.

Daallo Airlines: "Official website" 2022, retrieved 10.12.2022, from http://www.daallo.biz/.

Dahir, Abdi Latif: "Somalia Severs Diplomatic Ties with Kenya". *New York Times* 12.10.2021, retrieved 1.6.2023, from https://www.nytimes.com/2020/12/15/world/africa/somalia-kenya.html.

Delegation of the European Union to Somalia: "International partners joint statement on the situation in Laascaanood and Somaliland elections". *Delegation of the European Union to Somalia* 17.4.2023, retrieved 30.6.2023, from https://www.eeas.europa.eu/delegations/somalia/international-partners-joint-statement-situation-laascaanood-and-somaliland-1_en?s=153.

Demissie, Selam Tadesse: "Djibouti looks to Ethiopia to gauge its economic future". *Institute for Security Studies* 3.5.2021, retrieved 26.12.2022, from https://issafrica.org/iss-today/djibouti-looks-to-ethiopia-to-gauge-its-economic-future.

Desiderio Consultants Ltd: "Djibouti port loses traffic shares from neighbouring Ethiopia". *Desiderio Consultants Ltd. International Trade & Custom Regulations* 1.2.2022, retrieved 2.11.2022, from https://www.ddcustomslaw.com/index.php?option=com_content&view=article&id=587%3Adjibouti-port-loses-traffic-shares-from-neighbouring-ethiopia&catid=1%3Aultime&Itemid=50&lang=en.

DP World: "Ministry of Transport of Ethiopia and DP World sign MoU for the development of the Ethiopian side of the Berbera Corridors". *DP World* 6.5.2021, retrieved 27.12.2022, from https://www.dpworld.com/berbera/news/ministry-of-transport-of-ethiopia--dp-world-sign-mou.

Economist Intelligence Unit. "Kenya establishes consul-general's office in Somaliland". 6.5.2022, retrieved 1.6.2023, from https://country.eiu.com/article.aspx?articleid=1242081307&Country=Kenya&topic=Politics&subtopic=Forecast&subsubtopic=International+relations.

EUCAP Somalia: "EUCAP & Swedish Specialized Team train Somaliland Coast Guard Sweden should recognize Somaliland". *EUCAP Somalia* 18.5.2022a, retrieved 29.6.2023, from https://www.eeas.europa.eu/eucap-som/eucap-swedish-specialized-team-train-somaliland-coast-guard_en?s=332.

EUCAP Somalia: "#FieldVision Maritime security has a real impact on economic development, regional security and the stability of Somalia". *EUCAP Somalia* 5.7.2022b, retrieved 29.8.2023, from https://www.eeas.europa.eu/eucap-som/fieldvision-maritime-security-has-real-impact-economic-development-regional-security-and-stability_en.

European Union External Action: "EU-UN Joint Maritime Capacity Building Training in Somaliland". *European Union External Action* 16.12.2016, retrieved 20.12.2022, from https://www.eeas.europa.eu/node/17437_en.

Fabricius, Peter: "Somaliland's election boosted its theoretical case for recognition". *Institute for Security Studies* 11.6.2021, retrieved 1.7.2023, from https://issafrica.org/iss-today/somalilands-election-boosted-its-theoretical-case-for-recognition.

Freedom House: "Freedom in the World 2022". *Freedom House*, retrieved 6.6.2023, from https://freedomhouse.org/country/somaliland/freedom-world/2022.

Fund for Peace: "Fragile States Index 2023". *Fund for Peace*, retrieved 11.7.2023, from https://fragilestatesindex.org.

Geldenhuys, Deon: *Contested States in World Politics*. Palgrave Macmillan: New York, 2009.

Gerding, Jonas: "At Port of Berbera, Dubai invests in Horn of Africa shipping". *Deutsche Welle* 26.12.2022, retrieved 28.12.2022, from https://www.dw.com/en/at-port-of-berbera-dubai-invests-in-horn-of-africa-shipping/a-64198524.

Getachew, Addis: "Ethiopia objects to Egyptian base plans in Somaliland". *Anadolu Ajansi* 7.8.2020, retrieved 28.11.2022, from https://www.aa.com.tr/en/africa/ethiopia-objects-to-egyptian-base-plans-in-somaliland/1934835.

Ghorbal, Samy: "Terrorisme, piraterie: Djibouti, en première ligne". *Jeune Afrique* 4.7.2014, retrieved 22.2.2017, from http://www.jeuneafrique.com/50072/politique/terrorisme-piraterie-djibouti-en-premi-re-ligne/.

Godsall, Jon R.: "Richard Burton's Somali Expedition, 1854-55: Its Wider Historical Context and Planning". *Journal of the Royal Asiatic Society*, 11(2) 2001, pp. 135–173.

Guglielmo, Matteo: *Il Corno d'Africa: Eritrea, Etiopia, Somalia*. Il Mulino: Bologna, 2013.

Haji, Mohammed: "Conflict in disputed Las Anod dims Somaliland's diplomatic dreams". *Al Jazeera*, 10.5.2023, retrieved 29.6.2023, from https://www.aljazeera.com/features/2023/5/10/conflict-in-disputed-las-anod-dims-somalilands-diplomatic-dreams.

Hansard. UK Parliament: "UK Government Recognition of Somaliland. Volume 707: debated on Tuesday 18 January 2022". *Hansard. UK Parliament* 18.1.2022, retrieved 2.7.2023, from https://hansard.parliament.uk/Comm

ons/2022-01-18/debates/8DBF2CDF-6DDF-4E0A-A2C6-9D677628EBFB/
UKGovernmentRecognitionOfSomaliland.

Harper, Mary: *Getting Somalia Wrong? Faith, War and Hope in a Shattered State*. Zed Books: London/New York, 2012.

Hoch, Tomáš: "EU Strategy towards Post-Soviet De Facto States". *Contemporary European Studies* 6 (Jan.) 2011, pp. 69–85.

Horn Diplomat: "Somaliland Community in Sweden donates medical equipment to Beledweyne Hospital". *Horn Diplomat* 29.4.2023, retrieved 23.6.2023, from https://www.horndiplomat.com/2023/04/29/somaliland-community-in-sweden-donates-medical-equipment-to-beledweyne-hospital/.

Ingiris, Mohamed Haji: "We Swallowed the State as the State Swallowed Us": The Genesis, Genealogies, and Geographies of Genocides in Somalia". *African Security* 9(3)2016, pp. 237-258.

International Crisis Group: "Considering Political Engagement with Al-Shabaab in Somalia". *International Crisis Group*. Report no. 309/Africa, 21.6.2022, retrieved 17.12.2022, from https://www.crisisgroup.org/africa/horn-africa/somalia/309-considering-political-engagement-al-shabaab-somalia.

International Monetary Fund: "Djibouti: Requests for disbursement under the rapid credit facility and debt relief under the catastrophe containment and relief trust. Press release; staff report; and statement by the Executive Director for Djibouti". *International Monetary Fund* 5.2020. IMF Country Report No. 20/159, retrieved 22.12.2022, from https://www.imf.org/en/Publications/CR/Issues/2020/05/12/Djibouti-Requests-for-Disbursement-Under-the-Rapid-Credit-Facility-and-Debt-Relief-Under-the-49410.

Johnson, Martha C. / Smaker, Meg: "State Building in De Facto States: Somaliland and Puntland Compared". *Africa Today* 60 (4) 2014, pp. 3-23.

Kenez, Levent: "Official document shows Turkey classifies Somaliland as an independent state despite close ties with Somalia". *Nordic Monitor* 23.11.2021, retrieved 28.6.2023, from https://nordicmonitor.com/2021/11/official-document-shows-turkey-classifies-somaliland-as-an-independent-state-despite-close-ties-with-somalia/.

Kentros Klyszcz, Ivan Ulises: "Russia's thwarted return to the Red Sea". *Responsible Statecraft* 15.11.2020, retrieved 27.6.2023, from https://responsiblestatecraft.org/2020/11/15/russias-thwarted-return-to-the-red-sea/.

Ker-Lindsay, James: "Somaliland's Growing Crisis Threatens Stability Across the Horn of Africa". *World Politics Review* 31.3.2023, retrieved 29.6.2023, from https://www.worldpoliticsreview.com/somaliland-las-anod-fighting/.

Kłosowicz, Robert, Mormul, Joanna: "Interview with Prof. Amina Said Chiré" Djibouti Ville, March 19, 2017a. Unpublished.

Kłosowicz, Robert: *Konteksty dysfunkcyjności państw Afryki Subsaharyjskiej.* Wydawnictwo Uniwersytetu Jagiellońskiego: Kraków, 2017b.

Kłosowicz, Robert: "United States Africa Command – Balance of Activities during the Presidencies of George H. Bush, Barack Obama and Donald Trump". *Politeja* 19(1(76) 2022, pp. 255-284, DOI: 10.12797/Politeja.19.2022.76.13.

Kłosowicz, Robert / Mormul, Joanna: *Erytrea i jej wpływ na sytuację polityczną w Rogu Afryki.* Wydawnictwo Uniwersytetu Jagiellońskiego: Kraków, 2018.

Kosienkowski, Marcin / Ženková Rudincová, Kateřina: "Client De Facto States and Quasi-Patrons: Insights from the Relationship Between Somaliland and Ethiopia". *Ethnopolitics* Sept. 2022, pp. 1–21, DOI:10.1080/17449057.2022.2121470.

Lemkin Institute for Genocide: "Statement on the Isaaq Genocide Committed between 1987 and 1989 by the Somali Government". *Lemkin Institute for Genocide* 10.8.2022, retrieved 29.6.2023, from https://www.lemkininstitute.com/statements-new-page/statement-on-the-isaaq-genocide-committed-between-1987-and-1989-by-the-somali-government.

Lewis, Ioan: *Understanding Somalia and Somaliland.* Hurst&Company: London, 2009.

Lizak, Wiesław: *Afrykańskie instytucje bezpieczeństwa.* Wydawnictwo Naukowe Scholar: Warszawa, 2012.

Maasho, Aaron: "DP World launches expansion of port in Somaliland". *Reuters* 11.10.2018, retrieved 29.11.2022, from https://www.reuters.com/article/dp-world-somaliland-idUSL8N1WR6DY.

Makinda, Samuel M.: *Security in the Horn of Africa.* (The Adelphi Papers series, 32 (269)). Brassey's for the International Institute for Strategic Studies: London, 1992.

Mormul, Joanna: "Ethio-Djiboutian Relations in 21st century: towards New African Cooperation". *Politeja* 13. 3(42) 2016, pp. 263-285, DOI: 10.12797/Politeja.13.2016.42.16.

Neijnes, Kennet" "FieldVision | 'Maritime security has a real impact on economic development, regional security and the stability of Somalia. Our support is making a great difference'". *European Union External Action* 4.7.2022, retrieved 15.10.2022, from https://www.eeas.europa.eu/eeas/fieldvision-%E2%80%98maritime-security-has-real-impact-economic-development-regional-security-and_en.

Organization of African Unity: "Border Disputes Among African States" 1964. *Organization of African Unity.* The Assembly of Heads of State and Government meeting in its First Ordinary Session in Cairo, UAR, from 17 to 21 July 1964, AHG/Res. 16(I), retrieved 20.12.2022, from https://archives.au.int/

bitstream/handle/123456789/1092/AfricanBorderDispuites_E.pdf?seque nce=1&isAllowed=y.

Payton, Gary D.: "The Somali Coup of 1969: The Case for Soviet Complicity". *The Journal of Modern African Studies*, 18(3)1980, pp. 493–508.

Pegg, Scott / Berg, Eiki: "Lost and Found: The WikiLeaks of *De Facto* State-Great Power Relations". *International Studies Perspectives*, May 2014, pp. 267–286, DOI: 10.1111/insp.12078.

Rubin, Michael: "Turkey's Ties with Somaliland Must Be Reciprocal". *American Enterprise Institute* 1.1.2022, retrieved 28.6.2023, from https://www.aei.org/op-eds/turkeys-ties-with-somaliland-must-be-reciprocal/.

Samatar, Abdi Ismail: "The Production of Somali Conflict and the Role of Internal and External Actors". In: Bereketeab, Redie (ed.). *The Horn of Africa. Intra-State and Inter-State Conflicts and Security.* PlutoPress / Nordiska Afrikainstitutet: London/Uppsala, 2013, pp. 156–177.

Samir, Mohamed: "Somaliland says keen on stronger ties with Egypt". *Daily News Egypt* 18.7.2020, retrieved 26.6.2023, from https://www.dailynewsegypt.com/2020/07/18/somaliland-says-keen-on-stronger-ties-with-egypt/.

Seth, Michael J.: *Not on the Map. The Peculiar Histories of De Facto States.* Lexington Books: Lanham et al., 2022.

Shaban, Abdur Rahman Alfa: "As Somalia fumes at Guinea, Somaliland 'begs' for international recognition". *Africanews* 5.7.2019, retrieved 1.7.2023, from https://www.africanews.com/2019/07/05/as-somalia-fumes-at-guinea-somaliland-begs-for-international-recognition/.

Shaban, Abdur Rahman Alfa: "U.S. 'backs' Taiwan – Somaliland cooperation". *Africanews* 7.7.2020, retrieved 22.12.2022, from https://www.africanews.com/2020/07/10/us-backs-taiwan-somaliland-cooperation/.

Shire, Saad Ali: "Somaliland: Why we should be at the Commonwealth summit". *African Arguments* 16.4.2018, retrieved 29.6.2023, from https://africanarguments.org/2018/04/somaliland-we-should-be-at-the-commonwealth-summit-chogm/.

Skyscanner: "Official website" 2023, retrieved 22.6.2023, from https://www.skyscanner.pl.

Somaliland Central Statistics Department, Ministry of Planning and National Development: "Gross Domestic Product 2012-2020". *Central Statistics Department, Ministry of Planning and National Development* 2017, retrieved 27.6.2023, from https://slmof.org/wp-content/uploads/2021/10/Somaliland-GDP-2020-Report.pdf.

Somaliland Central Statistics Department, Ministry of Planning and National Development: "Somaliland in Figures 2021". *Central Statistics Department,*

Ministry of Planning and National Development Nov. 2022a, retrieved 6.7.2023, from https://slmof.org/wp-content/uploads/2023/05/SOMALIL AND-IN-FIGURES-2021.pdf.

Somaliland Central Statistics Department: "Official website" 2022b, retrieved 15.12.2022, from https://somalilandcsd.org/.

Somaliland Chronicle: "Egyptian Government Delegation Visits Somaliland". *Somaliland Chronicle* 14.7.2020, retrieved 22.12.2022, from https://somalila ndchronicle.com/2020/07/14/breaking-egyptian-government-delegation-vis its-somaliland/.

Somaliland Chronicle: "President Bihi Welcomes the United Arab Emirates Ambassador to Somaliland". *Somaliland Chronicle* 13.3.2021, retrieved 26.6.2023, from https://somalilandchronicle.com/2021/03/13/president-bihi-welcomes-the-united-arab-emirates-ambassador-to-somaliland/.

Somaliland official website. "Official website" 2022, retrieved 20.11.2022, from http://www.somalilandgov.com/.

Somaliland Standard: "The cross-border Berbera Corridor-linking Somaliland and Ethiopia nears completion". *Somaliland Standard* 29.6.2022, retrieved 20.10.2022, from https://somalilandstandard.com/the-cross-border-berbera-corridor-linking-somaliland-and-ethiopia-nears-completion/.

Somaliland Standard: "UAE Appoints a new representative to Somaliland". *Somaliland Standard* 13.3.2021, retrieved 26.6.2023, from https://somalilands tandard.com/uae-appoints-a-new-representative-to-somaliland/.

The Diplomat: "Taiwan, Somaliland Ties Growing Despite Diplomatic Isolation". *The Diplomat* 10.2.2022, retrieved 22.11.2022, from https://thediplomat.com/2022/02/taiwan-somaliland-ties-growing-despite-diplomatic-isolation/.

The East African: "Kenya's policy on breakaway Somaliland still intact – officials". *The East African* 24.1.2022, retrieved 1.6.2023, from https://www.theeastafri can.co.ke/tea/news/east-africa/omamo-kenya-policy-on-somaliland-still-int act-3692314.

The Mail and Guardian: "AU Supports Somali Split". *The Mail & Guardian* 10.2.2006, retrieved 20.12.2022, from https://mg.co.za/article/2006-02-10-au-supports-somali-split/.

Ukrinform: "25,000 tonnes of Ukrainian wheat delivered to Somali". *Ukrinform* 29.12.2022, retrieved 29.12.2022, from https://www.ukrinform.net/rub ric-economy/3643388-25000-tonnes-of-ukrainian-wheat-delivered-to-som ali.html.

United Nations – Office of Legal Affairs: "Vienna Convention on Diplomatic Relations" 18.4.1961. *United Nations - Office of Legal Affairs*, retrieved 9.12.2022, from   https://legal.un.org/ilc/texts/instruments/english/conventions/9_1_1 961.pdf.

Universitetet i Oslo: "Montevideo Convention on the Rights and Duties of States" 1933, retrieved 20.12.2022, from https://www.jus.uio.no/english/services/libr ary/treaties/01/1-02/rights-duties-states.xml.

U.S. Department of State: "Instability and Democratic Backsliding in Somaliland. Press Statement. Vedant Patel, Principal Deputy Spokesperson" 30.3.2023, *U.S. Department of State*, retrieved 30.6.2023, from https://www.state.gov/inst ability-and-democratic-backsliding-in-somaliland/.

Robert Kłosowicz

Chapter 10. Cooperation of Unrecognised States in International Relations on the Example of the Republic of Somaliland and the Republic of China (Taiwan). A Model for an Unofficial Approach to Diplomacy.[1]

Separated by thousands of kilometres and characterised by vastly different cultures, histories, and economies, Taiwan and Somaliland may initially appear to have little in common. However, akin to Taiwan, Somaliland emerged in the aftermath of a civil war, and the legacies of these conflicts continue to influence the political status of both nations. Since declaring independence from Somalia in 1991, Hargeisa, like Taipei, has endeavoured to assert its sovereignty, facing challenges of international recognition and opposition from their respective former states. Despite existing on the fringes of the global community, both *de facto states* strive to actively engage in international affairs. This chapter aims to analyse the extent to which Somaliland could adopt the political strategies employed by Taiwan, including the development of paradiplomacy, which has been tested over time to navigate the complexities of the international arena and mitigate the isolation stemming from lack of recognition. Drawing on a critical review of existing literature, documents, and press materials, as well as insights gathered from research visits to Somaliland in 2011 and Taiwan in 2023, this chapter seeks to explore potential parallels and lessons for Somaliland's diplomatic endeavours.

Keywords:*de facto states*, Somaliland, Taiwan, informal diplomacy

In recent decades, both Somaliland, since declaring independence from Somalia in 1991, and the Republic of China in Taiwan have primarily been attempting to secure their existence, as both states have in fact no international recognition and their independence is contested by the countries from which they seceded. Although they are forced to function on the margins of the international community, they do what they can to remain active participants in international relations. Separated by more than 8,000 kilometres and with very different cultures, histories and economies, the Republic of China (ROC) and the Republic

---

1   This chapter is the result of the research project financed by the National Science Centre (Narodowe Centrum Nauki), Poland, grant ID: 2017/25/B/HS5/00958.

of Somaliland have several notable similarities. Like Taiwan, Somaliland also emerged in the aftermath of a civil war, the consequences of which continue to shape the political status of the countries. Their independence is contested by countries that consider them to be their provinces. Interestingly, in the case of the Republic of China, it has not declared independence as it considers itself the only legitimate representative of China. Both *de facto states* were previously internationally recognised entities. The Republic of China was even one of the founding members of the United Nations until 1971. However, as a result of the political rapprochement between the People's Republic of China (PRC) and the USA in the early 1970s and pressure from Beijing, the Republic of China lost its international recognition, with Beijing claiming it to be a rebellious province of China and the people of Taiwan to be Chinese, only separated from mainland China as a result of historical accidents and political divisions resulting from the Cold War.[2]

The Republic of Somaliland has invoked historical rights since declaring independence in 1991 as Somaliland was a separate colony within the British Empire. After decolonisation, it was an independent internationally recognised state for a short time, until it entered into a state union with Somalia of its own accord in 1960. On 26 June 1960, the British protectorate of Somaliland gained independence and became a sovereign state, in line with the practice at the time under which international recognition was extended to newly decolonised states. In July 1960, Somaliland united with Somalia, comprising the area of the former Italian colony, to create a single state (Lewis 2009; Somaliland Official Website: "Official website", Web).[3]

---

2   In recent decades, there have been changes related to strengthening a distinct sense of identity among the Taiwanese people. This process was initiated by the chairman of the National Party (Kuomintang), President Lee Teng-hui (1988-2000). He made a fundamental reform of school textbooks, which had a serious impact on the consciousness of the younger generation and the way they perceived the island's identity. According to a survey conducted in Taiwan in September 2020, more than 80% of the residents questioned identified themselves as Taiwanese, regardless of their ethnic roots. At the same time, only 2% of respondents identified as Chinese. The results of the poll also showed that 80.5 percent support Taiwan's participation in international organisations and events under the name "Taiwan", while only 12 percent are opposed. When asked what name Taiwan should use when engaging in foreign affairs, 51.2 percent answered "Taiwan," 33.0 percent responded "Republic of China" (Everington 2020, Web).

3   Somalis also live in northern Kenya, in the Ogaden region of eastern Ethiopia, and in Djibouti, to the northwest of Somalia.

The Republic of China in Taiwan is located in East Asia mainly on the island of Taiwan off the coast of the People's Republic of China and also controls the archipelagos of Pescadores (Penghu), Kinmen and Matsu. It covers a total area of 35.9 thousand km^2 and has a total coastline of 1.5 thousand km. Taiwan is thus one of the smallest countries in Asia by area and ranked 139th worldwide. With 655 inhabitants per km^2, it has a population of 23.8 million (National Statistics Republic of China (Taiwan): "Statistical Tables 2020", Web; World Data, "Taiwan", Web). The origins of Taiwan as an actor in international relations can be traced to after the Communist victory in the Chinese Civil War, with the People's Republic of China declared in 1949. The losing side, i.e., the government of the Republic of China, left the communist-controlled Chinese mainland for the island of Taiwan, which remained (along with several nearby smaller islands) the only ROC-controlled territory. At the same time, even after moving to Taiwan, the ROC considered itself the only legitimate representative of China. Understandably, the new communist government of the PRC in Beijing introduced attempts to establish its own diplomatic contacts, and began to inform foreign governments that it considered itself the sole legitimate representative of China. This was a clear message to foreign governments that they had to choose whether to maintain official diplomatic relations with the government of the People's Republic of China in Beijing or with the government of the Republic of China in Taiwan. Beijing's diplomatic practice signified that when establishing diplomatic relations with any country, the PRC insisted that it sever diplomatic relations with the Republic of China in Taiwan. Therefore, as a result of what is referred to as the "One China" policy, the Republic of China in Taiwan is not recognised by the vast majority of countries in the world. Currently, it has the recognition of only 12 countries and the Vatican. These are mainly economically underdeveloped countries, primarily in the Pacific, Central America, and the Caribbean Sea, as well as the African Eswatini, also known as Swaziland. Most of the African countries that previously recognised Taiwan withdrew their recognition in the 1990s and 2000s: Liberia (1993), Lesotho (1994), Niger (1996), the Central African Republic (1998), Guinea Bissau (1998), South Africa (1998), Gambia (2013), São Tomé and Príncipe (2016), Burkina Faso (2018) (Trojnar 2015, pp. 131, 166; Ndiaga / Yu: "Taiwan loses second ally...", Web).

Somaliland is a secessionist region of Somalia, located in the Horn of Africa, sharing boundaries with the Gulf of Aden in the north, Somalia in the east, the Federal Republic of Ethiopia in the south-west, and the Republic of Djibouti in the north-west. It has a total surface area of about 177 thousand km^2 and a coastline that is 850 km long. According to government statistics, in 2021, it had a population of 4.3 million people (Ministry of Planning and National

Development / Central Statistics Department Hargeisa Somaliland: "Somaliland in Figures", Web). As the term itself indicates, the population of Somaliland consists of the Somali people, who share a common language, culture, and most are Sunni Muslims. In spite of national boundaries, all Somalis consider themselves to be one people. The largest clan family in Somaliland is the Isaaq making up 80% of the population (Lewis 2009, pp. 3-13).

Although Somaliland has in fact been independent since 1991, it still lacks international recognition. Somaliland has sovereign control over its borders, issues its own currency, maintains a foreign service and is governed by a democratically elected government, but the international community still recognises it as an autonomous region within Somalia, and the authorities in Mogadishu reject Hargeisa's aspirations for independence. The UN and the African Union have also consistently stood by the principle of *uti possidetis*, or the protection of the existing postcolonial state borders in Africa. Significantly, Somalia, from which Somaliland is attempting to break away, is in turn incapable of performing state functions and for years has been considered a highly dysfunctional (failed) state, leading in the rankings of dysfunctionality (Fragile States Index: "Country Dashboard (2008-2023)", Web; Kłosowicz 2017b, pp. 120-123).

As Somalia descended deeper and deeper into violence, lawlessness, and became an example of a failed state, Somaliland not only avoided being dragged into a fratricidal war, but clan elders disarmed the guerrillas, elected a consensual government from among themselves, established courts, a police force, the country's own currency, and adopted a new constitution. In time, it even introduced a democracy modelled on Western democracy, a three-party political system, and, since 2005, has had democratic parliamentary and presidential elections. The last type of election, previously unpractised in the country, was introduced to please the West and gain its official recognition (Harper 2012, pp. 135-136).

However, all these efforts have not had the desired effect of bringing the country international recognition. Meanwhile, as the authorities in Hargeisa argue, Somaliland's independence merely restores the colonial boundaries of the former British protectorate, incidentally of the same name, which does not violate the principle of *uti possidetis*. Somaliland authorities cite precedents of countries in Africa that, after previously merging into larger state unions, eventually decided to return to earlier borders: Egypt and Syria were merged into the United Arab Republic (1958-1971); Senegal and Mali were united as the Federation of Mali (1959-1960); Senegal and Gambia were merged into the Sénégambia Confederation (1982-1989); Eritrea officially separated from Ethiopia in 1993. Thus, according to the authorities in Hargeisa, since Somaliland voluntarily opted for unification with Somalia, it should also be able to opt out of such a state union (Carroll / Rajagopal 1993, pp. 662; Government of Somaliland: "Official website", Web).

Achieving international recognition has therefore been a major goal of the Somaliland government for 32 years, and to this purpose the Hargeisa authorities have made a number of visits to virtually all the capitals of the world's most influential countries. The lack of international recognition also hinders its daily existence and further threatens its security (International Crisis Group: "Considering Political Engagement", Web; Samatar 2013, pp. 172-173). Until recently, the political situation in Somaliland was relatively calm compared to Somalia, but unfortunately it has deteriorated in recent months (Hassani: "At Least 20 People Killed...", Web).

International recognition is therefore a key issue for Somaliland's continued "to be or not to be", as it seems that this *de facto state* may struggle to survive, especially in such a highly volatile region as the Horn of Africa and in the neighbourhood of a collapsed state like Somalia. This was very aptly stated by Somaliland's president in the term between 2010 and 2017, Ahmed Mohammed Mahamoud Silanyo:

> We need foreign recognition because that is the only way we will become a fully-fledged member of the international community. We cannot attend conferences organized by the United Nations and other organizations. We cannot benefit from programmes of the World Bank and other international bodies. We miss out on a lot by not being recognized. We have been very patient about this and we hope are patience will be rewarded very soon. If we are granted international recognition during my presidency, we would put on the biggest celebration the world has ever seen. (Harper 2013, p. 131)

Since Somaliland does not have international recognition, it is also not a member of international organisations. Although Somaliland is not a party to the Chicago Convention, it has air links with Ethiopia, Kenya and Djibouti (Somaliland Civil Aviation and Airports Authority: "Official website", Web; Daallo Airlines: "Official website", Web). Although the international community recognizes Somaliland as part of Somalia, the government in Hargeisa maintains informal representations in some countries. However, these missions do not have diplomatic status under the provisions of the Vienna Convention on Diplomatic Relations (Wolters Kluwer website (OpenLEX): *Konwencja wiedeńska*, Web).

Somaliland currently has representation in six African countries – Ethiopia, Djibouti, Egypt, Kenya, South Africa, and Tanzania; in North America – in Canada and the US; in six European countries – France, the UK, Sweden, Belgium, the Netherlands and Norway; in three Asian countries – the United Arab

Emirates, Yemen and Turkey, as well as in Australia. In addition, Somaliland maintains diplomatic relations with another *de facto state* that also lacks international recognition, Taiwan, which opened its embassy in the Somaliland capital in August 2020. Somaliland opened a representative office in Taipei in September of the same year (The Diplomat: "Taiwan, Somaliland Ties Growing…", Web). Additionally, Ethiopia, Djibouti, Kenya, Turkey, the United Kingdom, Denmark, and Taiwan maintain their representations in Somaliland (Somaliland Official Website: "Official website", Web; Somaliland Official Website: *The Recognition of Somaliland*, Web; Embassy Pages: *Representative Office of Somaliland in London*, Web). Visas are issued by Somaliland's diplomatic missions in London or Addis Ababa (Somaliland Official Website: "Official website", Web). Since 2020, Taiwan's representative office in Hargeisa began issuing visas to people travelling to Taiwan with Somaliland passports, whereas previously travel was only possible with Somali passports (Somali Dispatch, "Taiwan issuing visas…", Web). Although they do not fully control their territory, the Somali authorities are very strongly opposed to opening diplomatic missions in Somaliland. When plans to open a Kenyan consulate in Somaliland were announced in December 2020, it led to a break in Mogadishu's diplomatic relations with Nairobi as Somalia accused Kenya of trying to infringe upon the sovereignty, territorial integrity, political independence, and unity of Somalia. Eventually, however, the consulate was opened in May 2022 (Economist Intelligence: "Kenya establishes consul-general's office…", Web).

Paradiplomacy as an instrument of Taiwan's foreign policy as an unrecognised state

One of the most interesting issues in international relations related to *de facto states* is Taiwan's developed ability to conduct diplomacy as a foreign policy tool in the absence of international recognition. In this regard, Taiwan is blazing a trail for countries that are in a similar situation, and it can be observed that Somaliland is also trying to follow in Taipei's footsteps in this regard.

When Taiwan entered the international political arena in 1949, most of its foreign activities were official in nature. In the following years, however, the number of countries that established diplomatic relations with the PRC gradually increased and they consequently severed diplomatic ties with the Taipei government, with the result that gradually more and more of Taiwan's foreign activities took on a non-diplomatic character. A fundamental tipping point came in 1971, when the PRC took Taiwan's place in the UN. Several countries that had until then still maintained diplomatic relations with Taipei reacted to this event by establishing diplomatic relations with Beijing and severing ties with Taipei. Taiwan's rapid and progressive marginalisation in the international arena led to a re-evaluation in the approach to conducting foreign policy in the previous formula and was helped by changes associated with the evolution in international relations in the second half of the 20th century when extraterritorial "transsovereign contacts" of federation's state units flourished, i.e., there was an external empowerment of federation's components (Duchacek 1988, pp. 7-8). This was linked to the neoliberal paradigm of international relations in force in the 1970s, according to which not only states, but also non-state actors are considered subjects of international politics (Łuszczuk 2013, pp. 124-125). A few years later, the term "paradiplomacy" appeared, which began to be used in political science terminology in the second half of the 1980s to describe the dynamically developing activities of sub-state (regional) administrations in the international political arena at that time. Ivo D. Duchacek's texts supplemented by the analyses of other researchers led to the formation of the original concept of paradiplomacy (Duchacek 1984; Soldatos 1990). Some scholars associate the concept with the foreign activities of regional "higher level" administrative units, such as provinces, federal republics, counties or federal states, while others believe that paradiplomacy only includes the activities of sub-state units in relation to analogous (sub-state) actors abroad. In other studies, the concept of paradiplomacy also includes the foreign activities of sub-state units conducted in relation to foreign states, i.e., in relation to central governments (Wolff 2007; Duchacek 1988). Thus, the term paradiplomacy can be generally defined as a set of foreign activities of a non-sovereign regional sub-state entity that are carried out to promote its interests *vis-à-vis* other analogous entities abroad, as well as *vis-à-vis* foreign states and international organizations. It seems that this concept refers also to the situation in which Taiwan found itself and was in fact developed and put into practice very effectively by this state (Pajtinka 2017, pp. 46-47).

Since the loss of international recognition, Taiwan's foreign policy can be divided into official diplomatic activity, which it conducts with countries with which it has established diplomatic relations, and unofficial quasi-diplomatic or paradiplomatic activity, which Taiwan conducts with countries with which it does not have diplomatic relations. The differences between the diplomatic and paradiplomatic dimensions of Taiwan's foreign activities lie mainly in their formal and protocol aspects, while from the standpoint of their organisation and practical functioning, the differences are minimal (Pajtinka 2017, pp. 46-47).

For most countries in the world that maintain diplomatic relations with the government of the People's Republic of China, Taiwan is formally recognised as a province or non-sovereign sub-state unit. In contrast, for those countries that do not maintain diplomatic relations with the government in Beijing, the Republic of China is a sovereign state. This special "dual" status of Taiwan is also reflected in the existence of two types of foreign activities conducted by the country, which differ in nature. These include, on the one hand, the standard official diplomatic activities that Taiwan conducts as a state with other countries with which it has established official diplomatic relations, and, on the other hand, the unofficial quasi- or paradiplomatic activities with countries with which it does not have official diplomatic relations. In most cases, countries that have established diplomatic relations with the PRC have, from the beginning, maintained only unofficial (extra-consular) contacts with Taiwan, with Taiwan formally acting not as a state, but as a regional and sub-state entity. In contrast, in countries with which Taiwan maintains official diplomatic relations, all the representative offices of Taiwan operate under the official name of the Embassy of the Republic of China (or Consulate General of the Republic of China), the name commonly used for such offices in the diplomatic practice of other countries. However, unlike the diplomatic missions of other countries, the provisions of the Vienna Convention on Diplomatic Relations do not apply to Taiwan's diplomatic missions and their personnel, as the Taiwanese are not a party to this international treaty. The official designation of Taiwan's informal overseas missions, both its representations and offices, varies depending on the specific host country (Pajtinka 2017, pp. 46-47). Currently, Taiwan's unofficial representative offices operate under various official names around the world; most commonly as the "Taipei Economic and Cultural Office" or "Taipei Representative Office". For example, in Warsaw, there is the Taipei Representative Office in Poland, but the website address functions as www.taiwanembassy.org (Taipei Representative Office in Poland: "Official website", Web).

All of Taiwan's unofficial foreign representative offices, regardless of their category, have a similar organisational structure, largely resembling that of diplomatic missions or consular offices. From an organisational point of view, all of Taiwan's unofficial representative offices are under the administration of the Ministry of Foreign Affairs in Taipei, just like its diplomatic missions and consular offices. From the point of view of the legal situation, Taiwan's unofficial foreign representative offices do not have the status of diplomatic missions or consular offices, which means that various privileges and immunities under the provisions of the Vienna Convention on Diplomatic Relations do not apply. In practice, however, Taiwan's unofficial representations are granted – in some cases – a certain degree of privileges and immunities based on the host country's domestic regulations or a special bilateral treaty. The staff of Taiwan's unofficial representations do not enjoy diplomatic or consular status and they also do not use diplomatic or consular ranks. Similarly, the naming of individual positions does not apply "traditional" diplomatic terms, such as "economic attaché" or "cultural attaché," but instead "head of the economic department" or "head of the cultural department". Nonetheless, the staff of Taiwan's unofficial delegations are mostly career diplomats, for whom working in such delegations is part of their professional diplomatic career in Taiwan's foreign service, and they are employees of Taiwan's Ministry of Foreign Affairs. Staff members of Taiwan's unofficial representative offices are generally not considered members of the diplomatic or consular corps in the host country. In addition, Taiwan's unofficial delegations are not allowed to use national flags and coats of arms on their buildings or vehicles, as is the case with other diplomatic missions. All negotiations between Taiwan's unofficial delegations and the foreign ministries of host countries are usually referred to as "informal".

Nonetheless, it can be concluded that Taiwan's diplomatic activities from the point of view of organisation, institutional background and formal and protocol regulations of its practical execution do not differ significantly from the diplomatic activities carried out by most other countries. For Taiwan, it is highly significant that the host country, even if through a veiled, unofficial form of Taipei's representation, recognises it as a partner in political dialogue, which in turn can be interpreted as a sign of recognition of the political legitimacy of Taiwan's authorities (Pajtinka 2017, pp. 46-47).

Taiwan as a model for "Politics of Survival" in international relations

As mentioned earlier, the change in US policy toward the People's Republic of China has significantly affected the international position of the Republic of China in Taiwan. On the international level, a landmark moment was the announcement in February 1972 by Washington and Beijing of what is referred to as the Shanghai Communiqué, an announcement of the normalisation of relations between the two countries. On the issue of Taiwan, significant declarations were made, with the most important consequence being the recognition of Taiwan as a province of China:

> The U.S. side declared: The United States acknowledges that all Chinese on either side of the Taiwan Strait maintain there is but one China and that Taiwan is a part of China. The United States Government does not challenge that position. It reaffirms its interest in a peaceful settlement of the Taiwan question by the Chinese themselves. With this prospect in mind, it affirms the ultimate objective of the withdrawal of all U.S. forces

and military installations from Taiwan. (Office of the Historian: "203. Joint Statement Following Discussions...", Web)

Taiwan lost not only its seat in the UN but also its membership in international organisations and the support of its existing allies. Gradually, more countries withdrew their support. The Taiwanese authorities faced the need to change their foreign policy, with the aim to maintain relations with existing partners through cooperation on political, economic, scientific, technological, and cultural levels. Bilateral contacts – official and unofficial, direct and indirect – were all acceptable.

The state's new foreign policy strategy excluded only relations with communist states. However, this strategy did not provide the expected results and Taiwan gradually lost the international recognition of successive countries (Trojnar 2015, pp. 85-86). On 1 January 1979, full normalisation of relations between Beijing and Washington was established, with the consequent withdrawal of US recognition of the Republic of China. Washington and Beijing, in a joint communiqué, announcing the establishment of diplomatic relations and US recognition of the government of the People's Republic of China as the sole legitimate government of China:

> The United States of America and the People's Republic of China have agreed to recognize each other and to establish diplomatic relations as of January 1, 1979. The United States of America recognizes the Government of the People's Republic of China as the sole legal Government of China. (Office of the Historian: "104. Joint Communique on the Establishment of Diplomatic Relations...", Web)

However, some countries, after withdrawing recognition on the diplomatic level, continued to maintain close relations with Taipei on other levels with an emphasis on the economic sphere, as exemplified by Japan's policy towards Taiwan. The arrangement under which Japan maintained unofficial relations with Taiwan became known as the "Japanese formula" and was adopted by other states (Chiu Hungdah 2007, p. 24).

This collision with a new political reality necessitated a reorientation of foreign policy so that Taiwan could effectively resist marginalisation on the international arena, which was strenuously pursued by Beijing through political action. Thus, the primary objective in Taipei's post-1979 foreign policy was survival and the search for alternative means of international presence, which in turn opened the way for unorthodox diplomacy. The success of this method can be measured by the number of countries that maintained political relations with Taiwan or decided to cooperate on new terms, despite continued pressure from Beijing. The policy of setting up non-governmental delegations to maintain economic, trade and cultural relations worked well, and increasing amounts of countries accepted this new form of cooperation (Wang Yu San 1990, p. 8; Trojnar 2015, p. 94). In the 1990s, it was Taipei's foreign policy to internationalise Taiwan by seeking admission to the UN and other international organisations. At the time, Taiwan was celebrating economic success, which provided it with advantages in maintaining contacts with allies and attracting economically underdeveloped countries. Taiwan's flexible diplomacy strategy also included overseas visits by Taiwanese senior government officials. President Lee Teng-hui himself travelled abroad at the invitation of local authorities, officially for leisure purposes, as a result of which his trips became known as "golf diplomacy". President Lee was in fact a supporter of Taiwan's independence from the People's Republic of China, which in 1996 tried to prevent his election by staging military exercises off the island (referred to as Third Taiwan Strait Crisis). In July 1999, he risked Beijing's wrath when he described Taiwan's relationship with China as a "special state-to-state relationship", seeking to loosen ties with China but not a formal declaration of independence, meanwhile explaining that Taiwan was already effectively independent. He believed that any negotiations with the People's Republic of China should be conducted as negotiations between two sovereign states. He also sought to break cultural links in favour of developing a distinct Taiwanese identity (Blanchard /Lee 2020, Web). The consequence of this change in their approach was a situation in 2007, resulting in a radical change in Taiwan's approach when it asked the UN to process its application for full membership. This new strategy did not leave any doubt that Taiwan (not under the name "Republic of China") wanted to have its sovereignty legitimised by becoming a new member of the United Nations. UN Secretary-General Ban Ki-moon refused to accept the application on the grounds that "in accordance with [General Assembly Resolution 2758], the United Nations considers Taiwan for all purposes to be an integral part of the People's Republic of China" (Winkler 2020, Web).

Since 2008, the Taiwanese authorities have consistently pursued viable diplomacy, appealing to the universal values of democracy, freedom and peace, a policy also supported by soft power diplomacy, i.e., Taiwan's active involvement in humanitarian aid and cultural exchanges. All these Taiwanese experiences are in a way a trail already blazed for other unrecognised states such as Somaliland (Trojnar 2015, p. 165).

When diplomatic relations were established between Somaliland and Taiwan, Somalia condemned Taiwan and Beijing expressed outrage at the Somaliland authorities' actions. Chinese officials even went to Hargeisa and insisted that relations with Taiwan be severed. Indeed, Beijing sees Taiwan's relations with Somaliland as a potential threat to their "Belt and Road Initiative", aimed at reactivating the "New Silk Road" as a tool for their expansion, according to which they plan to develop sea and land trade routes through Asia, the Middle East and Africa (BBC 2021, Web). However, one has to ask what made the authorities in Hargeisa decide to take the bold but risky step of throwing down the gauntlet to a power that treats any attempt to establish contacts with Taipei as an openly hostile act. Was it not better for Somaliland to maintain proper relations with the Chinese giant and believe that it would gain tangible benefits from doing so? During my conversations with Somaliland's foreign minister and the speaker of Somaliland's parliament in February 2011, disappointment clearly resonated at China's support for Djibouti, evidenced by their investing heavily in port expansion and marginalising its southern neighbour. Moreover, there was a perception in Hargeisa that Beijing-backed Djibouti was actually not interested in recognising Somaliland, as this could attract foreign investment in, e.g., the expansion of Somaliland's ports, and would therefore create serious competition for Djibouti (Kłosowicz 2011). That Djibouti does not support Somaliland's bid to be recognised as independent was also confirmed in an interview with Prof. Amina Saïd Chiré, a professor at the University of Djibouti in 2017 (Kłosowicz 2017a).

Over the past decades, through a series of investments aimed towards Somaliland's neighbour to the north, Djibouti, China has sought to gain a monopoly in control over this important sea route and a dominant influence on political and economic relations with the countries of the region, above all Sudan and Ethiopia. Meanwhile, if it took advantage of its favourable strategic location, especially with a port in Berbera, Somaliland could create real competition for the maritime section of the "New Silk Road" along Africa's east coast. Taiwan, on the other hand, sees Somaliland as a first step in realising its ambitions in the region by treating it as a gateway to East Africa.

Hargeisa-Taipei relations are also supported by the US, which for years has viewed with increasing concern the gradual growth of Beijing's economic and political influence in this strategic region of the world (Shaban 2020, Web). Meanwhile, Somaliland does not have an international patron state like Taiwan does in the form of the US. Some scholars consider Ethiopia to be Somaliland's quasi-patron state, understood as a state that resembles patrons in their approach to *de facto states*, however, without providing security guarantees (Kosienkowski / Ženková Rudincová 2022). However, it seems that in the current situation, Addis Ababa, at best, can aspire to be a strong state in the Horn of Africa region, and is currently weakened by internal conflict and ethnic divisions and does not really have enough power to play any other role, let alone compared to the strength and importance of the USA (Kłosowicz 2015).

The geostrategic implications of Somaliland's position as regards its cooperation with Taiwan

One of Somaliland's hopes for international recognition remains its geopolitical location. Its 850 km-long coastline lies entirely on the Gulf of Aden and thus runs opposite the coast of Yemen. The distance between Berbera, Somaliland's main port, and Aden in Yemen is only 140 nautical miles. This location makes Somaliland's ports the region's only alternative to Djibouti in the basin of the Red Sea and Horn of Africa (Makinda 1992, pp. 3-8).

Somaliland's attractiveness to Taipei is also enhanced by the growing interest of countries in the region in the qualities of the *de facto state*'s strategic location. Somaliland's ports are increasingly becoming a focus of international interest and competition. The region's largest state, Ethiopia, was cut off from the sea by the secession of Eritrea and consequently lost important ports on the Red Sea (Massawa and Assab). Using the congested ports of Djibouti, through which 80 per cent of its exports and imports (including 95 per cent of its maritime trade) pass, is becoming more expensive every year (Selan Tadesse Demissie 2021, Web). This development is prompting Ethiopia to seek alternative options, consequently bolstering its economic relations with Somaliland. Another nation expressing interest in Somaliland's ports is the United Arab Emirates. In March 2018, the international logistics company Dubai Ports World, in collaboration with the governments of Somaliland and Ethiopia, entered into an agreement to expand and jointly manage the port of Berbera. Currently, the port is undergoing significant expansion efforts, and a highway is being constructed between the port and the Ethiopian capital (DP World: "Ministry of Transport of Ethiopia and DP World Sign MoU…", Web).

Another regional power interested in Somaliland's ports is Egypt, which is seen by the Somaliland authorities as a partner that can play an important role in gaining international recognition, as it is a major country in both Africa and the Arab world, which, according to the authorities in Hargeisa, can help in seeking international recognition in both the African Union and the Arab League. A Somaliland delegation visited Egypt in March 2020 and an Egyptian delegation reciprocated by visiting Hargeisa in July of the same year. The intensification of diplomatic contacts between Somaliland and Egypt invoked protests both from the Somali government and Ethiopia, the latter viewing it as an attempt to po-litically play up the conflict between Addis Ababa and Cairo in the dispute over the construction of a hydroelectric power plant on the Blue Nile (Somaliland Chronicle 2020, Web; Kłosowicz / Mormul 2018, pp. 170-171).

The development of political cooperation between Somaliland and Taiwan

Somaliland does not just want to be dependent on the regional powers of Ethiopia, Egypt or the money and influence of the Arabian Peninsula states. It also seeks to strengthen its political position by establishing diplomatic relations with other states, including the Republic of China as a *de facto state* with similar international status and corresponding problems. Initial relations date back to 2009 when the first unofficial meetings took place between representatives of the authorities of the two *de facto states*. At the time, the areas of cooperation only included maritime security, education, and health matters. In late 2019, an official delegation from the Ministry of Foreign Affairs of Taiwan travelled to Somaliland to initiate talks on establishing bilateral relations. In January 2020, a Somaliland delegation led by the deputy foreign minister travelled to Taiwan. In July 2020, Taiwan's Foreign Minister Joseph Wu announced that Taiwan had established diplomatic relations with Somaliland based on friendship and shared commitment to the common values of freedom, democracy, justice, and the rule of law. It seems that the prominence of this theme is not accidental, as its starting point is the assumption that the establishment of common ideological ground is crucial for effective interaction and cooperation between states. Both unrecognised states endeavour to construct a geocultural narrative primarily for external consumption, targeting world public opinion, particularly in Western states, through the aforementioned principles of freedom, democracy, and the rule of law. This narrative is complemented by a discourse on economic success, presented in the form of investment, which in turn is aimed at shaping domestic public opinion (Bakonyi & Darwich, 2023).

As already mentioned, both China and Somalia have condemned the establishment of diplomatic contacts between Somaliland and Taiwan, while the US National Security Council has supported Taiwan's initiative in East Africa. This is a severe blow to Beijing, which in recent decades has used its international influence and development assistance to gather support among African states for its efforts to eliminate Taiwan's presence in international politics. China has been investing in Djibouti ports for years in an effort to monopolise transhipment and shipping in this strategic region. Taiwan's steps are perceived in Beijing not only as a thwarting of its interests but also as a blatant provocation by an unrecognised state that does not want reunification with China (Shaban 2020, Web).

While the Taiwan-Somaliland partnership is thus far limited in scope, it represents a significant opportunity for both sides. For Hargeisa, Taiwan is expected to help Somaliland consolidate its young democracy, help expand its infrastructure, upgrade its economy, and develop its untapped natural resources. For Taipei, Somaliland could be a key anchor for expanding diplomatic contacts in Africa and exerting economic influence in a region dominated by the PRC.

For decades, discussions about Taiwan's international space have mainly focused on Taipei's shrinking list of official diplomatic partners as the PRC gradually deprived it of its diplomatic partners, one by one. The Taiwanese government made every effort to prevent the departure of its diplomatic partners. During Chen Shui-bian's time in power, these efforts took the form of "cheque book diplomacy" in an extreme version, as Taiwan resorted to providing more funds to partner governments than Beijing would offer. As relations with Somaliland have shown, Taiwan has found a way to establish international cooperation without formal ties. Today, Taiwan maintains limited, unofficial ties with many countries around the world. In many cases, this amounts to representation, usually staffed by a small contingent of diplomats and cultural attachés. Despite these limitations, the offices may provide a foundation for more expansive, unofficial relationships in the future. Such Taiwanese representative offices in Africa operate, for example, in South Africa, Nigeria, Kenya, Egypt and Algeria (Overseas Community Affairs Council, ROC Taiwan: "Taiwan External Trade Development Council", Web). The partnership between Taiwan and Somaliland is an example of just such a flexible political approach executed by Taiwan, as exchanges of small representations have quickly developed into a more meaningful diplomatic, economic, and cultural relationship. As the Taiwan-Somaliland relationship has shown, even the most unlikely and unofficial partnerships can be mutually beneficial if properly supported, and Taipei has proven its ability to expand its international space through unofficial partnerships.

Taiwan's cooperation with Somaliland within the scope of economy and public services

In comparing the economies of Taiwan and Somaliland, a sizeable gulf is observable when it comes to disparities in each of the economic indicators considered. The comparison of GDP per capita alone shows huge differences in the level of both economic development and the standard of living of the population. In 2021, the GDP per capita in the Republic of China in Taiwan was more than US$33,000, while in Somaliland it was US$775 in the same period, a ratio of 1:42 in favour of Taiwan (International Monetary Fund: "GDP per capita…", Web). Data on Somaliland's economic activity is scarce and difficult to come by. Somaliland's economy is driven by the private sector. The two most important sources of income and foreign exchange are remittances and livestock exports, with the port of Berbera being a key centre for the exports to Saudi Arabia, Yemen, and Oman. The most important components of the Somaliland economy's GDP are livestock – 30%, trade – 24%, and remittances from the Somaliland diaspora – 22%. Livestock is the main export commodity – 59% of revenues. Food insecurity and poverty remain widespread in many regions, affecting 30% of the population living in rural regions and 25% in urban areas. In addition, the country is plagued by low levels of investment and a low employment-to-population ratio amounting to 28% for men and 17% for women. Additionally, Somaliland's economy has been hit hard in recent years due to the COVID-19 pandemic, drought, and a locust infestation that devasted the region (Bashir 2021; Ministry of Planning and National Development of Somaliland / Central Statistics Department Hargeisa Somaliland: "Somaliland in Figures", Web).

As mentioned, Somaliland is largely dependent on access to the sea and its strategic location on the Gulf of Aden, with the main port of Berbera at the forefront. Thus, serving landlocked Ethiopia may have an impact on Somaliland's growing political and economic importance in the near future, and thus its chances of international recognition may also increase (Somaliland Times: "Ethiopia Bound Cargo Arrives…", Web). The jewel of the coast, the port of Berbera, originally built by the British, then modernised first by the Soviet Union and later by the United States, is Somaliland's window to the world, used to import most of the products the country needs. The expansion of the Berbera port is expected to multiply its capacity and elevate the surrounding logistics facilities to create a regional trading hub. It is predicted this will provide an economic boost for Somaliland and other countries in the Horn of Africa region, most notably Ethiopia. In Somaliland, the port of Berbera is expected to be one of the most important pillars of the economy and by 2035, trade revenues should account for 27% of GDP and 75% of Somaliland's total trade, which will indirectly translate into more than 50,000 jobs. Various sectors of the economy are expected to benefit from the expansion of the port and, in addition, trade through the port will increase the availability of goods for more than a quarter of Somaliland's population. The expansion of the port is expected to benefit various sectors of the economy and, in addition, trade through the port will increase the availability of goods for more than a quarter of Somaliland's population (British International Investment: "Port of Berbera…", Web).

In cooperation with Taiwan, Somaliland offers investment opportunities by highlighting its potential to become an important location in East Africa for Taiwan's African project. In the mining sector, Somaliland has great potential for foreign investment, including in the extraction of oil, natural gas, as well as coal (DW: "Somaliland, Taiwan expand ties…", Web). This cooperation is indeed gaining momentum, as shortly after the signing of the 2022 Energy and Minerals Cooperation Agreement, the first meeting of the Taiwan-Somaliland Joint Working Group on Cooperation in the aforementioned field was held in Hargeisa in March 2023. The event, co-chaired by Eugene YJ Chen, Director General of the Department of International Cooperation under the Ministry of Economic Affairs, and Fowsi Mohamed Farah, Director General at the Ministry of Energy and Minerals of Somaliland, discussed exploration in search of oil, gas and other mineral resources, as well as their possible extraction. They also discussed Taiwan's experience in oil exploration and production in Africa (Taiwan Today: "Taiwan, Somaliland hold first joint energy, mineral meeting", Web).

Taiwan's participation is also evident in assisting in the social sphere especially health care and education. Under the International Cooperation and Development Fund's (TaiwanICDF) Health Care Personnel Training Programme, Taiwan provides training to Somaliland health care workers and also educates Somaliland students in universities in Taiwan under the Taiwan Scholarship Programme. Taiwan, drawing on its rich experience in information and communication technology (ICT) development, is also offering assistance through its support of the Somaliland Innovation Zone as an ICT training centre. The zone will serve as an ICT training centre for interested public officials and citizens. Through ICT education, Taiwan can help bridge the digital divide between Somaliland and the world (Taipei Trade Office in the Federal Republic of Nigeria: "Somaliland Innovation Zone...", Web). In addition to government operations in Somaliland, there are also Taiwanese NGOs operating there, such as Root Medical Peace Corps, which has sent missions to Somaliland to operate free clinics in 10 regions (Horn Diplomat: "Taiwan, Somaliland vow to boost cooperation...", Web).

The Gulf of Aden and the region as a whole are rich in resources, including fish and seafood, which can benefit Somaliland's development and prosperity. The development of fisheries in the maritime sector and the sustainable exploitation of sea resources is therefore a key issue for the country in terms of food security, providing an alternative source to counter the country's ongoing food crisis caused by severe drought. Meanwhile, Somalia, from which Somaliland seceded, has Africa's longest coastline and has been mired in instability for the past decades, consequently facing numerous challenges related to insecurity, armed insurgencies, and difficulties in implementing the rule of law both on land and at sea. A particular challenge for the international community in recent years has been the fight against maritime piracy off its coasts. Therefore, the international community has been strongly committed to supporting the strengthening of Somali institutions in order to build a stable and secure society.

In the maritime sector, Somaliland's institutions need support to achieve compliance with international standards and a reputation as a reliable partner in search and rescue (SAR), as well as in dealing with environmental incidents. Maritime security is very important to Somaliland as it has a real impact on economic development, regional security, and the stability of the entire region. Therefore, missions to strengthen the Somaliland Coast Guard are important, including through providing training activities and equipment so that it can enforce the rule of law and maritime sovereignty, maintain order at sea and combat piracy, smuggling and illegal fishing. The training programme provides Coast Guard officers with a wide range of knowledge and tools to perform their duties effectively, including rescue service. It also supports the operationalisation of the country's emergency and maritime disaster response centre. Environmental protection is also a very important issue, as oil spills from passing vessels are extremely dangerous and have a devastating impact on the environment, human health, and the economy (Nicoloso 2016, Web).

Taiwan has been heavily involved in supporting maritime security cooperation. Among other things, the government in Taipei has contracted US maritime security solutions provider Oceans Beyond Piracy (OBP) to assist the European Union in setting up Somalia's first coastal surveillance radar network to help secure the Indian Ocean waters off the war-ravaged country in the Horn of Africa. Under a memorandum signed between the EU, OBP and Taiwan's representative to the EU, Taiwan has set aside US$166,000 for the establishment of the Somali Maritime Communications Initiative (MCI) to monitor vessel movements and coordinate the security operations of local coast guards and international navies involved in anti-piracy operations on the Indian Ocean coast near Somalia. The surveillance system operates from five Somali maritime communications and security centres, which have been established in the coastal towns of Berbera, Bosaso, Hobyo, Kismayo and the capital Mogadishu. The joint maritime security initiative helps to ensure the security of local shipping lanes and promote better port management practices in Somalia. The centres work with international maritime forces and local authorities to enhance the safety of seafarers operating in the region (Nkala 2015, Web).

Conclusions

Taiwan offers Somaliland assistance in agriculture, technology, education, healthcare, energy, infrastructure, and maritime security. Somaliland, in turn, has to offer its strategic location, a long coastline with an important port in Berbera, rich fishing grounds, natural deposits and tourism potential. According to the

Hargeisa authorities, the new partnership with Taiwan and related investments will strengthen Somaliland's political and economic position in international relations both regionally and globally. The Hargeisa authorities also wish to learn from the experience of Taiwan's "informal" diplomacy, which has worked well in recent years. In addition, for the Hargeisa government, the United States as Taiwan's political patron in the international arena through supporting Taiwan-Somaliland relations, can be a big boost to Somaliland's position. Taipei, for its part, hopes that by establishing close relations with Somaliland located in a very strategic region of Africa, it will be able to regain at least some of the influence lost over the past three decades to the People's Republic of China, which has effectively pushed Taipei out of Africa, and to establish a presence in this strategic region. Taiwan sees Somaliland as the first step in its ambitions in the region. As the Taiwanese representative in Somaliland, Allen Chenhwa Lou, recently stated, "Somaliland is Taiwan's gateway to East Africa. From here I represent Taiwan in 10 East African countries, including Kenya and Ethiopia" (BBC 2021, Web).

Following the example of Taiwan, increasing amounts of countries have opened offices in the Somaliland capital in recent years, including Turkey, Ethiopia, Djibouti, the European Union, and the United Kingdom. In addition, more recently, like Taiwan, other unrecognised countries have also become interested in establishing relations with the government in Hargeisa. However, it should be noted that not everyone in Somaliland supports such a government policy, wondering whether antagonising a superpower like China is too high a price to pay for relations with Taiwan, which – after all – is also an unrecognised state and treated by Beijing as an integral part of China. Some are even convinced that this is a huge mistake on the part of the Hargeisa government which Beijing will never forget (BBC 2021, Web). The words of Somaliland's foreign minister Essa Kayda Mohamoud in December 2021 are telling: "The philosophy of the relationship between Taiwan and Somaliland is we're in the same boat" (Kine 2021, Web).

Meanwhile, the relationship could be a problem not only for Somaliland. When Taipei established diplomatic relations with Hargeisa, the political situation in Somaliland seemed stable. Taiwan even referred to the relationship as "diplomatic recognition in waiting", while President Tsai Ing-wen called Taiwan and Somaliland "like-minded partners who share the values of democracy and freedom." (Feingold 2023). However, recent events in Somaliland do not look promising in terms of "common" values as the country's president, Muse Bihi Abdi, delayed the presidential elections that were to occur in 2022, freedom of the press is under threat, and hundreds have died in what has become practically a civil war. UN Refugee Agency called for humanitarian aid to assist the over 100,000 refugees that fled the fighting[4].

It should thus be asked to what extent the cooperation between Somaliland and Taiwan will succeed in arousing the interest of the international community in Somaliland's problems and whether it will bring the aim of statehood recognition closer. How much will this cooperation contribute to economic development? And to what extent is it possible to dream of Somaliland becoming the Taiwan of the Horn of Africa and, by replicating its model of development, succeeding in the same way?

References

Al Jazeera: "Somalia cuts diplomatic ties with Kenya citing interference", Al Jazeera 15.12.2020, retrieved 7.7.2023, from https://www.aljazeera.com/news/2020/12/15/somalia-cuts-diplomatic-ties-with-kenya-citing-interferences.

Author's Interviews with Somaliland Minister of Foreign Affairs, Mohammad Abdullahi Omar, and Chair of the Parliament of Somaliland, Abdirahman Mohamed Abdullahi, Hargeisa 27.2.2011.

Author's Interview with Amina Saïd Chiré, professor at the University of Djibouti, Djibouti, 19.3.2017a.

Bakonyi, Jutta / Darwich, May: *Imaginaries of Modernity in the Horn of Africa: Ports and Infrastructural Lifeworks.* (paper presented at the *European Conference on African Studies* in Cologne, 31.05.2023).

Bashir, Mohamed: *Somaliland Budget Analysis 2021*, 14.1.2021, retrieved 5.12.2022, from https://www.horndiplomat.com/2021/01/14/somaliland-budget-analysis-2021/.

BBC: "Somaliland and Taiwan: Two territories with few friends but each other", *BBC* 13.4.2021, retrieved 15.3.2023, from https://www.bbc.com/news/world-africa-56719409.

Bereketaeb, Redie (ed.): *The Horn of Africa. Intra-State and Inter-State Conflicts and Security.* Pluto Press: London 2013.

Blanchard, Ben / Lee, Yimou: "Taiwan's 'Mr Democracy' Lee Teng-hui championed island, defied China", *Reuters* 30.6.2020, retrieved 5.7.2023, from https://www.reuters.com/article/uk-taiwan-lee-obituary-idUKKCN24V29C.

---

4 See more in Chapter 9.

British International Investment: "Port of Berbera. Charting a stronger course for African trade with the rest of the world", *British International Investment*, retrieved 16.11.2022, from https://www.bii.co.uk/en/story/port-of-berbera/.

Carroll, Anthony J. / Rajagopal, B.: "The Case for the Independent Statehood of Somaliland", *American University International Law Review* 8.2/3, 1993, Art. 26, pp. 653-681.

Chiu Hungdah: "*The International Law of Recognition and the Status of the Republic of China*". In: Mosher, Steven W. (ed.): *The United States and the Republic of China: Democratic Friends, Strategic Allies and Economic Partners.* Transaction Publishers: New Brunswick and London 2007, pp. 13-30.

Daallo Airlines: *Official Website*, retrieved 10.12.2022, from http://www.daallo.biz/.

DP World: "Ministry of Transport of Ethiopia and DP World sign MoU for the development of the Ethiopian side of the Berbera Corridors", *DP World* 6.5.2021, retrieved 27.12.2022, from https://www.dpworld.com/news/releases/ministry-of-transport-of-ethiopia-and-dp-world-sign-mou-for-the-development-of-the-ethiopian-side-of-the-berbera-corridor/.

Duchacek, Ivo D.: "Multicommunal and Bicommunal Politics and their International Relations". In: Duchacek, Ivo D. / Latouche, Daniel / Stevenson, Garth (eds): *Perforated Sovereignties and International Relations: Trans-Sovereign Contacts of Subnational Governments.* Greenwood Press: New York, 1988, pp. 3-28.

Duchacek, Ivo D.: "The International Dimension of Subnational Self-Government", *Publius. The Journal of Federalism*, 14 (4) 1984, pp. 5-31.

DW: "Somaliland, Taiwan expand ties amid isolation", *DW* 2.9.2022, retrieved 20.5.2023, from https://www.dw.com/en/somaliland-taiwan-hail-special-relationship-amid-isolation/a-60708402.

Economist Intelligence: "Kenya establishes consul-general's office in Somaliland", *Economist Intelligence* 6.5.2022, retrieved 7.7.2023, from https://country.eiu.com/article.aspx?articleid=1242081307.

Embassy Pages: *Representative Office of Somaliland in London, United Kingdom*, retrieved 9.7.2023, from https://www.embassypages.com/somaliland-representativeoffice-london-unitedkingdom.

Everington, Keoni: "Only 2% of Taiwanese consider themselves 'Chinese'", *Taiwan News* 24.9.2020, retrieved 6.7.2023, from https://www.taiwannews.com.tw/en/news/4016119.

Feingold, Ross: "The Trouble with Taiwan's Diplomatic Allies: All too often, Taiwan looks the other way as its formal partners commit human rights abuses", *The Diplomat* 12.5.2023, retrieved 5.7.2023, from https://thediplomat.com/2023/05/the-trouble-with-taiwans-diplomatic-allies/.

Fragile States Index: "Country Dashboard (2008-2023)", retrieved 6.6.2023, from https://fragilestatesindex.org/country-data/.

Gerding, Jonas: "At Port of Berbera, Dubai invests in Horn of Africa shipping", *Deutsche Welle* 26.12.2022, retrieved 28.12.2022, from https://www.dw.com/en/at-port-of-berbera-dubai-invests-in-horn-of-africa-shipping/a-64198524.

Government of Somaliland: "Official website", retrieved 28.12.2022, from https://www.govsomaliland.org/.

Harper, Mary: *Getting Somalia Wrong? Faith, War and Hope in a Shattered State.* African Agruments: London, New York 2012.

Hassani, Abdiqani: "At least 20 people killed in clashes in Somaliland", *Reuters* 2.1.2023, retrieved 9.7.2023, from https://www.reuters.com/world/africa/least-20-people-killed-clashes-somaliland-2023-01-01/.

Horn Diplomat: "Taiwan, Somaliland vow to boost cooperation in maritime security, healthcare and education", *Horn Diplomat* 1.7.2020, retrieved 28.5.2023, from https://www.horndiplomat.com/2020/07/01/taiwansomaliland-vow-to-boost-cooperation-in-maritime-securityhealthcare-and-education/.

International Crisis Group: "Considering Political Engagement with Al-Shabaab in Somalia" (Report 309, Africa), 21.06.2022, retrieved 17.12.2022, from https://www.crisisgroup.org/africa/horn-africa/somalia/309-considering-political-engagement-al-shabaab-somalia.

International Monetary Fund: "GDP per capita, current prices, List 2021", retrieved 9.7.2023, from https://www.imf.org/external/datamapper/NGDPDPC@WEO/ADVEC/WEOWORLD/CHN/TWN.

Kine, Phelim: "On the Horn of Africa, a tiny 'country' has Congress' ear", *Politico* 21.12.2021, retrieved 6.6.2023, from https://www.politico.com/news/2021/12/21/somaliland-china-taiwan-congress-525842.

Kłosowicz, Robert: *Konteksty dysfunkcyjności państw Afryki Subsaharyjskiej.* (Studia nad rozwojem) Wydawnictwo Uniwersytetu Jagiellońskiego: Kraków, 2017b.

Kłosowicz, Robert: "The Role of Ethiopia in the Regional Security Complex of the Horn of Africa", *Ethiopian Journal of Social Sciences and Language Studies*, Jimma University, 2 (2) 2015, pp. 83-97.

Kłosowicz, Robert / Mormul, Joanna: *Erytrea i jej wpływ na sytuację polityczną w Rogu Afryki.* Wydawnictwo Uniwersytetu Jagiellońskiego: Kraków, 2018.

Kosienkowski, Marcin / Ženková Rudincová, Kateřina: "Client De Facto States and Quasi-Patrons: Insights from the Relationship Between Somaliland and Ethiopia", *Ethnopolitics* (20) 2022, pp. 1-21, DOI: 10.1080/17449057.2022.2121470.

Lewis, Ioan: *Understanding Somalia and Somaliland, Culture, History, Society*. Hurst and co.: London, 2009.

Łuszczuk, Michał: "Zastosowanie pojęcia 'paradyplomacja' w świetle ewolucji badan dyplomacji niesuwerennej". In: Surmacz, Beata (ed.): *Nowe oblicza dyplomacji*. Wydawnictwo UMCS: Lublin, 2013, pp. 124-125.

Makinda, Samuel. M.: *Security in the Horn of Africa*. (Adelphi Papers, 32 [269]). Brassey's for the International Institute for Strategic Studies: London, 1992.

Mengisteab, Kidane: *The Horn of Africa*. Polity Press: Cambridge, England, 2014.

Ministry of Planning and National Development / Central Statistics Department Hargeisa Somaliland: "Somaliland in Figures" November 2022, retrieved 6.7.2023, from https://slmof.org/wp-content/uploads/2023/05/SOMALIL AND-IN-FIGURES-2021.pdf.

National Statistics Republic of China (Taiwan): "Statistical Tables 2020", retrieved 6.7.2023, from https://eng.stat.gov.tw/News_Content.aspx?n=2401&s=231349.

Ndiaga, Thiam / Yu, Jess Macy: "Taiwan loses second ally in a month as Burkina Faso cuts ties", *Reuters* 24.5.2018, retrieved 20.4.2023, from https://www.reut ers.com/article/ozatp-uk-burkina-taiwan-idAFKCN1IP1V4-OZATP.

Nicoloso, Giulia: "EU and UN carry out maritime training with Somaliland Coast Guard", *Critical Maritime Routes Programme* 8.12.2016, retrieved 12.11.2022, from https://criticalmaritimeroutes.eu/2016/12/08/eu-un-carry-maritime-training-somaliland-coast-guard/.

Nkala, O.: "Taiwan to Fund Somali Coastal Radar", *Defence News* 17.9.2015, retrieved 29.04.2022, from https://www.defensenews.com/naval/2015/09/16/taiwan-to-fund-somali-coastal-radar/.

Office of the Historian: "203. Joint Statement Following Discussions with Leaders of the People's Republic of China, Shanghai, February 27, 1972", *Foreign Relations of the United States, 1969–1976*, 17 (China, 1969–1972), Doc. 203, p. 815, retrieved 5.7.2023, from https://history.state.gov/historicaldocuments/frus1969-76v17/d203.

Office of the Historian: "104. Joint Communique on the Establishment of Diplomatic Relations Between the United States of America and the People's Republic of China, January 1, 1979", *Foreign Relations of the United States, 1977–1980*, 1 (Foundations of Foreign Policy), Doc. 104, p. 505, retrieved 5.7.2023, from https://history.state.gov/historicaldocuments/frus1977-80v01/d104.

Overseas Community Affairs Council, ROC Taiwan: "Taiwan External Trade Development Council", retrieved 8.6.2023, from https://www.ocac.gov.tw/OCAC/Eng/Pages/Detail.aspx?nodeid=5903&pid=27139132.

Pajtinka, Erik: "Between Diplomacy and Paradiplomacy: Taiwan's Foreign Relations in Current Practice", *Journal of Nationalism, Memory & Language Politics*, 11(1), 2017, pp. 39-57, retrieved 6.7.2023, from DOI: https://doi.org/10.1515/jnmlp-2017-0003.

Samatar A. I.: "The Production of Somali Conflict and the Role of Internal and External Actors". In: Bereketeab, Redie (ed.): *The Horn of Africa. Intra-State and Inter-State Conflicts and Security*. Pluto Press: London, 2013.

Selam Tadesse Demissie: "Djibouti looks to Ethiopia to gauge its economic future", *Institute for Security Studies*, published 3.5.2021, retrieved 21.12.2022, from https://issafrica.org/iss-today/djibouti-looks-to-ethiopia-to-gauge-its-economic-future.

Shaban, Abdur Rahman Alfa: "U.S. 'backs' Taiwan – Somaliland cooperation", *africanews* 10.7.2020, retrieved 12.03.2020, from https://www.africanews.com/2020/07/10/us-backs-taiwan-somaliland-cooperation/.

Soldatos, Panayotis: "An Explanatory Framework for the Study of Federated States as Foreign-Policy Actors". In: Michelmann, Hans J. / Soldatos, Panayotis: *Federalism and International Relations. The Role of Subnational Units*. Clarendon Press & Oxford University Press: Oxford, England – New York, 1990, pp. 35–53.

Somali Dispatch: "Taiwan issuing visas to citizens with Somaliland passport", *Somali Dispatch* 25.8.2020, retrieved 29.5.2023, from https://www.somalidispatch.com/latest-news/taiwan-issuing-visas-to-citizens-with-somaliland-passport/.

Somaliland Central Statistics Department: "Official website", retrieved 30.12.2022, from https://somalilandcsd.org/.

Somaliland Chronicle: "Egyptian Government Delegation Visits Somaliland", *Somaliland Chronicle* 14.7.2020, retrieved 22.12.2022, from https://somalilandchronicle.com/2020/07/14/breaking-egyptian-government-delegation-visits-somaliland/.

Somaliland Civil Aviation and Airports Authority: "Official website", retrieved 22.11.2022, from https://caaa.govsomaliland.org/.

Somaliland Official Website: "Official website", retrieved 30.12.2022, from http://www.somalilandgov.com.

Somaliland Official Website: *The recognition of Somaliland. The legal case.* Retrieved 20.11.2022, from https://recognition.somalilandgov.com/wp-content/uploads/2013/01/The-recognition-of-Somaliland-The-legal-case.pdf.

Somaliland Times: "Ethiopia Bound Cargo Arrives at Berbera Port", *Somaliland Times*, retrieved 11.12.2022, from http://www.somalilandtimes.net/199/16.shtml.

Taipei Representative Office in Poland: "Official website", retrieved 8.7.2023, from https://www.taiwanembassy.org/pl_pl/index.html.

Taipei Trade Office in the Federal Republic of Nigeria: "Somaliland Innovation Zone will serve as a hub of ICT training for public officers and citizens who are interested in ICT learning" 15.10.2021, retrieved 8.6.2023, from https://www.roc-taiwan.org/ng_en/post/4587.html.

Taiwan Today: "Taiwan, Somaliland hold first joint energy, mineral meeting", *Taiwan Today* 16.3.2023, retrieved, from https://taiwantoday.tw/news.php?unit=6&post=234116.

The Diplomat: "Taiwan, Somaliland Ties Growing Despite Diplomatic Isolation", *The Diplomat*, 10.02.2022, retrieved 22.11.2022, from https://thediplomat.com/2022/02/taiwan-somaliland-ties-growing-despite-diplomatic-isolation/.

Trojnar, Ewa: *Tajwan. Dylematy rozwoju*. Księgarnia Akademicka: Kraków, 2015.

Wang Yu San: "Foundation of the Republic of China's Foreign Policy". In: Wang Yu San (ed.): *Foreign Policy of the Republic of China on Taiwan 1988-2000. An Unorthodox Approach*. Bloomsbury Academic: New York, 1990, pp. 1-12.

Winkler, Sigrid: "Taiwan's UN Dilemma: To be or not to be", *Brookings* 20.6.2020, retrieved 9.7.2023, from https://www.brookings.edu/articles/taiwans-un-dilemma-to-be-or-not-to-be/.

Wolff, Stefan: "Paradiplomacy: Scope, Opportunities and Challenges", *Bologna Center Journal of International Affairs*, 10 (Spring) 2007, pp. 141-150.

Wolters Kluwer website (OpenLEX): *Konwencja wiedeńska o stosunkach dyplomatycznych*, Vienna 18.4.1961, Dz.U.1965.37.232, version from 19.4.1965, retrieved 19.12.2022, from https://sip.lex.pl/akty-prawne/dzu-dziennik-ustaw/konwencja-wiedenska-o-stosunkach-dyplomatycznych-wieden-1961-04-18-16786459.

Woodward, Peter: *Crisis in the Horn of Africa. Politics, Piracy and the Threat of Terror*. Bloomsbury Academic: New York, 2013

World Data: "Taiwan", retrieved 6.7.2023, from https://www.worlddata.info/asia/taiwan/index.php.

Robert Kłosowicz, Edyta Chwiej

Chapter 11. *Proto-state* as a Consequence of Unfinished Decolonisation. The Case of Azawad and West Papua[1]

The chapter examines two geopolitical entities commonly referred to in the literature as proto-states: West Papua, which is part of Indonesia, and Azawad, situated within the territory of the Republic of Mali. Additionally, the case of Western Sahara is mentioned within a comparative context. The chapter aims to elucidate the aspirations of the inhabitants of these regions for independence, delineate the historical (both colonial and post-colonial) factors that have shaped their development, and expound upon the political and international implications associated with the failure to address their quest for independence. Furthermore, it examines the resulting consequences, both in terms of political dynamics and operational security, for these proto-states and their respective regions in Southeast Asia and Africa. The chapter employs comparative, genetic, and historical methods, alongside critical analysis of relevant literature, documents, reports, and statistical data.

Keywords: proto-state, Azawad, Western Sahara, Mali, West Papua, Indonesia

The chapter analyses two cases of *proto-state* territories to which the criteria of decolonisation, based on the principle of self-determination, were not applied – Azawad in Africa and West Papua in Southeast Asia. Additionally, the third case of Western Sahara is taken into consideration; however, due to the detailed discussion in previous chapters of this monograph, it is only mentioned in a comparative context with West Papua and Azawad. The territory of West Papua, comprising the provinces of Papua and West Papua, is now formally a part of Indonesia. In turn, Azawad occupies two-thirds of Mali, spanning over the southern portion of the Sahara Desert and the Sahel. Azawad was a short-lived, unrecognised state from 2012 to 2013. Western Sahara has been on the United Nations list of non-self-governing territories since 1963, following Spain's submission of information on Spanish Sahara under Article 73e of the Charter of the United Nations (United Nations, "Western Sahara" 2023).

---

1   This chapter is the result of the research project financed by the National Science Centre (Narodowe Centrum Nauki), Poland, Grant ID: 2017/25/B/HS5/00958.

There are many similarities between the situation in the Western Sahara and West Papua. Both territories were colonies and – due to the occupation of these territories by a larger neighbour – independence aspirations of their inhabitants were not taken into account in the decolonisation process. Western Sahara, as Spanish Sahara, was left at the mercy of its neighbours Morocco and Mauritania under the Madrid Accords ("Declaration of Principles on Western Sahara (Madrid Accords)" 1975). Then, it was occupied by Mauritania and Morocco – and since 1979, 80% of its territory has been occupied by Morocco. A similar situation occurred in West Papua during the colonial era of Dutch New Guinea, when in August 1962, under pressure from the United Nations (UN), the Netherlands accepted Indonesian terms and a ceasefire was signed. Two months later, both countries placed the disputed region under the temporary management of the United Nations Temporary Executive Authority (UNTEA). As previously agreed, the people of Western Sahara and Western Guinea were to decide for themselves the territory's future in a referendum held under the auspices of the UN. In both cases, the stronger neighbour occupied the territory and did not allow the local population a voice in self-determination. Unlike Morocco, Indonesia allowed the referendum to take place – but it was conducted improperly by the Indonesian government, and the result is considered invalid by the people of West Papua. Compounding this was the Cold War political context because both Morocco and Indonesia were in the political camp of the US and Western countries in the Cold War rivalry. Meanwhile, the standing practice of the United Nations General Assembly concerning Resolution 1514 (XV) and the right to self-determination "gives evidence of a new rule of international law whereby title to a colonial territory cannot be validly opposed to the claims of self-determination by the people of that territory" (Janki 2010). The rule of law, as elaborated by the court in the Western Sahara case, is that once the right to self-determination exists, the state claiming the territory must allow the people of the territory to make a free and genuine choice: "It seems hardly necessary to make more explicit the cardinal restraint which the legal right of self-determination imposes. That restraint can be summed up in a single sentence: It is for the people to determine the territory's destiny and the destiny of the people" ("Separate opinion of Judge H. C. Dillard, Western Sahara Advisory Opinion" 1975, p. 114).

The case of Azawad in the Republic of Mali is also the aftermath of the population's unacknowledged aspirations for self-determination. Not only did decolonisation disregard the rights of the inhabitants to their historic territory, but – in addition – the creation of independent African states (while maintaining artificial colonial borders) disrupted their previous way of life and economy. The community living in this territory was divided into several countries (Niger,

Mali, Algeria, Burkina Faso, Libya, Mauritania) (Maddy-Weitzman 2022, p. 89) and found themselves there as an ethnic minority, which was associated with social, political, and economic marginalisation. Both Azawad and West Papua can be classified as *proto-states* (i.e., a particular type of political entity) that is administratively organised, has a certain degree of autonomy and is usually built around a local ethnic group. *Proto-state* created by social and political movements rooted in a specific territory often strive for secession but have neither internal legitimacy nor international recognition (Griffiths 2016, p. 219).

West Papua

The problem of West Papua is not widely known to the public and there is still little information about what is actually happening in this region that is closed to human rights organisations and foreign journalists. Meanwhile, the human rights situation in the area is so severe that it deserves more attention not only from the international community, but also from international relations scholars. The issue of West Papua recently came to prominence after the armed group called the West Papua Liberation Army (*Tentara Pembebasan Nasional Papua Barat*, TPNPB), which is an armed wing of the Free Papua Movement (*Organisasi Papua Merdeka*, OPM), abducted Phillip Merthens – a New Zealand-born pilot – on 7 February 2023 in Nduga, Indonesia. As reported by local media, the TPNPB, led by local commander Egianus Kogoya, attacked a small Susi aeroplane after it landed and took the pilot hostage in a desperate attempt to draw world attention to the problem of the region's people (Wangge 2023).

The island of New Guinea is largely inhabited by Papuans, a diverse indigenous population speaking hundreds of languages and a history of settlement dating back tens of thousands of years. Papua New Guinea, the eastern part of New Guinea, has been an independent country since 1975. The western part of New Guinea is a territory under Indonesian occupation. Supporters of independence and most Papuans call the territory "West Papua"; however, in the 20th century, a series of colonial names were imposed on it – firstly, under Dutch rule (Dutch New Guinea or Netherlands New Guinea) and then under Indonesian occupation (*West Irian, Irian Barat*). West Papua covers an area of over 415,000 km^2, inhabited by approximately 5.43 million people ("The Indonesian Population Census" 2020). The indigenous inhabitants of this part of Indonesia are the Melanesians, divided into approximately 260 local ethnic groups (Ananta et al. 2016, p. 458). As previously mentioned, West Papua was a Dutch colony in the past; but, in 1962, under pressure from the United Nations, it was transferred to the temporary administration of Indonesia ("Indonesia and Netherlands

Agreement" 1962). In 1969, following UN recommendations, a referendum (im-properly conducted and not recognised by the local population) was held on the future status of the territory ('Act of Free Choice'), in which 1025 indigenous "representatives" (designated by the authorities in Jakarta) decided to annex West Papua to Indonesia (May 2021, p. 1). Papuans consider themselves ethni-cally, linguistically, and culturally distinct from the rest of the Indonesian archi-pelago and largely reject Indonesian rule. As a leaked US congressional research paper (2007) put it: "Many Papuans have a sense of identity that is different from the main [...] identity of the rest of the Indonesian archipelago, and many favour autonomy or independence from Indonesia" (White 2018).

The indigenous people of West Papua have sought to establish an independent state since the early 1960s. On 1 December 1961, the Morning Star flag (*Bintang Kejora*) was raised for the first time, which is celebrated symbolically as West Papua's Independence Day (Doherty, 2020). In 1965, the Free Papua Movement was established, who questioned the result of the 1969 referendum. In 1971, the independent Republic of West Papua was proclaimed; however, it has not been recognised by the Indonesian authorities or other countries in the region (May 2012, p. 2).

West Papua's independence efforts range from guerrilla warfare against the Indonesian administration to peaceful protests by civilians, and to making ap-peals to the international community for recognition[2]. OMP guerrilla units car-ried out attacks on Indonesian armed forces or infrastructure, often leading to brutal military campaigns against the local population. International organisa-tions criticise the Indonesian armed forces and services operating in West Papua for repression against the civilian population, unjustified arrests, torture, and violations of human rights (Human Rights Watch 2001). One of the Indonesian military's most serious operations was carried out in 1981, which alone resulted in the deaths of an estimated 2,500 to 13,000 indigenous West Papuans. How-ever, the estimates may be inaccurate because, as already mentioned, the Indo-nesian authorities control the flow of information and journalists' access to the western part of New Guinea (MacLeod 2016, p. 49).

In 1998, after the fall of President Suharto's government, a short period called the Papuan Spring began, when the people of West Papua began to demand their rights again. At the turn of May and June 2000, the Second Congress of the Peo-ples of Papua met, which rejected the decision of the 'Act of Free Choice', called

---

2   The independence of West Papua is supported by, among others, authorities of Vanuatu, Nauru, and Tuvalu.

on the international community to recognise an independent West Papua and punish the perpetrators of crimes against the indigenous inhabitants ("Resolution of the Second Papuan People's Congress" 2000). The Indonesian authorities rejected these demands, and in return, on October 22, 2001, they granted Special Autonomy (Indonesia: Law No. 21 of 2001) to the area of West Papua. Many residents of this area and their representative bodies negatively assessed the adopted regulations. Following the provisions of the Special Autonomy Law, decisions of the Indonesian authorities regarding West Papua should be consulted with the Papuan People's Assembly (*Majelis Rakyat Papua*, MRP) and the Regional People's Representative Council (*Dewan Perwakilan Rakyat Papua*, DPRP). Unfortunately, this provision was often ignored, an example of which is the decision of Indonesian president Megawati Sukarnoputri in 2003 to divide the territory into two provinces, Papua and West Papua (Hasibuan 2022, p. 151).

An important goal of the Special Autonomy was to improve the living conditions of the inhabitants of West Papua, considered one of the poorest provinces of Indonesia. It is worth mentioning that the western part of New Guinea is rich in natural resources (wood, fish) and raw materials such as gold and copper (Ananta et al. 2016, p. 462). However, even before the territory was formally annexed to Indonesia, President Suharto's administration signed an agreement with the US company Freeport-McMoRan Inc. (in 1967) regarding the exclusive exploitation of West Papua's resources. When signing the agreement, no care was taken to protect indigenous people's living conditions or compensate them for land exploitation and devastation of the natural environment (Nurfaiza 2019, p. 206). The importance of this cooperation for the Indonesian authorities can be demonstrated by the fact that the Indonesian security forces provide external protection of the mine, access roads and all infrastructure (Schulman 2016).

In the twenty years of the Special Autonomy, approximately US ($) 7.4 billion has been allocated to the development of West Papua (Nurbaiti 2020). According to experts, these funds positively impacted and contributed, among others, to reducing poverty levels, decreasing unemployment, and increasing the human development index. However, West Papua is still one of Indonesia's poorest and least developed parts. The effective use of these funds was hampered, among others, by the lack of identification of priority projects, socio-political barriers and low level of social and human capital (lack of education, high level of illiteracy, lack of access to health care and basic services) (Hasibuan 2022, p. 156).

In 2020, sixteen Papuan groups under the Papuan People's Petition movement (PRP, *Petisi Rakyat Papua*) expressed opposition to the continuation of the Special Autonomy. However, they demanded that talks be held regarding the further status of this area (Nurbaiti 2020). Despite this, on 15 July 2021, the

Special Autonomy status for West Papua was extended by President Joko Widodo (Costa da, Lamb 2021). Additionally, as of June 2022, the Indonesian part of New Guinea has been divided into five provinces: Papua, West Papua, South Papua, Central Papua, and the Highlands (Bambani 2022). Moreover, in November of that year, the Indonesian government created Southwest Papua Province (Paat 2022). Residents of this region fear that this will further increase the central government's control over the entire territory.

A serious challenge for the future of the indigenous people of West Papua is the transmigration programme conducted by the Indonesian authorities since the early 1970s. Officially, the idea was to move people from more crowded places, such as the islands of Java or Bali, to less populated areas (Ananta et al. 2016, p. 463). The new settlers were supported by the government. They often received lucrative positions (newcomers replaced native inhabitants working in the administration and services), as well as land previously belonging to the inhabitants of West Papua (Sienkiewicz 2020, p. 28). Spontaneous migrations also intensified, especially from the island of Java. The large influx of migration has led to the displacement and relocation of Papuans, increasing among them a sense of common identity and resentment towards newcomers, treating them as a tool in the hands of the authorities trying to change the population structure of the revolting province (Ananta et al. 2016, p. 463). The religious structure of the West Papuan people, who are mostly Christian or practise animism, is also changing. With the arrival of migrants from other Indonesian islands, the number of Muslims has been increasing – in the early 1970s, they made up about 4% of the population, while in the early 2000s, they made up about ¼ of the population of West Papua (Sienkiewicz 2020, p. 33).

The West Papuan people's aspiration to have their own state, human rights violations, and severe repression[3], as well as difficult living conditions, not only challenge the indigenous population, but also affect the situation in the region. One of the most serious challenges is uncontrolled migration both within the territory and beyond its borders. The largest wave of refugees from West Papua occurred between 1984 and 1986, when some 12,000 people arrived in neighbouring Papua New Guinea in search of refuge (May 2021, p. 6). Previously, between 1962 and 1969, the Australian administration of Papua New Guinea recorded approximately 4,000 people who came from West Papua (Glazebrook 2008, pp. 5-6).

---

3 For example, for raising the Morning Star flag, residents of West Papua can face up to fifteen years in prison (Silva, 2017)

Illegal border crossings have been a major problem in relations between Indonesia and Papua New Guinea for many years. Authorities in both countries lacked effective means of patrolling the vast and difficult-to-access border. The Indonesian side criticised the government in Port Moresby for failing to counter the OPM guerrillas setting up camps on the other side of the border. In turn, the authorities of Papua New Guinea were concerned about numerous incursions by the Indonesian armed forces into its territory in pursuit of OPM fighters or sympathisers. Following these incidents, a Treaty of Mutual Respect, Friendship and Cooperation was signed in 1987 to regulate, among others, the protection of the common border (May 2021, p. 6).

The large and sudden influx of refugees has necessitated a response from the Papua New Guinean authorities in collaboration with the Office of the United Nations High Commissioner for Refugees (UNHCR). It was decided that refugees from West Papua would be transferred from seventeen informal camps to the East Awin camp, located approximately 120 kilometres east of the border with Indonesia (Glazebrook 2008, pp. 5-6). Eventually, around 2,500 people settled in the East Awin camp. After six months of stay, they could apply to the Papua New Guinea authorities for a residence permit, which is renewed every three years (Rummery 2004). However, most people preferred to stay close to the border zone, their land, and their families on the other side of the border. According to estimates, from 5,500-7,000 people live in makeshift villages along the Fly River – the border between Papua New Guinea and West Papua. Living conditions are difficult in this region; access to services, education and work is very limited due to the unregulated legal status of these people. Refugees compete with residents of Papua New Guinea for water and food. However, the supply of these resources is limited, and a particular problem concerns water poisoned by industrial waste from mines (Chandler 2019). Additionally, approximately 2,500 refugees from West Papua live in the cities of Papua New Guinea. Just like in the border areas, they live in difficult conditions due to the lack of consent from local authorities for legal stay. Only a few can afford the cost of naturalisation, which is more than USD 4,000 (MacLean 2013).

Difficult living conditions affect not only refugees from West Papua, but also many citizens of Papua New Guinea. About 84% of the inhabitants work in the agricultural, fishing and forestry sectors (World Bank Group 2022). Almost ¼ of the country's population of approximately 9.5 million people lives below the poverty line (CIA World Factbook 2022). In terms of GDP per person, Papua New Guinea ranks 182nd in the world. According to World Bank data, approximately 60% of people living in rural areas do not have access to clean drinking water, and 80% do not have access to electricity and sanitary facilities (World

Bank Group 2022). In such conditions, the presence of a large group of migrants from West Papua may lead to tensions and conflicts.

Conflict spillover is another challenge stemming from the situation in West Papua, where clashes between OPM fighters and indigenous populations occur frequently with Indonesian armed forces and law enforcement agencies. Additionally, demonstrations and riots have been witnessed in other regions of Indonesia. The most recent major unrest, occurring in August and September 2019, was even labelled as an 'uprising'. They covered many cities in Indonesia, including Jayapura, Sentani, Ternate, Ambon, Bandung, Yogyakarta, Jakarta, and Malang (a total of 87 demonstrations and clashes with the police and armed forces took place, of which 17 outside the territory of West Papua) (Koman, 2020). The violence escalated following the events of 16 August 2019, when over forty Papuan students were arrested by police in Surabaya (Java) following reports that they had damaged the Indonesian flag. According to witnesses, there were also racist attacks against students by Indonesian nationalists who called them "monkeys", "pigs" and "dogs" (Lamb 2019).

Most riots, protests and clashes with Indonesian forces took place on the territory of West Papua, where, in Manokwari, the local parliament building was set on fire and, in Sorong, a crowd attacked the local airport, damaging the terminal building (Lamb 2019). According to estimates, the Indonesian authorities have deployed at least 6,500 additional police and military personnel to West Papua to suppress the 'uprising'. It is known that by 23 September 2019 61 people were killed during the clashes, including 35 indigenous inhabitants of West Papua, and at least 284 civilians were injured. In addition, at least 22,800 civilians were displaced during the 'uprising' period (Koman 2020). However, the estimates may be incomplete as the Indonesian authorities have once again imposed restrictions on the Internet and blocked journalists' access to protest sites (Lamb 2019).

These events had a wide impact not only in the Southeast Asian region. The governments of Australia, Solomon Islands and Vanuatu, as well as the acting United Nations High Commissioner for Human Rights (former Chilean President Michelle Bachelet), have called on the Indonesian authorities to talk to the people of West Papua and protested against violence and human rights violations ("Comment by UN High Commissioner for Human Rights Michelle Bachelet on Indonesia - Papua and West Papua 2019").

In today's reality, West Papua is the scene of one of the longest-running military occupations in the world. Human rights violations are widespread, and intimidation and torture are a modus operandi of Indonesian security forces. A report prepared by Yale Law School for the Indonesian Human Rights Campaign concluded that "available evidence clearly demonstrates that the Indonesian government has committed genocide against the West Papuans" ("Human rights in West Papua" 2016). Probably, over 100,000 Papuans have died due to repression by Indonesian security forces since the 1960s (White 2018). In the years leading up to the 1969 Free Choice Act, the West was aware of the reality of Indonesian rule and the fact that Papuans were in the vast majority in favour of independence. However, Western powers tolerated and even supported the Indonesian occupation throughout the Cold War, providing Indonesia with moral, diplomatic, and military support for its rule in Papua. Moreover, the governments of Australia and Great Britain are currently financing and training the Indonesian anti-terrorist police unit Densus 88, deployed in West Papua (White 2018).

In recent years, however, a change in the approach to the problem of West Papua has been noticeable. Some countries in the Pacific region, such as Vanuatu, provide support for independence aspirations. The country's Foreign Minister, Ralph Regenvanu, reaffirmed Vanuatu's support for West Papua in its efforts at the United Nations to complete decolonisation and achieve independence. Vanuatu's strong support for the independence of West Papua is based on the fundamental principles of national self-determination (Kaiku 2019). In June 2023, joint talks between Vanuatu and Indonesia were held in Jakarta, with the issue of West Papua at the top of the agenda ("Indonesia creates new committee on Papua after talks with Vanuatu" 2023). The international solidarity movement with the people of West Papua is also growing yearly. For example, the Norwegian Support Committee for Western Sahara officially expresses solidarity with the people of West Papua and their fight for self-determination, demanding that Indonesia end its occupation of West Papua and allow the inhabitants of this region to hold a referendum in which they will decide their own future (The Norwegian Support Committee for Western Sahara 2011). The international change goes hand in hand with the internal consolidation of the independence movement, which was reflected (for the first time since the beginning of the Indonesian occupation) in 2014 by the unification of Papuan independence organisations under the government of the United Liberation Movement of West Papua (ULMWP). Leaders of the independence movement hope that, as in the case of East Timor, which gained independence in 1999 after 25 years of Indonesian occupation, and Bougainville, which voted for independence in a referendum organised in 2019 to separate from Papua New Guinea, the same will be the fate of West Papua in the future[4].

---

4   In the referendum held in 2019, 98% of voters voted in favour of independence. As a result, by 2023, the Bougainville authorities will take over most of the competences

Azawad

The area of northern Mali is called Azawad, and the name comes from the Berber word "Azawagh", which means "dry riverbed" (a northern tributary of the Niger River once flowed through this bed). In some literature, the word is translated as "Azawagh" meaning "land of nomadic pastoralism". The region is inhabited mainly by the Tuareg people. During decolonisation in 1960, the French annexed this area to the newly established state of Mali, which the Tuaregs never accepted, aspiring to gain political independence.

During the decolonisation of Africa, the principle of *uti possidetis iuris* was adopted at the forum of the Organisation of African Unity (OAU) in 1964, which was to guarantee the inviolability of the borders of the newly established states and prevent conflicts between African states. However, from the beginning, separatist tendencies became visible, either caused by the desire to unite ethnic groups separated by colonial (and now state) borders or to gain independence by occupying regions rich in natural resources. Already in the first days of the creation of independent states in Sub-Saharan Africa, there were internal fights, as exemplified by the civil war in the Belgian Congo and the unsuccessful secession of Katanga. The principle of *uti possidetis* took on particular importance during the decolonisation of Africa and was a supported practice for many years, with the Organisation of African Unity categorically opposing any secession of territories that were part of African states. However, the history of the last 50 years has shown that separatist tendencies are still alive in many African countries, and the problem of secessionism in the context of post-colonial borders is still valid, as evidenced by the examples of separatist movements, among others, in Azawad.

The Tuaregs are among the Berber peoples who predominantly maintain a nomadic and cross-border lifestyle, migrating across countries in the Sahara region. However, during the period of French colonial rule in West Africa, this issue was not as pronounced as it became after decolonisation. Following decolonisation, their territories were divided by the establishment of new states, namely Algeria, Libya, Mali, Niger, and Burkina Faso. The division of the Sahara between the newly established states resulted in the closure of seasonal grazing routes, which were the main occupation of the Tuaregs and their nomadic lifestyle. Moreover, power was transferred to other people, and new elites were

from the government of Papua New Guinea, and the new state is to be proclaimed in 2027.

installed. In the case of Mali, it was the Bambara people who dominated the country (6.9 million – i.e., approximately 33% of the population) ("Bambara in Mali"). The consequence was the refusal of the Tuaregs to recognise the border divisions and the socialist system of power introduced by the leader of the independence movement, Modibo Keïta. He distanced himself from France and established close relations with communist countries by introducing a planned economy, which consequently led to the first Tuareg rebellion, which broke out in 1963 (Boilley 2011, p. 152).

Traditional authority in the form of chiefdoms or kingdoms is a phenomenon that often occurs in Africa and functions simultaneously within the state, actually fulfilling its tasks in the regions. This is particularly relevant in weak, poor states where the central authority does not have full control over the regions, especially those on the outskirts. The Sahel countries, which include Mali, are defined by such conditions. The power of tribal or clan leaders is regional in nature and enjoys great legitimacy among the community, and by resolving disputes, managing land or cultivating local culture, it exercises power in the peripheries more effectively than state structures (Trzciński 2017, pp. 14-15). Due to their nomadic lifestyle and good knowledge of the desert, the Tuaregs can freely cross the state borders established in the Sahara, bypassing the main roads and border control points. The pauperisation and marginalisation of the Tuaregs have historically contributed to several rebellions in the Sahel-Saharan region between 1962 and 1964 (Mali), between 1990 and 1995 (Mali, Niger), in 2007-2009 (Niger, Mali), and the largest one in 2012 in Azawad, Mali. It is worth noting that separatism was also supported by external actors, the main role being played by the leader of Libya, Muammar Gaddafi. In 2005, he began implementing his concept of uniting all nomadic tribes inhabiting the Sahara area under the banner of the borderless Islamic Republic of the Sahara, hoping that it would become the leader of all the people living in this area. In 2006, in his own style, the Libyan dictator announced the establishment of the Popular and Social League of the Great Sahara Tribes in Timbuktu. By declaring all borders dividing the Sahara completely artificial, thus encouraging the Tuaregs of Algeria, Mali, and Niger to unite and rise[5]. The consequence of this policy will be the subsequent Tuareg revolt and the creation in October 2011 of the National Movement for the Liberation of Azawad (*Mouvement national pour la libération de l'Azawad*,

---

5   Currently, the unifying idea of Islamic terrorism is being realised in this area in the form of the Islamic State in the Greater Sahara (ISGS) which has been functioning since 2015 (United Nations Security Council 2023).

MNLA) (Bongard, Bellal 2021), which, together with Islamic armed groups including Ansar Dine, Al-Qa'ida in the Islamic Maghreb (AQIM) and the Movement for Oneness and Jihad in West Africa (*Mouvement pour l'unicité et le jihad
en Afrique de l'Ouest*, MUJAO) initiated a series of attacks against government
forces in the north of the country[6]. These events were a direct consequence of the
fall of the Gaddafi regime in Libya in October 2011, when Tuareg fighters in his
service returned to Mali with weapons obtained from Libyan warehouses, which
enabled them to start fighting for the independence of Azawad in January 2012.
As a result of the Tuareg revolt from January to March 2012, the central authorities lost control over several cities, and the rebels gained control over most of
Azawad, with the most important cities in the north: Kidal, Gao, and Timbuktu.
Fights in the north of the country caused destabilisation in Mali, a military revolt
in Bamako and a coup that overthrew President Amadou Toumani Touré. The
Tuaregs took advantage of this situation and on 6 April 2012 they announced the
end of military operations against the Mali authorities and the declaration of independence of Azawad as *État indépendant de l'Azawad*, covering the northern
part of Mali ("Tuaregs claim 'independence' from Mali" 2012). The declaration
of independence was also a collection of all the grievances of the Tuaregs against
both the former colonial authorities (the annexation of Azawad to Mali without
the consent of the Tuaregs) and the Malian government (50 years of misrule,
corruption, discrimination, humiliation, expropriation, and inhuman treatment
that threatened the existence of the people of Azawad) (Moseley 2012). The international community was then called on to recognise the new state, which
declared respect for the borders of neighbouring countries. In its declaration,
the National Movement for the Liberation of Azawad referred to the "right of
nations to self-determination" and, at the same time, assured that the "new, independent state of Azawad" would not seek to further expand its territory at the
expense of Mali or other countries ("Declaration of Independence of Azawad"
2012). Decisions to announce the establishment of the Azawad state with an area
of 850,000 km^2 (two-thirds of Mali's territory) was taken after the historic city of
Timbuktu was occupied virtually without a fight ("Azawad - a new country on
the map of Africa?" 2012). The declaration of Azawad's independence was also
confirmation of the unilateral termination of military operations by the MNLA,
as the objective of ending the "Malian occupation" had been reached (Keating

---

6   The United Nations Multidimensional Integrated Stabilisation Mission in Mali
    (MINUSMA) was established by Security Council resolution 2100 of 25 April 2013
    (MINUSMA 2023).

2012). To reassure international public opinion, fearing the strong influence of Muslim fundamentalists among the Tuaregs, it was announced that a constitution would be enacted to ensure religious freedom in Azawad.

Both the European Union and the African Union have not recognised 'Azawad's independence. Moreover, the MNLA quickly conflicted with Islamist groups with completely different goals. Unlike the MNLA, which sought to establish an independent secular state, Muslim organisations wanted to establish a religious state and introduce Sharia law. This resulted in renewed fighting in Azawad at the end of 2012, with Islamic radicals defeating the Tuaregs and driving them out of the main towns. In a short time, Al-Qa'ida in the Lands of the Islamic Maghreb (AQIM), the Movement for Oneness and Jihad in West Africa and Ansar Dine took control of the entire Azawad, introducing their own orders and law based on Sharia. Due to the threat of the emergence of an Islamic state in Africa ruled by fundamentalists from Azawad, a plan was developed to reconquer this area by the West African states associated with the Economic Community of West African States (ECOWAS), with the military support of France (*Opération Serval*) (Boeke, Schuurman 2015). The plan was approved in December 2012 by the UN Security Council. After the withdrawal of French troops, the United Nations Multidimensional Integrated Stabilization Mission in Mali (MINUSMA) ("The United Nations Multidimensional Integrated Stabilization Mission in Mali" 2023) peace support forces took control. In this way, the unrecognised state of Azawad lasted only a few months (from the beginning of April 2012 to January 2013). In June 2013, the government of Mali and the Tuareg rebels signed a peace agreement, which included, among others, an immediate ceasefire and ensuring conditions for organising elections ("Mali: UN officials welcome accord between Government and Tuareg rebels" 2013).

However, persistent fighting in northern Mali between armed groups proves the fragility of the earlier compromise and shows that Azawad's status as an integral part of the Malian state is still contested. On the one hand, the international community formally supports the sovereignty and indivisibility of Mali. Still, on the other hand, there are opinions that the current Malian state is so weak that it does not properly fulfil its functions and does not fully control its territory. The inability of the central government to exercise effective power in Azawad and the active functioning of terrorist groups in this area constitutes a threat of destabilisation in neighbouring countries and must raise consideration whether this form of functioning of this region as an uncontrolled area (*black spot*) should take place and wouldn't it be better in such a situation for Azawad, for Mali, for neighbouring countries and the international community to create an independent state exercising real and effective power (Baldaro, Raineri 2020).

Azawad remains immersed in a low-intensity conflict involving non-state actors, local security forces and external actors. Following the history and development of Azawad and the complex and evolving relationship that exists between the rebels seeking to establish a state and the jihadist groups, one can see the current state of deadlock in the conflict, which appears to represent only a temporary and highly unstable arrangement, paving the way for the high probability of further attempts to establish a *parastatehood* (Baldaro, Raineri 2020). Furthermore, if the Tuaregs continue to feel marginalised and harmed in Mali they may come into closer contact with Islamic fundamentalist and terrorist groups and then an uprising – Sahelistan[7], might take place (Buchalik 2014, p. 18). These opinions are not unfounded, especially in a situation where military coups have taken place in Mali, Niger and Burkina Faso, and the authorities have no legitimacy in power and, moreover, chaos reigns in these countries – further fuelled by Wagner's Russian mercenary group (Madowo, Gretener, John 2023).

Instability in the Azawad region is linked to security threats, especially through the terrorist activities of Islamic fundamentalist groups and organised crime related to smuggling goods (including drugs) and people. An increase in terrorist activities occurred in northern Mali in the late 1990s. At that time, militias of the Algerian Salafist Group for Preaching and Combat (*Groupe Salafiste pour la Prédication et le Combat*, GSPC)[8] began to cross the Algerian-Malian border and build influence in Azawad after the Algerian security services gradually limited its activities in southern Algeria through effective anti-terrorist activities ("Al-Qa'ida in the Lands of the Islamic Maghreb (AQIM)"). Over time, members of this terrorist group began to infiltrate the local Arab-Berber population, which was also related to cultural affinity and the local population's reluctance to rule in Bamako. Terrorists often also entered local Tuareg communities through marriage, which allowed them access to known smuggling routes and facilitated the acquisition of new recruits through clan ties ("Libya, Extremism, and Consequences of Collapse" p. 15). Terrorist groups, establishing cooperation with members of local criminal organisations, became involved in the profitable practice of smuggling cocaine from South America through Azawad to

---

7   The concept of Sahelistan was introduced by Samuel Laurent in his book *Sahelistan: de la Libye au Mali, au coeur du nouveau jihad*. It refers to the narrative about proliferation of jihadism in the area that runs from Mauritania through Mali, Niger, Nigeria, Chad, Sudan, Ethiopia, and Eritrea to Somalia. See Laurent 2013.

8   The GSPC was renamed in January 2007 after the group officially joined al-Qa'ida in September 2006.

Europe, which provided them with funds for further activities and the expansion of structures[9].

The development of drug trafficking in this region has been observed since the beginning of the 21st century, when, due to the weakening of the Colombian cartels, control over cocaine exports was taken over by Mexican cartels. They were looking for new sales markets and safer transport routes. The said cocaine smuggling route leads from South America to the ports and airports of West African countries (especially the Republic of Guinea and Guinea Bissau). Then, the drugs arrive in convoys to important centres in the north of Mali (Kidal, Timbuktu, and Gao), from where they are transferred to Algeria and Niger and then to Europe (Musilli, Smith, 2013). Smugglers choose this route due to several factors as it leads through vast, uninhabited territories that are practically beyond the control of the authorities and services. An important factor is also the weakness of state institutions in most countries through which cocaine is smuggled, limited financial resources allocated to the fight against drug trafficking, a lack of appropriate training officers in combating this practice and the potential ease of bribery of officials – including people associated with the justice system (Musilli, Smith, 2013). The profits from drug sales are enormous: according to estimates, a kilogram of cocaine purchased in Latin American countries for EUR 2,000 to EUR 3,000 can be sold in Europe for about EUR 60,000 ("An Atlas of the Sahara-Sahel. Geography, Economics, Security" p. 231).

The Republic of Mali, especially its northern part, is also on the route of illegal trade in fuels, cigarettes, and cars (mainly from Europe and North African countries)[10]. Particularly important is the trade route for tobacco products, which go from Asia to Mauritania and the countries located on the Gulf of Guinea (especially Benin). From there, they are smuggled through Mali to the Maghreb countries, where these goods are subject to high taxes. Approximately 10% of global tobacco production is estimated to pass through this route. This practice brings criminal organisations and terrorist groups operating in Mali an annual income of approximately USD ($) 1.5 million ("An Atlas of the Sahara-Sahel. Geography, Economics, Security" pp. 229-231).

---

9   The UN estimates about 18 tonnes of cocaine, with an estimated street value of $1.25bn, crosses West Africa every year – nearly 50% of all non-US-bound cocaine (Hirsch, 2013).

10   According to estimates, the annual amount of fuel (mainly diesel) smuggled across the border between Mali and Algeria is approximately 29 million litres ("An Atlas of the Sahara-Sahel. Geography, Economics, Security" p. 227).

After the failure of the uprising in Azawad in 2012, fundamentalists began to consolidate their forces and create new bases from which they carried out attacks on military facilities and abducted foreigners. In August 2013, some terrorist groups merged to create Al-Mourabitoun in Mali, which quickly became one of the most dangerous terrorist organisations in the region; their stated goals are to "unite all Muslims from the Nile to the Atlantic in jihad against Westerners" ("Al-Qaida in the Lands of the Islamic Maghreb (AQIM)"). In November 2015, armed with machine guns and grenades, Al-Mourabitoun fighters stormed the Radisson Blu hotel in the capital Bamako, where they took about 170 hostages. An attempt to rescue them led to the death of 20 of them. In January 2017, a vehicle filled with explosives was detonated at the military base in Gao, killing over 50 Malian soldiers and former Azawad rebels cooperating with them under the peace agreement ("Al-Qaeda affiliate claims Mali car bomb attack in Gao").

Terrorist groups in Azawad also seek to escalate ethnic violence by attacking the Dogon and Bambara civilian population to deepen regional chaos and exacerbate ethnic tensions. The ultimate goal of the activities of terrorist groups is to paralyse state institutions through closing schools, preventing the operation of offices and courts and isolating security service facilities. As a result, much of northern Mali has become a place of economic stagnation and deepening humanitarian problems ("Education Under Attack 2018 – Mali").

The illegal trade in drugs, weapons, fuel, and tobacco products also deepens the economic, social, and political problems of this region. It not only provides profit to criminal organisations but is also a source of income for many people in Mali, one of the poorest countries in the world. According to data from the African Development Bank Group, in 2022, poverty affected about 45% of the country's population (about 9.8 million people) ("Mali Economic Outlook 2023"), and about 7.5 million people (over one-third of the population) needed humanitarian aid ("World Population Prospects", 2022). Not without significance is the fact that Mali's society is very young. The median age of the population is 15 years, and the percentage of the population under the age of 24 is as much as 67% of the population ("World Population Prospects" 2022). Unfortunately, the authorities of most Sub-Saharan African countries are unable to meet the important needs of the rapidly growing population, such as broadly understood security (including economic and social), a sufficient number of jobs, access to services or appropriate infrastructure. According to estimates, only 10% to 20% of people in a given age group can find employment in the labour market. Therefore, other people benefit from family support, operate in the grey zone, migrate in search of better living conditions, or decide to join a criminal or terrorist group, which provides them with easy, although illegal, income and potential advancement in the social structure ("An Atlas of the Sahara-Sahel. Geography, Economics, Security" pp. 234-235).

The emergence of new, influential criminal groups also significantly changes the existing social structure of Mali (based on family and clan relationships) and undermines the territorial division of the sphere of influence (especially in the area of Azawad) (Musilli, Smith 2013). Leaders of criminal organisations take the place of local leaders, which leads to the disruption of existing alliances and the weakening of traditional forces (Strazzari 2015). There are increasingly frequent clashes between groups competing for spheres of influence and control over drug trafficking routes, violence is increasing and the number of victims of such conflicts is on the rise (World Drug Report 2023, pp. 186-189).

It is worth mentioning that funds from illegal activities are also used to corrupt local officials to obtain political benefits for criminal and terrorist groups. These funds also financed services for the local population in order to gain supporters and support (Musilli, Smith 2013). Criminal organisations that offer work and sometimes replace state institutions have gained a certain form of social legitimacy. Criminal networks and terrorist groups are undermining trust in the central government in northern Mali, and the local community is becoming increasingly dependent on income from illegal activities. At the same time, the region's economic stagnation is deepening because foreign investors do not want to invest capital due to the lack of security and the weakness of state institutions (Strazzari 2015).

In such conditions, another form of illegal trade flourishes in Mali: human trafficking. This phenomenon is even more terrifying because most of the victims of this criminal practice are children. They are mainly used for work and providing sexual services ("Global Report on Trafficking in Persons", 2020, pp. 165-170). Human traffickers exploit boys from Mali and other countries in the region (Guinea, Burkina Faso, Côte d'Ivoire, Senegal) to work in agriculture, gold mines, domestic work, the informal trade sector, and they also force them to beg. Girls and women are forced into domestic and agricultural work and exploited for sexual services not only in Mali, but also in Gabon, Libya, Lebanon, and Tunisia. In addition, terrorist organisations and armed groups recruit and use children in combat, forcing them to carry weapons, guard prisoners, conduct patrols, spy, and even engage in sexual slavery through forced marriages to members of these groups ("2022, Trafficking in Persons Report: Mali").

Conclusion

The cited cases of Azawad, West Papua and Western Sahara have different sta-
tuses determined by the UN and the international community. Their perspective on independence also differs. In the case of West Papua, this issue seems to
be the most optimistic. Supporters of West Papuan independence advocate for
classifying West Papua as a Non-Self-Governing Territory because this designation places responsibilities on Indonesia, which would serve as the "administering state". Administering states are obligated to recognise the interests of the
inhabitants of these territories and implement effective measures to protect and
ensure the inalienable rights of the people. These requirements would mean that
Indonesia could no longer use most of its repressive measures and would have
to be more open to dialogue on independence. Finally, and most importantly,
the function of the administering authorities is to help the territory develop self-
governance for the ultimate goal of decolonisation. This means that Indonesia
would be obliged to create and develop free political institutions in West Papua
in preparation for independence. It is true that Western Sahara has had such
a status in the UN since 1963, but it has not changed its situation much. The
authorities in Rabat are not thinking of any concessions on self-determination,
as demonstrated by the blocking of the possibility of a referendum and the policy
of accomplished facts by colonising the Western Sahara area and building a wall
separating 80% of the occupied territories with all major urban centres, the coast,
and the area where natural resources are located. Despite the status of Western
Sahara, defined by the UN as a non-self-governing territory, in the scientific debate, it is sometimes referred to as a hybrid of a parastate and a state-in-exile
(Fernández-Molina, Ojeda-García 2020). The Indonesian authorities, like the
Moroccan authorities in Western Sahara, are carrying out an operation to encourage people from other parts of the country to emigrate to West Papua, which
is gradually changing the ethnic structure of this area. However, West Papua is
better positioned to achieve independence than Western Sahara. Azawad faces
significant challenges, exacerbated by divisions within Tuareg society, particularly between proponents of establishing a secular state and fundamentalists
advocating for a religious state governed by Sharia law, which is perceived by the
international community as affiliated with Islamic extremists. Furthermore, recent developments in Mali, including the junta's governance, as well as the situation in neighbouring countries with substantial Tuareg populations, do not bode
well for the inhabitants of the Azawad region. Whatever the fate of the people of
the areas in question, they are paying a high price for the unfinished process of
decolonisation and the prevailing principle in international relations, in which

there is a tendency to maintain the integrity of states at all costs, even at the expense of people striving for self-determination, who have every reason to do so.

References

"2022 Trafficking in Persons Report: Mali", U.S. Department of State retrieved 4.9.2023 from https://www.state.gov/reports/2022-trafficking-in-persons-rep ort/mali/

Ananta, Aris et al., "Statistics on Ethnic Diversity in the Land of Papua, Indonesia: Ethnic Diversity in Land of Papua", *Indonesia, Asia & the Pacific Policy Studies*, Vol. 3, 2016, pp. 458-474.

"An Atlas of the Sahara-Sahel. Geography, Economics, Security", OECD, 2014, retrieved 1.9.2023 from https://www.oecd.org/development/an-atlas-of-the-sahara-sahel-9789264222359-en.htm

"Al-Qaeda affiliate claims Mali car bomb attack in Gao", *BBC News* 18.1.2017, retrieved 30.8.2023 from https://www.bbc.com/news/world-africa-38663693

"Al-Qa'ida in the Lands of the Islamic Maghreb (AQIM)", Counter Terrorism Guide, retrieved 30.8.2023 from https://www.dni.gov/nctc/groups/aqim.html

"Al Mourabitoun", Mapping Militant Organizations - Stanford University 2018, retrieved 1.9.2023 from https://cisac.fsi.stanford.edu/mappingmilitants/profi les/al-mourabitoun

"Azawad-nowe państwo na mapie Afryki?", *Wprost*, 6.4.2012, retrieved 27.8.2023 from http://www.wprost.pl/ar/315120/Azawad-nowe-panstwo-na-mapie-Afryki/

Baldaro, Edoardo, / Raineri, Luca, "Azawad: A Parastate Between Nomads and Mujahidins?" *Nationalities Papers*, 48(1) 2020, pp. 100-115. doi:10.1017/nps.2019.62

Bambani, Arfi, "Indonesia to Form Three More Provinces in Papua, Becomes Five", 28.6.2022, retrieved 15.12.2022 from https://www.theindonesia.id/news/2022/06/28/193000/indonesia-to-form-three-more-provinces-in-papua-becomes-five

"Bambara in Mali", Joshua Project, retrieved 15.09.2023 https://joshuaproject.net/people_groups/10617/ML

Boeke, Sergei, / Schuurman, Bart, "Operation Serval: the French Intervention in Mali", 28.7.2015, retrieved 14.4.2023 from https://www.leidensecurityandgl obalaffairs.nl/articles/operation-serval-the-french-intervention-in-mali

Boilley, Pierre, "Geopolitique africaine et rebelions touaregues, Approches locales, approaches globales, (1960-2011)", *L'annee du Maghreb*, VII, 2011, pp. 151-162.

Bongard, Pascal, Bellal, Annyssa, "From Words to Deeds: A Research Study of Armed Non-State Actors' Practice and Interpretation of International Humanitarian and Human Rights Norms", Academy of International Humanitarian Law and Human Rights, 3.2021, retrieved 9.9.2023 from https://words2deeds.org/wp-content/uploads/2021/07/Case-Study-MNLA.pdf

Buchalik, Lucjan, "Samozwańczy Azawad kontra Republika Mali. Konflikt widziany oczami etnologa", Forum Politologiczne, t. 17, Olsztyn 2014, pp. 195-221.

Chandler, Jo, "Refugees on their own land: the West Papuans in limbo in Papua New Guinea", The Guardian, 30.11.2019, retrieved 22.12.2022 from https://www.theguardian.com/world/2019/dec/01/refugees-on-their-own-land-the-west-papuans-in-limbo-in-papua-new-guinea

Comment by UN High Commissioner for Human Rights Michelle Bachelet on Indonesia (Papua and West Papua) 2019, retrieved 22.12.2022 from https://www.ohchr.org/en/press-releases/2019/09/comment-un-high-commissioner-human-rights-michelle-bachelet-indonesia-papua

CIA World Factbook 2022, "Papua New Guinea" retrieved 22.12.2022 from https://www.cia.gov/the-world-factbook/countries/papua-new-guinea/

CIA World Factbook 2023, "Mali" retrieved 22.12.2022 from https://www.cia.gov/the-world-factbook/countries/mali/

Costa, Augustinus B. da, / Lamb, Kate, "Indonesia parliament passes revised autonomy law for restive Papua", Reuters, 15.6.2021 retrieved 21.12.2022 from https://www.reuters.com/world/asia-pacific/indonesia-parliament-passes-revised-autonomy-law-restive-papua-2021-07-15/

"Declaration of Principles on Western Sahara (Madrid Accords)" 1975, United Nations Peacemaker, retrieved 30.8.2023 from https://peacemaker.un.org/sites/peacemaker.un.org/files/MA-MR   ES_751114_DeclarationPrinciplesOnWesternSahara_0.pdf

"Deklaracja Niepodległości Azawadu", 6.4.2012, retrieved 30.8.2023 from http://www.mnlamov.net/component/content/article/169-declaration-dindependance-de-lazawad.html

Doherty, Ben, "West Papua independence leaders declare 'government-in-waiting", The Guardian, 1.12.2020, retrieved 15.12.2022 from https://www.theguardian.com/world/2020/dec/01/west-papua-independence-leaders-declare-government-in-waiting

"Education Under Attack 2018 – Mali", UNHCR, 11.5.2018, retrieved 1.9.2023 from https://www.refworld.org/docid/5be9430813.html

Fernández-Molina, Irene, Ojeda-García, Raquel "Western Sahara as a Hybrid of a Parastate and a State-in-Exile: (Extra)territoriality and the Small Print of

Sovereignty in a Context of Frozen Conflict", *Nationalities Papers,* 48(1), 2020, pp. 83-99, doi:10.1017/nps.2019.34

Glazebrook, Diana, "Permissive Residents. West Papuan Refugees living in Papua New Guinea", ANU E PRESS 2008.

"Global Report on Trafficking in Persons" 2020, United Nations Office of Drugs and Crime retrieved 4.9.2023 from https://www.unodc.org/documents/data-and-analysis/tip/2021/GLOTiP_2020_15jan_web.pdf

Griffiths, Ryan D. "Age of Secession: The International and Domestic Determinants of State Birth", Cambridge University Press 2016.

Hasibuan, Sarah N., "Special Autonomy in Papua and West Papua", *Bestuurskunde: Journal of Governmental Studies,* 2(2) 2022, pp. 145-158.

Hirsch, Afua, "Cocaine flows through Sahara as al-Qaida cashes in on lawlessness", *The Guardian,* 2.5.2013, retrieved 30.8.2023 from https://www.theguardian.com/world/2013/may/02/cocaine-flows-through-sahara-al-qaida

"Human rights in West Papua", International Parliamentarians for West Papua, retrieved 28.8.2023 from https://www.ipwp.org/human-rights-in-west-papua/2016

Human Rights Watch, "Violence and Political Impasse in Papua", Vol. 13, No 2(C), 2001, retrieved 20.12.2022 from https://www.hrw.org/reports/2001/papua/PAPUA0701.pdf#

"Indonesia and Netherland Agreement concerning New West Guinea (West Irian)" 1962, United Nations, retrieved 15.12.2023 from https://peacemaker.un.org/sites/peacemaker.un.org/files/ID%20NL_620815_AgreementConcerningWestNewGuinea.pdf

"Indonesia creates new committee on Papua after talks with Vanuatu", 22.6.2023, retrieved 28.8.2023 from https://www.rnz.co.nz/international/pacific-news/492438/indonesia-creates-new-committee-on-papua-after-talks-with-vanuatu

"Indonesia: Law No. 21 of 2001, On Special Autonomy for the Papua Province", UNHCR, retrieved 20.12.2023 from https://www.refworld.org/docid/46af542e2.html

Janki, Melinda "West Papua and the Right to Self-determination Under International Law", *West Indian Law Journal* Vol 34 No. 1 2010, retrieved 29.8.2023 from https://www.ipwp.org/wp-content/uploads/2016/04/West_Papua_and_the_right_to_self-determination_under_international.pdf

"Islamic State in the Greater Sahara (ISGS)", United Nations Security Council, retrieved 14.4.2023 from https://www.un.org/securitycouncil/content/islamic-state-greater-sahara-isgs

Kaiku, Patrick, "Why Vanuatu Supports West Papuan Independence", *Daily Post* 20.2.2019, retrieved 28.8.2023 from https://www.dailypost.vu/news/why-vanuatu-supports-west-papuan-independence/article_b5563f63-a45c-5c59-baee-af2f274a1287.html

Keating, Joshua "Can Azawad win international recognition?", *Foreign Policy*, 5.4.2012, retrieved 28.8.2023 from https://foreignpolicy.com/2012/04/05/can-azawad-win-international-recognition/

Koman, Veronica, "The 2019 West Papua Uprising. Protests against racism and for self-determination", 2020, retrieved 22.12.2022 from https://www.tapol.org/sites/default/files/sites/default/files/pdfs/The%202019%20West%20Papua%20Uprising.pdf

Lamb, Kate "West Papua protests: Indonesia deploys 1,000 soldiers to quell unrest, cuts internet", *The Guardian*, 22.8.2019, retrieved 23.12.2022 from https://www.theguardian.com/world/2019/aug/22/west-papua-protests-indonesia-deploys-1000-soldiers-to-quell-unrest

Laurent, Samuel "Sahelistan: de la Libye au Mali, au coeur du nouveau jihad", Seuil: Paris 2013.

"Libya, Extremism, and Consequences of Collapse", The Soufan Group - Africa Centre for Strategic Studies 2016, retrieved 30.8.2023 from https://africacenter.org/wp-content/uploads/2019/12/Libya-Extremism-and-the-Consequences-of-Collapse-Soufan-Group.pdf

MacLean, Dana, "Papua New Guinea: Refugees and advocates call for greater legal rights", Jesuit Refugee Service, Asia Pacific, 2013, retrieved 23.12.2022 from https://apr.jrs.net/en/story/papua-new-guinea-refugees-and-advocates-call-for-greater-legal-rights/

MacLeod, Jason "Citizen media and civil resistance in West Papua", *Pacific Journalism Review*, 22(1) 2016, pp. 38-51.

Maddy-Weitzman, Bruce "Amazigh Politics in the Wake of the Arab Spring", University of Texas Press: Austin 2022.

"Mali Economic Outlook 2023", African Development Bank Group retrieved 1.9.2023 from https://www.afdb.org/en/countries/west-africa/mali/mali-economic-outlook

"Mali: UN officials welcome accord between Government and Tuareg rebels", United Nations News, 18.6.2013, retrieved 30.8.2023 from https://news.un.org/en/story/2013/06/442632

Madowo, Larry, Gretener, Jessie, John, Tara, "A Niger coup leader meets with Wagner-allied junta in Mali", *CNN*, 2.8.2023, retrieved 30.8.2023 from https://edition.cnn.com/2023/08/02/africa/niger-coup-mali-wagner-intl-afr/index.html

May R. J., "Fifty Years after the „Act of Free Choice" – The West Papua in a Regional Context", *Department of Pacific Affairs, Discussion Papers* 2021/1, pp. 1-24.

MINUSMA 2023, The United Nations Multidimensional Integrated Stabilization Mission in Mali retrieved 14.4.2023 from https://minusma.unmissions.org/en/history

Moseley, William G. "Mali: Azawad - the Latest African Border Dilemma", 18.4.2012, retrieved 30.8.2023 from http://allafrica.com/stories/201204190 699.html?page=4

Musilli, Pietro, Smith, Partick, "The lawless roads: an overview of turbulence across the Sahel", Norwegian Peacebuilding Resource Centre, 6.2013, retrieved 1.9.2023 from https://www.files.ethz.ch/isn/165438/e2cc78a2ce149 944b9a35b4ce42759b9.pdf

Nurbaiti, Alya "Papuan groups voice opposition to special autonomy status", *The Jakarta Post*, retrieved 21.12.2022 from https://www.thejakartapost.com/news/2020/07/06/papuan-groups-voice-opposition-to-special-autonomy-sta tus.html

Nurfaiza, Martha W. "Transnational Corporations and West Papua: A Friend or Foe for Indigenous People of This Region?" [In:] McIntyre-Mills, Janet, / Room, Norma R. A. (eds.) *Mixed Methods and Cross Disciplinary Research. Towards Cultivating Eco-systemic Living*, Springer, 2019, pp. 205-210.

Paat, Yustinus, "Indonesia Adds Four New Provinces to 38 Overall", *"Jakarta Globe"* 17.11.2022, retrieved 21.9.2023 from https://jakartaglobe.id/news/indonesia-adds-four-new-provinces-to-38-overall

"Resolution of the Second Papuan People's Congress – 4th June 2000", retrieved 27.12.2022 from https://www.freewestpapua.org/documents/resolution-of-the-second-papuan-peoples-congress-4th-june-2000/

Rummery, Ariane, "In PNG, refugees from Indonesia's Papua province start complex journey to new home", UNHCR, 1.10.2004, retrieved 23.12.2022 from https://www.unhcr.org/news/latest/2004/10/415d4df44/png-refugees-indonesias-papua-province-start-complex-journey-new-home.html

Schulman, Susan "The $100bn gold mine and the West Papuans who say they are counting the cost", *The Guardian*, 2.11.2016, retrieved 28.12.2022 from https://www.theguardian.com/global-development/2016/nov/02/100-bn-dol lar-gold-mine-west-papuans-say-they-are-counting-the-cost-indonesia

Searcey, Dionne, Nossiter, Adam, "Deadly Siege Ends After Assault on Hotel in Mali", *The New York Times*, 21.11.2015, retrieved 1.9.2023 from https://www.nytimes.com/2015/11/21/world/africa/mali-hotel-attack-radisson.html

"Separate opinion of Judge H. C. Dillard, Western Sahara Advisory Opinion", 1975, pp. 108-118, retrieved 30.8.2023 from https://www.icj-cij.org/public/files/case-related/61/061-19751016-ADV-01-07-EN.pdf

Sienkiewicz, Simona, "Religion and Internal Migrations in the Processes of Indonesianisation and Islamisation of West Papua", *Annales UMCS*, Sectio K – Politologia, Vol. 27, No 1., 2020, pp. 25-42.

Silva da, Chantal, "West Papua flag day: Why people around the world are raising the colours of a country that doesn't exist", *Independent* 1.12.2017, retrieved 28.12.2022 from https://www.independent.co.uk/news/world/asia/west-papua-flag-day-indonesia-independence-separatists-illegal-oxford-raised-world-locations-support-a8085286.html

Strazzari, Francesco, "Azawad and the rights of passage: the role of illicit trade in the logic of armed group formation in northern Mali", Norwegian Peacebuilding Resource Centre, 1.2015, retrieved 4.9.2023 from https://www.files.ethz.ch/isn/192065/Strazzari_NOREF_Clingendael_Mali_Azawad_Dec2014.pdf

"The Indonesian Population Census" 2020, United Nations, retrieved 19.12.2022 from https://unstats.un.org/unsd/demographic-social/meetings/2021/egm-covid19-census-20210209/docs/s03-04-IDN.pdf

The Norwegian Support Committee for Western Sahara, "Free West Papua!" 31.3.2011, retrieved 29.8.2023 from https://vest-sahara.no/en/archive/1652

The United Nations Multidimensional Integrated Stabilization Mission in Mali, retrieved 30.8.2023 from https://peacekeeping.un.org/en/mission/minusma

Trzciński, Krzysztof, "A few introductory remarks to research on the contemporary role of traditional authority in the countries of Sub-Saharan Africa", *Political Sciences Forum*, INP UWM Olsztyn 2017, vol. 22, pp. 11-30.

"Tuaregs claim 'independence' from Mali. Rebel group proclaims "independence of Azawad" following gains in northern Mali, as Algerian consulate staff abducted", *Al Jazeera*, 6.4.2012, retrieved 30.8.2023 from https://www.aljazeera.com/news/2012/4/6/tuaregs-claim-independence-from-mali

United Nations, "Western Sahara" 2023, retrieved 30.8.2023 from https://www.un.org/dppa/decolonization/en/nsgt/western-sahara

USAID – Mali, United States Agency for International Development, 2023 retrieved 4.9.2023 from https://www.usaid.gov/humanitarian-assistance/mali

White, Connor "Explainer: What's Going On in West Papua?", 1.12.2018, retrieved 28.8.2023 from https://newnaratif.com/explainer-whats-going-on-in-west-papua/

Wangge, Hipolitus, "Why Indonesia fails to address the West Papua conflict", *Al Jazeera*, 14.3.2023, retrieved 28.8.2023 from https://www.aljazeera.com/opinions/2023/3/14/why-indonesia-is-losing-the-west-papua-conflict

"World Drug Report" 2023, United Nations Office of Drugs and Crime retrieved 4.9.2023 from https://www.unodc.org/res/WDR-2023/WDR23_Booklet_2.pdf

"World Population Prospects" 2022, Population Division of the Department of Economic and Social Affairs of the United Nations retrieved 4.9.2023 from https://population.un.org/wpp/

Robert Kłosowicz, Joanna Mormul

Conclusions

The issue of *de facto states* or unrecognised states has been more commonly associated with post-Soviet states, as well as certain regions in Europe and Asia, rather than with Africa. Presently, there are only two entities on the African continent that can be classified as *de facto states* – Western Sahara (the Sahrawi Arab Democratic Republic) and Somaliland, although the former does not meet all the criteria outlined by the majority of researchers interested in this phenomenon. *De facto states* lack external sovereignty; however, they continually seek a niche for themselves within an international system based on external sovereignty. While they may not always feature prominently among globally recognised challenges, the media frequently reports on their issues, often in the context of security concerns, regional instability, and the struggle for influence among global powers.

The challenges encountered by unrecognised states have tangible repercussions for their neighbours, entire regions, and even the international order within the realm of international relations. Unresolved territorial or ethnic conflicts surrounding *de facto states* pose significant challenges to regional and global stability, and the international community does not always succeed in finding adequate responses to these challenges. Many unrecognised states exist in a state of uncertainty and have been characterized as entities whose lack of international recognition remains unresolved or appears irresolvable. Dissatisfied with their status, which is further threatened by the fact that their internal sovereignty is not acknowledged *de jure*, they find themselves engaged in an ongoing struggle to safeguard their existence. Despite their potential, they are relegated to the periphery of the international legal system. However, it should be noted that the greater the number of actors recognising a *de facto state*, the more stable its international legal position appears to be.

This volume aims to explore the place and role of contemporary unrecognised states in Africa within international relations on the continent and beyond, with a focus on Western Sahara and Somaliland. However, when necessary for analysis, it also reflects on other, often ephemeral, historical examples of *de facto states* in Africa or compares selected cases with seemingly distant ones, such as West Papua's desire to secede from Indonesia. As demonstrated in the case studies used to illustrate the challenges of *de facto states* and emphasised in almost every chapter of this monograph, historical perspective is crucial for understanding the phenomenon of unrecognised states, not only in Africa.

In general, on the African continent, three scenarios can be distinguished regarding the emergence of unrecognised states: 1. the outcome of an initial decolonisation process (Rhodesia, Cabinda, Western Sahara), 2. the dissolution of highly dysfunctional (collapsed/failed) states (Somaliland), and 3. the act of secession resulting from previous armed conflicts (Eritrea, South Sudan, Katanga, Biafra, Azawad). Several African *de facto states* were reintegrated into their "mother states" as a result of armed actions (Katanga, South Kasai, Biafra, Cabinda), while others appeared to be purely episodic from the outset and had little chance of prolonged existence. Notably, unrecognised states are often situated on the so-called periphery, which sometimes leads to their being overlooked until situations escalate and attract the attention of the international community and the media, albeit temporarily. Examples include the recent situation in Nagorno-Karabakh and on the border between Mauritania and Western Sahara, which is under Moroccan control, that commenced in late 2020 (known as Guerguerat crisis).

Due to the lack of international recognition, *de facto states* are often perceived as anomalies and are isolated by the international community. However, they still require the establishment of relations with recognised states in the international system. In the domain of international relations and foreign policy, despite lacking international recognition, *de facto states* can forge and sustain international relations with sovereign states, international organisations, or other actors in the international system, such as NGOs or other *de facto states*. They may utilise official channels through liaison offices, as well as various tools of paradiplomacy, such as commercial offices or diaspora networks. Securing support from other states or even patronage is crucial in their pursuit of international recognition, as they seek external assistance not only to ensure their survival but also to promote economic development and enhance the well-being of their citizens. Surprisingly, they can also have broadly outlined goals of their foreign policy, as seen in the case of the Sahrawi Arab Democratic Republic, which projects a certain role in shaping international relations on the African continent in the future. The reality, however, is much more pragmatic. Sahrawi activities, also in the area of international politics, depend to a large extent on the aid (including diplomatic support) provided by Algeria, which plays the role of a patron state for Sahrawi statehood. Furthermore, the question of Western Sahara is highly politicised in international relations, not only in the Maghreb region but also throughout North Africa and globally, making it difficult for the Sahrawi Arab Democratic Republic to achieve their foreign policy objectives. These divisions in the Western Saharan stance were already visible during the Cold War era, greatly polarizing not only the Maghreb region but also the entire African continent, a fact repeatedly reflected in the Organisation of African Unity and later, the African Union.

Last but certainly not least is the plight of the people inhabiting the disputed areas of unrecognised states. These individuals, described in the quote by Thomas de Waal in the introduction to this volume as those who "fall between the cracks", include thousands of Sahrawis who have resided in refugee camps in south-western Algeria for nearly fifty years, as well as the displacement of over 100,000 Armenians from Nagorno-Karabakh (Republic of Artsakh) in September 2023. The inhabitants of unrecognised states often bear the brunt of secession, the un-finished process of decolonisation, or the quest for self-determination and in-dependent existence in a world where the prevailing principle in international relations is to prioritise the preservation of state integrity at all costs. Once again, using the SADR example, for the Sahrawis living on the Algerian soil, who have few other choices than staying in exile, the refugee camps in the Tindouf prov-ince in Algeria have become a substitute for their own statehood, a type of *ersatz state* and a kind of test of perseverance for both the rulers and the ruled, and – at the same time – an expression of the durability of the idea of Western Saharan independence, an act of courage and, at the same time, persistence.

Biographical notes

Robert Kłosowicz, Professor at the Institute of Political Science and International Relations at the Jagiellonian University in Kraków, Poland; Director of the Jagiellonian Research Centre for African Studies. His research interests concentrate on the relationship between diplomacy and the armed forces, international security, and military conflicts in Sub-Saharan Africa, as well as dysfunctional and *de facto states*.

Joanna Mormul, Ph.D., Assistant Professor at the Institute of Political Science and International Relations of the Jagiellonian University in Kraków, Poland; Secretary of the Jagiellonian Research Centre for African Studies. Her research focuses on dysfunctional states, socio-political transformations in post-conflict societies, and regional separatism in Africa.

Edyta Chwiej, Ph.D., Assistant Professor at the Institute of Political Science and International Relations of the Jagiellonian University in Kraków, Poland. Her primary areas of interest encompass policy issues in the international relations of the Western Hemisphere, Polish foreign policy post-1989, and global demographic challenges.

Agnieszka Czubik, Ph.D., attorney-at-law, Assistant Professor at the Institute of Political Science and International Relations of the Jagiellonian University in Kraków, Poland. She specialises in issues related to the international protection of human rights and international public law. From 2005 to 2009, she served as a case lawyer at the Registry of the European Court of Human Rights in the Council of Europe. Her research interests also extend to contemporary human rights challenges emerging on the African continent.

Ewa Szczepankiewicz-Rudzka, Ph.D., Assistant Professor at the Institute of Political Science and International Relations of the Jagiellonian University in Kraków, Poland. Her scholarly interests encompass the modern history of the Maghreb countries within the framework of political, social, and cultural transformations, European Mediterranean policy, and theories of democratisation.

Kateřina Ženková Rudincová, Ph.D., Assistant Professor at the Department of Human Geography and Regional Development of the University of Ostrava, Czechia. Her research has focused on international relations, politics, conflict, and human rights in Africa, with particular emphasis on political developments in the *de facto state* of Somaliland and South Sudan.

Index

INTERNATIONAL RELATIONS IN ASIA, AFRICA AND THE AMERICAS

Edited by Andrzej Mania & Marcin Grabowski

www.peterlang.com